T0321216

Electronic Hive Minds on Social Media:

Emerging Research and Opportunities

Shalin Hai-Jew
Kansas State University, USA

A volume in the Advances in
Social Networking and Online
Communities (ASNOC) Book Series

Published in the United States of America by
    IGI Global
    Information Science Reference (an imprint of IGI Global)
    701 E. Chocolate Avenue
    Hershey PA, USA 17033
    Tel: 717-533-8845
    Fax: 717-533-8661
    E-mail: cust@igi-global.com
    Web site: http://www.igi-global.com

Library of Congress Cataloging-in-Publication Data

Names: Hai-Jew, Shalin, author.
Title: Electronic hive minds on social media : emerging research and
  opportunities / by Shalin Hai-Jew.
Description: Hershey, PA : Information Science Reference, [2020] | Includes
  bibliographical references and index.
Identifiers: LCCN 2019000517| ISBN 9781522593690 (h/c) | ISBN 9781522593713
  (eISBN) | ISBN 9781522593706 (s/c)
Subjects: LCSH: Swarm intelligence. | Online social networks--Research. |
  Social influence.
Classification: LCC Q337.3 .H34 2020 | DDC 302.30285--dc23 LC record available at https://lccn.
loc.gov/2019000517

This book is published in the IGI Global book series Advances in Social Networking and Online Communities (ASNOC) (ISSN: 2328-1405; eISSN: 2328-1413)

British Cataloguing in Publication Data
A Cataloguing in Publication record for this book is available from the British Library.

All work contributed to this book is new, previously-unpublished material.
The views expressed in this book are those of the authors, but not necessarily of the publisher.

For electronic access to this publication, please contact: eresources@igi-global.com.

Advances in Social Networking and Online Communities (ASNOC) Book Series

ISSN:2328-1405
EISSN:2328-1413

Editor-in-Chief: Hakikur Rahman, Institute of Computer Management and Science, Bangladesh

MISSION

The advancements of internet technologies and the creation of various social networks provide a new channel of knowledge development processes that's dependent on social networking and online communities. This emerging concept of social innovation is comprised of ideas and strategies designed to improve society.

The **Advances in Social Networking and Online Communities** book series serves as a forum for scholars and practitioners to present comprehensive research on the social, cultural, organizational, and human issues related to the use of virtual communities and social networking. This series will provide an analytical approach to the holistic and newly emerging concepts of online knowledge communities and social networks.

COVERAGE

- Communication and Agent Technology
- Methods, Measures and Instruments of Knowledge Management
- Knowledge as a Competitive Force
- Strategic Management and Business Process Analysis
- Communication and Management of Knowledge in R&D Networks
- Leveraging Knowledge Communication in Social Networks
- Challenges of Knowledge Management
- Technology Orientation and Capitalization of Knowledge
- Social Models to Design and Support Knowledge Intensive Collaborative Processes
- Epistemology of Knowledge Society

IGI Global is currently accepting manuscripts for publication within this series. To submit a proposal for a volume in this series, please contact our Acquisition Editors at Acquisitions@igi-global.com or visit: http://www.igi-global.com/publish/.

Titles in this Series

For a list of additional titles in this series, please visit:
https://www.igi-global.com/book-series/advances-social-networking-online-communities/37168

For an entire list of titles in this series, please visit:
https://www.igi-global.com/book-series/advances-social-networking-online-communities/37168

701 East Chocolate Avenue, Hershey, PA 17033, USA
Tel: 717-533-8845 x100 • Fax: 717-533-8661
E-Mail: cust@igi-global.com • www.igi-global.com

Table of Contents

Preface

A preface, for me, is something written at the end, once a book manuscript has achieved final form and needs a lead-in, a bridge from outside the text in. After all, why write a preface to a book that does not exist yet? At best, this would offer a "personality frame" approach to an elusive topic about which there is not yet any proof-of-concept. At worst, time will have been wasted, and a dangling preface exists in the world, as part of the Great Unread. Regardless, for this project, going with a "research journal" approach to this prefatory writing seems to make more sense because of the nature of the topic.

An "electronic hive mind" (EHM) is a notional concept that may or may not be operationalized in the world (Figure 01). The power of the hypothesizing and exploratory stages is in the breadth of the thinking that may be engaged. However, this process itself is somewhat messy. The writing will occur in multiple phases, and as the author is learning, she will likely have to return to revise or qualify earlier thinking. And yet, the earlier thoughts themselves may show the power of naïve thinking about a topic, and locking in a concept or practice may not be optimal. A research journal approach then sheds light on the evolution of the thinking and the work in this research text.

Figure 1. An electronic hive mind

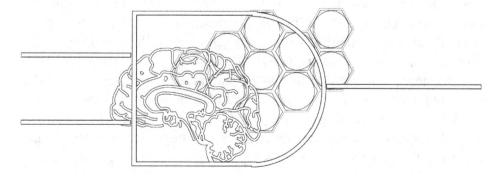

PHASE 1: THE PRE-WRITING PERIOD (CONCEPTUALIZATION AND GESTATION FROM LATE JULY TO EARLY OCT. 2018)

It seems foolish to begin a book about a phenomenon that is not yet defensibly established and that is only really a notional idea. Used colloquially, a "hive mind" is comprised of a number of people who "share their knowledge or opinions with one another, regarded as producing either uncritical conformity or collective intelligence," according to Google dictionary. A secondary definition is from science fiction and is defined as "a unified consciousness or intelligence formed by a number of alien individuals, the resulting consciousness typically exerting control over its constituent members" (with a Borg Queen offered as an example) ("hive mind," Oct. 9, 2018). An "electronic hive mind," at least initially, is defined conceptually in the following way:

a synchronous temporal and informal patchwork of emergent shared social consciousness (held by geographically distributed people, cyborgs, and robots) enabled by online social connectivity (across a range of social media platforms on the Web and Internet), based around various dimensions of shared attractive interests.

This definition touches on some basic criteria for an "electronic + hive + mind," in its various parts and in its combinatorial complexity. An EHM is not about consensus or agreement around the topic but about interest. Also, while there are social aspects to EHMs, the links tend to be weak when they do exist, but a majority of the interactions is thought to be through information-sharing (one-to-many, few-to-few). While social networks may exist in EHMs, EHMs should not be conflated with social networks (with much higher levels of connectivity). However, an implication of the "hive" is that mutual engagement around a topic may lead to massthink or massmind, group-based conceptualizing of a topic resulting in shared stances, opinions, limiting paradigms, mass coordination, and potential mass actions. Massmind can be about non-thinking and selective forgetting as much about thinking and remembering. In an earlier work based around a mapped "cybersecurity" EHM, this was more particularly defined as "a sentient and potent mass entity with potential for various types of concentrated mass action as well as dispersed smaller-unit actions, among others" (Hai-Jew, 2019, p. 210). The "sentience" suggested here is somewhat embodied in parts of the human membership and in parts of the sociotechnical spaces supporting the distributed "electronic" hive mind, but there is no assumption that any of the members (or groups of members) or the social technology achieve or contain the full awareness of the whole. This is especially so since an electronic hive mind is "inclusive of all potential members, no matter what their level of expertise" (Hai-Jew, 2019, p. 211). Within an EHM, there may be various clusters of differing consciousness(es) and unique interests. Indeed, the EHM exists in each person as well, influenced individually by the ideas he or she understands, takes in, experiences, and activates in the imagination and the real world.

A core assumption is that EHMs do not form for no reason but are ways for people to meet their needs individually and in groups. These may be needs for learning, for socializing, for social recognition, for entertainment, for social participation, for survival, and other factors. As such, a number of different "seeds" exist for the origination of electronic hive minds and their continuance. A rough perusal of what is in the world might suggest some examples of EHM seeding types (based on the 5Ws and 1H):

Who

- **Personalities** (human and non-human, real and non-real, individual and group, and others)
- In-world **identities**, online identities

What

- Various **topics** (political topics, social topics, personal topics, geographical regional topics, and others)
- Various **events**
- Shared interests and **practices** (commercial and non-commercial, lifestyles, and others)
- Various **brands**

When

- Various **time-based occurrences** and events (named and unnamed, and others)

Where

- **Locational issues** and **occurrences**

Why

- **Motivational** pursuits (self-actualization, socializing, entertainment, learning, and others)

How

- **Learning**, skills acquisition, skills maintenance, prevention of skills decay
- Maintenance, **risk mitigation,** disaster prevention, and others
- **Problem-solving**, troubleshooting
- **Activities** (individual and mutual), and others

The rest of this definition is "TBD" (to be determined), and a more empirically supported definition will be one of the objectives of this text. If this reads as "fragile," that's because it is. I do assume that there are analog (non-digital) hive minds, too, although most of these would be mediated by information and communication technologies (ICT), unless the human hive is a physically local and small one with co-located members.

A basic assumption of the electronic hive mind is that anything that touches more than one person at some point has to have some public facing side, and in the current age, the "public" often involves electronic presences via the Web and Internet. This means that if a hermit wanted to reach an audience, he or she would have to go public at some point. Technologically and practically, it is very hard to create public messaging to appeal to particular narrowcast audiences without also showing one's hand to a larger audience of potential observers (including researchers).

A book project is virtually never a *fait accompli*, no matter how alluring a concept. [I am reminded of the fictional character Dominick Cobb's comment, "An idea is like a virus, resilient, highly contagious. The smallest seed of an idea can grow. It can grow to define or destroy you." This is from screenplay author and film director Christopher Nolen in his 2010 film *Inception.*] No matter the uncertainty about this work, a book for me starts with an idea that has traction and resilience; it feeds obsessiveness. Then, what follows is a lot of work to test that theory of whether there is a *there*. The concept of an EHM at this moment is amorphous and somewhat formless, based on an elusive analogy of online social thinking to the human mind (as a social mind). This work will be experimental. In this project as in all others, there are breakpoints at which a "go" or "no-go" decision will ultimately have to be made. However, at the beginning, the sky is always blue, and the sun is out, and all things are possible.

Before any solid work towards this effort, I think it would help to explain the attraction of the concept. An electronic hive mind (EHM) is alluring because it captures the sense of a thinking, feeling, willful, purposive, mass social/anti-social/asocial opinionating group-human "personality" connected by socio-technical means and triggered by any number of things. This consciousness is both an individual and a collective one, and while there are sci-fi elements to this, I do not mean this as anything approaching the concept of a singularity (a moment when an artificial intelligence affects humanity collectively irreversibly by affecting their collective consciousness and existence). This also does not refer to any sort of super-consciousness *per se* (no singularity comparisons) or about "wisdom of crowds" as its own phenomenon, but this is also not just about a group of people collaborating. For me, there is a mix of people and learning and technology, which is a nexus that I have worked within for years. This is also about using empirical data from the natural world based on available digital residua, mostly from a slice-in-time frame, and without an N = all (which would be truly "big data"). While the datasets are multimodal, and while big data (book corpora searches, mass search data) are accessed (albeit in "non-consumptive" ways that do not enable readability of or direct access to the underlying data), the data gathering may be better termed "data grazing" and "data nibbling" given how little of a full set is actually acquired. Ideally, a full sweep of data could be collected for analysis. From the collection, deductive observations may be made, and inductive hypotheses may be arrived at. Ad hoc and post hoc hypothesizing may be engaged to arrive at plausible understandings of the collected information. The EHM data may inform follow-on research. The research frame is subjective and interpretive, combining mixes of top-down and bottom-up data coding. It is unclear currently how reproducible this work may be or how much "noise" will be swept up with "signal."

The single idea of people coalescing around shared interests (even if they fundamentally disagree on aspects of the issue) via social media platforms is *passé*. The concept of groups messaging information to each other in a complex world is also not newsworthy. The observation that people coordinate via online means and then take action online and offline does not offer a Eureka moment. The notion that people in groups have various interests and express those interests in the hopes of swaying others is not news. The novelty of this approach is not in the idea of massminds. After all, people regularly attribute to markets various sentiments about particular in-world events to explain stock price movements; they attribute to collective entities particular personalities (nations, international and multinational organizations, companies, and other groupings). What may be pseudo-original is in the concept of electronic + hive + mind and the uses of some analytical approaches to understanding how these may manifest and affect the world.

WHAT TO STUDY

To Repeat: Is there a *there?* The *there* in "electronic hive minds" comes about in the following aspects:

- The definition of what makes an "electronic hive mind" and the analogical comparisons with the individual's mind and group mind research;
- Its parts and respective functions in real space;
- Its capabilities of EHM cognition, learning, reasoning, decision-making, imagination and fantasy, conscious / unconscious / subconscious, conscience and applied values, "personalities," memory and forgetting, and other aspects;
- The global and multi-lingual, multi-geographical, multi-cultural, and Web-informed aspects of the EHM;
- The informal vs formal EHMs, the natural self-organizing emergent EHM vs. the strategic and planned ones;
- Its calls to actions and the responsiveness of its "body" or members;
- Its evolution over time;
- Its evolving members, foremost humans, but also "cyborgs" (human-embodied and semi-automated social media accounts) and "bots"/ automated agents (and their motivations and their contributions); and
- Ultimately, whether an "electronic hive mind" is more than the sum of its parts.

How are attentional resources distributed in an EHM? How is information processed? How does learning occur? How does forgetting (not remembering, unlearning, writing over memories) occur? Are there times when the EHM is unthinking? What are proclivities of particular EHMs? How much can the respective stakeholders and participants in an EHM be identified (at least by interests, and maybe, to a person through personally identifiable information or "PII")? Are there times when EHMs fall into mad "loves" and mad "likes" that bypass the executive functions? How much accurate and inaccurate information is shared among the members of an EHM? Are there differences between EHMs based on size? Are there different types of EHMs, and what are consistent ways to identify these types? For example, are there different types of EHMs based on personalities, identities; topics, events, practices, brands; time-based occurrences; locational issues and occurrences; motivational pursuits; (and) processes like learning, risk mitigation, problem-solving, (and) activities. Do EHMs enable mass unthinking actions and reaping whirlwinds and destruction?

To explore this issue, it seemed like it would make sense to apply the concept to a variety of actual real-world cases to see if the methods could offer sufficient coherence to this phenomenon. In alignment with this approach, the initial chapter will lay the groundwork for the concept, and the follow-on chapters will involve real-world cases of applied EHMs.

Research Methods and Data Analysis

Another point of interest has to do with what is practically knowable about electronic hive minds based on public "trace" data [capturable using the affordances of the application programming interfaces (APIs) of the respective social media platforms and proprietary commercial software and open-shared freeware], and further, what may be understood using computational text and digital content analyses alongside human analysis? Is this even a workable research approach? How confident can one be of these respective assertions, and are there ways to compare the known with what is knowable and to extrapolate unknowns (and maybe unknown unknowns)? How can biasing analytic factors, like "survival bias," be mitigated for, given silences and unavailable data?

In this sense, this work is built on prior research on human psychology, information processing, social psychology, human decision-making, human cognition, social network analysis, and other relevant fields. The seeding topics that will be used to study various aspects of an EHM will be "social" topics, beyond the interests of an individual or "isolate" node. Some early hypothesizing might suggest the following:

- Different types (based on the reasons for why people connect as an online group with some shared interests) of electronic hive minds online may be identifiably unique from other types. They may differ in terms of structure, messaging, membership, activities, and other aspects.

- EHMs may have different time aspects—in terms of how they originate and why, how they maintain over time, and other aspects. What does a basic EHM look like in its early phases? What re ways that EHMs are fed and nurtured over time? What strengthens them, and what weakens them over time? How do these sunset? How long do these usually last? What are some defining events for respective EHMs? What are some common general trajectories?

These are some initial and untested questions. As the work progresses, more questions will certainly arise, and some initial questions may be found to be too far outside the possible at this present moment, with the current methods and technologies. [That said, I am beginning with a dozen or so different methods and technologies that have traction in this space. The approaches will include the following: search data (Google Correlate); large-scale formal corpus data (Google Books Ngram Viewer); ephemera (#hashtag networks); virtual communities data (social networks, virtual groups, and others, from social networking sites, microblogging sites, and others); social data (from news sharing sites, crowd-sourced encyclopedias, video sharing sites), and others. These will also include multimodal data: text, hashtags, audio, video, imagery, and other digital forms. More on these will follow in the respective chapters. The draft Table of Contents is also in a very nascent form. The early version that I sent to the very able Jordan Tepper, Assistant Development Editor at IGI Global, was such an embarrassment of in-definition that I would not have likely met that suggested deadline with a very early draft had I not worked with her before on other projects.]

Even if all the prior is attainable, typical questions for any research goes, "So what? And?" In other words, what is the relevance of mapping "electronic hive minds" and potentially understanding this phenomenon better (if it is indeed a phenomenon and not a reified pseudo-phenomenon)? Some early thinking on this is that these approaches may help researchers better understand social phenomena online and better forecast social changes. This work may point to ways to better evolve electronic hive minds for more accurate and efficient cognition and decision making, collaboration, and problem-solving. These methods may provide ways to improve the power of human sensor networks—or observing human messaging to understand how events may unfold.

PROJECT STARTS

Work on this project has been going on since early 2018, when I first wrote a chapter titled "The Electronic Hive Mind and Cybersecurity: Mass-Scale Human Cognitive Limits to Explain the 'Weakest Link' in Cybersecurity," which ran in a book titled *Global Cyber Security Labor Shortage and International Business Risk* (edited by Bryan Christiansen and Agnieszka Piekarz, and published in October 2018, with a copyright year of 2019). The concept of an electronic hive mind met my requirements for the earlier work, but then, it persisted in my thinking. The idea was not yet done with me. In early Fall 2018, I signed a contract for yet another book, and I actually started work several months later once I had met prior commitments with earlier deadlines. In this early stage, I do not know if the work will be like climbing a hillock or a mountain. I have no idea if this work will come to reality or remain an inchoate and elusive idea. Sometimes, though, there is value to even asking a question, and the attractiveness of the concept is enough to carry it—for the next little while. At best, this exploratory work may be helpful in highlighting an online/offline phenomenon; at worst, this will have been a fun misadventure.

PHASE 2: CHAPTER DEVELOPMENT AND DRAFTING (LATE OCT. – DEC. 2018)

How the respective chapters were conceptualized initially is based on different aspects of mind (awareness, decision making, personality, and so on), especially those that have some way of translating in a group or collective sense. Then, once foundational research was done, target electronic hive minds were identified for the particular areas of study. As research occurred both in the formal published realm and in the social media spaces, the conceptualizations for each chapter evolved. For each chapter, there were attempts to achieve the following: originality, varying complementary research methods, different technological tools, and others, so that something novel could be brought to the forefront for each. While a number of different EHMs were analyzed, all were done so provisionally and partially and non-definitively, but with the idea that each would offer some transferable insights…about the phenomenon of EHMs and about researching them. This collection is of a number of case studies.

The idea of the analyses was to shed light on research processes and to enable some initial hypothesizing. In none of these contexts was the research scale inclusive of an N = all to even begin to capture some of the complex dimensions. Also, the analyses are based not only on partial (often recent) data but on subjective interpretive lenses in some cases (along with mass search data, mass book data, computational text analysis and some other types of reproducible research).

For a researcher, an idea has to be somewhat compelling and alluring to have value. The risk, though, is to fall in love with an idea so much that one ends up reifying it with follow-on work that is not sufficiently self-critical and skeptical. An electronic hive mind (EHM) is built on an abstract concept, with little research about how to concretize it. These early works at capturing glimpses of EHMs may make it seem more solid and realized than it is currently. And yet, I will say that there is something of a "there" there.

The original book proposal was a mere idea, and it was not until months later that a very rough and early outline was sent to the publisher. At that time, the book was conceptualized as nine chapters around the topic of electronic hive minds (EHMs) based on certain forefronted features of human minds (albeit as collectives), such as these concepts: top-of-mind, subconscious, unconscious, disposition and personality, intelligence quotient, emotional intelligence, executive functions, delusions, forgetting, decision making and action taking, threat awareness (and mitigation), and innovations. If I had not had a prior online-mediated working relationship with the professional at the publisher, I would have been wholly embarrassed and stricken to have sent something so rough and undeveloped. Having been through the creative process before and having conducted research before, I was sufficiently comfortable that something would come of the initial proposed outline. Call it experience-based and informed intuition.

In terms of the actual specific topics selected, there were clear efforts to strive for something with sufficient broad scope. I knew that I would not be mapping any EHMs definitively because of the lack of comprehensive data and the lack of more comprehensive data analytics methods. The data for all the EHMs explored were slice-in-time data, without anywhere near an N = all and nothing truly longitudinal. The limitations of subjective framing have to be considered. The research methods were hybrid, involving both qualitative and quantitative analytics methods, and manual and auto-coding. For each chapter, I strove to explore a different aspect of EHMs, and I strove to use some new research or analysis approaches (even though some research methods recurred, necessarily). Along the way, I qualified assertions and strove not to go beyond where the social and other data allowed. I tried to identify new insights about EHMs in each chapter as well.

During the work, which spanned about half a year, I was constantly aware of the slippage of time. This was especially so because of required dependencies for accessing social data (text, imagery, quantitative data, and others) from social media platforms and the Social Web. For example, a social media platform changed ownership in one case. In several others, browser add-ons were no longer functioning on a new laptop with a newer operating system and updated web browsers, so I had to go to an older backup machine to acquire data. In several cases, the companies behind the application programming interfaces (APIs) of social media platforms changed terms of use, rendering some access points useless.

The extended Table of Contents follows:

AN EXTENDED TABLE OF CONTENTS (TOC)

Preface
Chapter 1: Early Mapping of "Electronic Hive Minds" on the Web and Internet

An "electronic hive mind" (EHM) is conceptualized as a type of temporally limited social consciousness (held by people, cyborgs, and robots) around shared interests, enabled by social media and information and communication technology (ICT). EHMs may be understood partially through combined prior research in the areas of social psychology and social media. Other research work is novel and requires the application of a range of methods and technologies to identify EHMs from publicly available social media residual data, in various digital modalities. To this end, some initial mapping techniques to understand EHMs will be shown.

Chapter 2: Ferreting Out Silences and Invisibilities in Electronic Hive Minds – Identifying Absent/Non-Present, Latent/Hidden, and Shadowed/ Obfuscated Messaging

An electronic hive mind (EHM), as a distributed swarm intelligence, is about shared information and resources, and the interactions around those elements. A lesser-studied aspect in such electronic-enabled collectives involves unshared information, silences, withholdings, and other invisibilities. What is shared depends on socio-technical systems and how people engage and think socially, and these factors result in various absences, latencies, and shadowing of messaging. Here, an early mechanism-based approach is taken to understand the inflows and outflows of information from an EHM and areas where messages may be unformed, dropped, misapprehended, or obfuscated, resulting in knowledge gaps. Finally, this thought experiment suggests that EHMs should be understood as constructs with shimmering and incomplete versions of reality, and "what you see is all there is" (WYSIATI) would be an illusory approach.

Chapter 3: Defining Collective Personalities, Dispositions, Temperaments, and Moods of Electronic Hive Minds

An electronic hive mind, a temporal shared consciousness (or massmind) of people interacting through online communications technologies and other means, may be thought of as having collective personalities, dispositions, and temperaments. These human-based features may be seen from various dimensions:

- The public (and private) messaging (textual, imagistic, audio, video, and multimodal elements)
- The collective culture(s) and practices
- The human membership and member motivations
- The group actions (virtual and in-world)
- The sociotechnical systems, and others

This early work explores some dimensions of collective and more stable personality, dispositions, and temperament that may be inferred form EHMs, as well as more transitory moods. These aspects of EHMs may inform on future actions and provide a predictive function.

Chapter 4: Frugal Living for Our Collective and Mutual #bestlife on a Distributed and Global Electronic Hive Mind

What is not as commonly identified as an optimal life #bestlife is living #frugal, and yet, there is a global electronic hive mind about how to live sparingly based on highly variant local realities. There are blogs about living on a shoestring, stretching funds, cooking in, engaging in a DIY economy (bartering with like-minded others), living off-the-grid, taking low-cost and simple vacations, maintaining a food garden, raising food animals, and forgoing the more spendy aspects of modern living. The narrative goes that saving up and retiring early enables low-pressure and intentional lifestyles (and an ability to focus on family and friends), low-carbon footprints (with low impacts on the environment), and the embodiment of a frugal virtue. This work explores what a #frugal living EHM looks like and how it brings together people around shared values and lifestyle practices for personal peace of mind, social justice and long-term sustainability.

Chapter 5: Buy/Hold/Trade or Sell/Divest/Disengage – Using Executive Functions in Electronic Hive Minds for Decision Making Around Cryptocurrencies

An electronic hive mind (EHM) can be a distributed virtual community and a mental space for information-gathering, analysis, and ultimately, decision making; it can play the role of executive functioning (in the same way a frontal lobe does for a human brain) and inform real-world actions. To see how this might function, the EHM around cryptocurrencies was explored from multiple social media platforms. This topic addresses an issue that is not fully defined and is of broad-scale mainstream interests. Cryptocurrencies may be everything from virtual ephemera and hot promises to a life-changing innovation. As a phenomenon, it has instantiated in different ways around the world, with cryptocurrency "farming" centers, nation-state-issued cryptocurrencies, government efforts at regulating such exchanges, and volatile gains and losses for cryptocurrency speculators and investors. How people engage with cryptocurrencies can affect their real-world net worth as well as other aspects of their lives, so this is not merely a theoretical issue but one with real-world impacts.

Chapter 6: Being and a Trolling State of Electronic Hive Mind – (1) Organically Emergent/Evolved Troll Groups and (2) Created/Instrumented Troll "Armies"

Trolling others, broadly defined as communicating provocative messages (and even threats) online, has been a pervasive part of the Web and Internet and even Information and Communications Technology (ICT). While many consider trolling a net negative, some do suggest that it provides counter-viewpoints, encourages caution in mainstream participants online, and broadens conversations. This work studies trolling as a state of electronic hive mind and being, in two main forms: (1) organically emergent, decentralized, and organically evolved troll coalitions for both personal member and group interests, and (2) created, instrumented, centrally supported / funded "troll armies" created for political and other purposes. Through the prism of "trolling," a part of the electronic hive mind will be explored, the pathologically aggressive, angry, aggrieved, and vengeance-seeking side.

Chapter 7: Consigned to Temporal or Permanent Oblivion? Mass Remembering and Forgetting in Electronic Hive Minds

Mass and partial forgetting in electronic hive minds (shared consciousness enabled through socio-technical spaces, social media, and information and communications technology [ICT]) is conceptualized as something gradual and organic based on the functions of human memory and accelerated in other cases, depending on the adaptive needs of the EHM. How EHMs form, the proclivity to certain attitudes, favored meta-narratives, the exposure to a wide range of ideas (vs. filter bubbles), and other aspects affect what is retained and what is forgotten. This early work explores some of the nature of forgetting in EHMs. This sheds some light on how some EHMs may coordinate to maintain memory on "critical issues" and "issues of facts" and the roles of those who act as "folk" historians and commemorators and the roles of technology as affordance/enablement and constraint. This work focuses on the hard effort of maintaining collective memory in the ephemera of transient EHMs. Methods for identifying blind spots and invisible spaces in memory in EHMs are suggested, and this method is applied in a walk-through of a portion of a star-based fandom and followership-based EHM.

Chapter 8: Micro- to Meso- to Macro-Scale Coordinated Individual and Group Action(s) on Electronic Hive Minds

So many of human endeavors are dependent on others' actions and interests. On an electronic hive mind (EHM), coordination online may spark and sustain actions by the body (the members of the EHM). Such coordination occurs over a range of human endeavors and continuously at different scales: micro (individual, dyadic, and motif levels), meso (small to large groups), and macro (system-wide, societal, web-scale levels). This work explores EHMs as planned-action entities and offers some early insights about some common practices, based on multiple exemplars and the application of abductive logic.

Chapter 9: Expanding the Imagination, Thinking, Knowledge, and Relevant Skills – True Innovation With Electronic Hive Minds?

"Creatives" online, those who innovate as a regular part of their work and lifestyles, are likely one of the most diverse electronic hive minds online, with often highly dissimilar and heterogeneous members. As a general group, they are specialists in their respective areas but often engage online with professionals in their respective communities of expertise as well as with others in disparate fields in order to benefit from the cross-fertilization of ideas. They are by nature and practice exploratory and often sharing. What does the pursuit of inspiration look like for the distribute EHMs based around creative work?

Conclusion

The resulting chapters address many of the initial concepts in the early brainstorm. And it may be that the first work of the series about the cybersecurity EHM (Hai-Jew, 2019) is the one that dealt with threat awareness and response.

PHASE 3: THE SPRINT TO THE WRAP-UP (MAR. 2019)

Once the initial drafts were completed by December, 2018, they were set up to be reviewed in a double-blind context by two reviewers, as all IGI Global Research Insight imprint books are. In late February, the two reviews were sent to the author, who made changes based on those comments. Of special import were changes to the Conclusion, with ethical considerations to explore electronic hive minds online.

The ambition of this work, from early days, was to explore the concept of "electronic hive minds" to see what was knowable and how well these could be tentatively explored across a number of platforms. Given the complexity of the endeavor and the lack of resourcing that could be put into this project, *Electronic Hive Minds on Social Media: Emerging Research and Opportunities* was conceptualized as a theorized work with some light research to backstop the effort. This would provide some very light early flirtation with EHMs, to suggest some early ways forward.

What can readers expect from this book? They can expect a creative approach that explores some light aspects of EHMs, with plenty of ideas for advancing this work by moving an existing chapter forward, asking relevant research questions in different ways, harnessing different methods and technologies to understanding EHMs, identifying peripheral areas of interest, and so on. It is hoped that these works are not only insightful but enjoyable to explore. In this spirit, I am grateful for your interest.

At the end of this text, the Conclusion contains the additional phases of this work. It captures some summary insights about electronic hive minds as they instantiate in the world. It offers musing on ethical considerations to achieve this research work. This book is built on unobtrusive research that uses trace data available through online forage. Perhaps more directly engaged elicitation of information and other forms of research would enable different and additional insights.

Shalin Hai-Jew
Kansas State University, USA
January 2019

REFERENCES

Hai-Jew, S. (2019). The electronic hive mind and cybersecurity: Mass-scale human cognitive limits to explain the 'weakest link' in cybersecurity. In *Global Cyber Security Labor Shortage and International Business Risk* (pp. 206–262). Hershey, PA: IGI Global. doi:10.4018/978-1-5225-5927-6.ch011

Hive Mind. (2018, Oct. 9). In *Google dictionary*. Retrieved Oct. 9, 2018, from https://www.google.com/search?q=Dictionary#dobs=hive%20mind

Acknowledgment

This is for R. Max, Lily, and Asher, remarkable individuals all!

Thanks to IGI Global for the opportunity to pursue this work of exploring electronic hive minds. There is a lot to be said for the necessary trust on which to build a project that involves this much effort! Thanks to Jordan Tepper, Assistant Development Editor at IGI Global, for shepherding this project through this book writing process, the double-blind peer review, the revision, and the proofing work. Also, thanks to Jan Travers or the contract. I am deeply grateful to the two anonymous peer reviewers for their encouragement, insights, and good humor. Their ideas improved this work. I appreciate their professional empathy, which goes a long way.

This project was proposed back in July 2018, was started in October 2018, and finalized in early March 2019.

Chapter 1
Early Mapping of "Electronic Hive Minds" on the Web and Internet

ABSTRACT

An "electronic hive mind" (EHM) is conceptualized as a type of temporally limited social consciousness (held by people, cyborgs, and robots) around shared interests, enabled by social media and information and communication technology (ICT). EHMs may be understood partially through combined prior research in the areas of social psychology and social media. Other research work is novel and requires the application of a range of methods and technologies to identify EHMs from publicly available social media residual data in various digital modalities. To this end, some initial mapping techniques to understand EHMs will be shown in this chapter.

INTRODUCTION

It was the summer of 1999, and people were starting to realize that the internet and the web were becoming a new, dynamic circulatory system for information, coordination, and life itself. - David Auerbach's Bitwise: A Life in Code (2018, p. 4)

DOI: 10.4018/978-1-5225-9369-0.ch001

The idea of an "electronic hive mind" emerges as a natural convergence between information and communication technologies (ICT) and people, who have in the past decades have used such technologies to intercommunicate, socialize, follow / like / emulate (meme-ing) / troll each other, share digital contents, collaborate, co-design, and co-act (Figure 01), as expressed in this Venn diagram. A part of this intersection has been referred to as the "cyber-physical convergence" (Conti, et al., 2012) or cyber-physical confluence. Whatever people have done and do in the real world, they often have some equivalency in the online one. Researchers have found that people tend to build egocentric social networks online that mirror the offline world (Dunbar, Arnaboldi, Conti, & Passarella, 2015). For many, their online existence may be even more salient and top-of-mind than their physical one. An early and tentative definition of this electronic hive mind (EHM) describes it as "a sentient and potent mass entity with potential for various types of concentrated mass action as well as dispersed smaller-unit actions, among others" (Hai-Jew, 2019, p. 210). This early work suggests a nascent view of a notional and practical EHM.

An electronic hive mind is enabled by humanity's hyperconnectivity through ICT technologies that enable them to share information and digital contents (and moneys and physical contents) in near real-time. This history-making enablement enables people from a wide geographical area (global) to interconnect. The human tendencies to filter information to see generally what they prefer and their confirmation bias (a form of built-in cognitive bias) may mean that people may "mind-meld" with other homophilous thinkers (those who prefer others with similar likes) regarding particular in-world phenomena, for short bursty periods or for longer term ones. The "hive" aspects of this suggest some sort of organization, with people and small groups and larger groups playing unique roles within the hive—to enable information collection, decision making, and leadership, among other needs. Another aspect of a "hive" may be its busyness, potentially bordering on frenzy, depending on particular social issues and senses of focus. And there is also something of the sense of swarm logic, the thinking and acting as a group, with the subsumation of the individuals into the hive and potentially mass suggestibility and mass action—that is so alluring about this concept.

Broadly speaking, EHMs are thought to coalesce around shared interests, based in part on individual and group/social motivations, which are sufficiently inspiring to encourage continuing engagement, at least for a time.

More formally, an early working definition of an "electronic hive mind" (EHM) is the following:

Figure 1. "Electronic hive mind" from a confluence of ICT and people

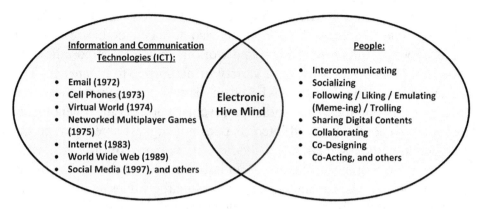

"Electronic Hive Mind" from a Confluence of ICT and People

a synchronous temporal and informal patchwork of emergent shared social consciousness (held by geographically distributed people, cyborgs, and robots) enabled by online social connectivity (across a range of social media platforms on the Web and Internet), based around various dimensions of shared attractive interests.

This is informed in part by concepts from social network analysis practices but also applied research in the social media platform spaces. It would help to parse out the various elements a little now, and the rest of the book will be used to explore what various aspects mean based on how such minds instantiate. The definition suggests that humans, cyborgs (social media accounts comprised of both humans and automated agents), and robots (automated agents / scripts used to run social media accounts) may achieve moments of shared consciousness based on online interactivity. (This is not to say that scripted agents have "cognition" or "self-awareness" but that the technologies contain the information that may be analyzed. This does suggest that humans have dependencies on technologies to enable an EHM, and consciousness is not only situated in the humans alone but externally to some degree, in inanimate technologies. Technologies augment and extend human minds—as individuals and as collectivities and groups. This may be informed by the "extended mind" concept, which suggests that external elements beyond the individual agent may extend the person's consciousness (Wilson, 2005, p. 230).]

The length of shared consciousness may be short-term or longer term, and these may not necessarily mean agreement or consensus, but only shared awareness. The "electronic hive mind" is also at once a connected hive of people, cyborgs, and robots ('bots) that work in some sort of coordination across the Web and Internet, on a variety of platforms, to co-engage. The core rationales for EHMs to exist is based on shared interests—whether about core issues, personalities, social practices, events, work, or other phenomena. The "attractiveness" of shared interests does not suggest agreement on the topic, only that the issue attracts the various participants of the EHM, even as they may hold opposite stances on an issue (or even if the agency of the participating "ego" is machine-based, expressing the values and interests of the developer or the funder behind the developer of the scripted agents and social media platform accounts). As is typical of social media relationships, most are assumed to be thin ties, without deeper connections in the real world and real life (RL). The assumption is that the ties exist as long as the individual interests are being met and the mind stays healthy and productive. Then, after a time, individuals (isolates), small groups (motifs), and larger groups (sub-networks) will break off, and then the electronic hive mind either reconstitutes itself through re-definition, or it dissipates, and its members find other interests. There is also the assumption that the respective individual "egos" that play a role in the network will be members in multiple electronic hive minds depending on their interests (to match the interests of complex human beings). Membership is non-exclusive, and the connections are informal and self-organizing in some cases (and formal and consciously structured and organized in others). This space is conceptualized as highly dynamic and constantly evolving, with alliances coalescing for a time and then dissipating, with some EHMs gradually dissipating…and others imploding with fanfare and human attention. The assumption is that EHMs continue as long as they continue to meet human needs, but if needs evolve, these will dissipate. The online spaces, though, are fairly "easy come, easy go," and "ghosting" people in online relationships is no difficult feat (it only requires going silent and / or ditching social media accounts.)

A final early assumption is that some EHMs may be obvious and named and high-profile, and others may be less obvious and require some exploration to find. Concomitant to this latter assumption, there is the idea that some EHMs will be sufficiently hidden and elusive so as to be invisible for researchers using only public data and publicly available tools. Any mapping will be incomplete. The concept of "finding" EHMs suggests that they are already extant in the world and just need to be seen, but that interpretation may be limiting. After all, there is some degree of reification here of an abstraction, the filling in of an idea with found data, in an *ex nihilo* or "out of nothing" approach. An optimal understanding is that this work is somewhere in between finding an extant object and reifying the somewhat-immaterial concept. Ideally, by the time this authored text is complete, there will be a clearer sense of which of the two polarities is more accurate for EHMs.

The central analogy in this work involves the human mind, which is something other than the brain but is enabled by the brain. The formal definition of a "mind" somewhat abstract: "the element of a person that enables them to be aware of the world and their experiences, to think, and to feel; the faculty of consciousness and thought; a person's intellect" ("Mind," Oct. 11, 2018). In Wikipedia, a "mind" is

a set of cognitive faculties including consciousness, perception, thinking, judgement, language, and memory. It is usually defined as the faculty of an entity's thoughts and consciousness. It holds the power of imagination, recognition, and appreciation, and is responsible for processing feelings and emotions, resulting in attitudes and actions ("Mind," Oct. 8, 2018).

An electronic hive mind, like software, exists over a technological infrastructure with its affordances and enablements as well as its constraints. Others have compared such technological understructures as electronic nervous systems. Human activities on these platforms and networks have been described as human sensor networks, ripe for surveillance and sousveillance (by its own members as self- and other-informants). [People in an electronic hive mind may not be aware that they are in one. They may not realize that they are a small part of something much larger than themselves. They may engage from within any number of social media platforms and forms of ICT. The concept is that small connections and weak links and light messaging may indeed coalesce into a dynamic outside of the people participating and well beyond the control of their members, singly or in groups.] An electronic hive mind is fundamentally cyborgian, comprising both humans and technologies. And when people are engaging in social ways, there are also cultural influences to the EHMs. The focus on a mind enables engagement with people's interests on a range of psychological and socio-psychological features (intelligence, personality, ethics, sociality, and others), while building on brain-and-body-based capabilities, including perception, cognition, learning, decision making, and others. This approach enables discussing mindsets, habits and routines, top-of-mind issues, emotions, moods, the conscious/subconscious/

unconscious, the pursuit of pleasure-seeking or hedonic pursuits, mental pain avoidance, mental blindspots, illusions and delusions, presumptions, cognitive biases, passions, convictions, sentiments, affections, schadenfreude, and other variations—from a social crowd-source collectivized perspective. The hope is not to just see EHMs in activated hot states and intensifications but also in cool ones.

Operationalizing the mapping of EHMs is a challenge. There is not a clear definition of understanding membership within EHMs, the harnessed social media platforms underpinning respective EHMs, the in-group and out-group definitions of membership for EHMs, which members are central vs. which are peripheral, and other aspects. The "mapping" or "mind reading" of EHMs is described as credibly identifying and describing respective EHMs: their objectives, their modus operandi, their membership (and leadership, in whatever form), their messaging, their personalities, their resources, their histories, their functions, their impacts, and other elements. This involves learning how these originate, evolve, engage, and end. This research would ideally inform on how EHMs may be identified and observed, with accuracy and confidence. It is hard to know yet the practical limits of this knowledge and also how confident one can be of the assertions.

This analogy of an EHM is not fully carried forward. In some ways, the mind is disembodied (cyber), but in another, it is fully embodied (via people). A "mind" is an ephemeral concept, situated in the biological physical and the social-cultural and also in the spiritual, but it is also unsituated and elusive, without emplacement.

This assumes a combined brains-and-bodies approach given the sociality of EHMs. And technological affordances stand to magnify interactivity, memory, and other aspects of human connectivity and collaboration. Finally, there will be some explorations that play off of brain capabilities, such as the alluring concept of the "lizard brain" or the "triune brain" or the ancient early-evolution brain…and an inferred mind from that baser and more ancient part of human mental processing.

Optimally, once this chapter and book manuscript are completed, there may be a more pithy and less unwieldy definition that can be operationalized.

The main focuses of this chapter then are to review some of the published research that relate to this concept of an electronic hive mind and then to go through some generic walk-throughs of how to collect public data from various social media and other relevant platforms to start sketching the outlines of an electronic hive mind. This will show ways to understand a hive mind on a platform and between platforms. Then, too, this work will show not only ways to capture summary data but also more zoomed-in in-depth data.

Technologies Employed

In this work, various technologies were used for the data extractions and data visualizations. These include Google Correlate; Google Books Ngram Viewer; Network Overview, Discovery and Exploration for Excel (NodeXL); NVivo 12 Plus, and others. Several social media platforms are accessed here, including Wikipedia and Flickr. More on the respective data analytics approaches will follow.

REVIEW OF THE LITERATURE

Early work in human psychology dates back to the 1870s, with the world's first psychologist, Wilhelm Wundt; social psychology dates back to 1898, with the world's first "social psychology" researcher, Norman Triplett. From early days, people have been seen as both individuals and as social beings in relation to others. As to where human minds come from, researchers describe fundamental assumptions: "The human mind is the product of evolution, and the human mind is shaped by culture. These conclusions are, we think, unassailable" (Norenzayan, Schaller, & Heine, 2010, p. 2).

A core social skill involves a phenomenon called "theory of mind" (colloquially known as "mentalizing" and as unschooled or amateur "folk psychology") which involves reasoning about one's own and others' mental states by interpreting observations of interpersonal cues and other signals and making inferences, in order to predict others' behaviors (Premack & Woodruff, Dec. 1978). The imputation of others' internal states, which are not directly observable, requires astute observations, human understandings, and empathy. People ascribe minds to others in somewhat idiosyncratic ways:

Perceiving others' minds is a crucial component of social life. People do not, however, always ascribe minds to other people, and sometimes ascribe minds to non-people (e.g. God, gadgets)…Causes of mind perception stem both from the perceiver and perceived, and include the need for social connection (perceiver) and a similarity to oneself (perceived). (Waytz, Gray, Epley, & Wegner, 2010, p. 383)

When thinking of other people's minds, people focus on two dimensions: "experience (the capacity to sense and feel) and agency (the capacity to plan and act)" (Gray et al., 2007, as cited in Waytz, Gray, Epley, & Wegner, 2010, p. 383). These two dimensions "experience…and agency" were extracted by factor analysis to better understand people's mind perception and their moral judgments (Gray, Gray, & Wegner, 2007). (One of the core elements of the fundamental attribution error is people's tendencies to explain a person's behavior based on their internal disposition and to neglect consideration of the larger context.) Individual skill with theory of mind is thought to enhance people's social interactions and cooperate work, and similarly, group skills with theory of mind enhances "collective intelligence," both online and face-to-face and group tasks (Engel, Woolley, Jing, Chabris, & Malone, 2014). Theory of mind informs group members on how to engage in group social interactions and especially in "highly impoverished communication channels such as many online environments" and enhances task performance ultimately (Engel, Woolley, Jing, Chabris, and Malone, 2014, p. 4). In longer term time periods, theory of mind is thought to enable humans to "cognize the world in ways leading to the creation and use of natural languages, complex tools and technologies, mathematical symbols, graphic symbols from maps to art, and complicated social institutions such as governments and religions," which are "collective cultural products" (Tomasello & Rakoczy, 2003, p. 121). While there may be some universals, cultural backgrounds and traditions may unduly affect "folk psychological interpretations" of others' intentions (Lillard 1998, p. 7).

"Group mind," the "collective consciousness," "the collective mind," and other references point to the understanding of shared collective thinking and feeling, with collectives acting as semi-autonomous agents. In this conceptualization, groups are somewhat more than the sum of its individual parts, and experiences are created and shared as social entities. There are true interdependencies, beyond simple aggregations (Dijkstra, Bouman, Bakker, & Assen, 2018). Groups have agency in the ways that some individuals have agency (Allport, 1962, p. 3), and "personification" has been applied to groups (Allport, 1962, pp. 3 - 4). Early thought may have situated groupness in "individual facts"…and existing "cognitively *within the individual*" (Asch, 1952b, as cited in Allport, 1962, p. 6), but more recent thought suggests something more: the idea of "crowd mind" and crowd actions (Allport, 1962, p. 6). One researcher writes:

Instead of saying that a group incorporates (or is composed of) many individuals, we would do almost better to say that an individual incorporates many groups. One group has salience for him (that is, he is present in it or acting in terms of it) at one time, and another has salience at another time. When not salient for the individual, a group to which he belongs could be said to be represented in his own organism as sets, latent meanings, or stored memories (Allport, 1962, p. 25).

Individual minds are augmented by group minds, a concept from "the biological and social sciences that have appealed to the idea that groups have minds" (Wilson, 2005, p. 227). Individuals are informed by emergent norms of collective behavior and their social relationships (Aguirre, Wenger, & Vigo, June 1998, p. 301). Organizations are thought to have capabilities for learning and strategy (Senge, 1990, 2006). They are thought to engage experience, imagination, and reasoning, such as companies engaging in "entrepreneurial theorizing" [involving "(1) the triggering role of experiential and observational fragments; (2) the imagination of possibilities; and (3) reasoning and justification" and systematized testing of theories in the world (Felin & Zenger, 2009, p. 127).] If "chance favors the connected mind" (Johnson, 2010), interconnections themselves may favor electronic hive minds by introducing diversity and heterogeneity that may feed innovations.

Collective minds have been harnessed for a variety of purposes beyond innovations. In high-risk work places, people train heavily to create a collective sense of a context, so they can manage risks and maintain safety and uphold "organizational performance in situations requiring nearly continuous operational reliability" (Weick & Roberts, Sept. 1993, p. 357). In this context, a collective mind is defined as "a pattern of heedful interrelations of actions in a social system" (Weick & Roberts, Sept. 1993, p. 357). (The prior research was based on flight operations on aircraft carriers.) Here, "organizational mind" is comprised of "collective mental processes in organizations" (Weick & Roberts, Sept. 1993, p. 357). Thinking as part of a group suggests that individuals have real-time awareness of their own roles and those of their colleagues and peers, in a systems way, so they can cooperate effectively across joint actions. Here, "mind" is conceptualized as a "disposition to heed" (Weick & Roberts, Sept. 1993, p. 361) or a kind of social mindfulness; collective mind is "located" in the process of interrelating (Weick & Roberts, Sept. 1993, p. 365), and people are socialized and re-socialized into this through the "candor and narrative skills of insiders and the attentiveness of newcomers" (p. 368). Individual and collective minds interact through "social representations, symbolic systems, practices and sense making" (Tateo & Iannaccone, 2102, p. 57). In some ways, digital artifacts may be used in stigmergy (defined as "signs that do the work" by Pierre-Paul Grassé in 1959) processes as signs left in the environment to enable people to self-organize around those activating messages (Dron 2007, p. 203).

Collective reputations are comprised of "group reputation as an aggregate of individual reputations" (Tirole 1996, p. 1), among others. The elements that help a team function smoothly: trust, (constructive) conflict, commitment, accountability, and attention to results (Lencioni, 2002, p. 97). Virtual work teams purposefully strive to create collective minds in order to "coordinate and interrelate their knowledge and actions in order to perform their tasks" (Yoo & Kanawattanachai, 2001, p. 190).

Costs to Human Coordination and Massing

Another insight from the research literature is that creating human coalitions is not costless—either to create or to maintain. There are natural limits to people's "economy of attention" in fairly close alignment with Dunbar's number, even in terms of how people interact online (Goncalves, Perra, & Vespignani, 2011). There may be tensions between members of an EHM, with frictions from in-group and out-group perceptions and natural disagreements. The relative size of a group sometimes serves as a proxy for its "level of collective action" as a simple metric (Oliver & Marwell, 1988, p. 1). If costs can be controlled, group size is not a limiting factor for collective action:

Many sociologists incorrectly believe that larger groups are less likely to support collective action than smaller ones. The effect of group size, in fact, depends on costs. If the costs of collective goods rise with the number who share in them, larger groups act less frequently than smaller ones. If the costs vary little with group size, larger groups should exhibit more collective action than smaller ones because larger groups have more resources and are more likely to have a critical mass of highly interested and resourceful actors. The positive effects of group size increase with group heterogeneity and nonrandom social ties. Paradoxically, when groups are heterogeneous, fewer contributors may be needed to provide a good to larger groups, making collective action less complex and less expensive) (Oliver & Marwell, 1988, p. 1).

This expense exists even when some costs are borne by other entities, such as the social media platforms that often offer free hosting services (in exchange for the user information, user access, and advertising dollars). Engaging in an electronic hive mind requires, at minimum, attentional energy, time, and effort. Of course, members may choose to not engage. Technologically, it is possible to join a social media platform with minimal information, and stay a passive member without engaging, except occasionally. These are colloquially called "lurkers." If there were a continuum of engagement, at the other extreme may be the main contributors (the 20% in the Pareto principle or "the law of the vital few"), who are responsible for 80% of the effects. These are the individuals who support the endeavors of the hive mind with work (research, content development, and even hyper-sharing) and investments (various material resources). These individuals invest actual mind space into the endeavors, and they may provide original digital contents. Some on this end of the continuum may provide leadership. In the middle may be those who share links, free-ride news sources, and offer contents now and again. These general tendencies towards particular roles may vary. Based on individuals' actions, there may be emergence of larger scale patterns that describe the particular EHM. The routines and subroutines of the various human and automated actors in socio-technical spaces may be somewhat observable from the outside (and much more readily available potentially from the inside, based on how the systems are constructed and what sorts of data logging is done). The dynamism of a space may mean that lurkers may take a forefronted view at times based on their capabilities and positionality and experiences, among other things. If an electronic hive mind is comprised in part of "mind space," the individuals and groups who contribute share their intelligence, passions, and personalities. Lurkers may not always be in those roles although equilibriums may occur.

While there is a literature review indicating some "priors" that indirectly inform this concept, this is not a foregone path or conclusion.

ON SOCIAL MEDIA

The *residua* from social media interactions may be studied to inform this phenomenon.

From a Crowd-Sourced Encyclopedia

Some informational resources from social media may speak to the idea of hive minds. Figure 02 shows a "Hive_mind" article-article network on Wikipedia, at one degree. [Wikipedia, of course, is a massive crowd-sourced encyclopedia on the Web. Its English version had 5,732,442 articles in the English version at the time of the data extraction ("Wikipedia:Size of Wikipedia," Oct. 1, 2018), which suggests why it may be informative through article network structures.] These evoke the outlinks from the target article in the middle, with ties to concepts like "universal mind," "collective consciousness," "swarm intelligence," "collective intelligence," and the derogatory label of "sheeple," probably to indicate unthinking followership.

At 1.5 degrees out, the concepts become more diffuse, and the network becomes much larger (with 14 identified clusters extracted using the Clauset-Newman-Moore clustering algorithm). This network also includes some 1400 articles. In Figure 03, the respective high-level labels have been pulled out for each group, and the network graph is broken out into clusters (of alters and their respective 1-degree article-article ties). The more particular links evoke ideas of mass behaviors and capabilities.

Figure 2. "Hive_mind" article-article network on Wikipedia (1 deg.)

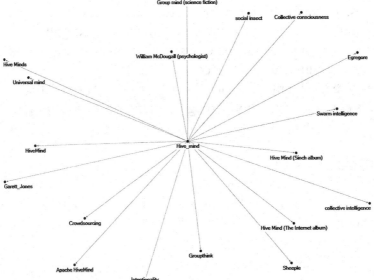

Figure 3. "Hive_mind" article-article network on Wikipedia (1.5 deg.)

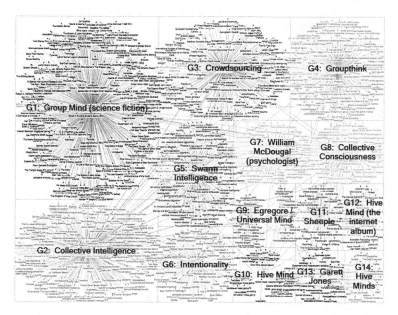

From an Image-Sharing Social Media Platform

On Flickr, it is possible to extract related tags networks. These tags are created by those who upload image contents to share on the site and others who use the site. The site also enables auto-tagging (the application of descriptive labels or tags to uploaded imagery) based on machine vision. There were no tags for "electronic hive mind," or "hive mind," but there were for the single elements: "electronic," "hive," and "mind." Interestingly, these separate elements were still evocative of insights, through combinations of words and imagery. Figure 04 was created from a 1.5 degree related tags network around "electronic." This data visualization evokes technology, energy, liveness, people, and crowds. The groups were created using the Clauset-Newman-Moore clustering algorithm.

"Hive," as a folk tag, evokes a rich range of co-occurring descriptor tags on the platform and more literalist aspects of hives. The images are thumbnails assigned by Flickr to represent the respective tags (Figure 05). Together, these evoke busyness, bees, emergent organization, and product (honey), among others.

Figure 4. *"Electronic" related tags network on Flickr (1.5 deg.)*

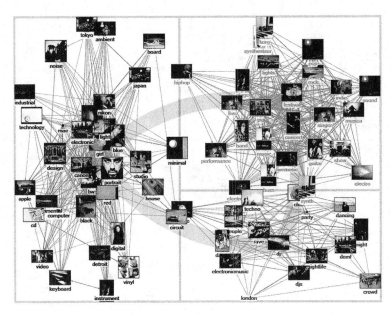

Figure 5. *"Hive" related tags network on Flickr (1.5 deg.)*

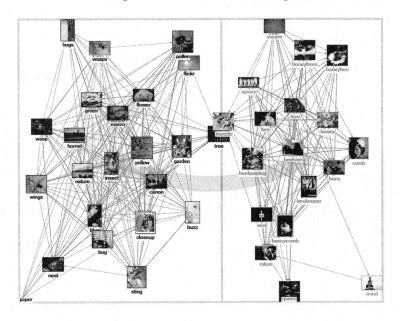

A search for "mind" related tags on Flickr at 1.5 degrees results in Figure 06. Here, a "mind" evokes the following: "heart," "soul," "spirit," "life" (animating), and other aspects. In this data visualization, the Fruchterman-Reingold layout algorithm is used for the clusters within each group, as it was for the others in this set.

From Mass-Scale Search Data

Interestingly, a basic search of "electronic hive mind" on Google Search resulted in 353 results (on Oct. 10, 2018), so it is not a widely known term (Figure 07). This author's prior publication in a cybersecurity text was an early use of the term and may have been the first use of the term, earlier this year. In terms of the found images from the "electronic hive mind" search, the image set was generally non-coherent albeit focused around technologies, robotics, online games, and some technologists and celebrities (Figure 08). This latter is included to convey the idea of the value of multimodal approaches to this research because data on the web is not only structured but semi-structured (and inclusive of imagery, audio, video, slideshows, multimedia publications, games, simulations, and much more than text).

Figure 6. "Mind" related tags network on Flickr (1.5 deg.)

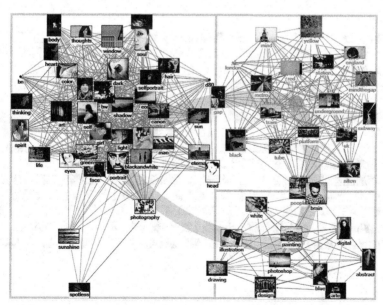

Figure 7. "electronic hive mind" search on Google Search

Figure 8. "Electronic hive mind" on Google image search (zoomed-out view)

On Google Correlate, "hive mind" results in a list of co-searched terms, but this list is not a particularly coherent or cohesive one. There are references to some social media elements and some internationally known car brands. It would be difficult to try to string together a narrative around this information. The word associations are not deeply revelatory in a way a Freudian slip or word association might be. (This approach, though, can and has worked in other applications.) The words that were correlated with "hive mind" for Google Searches from January 2003 to the present on Google Correlate (on Sept. 9, 2018) were the following (in descending order):

0.8538 2010 kia
0.8537 download teamviewer
0.8536 grow tents
0.8534 2010 dodge
0.8527 2010 ford explorer
0.8517 2010 dodge charger
0.8514 是 什么 意思 (shi shenme yisi)
0.8505 hunter facebook
0.8499 –
0.8495 porhub
0.8492 cook facebook
0.8491 someone you love
0.8489 how do you say i
0.8488 in facebook
0.8487 lemon skunk
0.8482 gelbooru
0.8480 displayport to vga
0.8478 4399
0.8476 you in french
0.8475 after a break up
0.8472 scott facebook
0.8466 bible verse of the day
0.8464 2010 explorer
0.8463 facebook st
0.8463 pon hub
0.8461 什么 意思 (shenme yisi)
0.8460 ninjatrader
0.8460 prn hub
0.8455 business on facebook

0.8455 orn hub
0.8453 displayport to dvi
0.8451 in one ear
0.8450 northwest pharmacy
0.8447 t3500
0.8445 kbid
0.8439 2010 kia forte
0.8436 easeus
0.8434 call people
0.8432 u say
0.8431 wild dog food
0.843 0rose facebook
0.8426 sankaku
0.8425 mini displayport
0.8424 say happy birthday in spanish
0.8417 how to say i
0.8416 bauer facebook
0.8413 recovery image
0.8413 nano receiver
0.8413 tv trope
0.8410 2010 ford focus
0.8410 precision t3500
0.8409 topics to talk about
0.8407 facebook friend request
0.8404 support phone number
0.8403 surgery recovery
0.8402 grow room
0.8402 create facebook
0.8397 get them
0.8395 2010 ford edge
0.8394 2010 hyundai elantra

Finally, it is possible to search for terms that exist in books published from the 1800s through 2000 that have been scanned into Google's repositories through their Google Books Ngram Viewer. Figure 09 shows low usage of the term "hive mind" and "hive," as compared to "mind." And there were no appearances of "electronic hive mind."

Figure 9. "Hive mind, hive, mind, electronic hive mind" on Google books ngram viewer

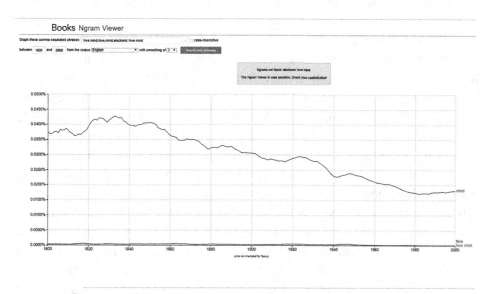

This approach of including data from social media gives a taste for some of the approaches that follow in the other chapters. These approaches are not comprehensive by any means, and these will not be the only sources used.

What is more important first is to define a basic sequence for how this exploration will work for discovering electronic hive minds on social media.

MAPPING ELECTRONIC HIVE MINDS ACROSS THE WEB AND INTERNET

Again, the basic working definition of an electronic hive mind is the following:

a synchronous temporal and informal patchwork of emergent shared social consciousness (held by geographically distributed people, cyborgs, and robots) enabled by online social connectivity (across a range of social media platforms on the Web and Internet), based around various dimensions of shared attractive interests.

One approach is to explore disparate social media and ICT platforms to see if there is a sense of "group entitativity" (coherence or organization) (Campbell, 1958; Hamilton & Sherman, 1996, as cited in Cikara, Bruneau, Van Bavel, & Saxe, 2014, p. 112).

What then are some ways to look for and identify electronic hive minds? What are ways to informatize the information? A very basic ten-step work sequence follows in Figure 10. This sequence begins with either a concept or exploratory research or both. Once there is an initial idea of a possible EHM or signs of one from the exploratory research, the next step is to design a multi-track research plan, identify relevant social media and ICT (data) sources, capture the multimodal data, clean the data, code the data, create data visualizations, explore and analyze the data, continue the research, validate or invalidate the electronic hive mind, write up the research, and present. In the steps, there are many assumptions about the types of social media, the types of multimodal collectible data, and the types of analytical approaches. It is beyond the purview of this initial chapter to address these, but these will be explored in depth in the following chapters. Also, within the large space related to EHMs, there are a number of approaches. In the spirit of parsimony, however, this visual sequence will suffice.

Even though a step-by-step work sequence is described here, the real-world processes themselves may be more complex than this visual might suggest. Certainly, achieving the actual results will often take a high amount of work and effort.

DISCUSSION

A basic starting point is with the working definition of an EHM: "a synchronous temporal and informal patchwork of emergent shared social consciousness (held by geographically distributed people, cyborgs, and robots) enabled by online social connectivity (across a range of social media platforms on the Web and Internet), based around various dimensions of shared attractive interests." Even though this is unwieldy, it may be useful to use this at least initially and until a more efficient and operationalized definition is developed.

An initial definition of an electronic hive mind? The initial intuition suggests that an electronic hive mind is comprised of some distributed coalescence of people around an issue and / or practice online forming some sort of entity (entitivaty), not in agreement or consensus or dissensus, but interest and focus. The members may have different individual and shared agendas. The

Figure 10. Exploring the online space for electronic hive minds (EHMs)

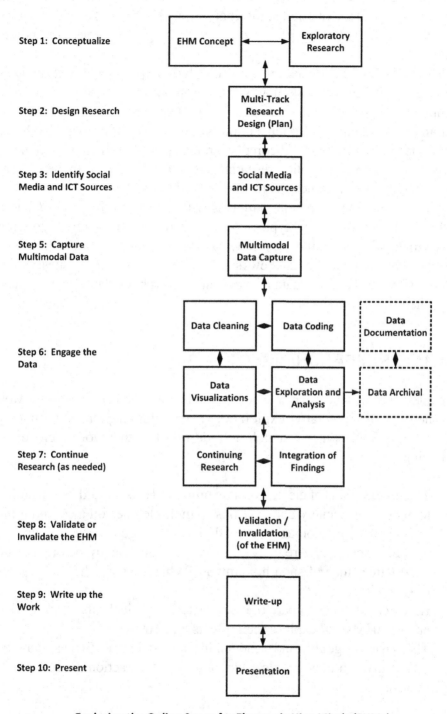

Exploring the Online Space for Electronic Hive Minds (EHMs)

coalescence may be sudden or gradual. But some shared engagement with the topic holds the hive mind somewhat loosely (or tightly) as a temporary body. In the colloquial, an EHM becomes a "thing." These seem to be the essentials.

The research approaches are informed by computational text analysis methods, including network analysis, content analysis, sentiment analysis, computational linguistic analysis, and related approaches. Manual coding, for text and image analysis also have important roles. The various methods are back-stopped by theory and theoretical frameworks, but the main emphasis in this text will be on applied research. The topical focus of the particular research will also influence the theory applied to the work.

What sorts of social media platforms will be used for this work? These will include the following types: social networking sites, microblogging sites, crowd-sourced online encyclopedias, online survey research platforms, learning management systems, news sharing sites, image-sharing sites, video-sharing sites, mass-search data research sites, mass book data research sites, and others.

FUTURE RESEARCH DIRECTIONS

The questions raised earlier may be answered in a wide variety of ways well beyond some of the tentative explorations here in this chapter and ultimately in the book. Some other research not addressed in this work include the following:

- The full lifespans of electronic hive minds (EHMs) would be intriguing to explore, especially comparisons of multiple ones on a certain topic or concept or phenomenon, or within a certain geographical space, or culture, or peoples. Are there early triggers that lead to the origination and maintenance of such hive minds? What are some lifespan events of such hive minds?
- Researchers may compare the various technological substructures that enable EHMs and explore their effects on EHMs.
- The visions, goals, and leadership of distributed EHMs may be informative on how people collaborate and take action on agendas of interest.

- Various types of EHMs may be mapped in more depth. What are the various types, and what are some logical ways to categorize these?
- Historical and "extinct" EHMs may be studied for other insights that may be shed on historical phenomenon and personages.
- Exploring how ideas percolate through EHMs and enable in-world effects would be powerful to study. For example, where did ideas originate from, and how did they evolve over time? Which members were brought into the discourse? How did plans originate? How were plans executed? How were plans funded (if relevant)?
- Taking an "ego" view of a "node" in an EHM may provide a human-embodied sense of the experience of being in an EHM. Or small-group studies of "motifs" and "subgroups" in EHMs may be researched per the "entity" experienced views.
- Are there "Dunbar Numbers" (Dunbar, 2010) for the natural sizes of EHMs supported by various social technologies? If so, what are reasonable explanations for why particular EHMs are particular sizes and not others? What are some methods for going beyond natural limits of size coordination (if these exist)? Are there size patterns of EHMs based on topics?
- Even if the public data collected were an N = all, researchers have imperfect insight into the phenomenon because such EHMs are comprised also of private data, real-space channels, and other ways of knowing. What are ways to go beyond publicly available data for this research, such as direct elicitations or legal access of private data (such as from service providers)? What are extensions to askable questions based on these extended approaches? And is a near-panopticon approach desirable?
- What are ways to accurately and practically infer invisible EHMs, with offline presences, hidden information, *note verbales*, encrypted communications, and other approaches?
- In EHMs engaging in high-risk high-reward endeavors, what are ways to detect manipulations, *agent provocateur* actions, and frauds?
- If EHMs are mapped for predictivity, what are some effective methods? What are ways to increase the accuracy of the predictions?
- Digital memory is theoretically available forever, but human memory is selective and incomplete and "plastic" (malleable). Perhaps future research in this area may be about the roles of forgetting in an EHM and why it occurs.

- What are practical ways to understand the personality of an electronic hive mind? What are ways to understand a collective unconscious? A collective subconscious? An EHM conscience?
- Are there ways to validate or invalidate the findings about an EHM at a particular point in time? Or cumulatively over time for a historical EHM?

Ultimately, the questions will come back to "So what? And?" The relevant applications of understanding EHMs are potentially many—to know how people coalesce around shared interests across social media and ICT platforms and to predict group behaviors (whatever the ranges of super-conscious group sizes, from micro to meso to macro).

CONCLUSION

This first chapter introduces the idea of the electronic hive mind and offers an initial definition of what these may be. The concept is notional, and the definition is conception-based and generally at this moment untested. As-yet, there is no direct operationalization of the term for research purposes. One of the main purposes of this book is to explore EHMs as a phenomenon and operationalize this approach. Ultimately, the standard here is to capture the best attainable version of electronic hive minds, with the available skills, methods, and technologies at present. In the asking of questions, the idea is to go as bold and relevant as possible in order to ask engaging questions, even if they may not be directly answerable currently.

REFERENCES

Allport, F. H. (1962). A structuronomic conception of behavior: Individual and collective. 1. Structural Theory and the master problem of social psychology. *Journal of Abnormal and Social Psychology*, *64*(1), 3–30. doi:10.1037/h0043563 PMID:13860640

Cikara, M., Bruneau, E., Van Bavel, J. J., & Saxe, R. (2014). Their pain gives us pleasure: How intergroup dynamics shape empathic failures and counter-empathic responses. *Journal of Experimental Social Psychology*, *55*, 110–125. doi:10.1016/j.jesp.2014.06.007 PMID:25082998

Conti, M., Das, S. K., Bisdikian, C., Kumar, M., Ni, L. M., Passarella, A., ... Zambonelli, F. (2012). Looking ahead in pervasive computing: Challenges in the era of cyber-physical convergence. *Pervasive and Mobile Computing*, *8*(1), 2–21. doi:10.1016/j.pmcj.2011.10.001

Dijkstra, J., Bouman, L., Bakker, D. M., & Assen, M. A. L. M. (2018). (in press). Modeling the micro-macro link: Understanding macro-level outcomes using randomization tests on micro-level data. *Social Science Research*, 1–9. PMID:30466880

Dron, J. (2007). The teacher, the learner and the collective mind. *AI & Society*, *21*(1-2), 200–216. doi:10.100700146-005-0031-4

Dunbar, R. (2010). *How many friends does one person need? Dunbar's Number and other evolutionary quirks*. Cambridge, MA: Harvard University Press.

Dunbar, R. I. M., Arnaboldi, V., Conti, M., & Passarella, A. (2015). The structure of online social networks mirrors those in the offline world. *Social Networks*, *43*, 39–47. doi:10.1016/j.socnet.2015.04.005

Engel, D., Woolley, A. W., Jing, L. X., Chabris, C. F., & Malone, T. W. (2014, December 16). Reading the mind in the eyes of reading between the lines? Theory of Mind predicts collective intelligence equally well online and face-to-face. *PLoS One*, *9*(12), e115212. doi:10.1371/journal.pone.0115212 PMID:25514387

Felin, T., & Zenger, T. R. (2009). Entrepreneurs as theorists: On the origins of collective beliefs and novel strategies. *Strategic Entrepreneurship Journal*, *3*(2), 127–146. doi:10.1002ej.67

Goncalves, B., Perra, N., & Vespignani, A. (2011). Modeling users' activity on Twitter networks: Validation of Dunbar's Number. *PLoS One*. doi:10.1371/journal.pone0022656 PMID:21826200

Gray, H. M., Gray, K., & Wegner, D. M. (2007, Feb.). Dimensions of mind perception. *Science*. Retrieved from http://science.sciencemag.org/content/315/5812/619

Hai-Jew, S. (2019). The electronic hive mind and cybersecurity: Mass-scale human cognitive limits to explain the 'weakest link' in cybersecurity. In *Global Cyber Security Labor Shortage and International Business Risk* (pp. 206–262). Hershey, PA: IGI Global. doi:10.4018/978-1-5225-5927-6.ch011

Hayes, J., & Allinson, C. W. (1998). Cognitive style and the theory and practice of individual and collective learning in organizations. *Human Relations, 51*(7), 847–871. doi:10.1177/001872679805100701

Johnson, S. (2010). *Where Good Ideas Come From: The Natural History of Innovation*. New York: Penguin Group.

Lencioni, P. (2002). *The Five Dysfunctions of a Team: A Leadership Fable*. San Francisco: Jossey-Bass.

Lillard, A. (1998). Ethnopsychologies: Cultural variations in Theories of Mind. *Psychological Bulletin, 123*(1), 3–32. doi:10.1037/0033-2909.123.1.3 PMID:9461850

Macintyre, B. (2016). *Rogue Heroes: The History of the SAS, Britain's Secret Special Forces Unit that Sabotaged the Nazis and Changed the Nature of War*. New York: Crown Publishers.

Markus, H. R., & Kitayama, S. (1994, October). A collective fear of the collective: Implications for selves and theories of selves. *Personality and Social Psychology Bulletin, 20*(5), 568–579. doi:10.1177/0146167294205013

McPhail, C. (1989, Autumn). Blumer's Theory of Collective Behavior: The development of a non-symbolic interaction explanation. *The Sociological Quarterly, 30*(3), 401–423. doi:10.1111/j.1533-8525.1989.tb01528.x

Mind. (2018, Oct. 11). In *Google dictionary*. Retrieved Oct. 11, 2018,

Mind. (2018, Oct. 8). In *Wikipedia*. Retrieved Oct. 11, 2018, from https://en.wikipedia.org/wiki/Mind

Norenzayan, A., Schaller, M., & Heine, S. J. (2010). Introduction. In *Evolution. Culture, and the Human Mind* (p. 2). New York: Psychology Press.

Oliver, P. E., & Marwell, G. (1988, February). The paradox of group size in collective action: A theory of the critical mass. II. *American Sociological Review, 53*(1), 1–8. doi:10.2307/2095728

Premack, D., & Woodruff, G. (1978, December). Does the chimpanzee have a theory of mind? *Behavioral and Brain Sciences, 1*(4), 515–526. doi:10.1017/S0140525X00076512

Senge, P. M. (2006). The Fifth Discipline: The Art & Practice of the Learning Organization. New York: Doubleday. (Originally published 1990)

Size of Wikipedia. (2018, Oct. 1). In *Wikipedia*. Retrieved Oct. 11, 2018, from https://en.wikipedia.org/wiki/Wikipedia:Size_of_Wikipedia

Tateo, L., & Iannaccone, A. (2012). Social representations, individual and collective mind: A study of Wundt, Cattaneo and Moscovici. *Integrative Psychological & Behavioral Science*, *46*(1), 57–69. doi:10.100712124-011-9162-y PMID:21494777

Theory of mind. (2018, Oct. 10). In *Wikipedia*. Retrieved Oct. 10, 2018, from https://en.wikipedia.org/wiki/Theory_of_mind

Tirole, J. (1996). A Theory of Collective Reputations (with applications to the persistence of corruption and to firm quality). *The Review of Economic Studies*, *63*(1), 1–22. doi:10.2307/2298112

Tomasello, M., & Rakoczy, H. (2003, April). What makes human cognition unique? From individual to shared to collective intentionality. *Mind & Language*, *18*(2), 121–147. doi:10.1111/1468-0017.00217

Waytz, A., Gray, K., Epley, N., & Wegner, D. M. (2010). Causes and consequences of mind perception. *Trends in Cognitive Sciences*, *14*(8), 383–388. doi:10.1016/j.tics.2010.05.006 PMID:20579932

Weick, K. E., & Roberts, K. H. (1993, September). Collective mind in organizations: Heedful interrelating on flight decks. *Administrative Science Quarterly*, *38*(3), 357–381. doi:10.2307/2393372

Wilson, R. A. (2005). Collective memory, group minds, and the extended mind thesis. *Cognitive Processing, 6*, 227 – 236. DOI doi:10.100710339-005-0012-z

Yoo, Y., & Kanawattanachai, P. (2001). Developments of transactive memory systems and collective mind in virtual teams. *The International Journal of Organizational Analysis*, *9*(2), 187–208. doi:10.1108/eb028933

KEY TERMS AND DEFINITIONS

Electronic Hive Mind: A synchronous temporal and informal patchwork of emergent shared social consciousness (held by geographically distributed people, cyborgs, and robots) enabled by online social connectivity (across a range of social media platforms on the web and internet), based around various dimensions of shared attractive interests.

Homophily: A human tendency to associate and bond with others who are similar to themselves.

Reification: Act of making an abstract idea real or concrete.

Chapter 2

Ferreting Out Silences and Invisibilities in Electronic Hive Minds:
Identifying Absent/Non-Present, Latent/Hidden, and Shadowed/ Obfuscated Messaging

ABSTRACT

An electronic hive mind (EHM), as a distributed swarm intelligence, is about shared information and resources and the interactions around those elements. A lesser-studied aspect in such electronic-enabled collectives involves unshared information, silences, withholdings, and other invisibilities. What is shared depends on socio-technical systems and how people engage and think socially, and these factors result in various absences, latencies, and shadowing of messaging. Here, an early mechanism-based approach is taken to understand the inflows and outflows of information from an EHM and areas where messages may be unformed, dropped, misapprehended, or obfuscated, resulting in knowledge gaps. Finally, this thought experiment suggests that EHMs should be understood as constructs with shimmering and incomplete versions of reality, and "what you see is all there is" (WYSIATI) would be an illusory approach.

DOI: 10.4018/978-1-5225-9369-0.ch002

INTRODUCTION

If the modern age is about wide access to information and fast sharing by many, it is also about mass silences and invisibilities, information that is absent, latent, or shadowed. In electronic hive minds (EHMs), this informational incompleteness may be based on design features of socio-technical technologies and how people engage on them as well as how people process information. Such incompleteness is partially a factor of intentional and unintentional processes. This thought piece does not suggest that being all-knowing is the ultimate goal; rather, it merely suggests the importance of being aware of the reality of non-included and hidden / occluded information in EHMs, for more accurate and less naïve engagement with this phenomenon.

REVIEW OF THE LITERATURE

Exploration of various types of electronic hive minds (EHMs), in their various forms, shows that the shared information is partial, depending on the membership and what they choose to share, in part (Hai-Jew, 2019). Those who run the respective social media platforms "set its rules" (Singer & Brooking, 2018, p. 21) and also affect what may or may not be shared through them for different EHMs. The social groupings found online vary in terms of their homogeneity and their heterogeneity, their homophilous or heterophilous aspects, and other dimensions. When people make social connections, offline and offline, it is often based on preferential connections, resulting in assortativity or assortative mixing. On social networks, attractiveness can be parlayed into social capital. Those who are more attractive can "exploit social network opportunities differently than less attractive people and, consequently, their networks will comprise more beneficial features" (O'Connor & Gladstone, 2018, p. 42). People apparently have natural limits to the numbers of people they can include in their social networks (or "trust networks"), topping out at about 150, based on the Dunbar number.

The number of people we know personally, whom we can trust, whom we feel some emotional affinity for, is no more than 150, Dunbar's Number. It has been 150 for as long as we have been a species. And it is 150 because our minds lack the capacity to make it any larger. (Dunbar, 2010, p. 4).

In immersive virtual worlds, where people may engage in more full sensory ways, people may be more susceptible to the "immersive parasocial" or the illusion of the existence of a (non-existent) two-way relationship with another person represented through a digital avatar (Hai-Jew, Sept. 2009). This suggests that those with large followings may have outsized impacts on what others think, say, and act.

On social media platforms, people share information, socialize with others, build and maintain relationships, strive to find support for their actions, and spark others' to actions. They may manifest differently on different social media platforms depending on the technological affordances there and the sense of community and the individuals and groups there. They may lurk in some spaces or engage heavily in others.

One way to understand sociality online is to explore electronic hive minds, described as

a synchronous temporal and informal patchwork of emergent shared social consciousness (held by geographically distributed people, cyborgs, and robots) enabled by online social connectivity (across a range of social media platforms on the Web and Internet), based around various dimensions of shared attractive interests. (Hai-Jew, 2019, Preface, Electronic Hive Minds…)

It is possible to explore EHMs in part by the contents that are shared and are publicly available, with the understanding though that some of the contents are manifest and some latent.

Another methodological question at the outset is whether a study will examine the manifest (visible at the surface level or literally present in the text) or latent (having a deeper meaning implied in the text) content of the text or a combination. Manifest content is identified using coding and key word searches and can be recorded in frequencies such as word counts. Latent content, although amenable to objective coding processes, is more complex and requires developing constructs and drawing conclusions to add broader meaning to the text. It is generally easier to conduct a CA (content analysis) of the manifest content of a message, but latent content is often the more interesting and debatable aspect of communication (Kondracki, Wellman, & Amundson, 2002, p. 225)

In terms of latencies, there are "known unknowns," such as hidden personal and group histories, hidden relationships (online and offline) among members, hidden identities (people, cyborgs, and robots/scripted agents), hidden private messaging, related in-world events, untruths, maliciousness (expressed as messaging, malware, and other forms), plots, and others. Influential roles of individuals on social networks may be hidden from most, with these individuals known as "hidden influential" ones (Baños, Borge-Holthoefer, & Moreno, 2013). The roles of such individuals "can make chain reactions turn into global cascades" (Baños, Borge-Holthoefer, & Moreno, 2013, p. 9). There may be "hidden friendships" because some individuals may have "properties that aren't socially acceptable" and may result in "detrimental consequences" to the individual (Preibusch, 2009, p. 336). In other words, people may have reasons to hide aspects of both themselves and their acquaintances, depending on the social norms of the individuals in a social network.

Some information may only be seen by those who run the respective social media platforms and have access to private information or big data analytics approaches (with an N = all). Some may only be seen by applying particular data analytics methods to particular data, to better map social relationships several degrees out, in longitudinal time, with particular questions in mind. There is a wide range of common data mining techniques in exploring social media, but these are by no means exhaustive (Injadat, Salo, & Nassif, 2016). The respective data mining and analytics methods may highlight particular aspects of data, but they do not enable full access to what may be knowable and what may be latent.

Some latencies may be more hidden than typical ones, such as "lesser-known unknowns" and even "unknown unknowns": hidden incentives, hidden coordination, hidden technologies, in the service of larger-scale plots. In a majority of cases, latencies can be left to remain hidden; however, in other cases, seeing what is not presented and understanding the reasons why these latencies are hidden may be important.

EXPLORING THE SILENCES AND INVISIBILITIES IN ELECTRONIC HIVE MINDS

It may help to define the voices and visibilities of electronic hive minds (EHMs) first. Broadly speaking, these are the ideas and informational resources easily available in an EHM and broadly salient, even top-of-mind. These topics do not have to be timely. Some may even be historical. All said, the members of an EHM are generally aware of the respective informational contents, whether values, principles, history, data, or other forms of knowledge. (This is even as EHMs have transient membership and change socio-technical platforms used to connect and share and collaborate. "Swarm intelligence" is also by definition somewhat distributed and somewhat locally limited, and it is in the swarm that competitive advantage is thought to lie, particularly for the identification of accurate information from delimited options and some group processes in "stigmergic" trails.)

The silences and invisibilities in electronic hive minds may come from the socio-technical technologies, people, and interactive combinations from the prior two. Different reasons for such hidden messaging apply in the context(s) of absent/non-present, latent/hidden, and shadowed/obfuscated messaging. The EHM silences may range on a continuum from accidental to purposeful; they may range from the non-obvious to the obvious. Some of these early understandings have been captured in Table 1.

Given the various non-comprehensive listing above, there are any number of steps in a process where information may be absented, hidden, or obfuscated. (Figure 01) This is especially so given that various EHMs have different *raison d'être*. EHMs themselves can be their own filter bubbles. At any point, information may also be muted, deleted, ignored, hidden, supplanted, or mutated.

Cold Approach Analyses to EHM Silences and Invisibilities

Approaching an EHM cold and understanding its particular "silences" and "invisibilities" can be challenging. One simple approach is to document what the main topics are (such as through computational topic modeling and human coding) and to posit respective unaddressed topic that one would assume would be relevant and / or interesting for the particular EHM. [This would benefit from having content experts in the particular area(s) of focus.]

It may help to further map where the sources of information are from, what vetting is applied to that information, and the information that survives that vetting process and is promoted to high level consciousness.

Table 1. Types of Silences and Invisibilities of Electronic Hive Minds based on Socio-Technical and Human Factors (including Absences, Latencies, and Shadowing)

Electronic Hive Mind (EHM) silences and invisibilities	Socio-technical technological reasons	Human (individual and social) reasons	Combined socio-technical technological and human individual and social reasons
Part 1: Absent / Non-present Messaging			
1. (Messaging) inaccessible (difficult or impossible to access and process)	• Socio-technical system designs • Playability on the technology systems (technological constraints, technological lack of capabilities) • Speed of message disappearance or unavailability • Provision of private channels (and the encryption that enables these)	• Perceptability by human senses • Foreign or non-native language challenges • Cultural barriers to understanding	• How people interact online via social media platforms and information and communications technology (ICT)
2. (Messaging) not included (unexpressed, unspoken, unshared)	• Socio-technical system designs • End user license agreements (EULAs) for socio-technical systems • Enforcement of rules (through human and automated means) • Privacy protections for users • Barriers to joining social networks • Technological barriers to the expression of the digital messaging • Costs to the expression of the digital messaging	• Social norms • Cultural norms • Social dynamics • Meta narratives • Value systems	• How people interact online via social media platforms and information and communications technology (ICT) • Offline relationships (which are non-declared in online spaces)
3. (Messaging) rejected from inclusion	• Scripted moderator oversight on various online groups • Enforcement of EULAs	• Moderator oversight on various online groups • Human reportage of offensive or inappropriate messaging	• Laws • Policies • License agreements • Cultural reasons • Meta narratives
Electronic Hive Mind (EHM) silences and invisibilities	**Socio-technical technological reasons**	**Human reasons**	**Combined socio-technical technological and human reasons**
Part 2: Latent / Hidden Messaging			
4. (Messaging) included but not noticed	• Single-mentions and other low-frequency mentions in the "long tail" of social messaging	• Focus on other more dominant top-of-mind topics • Member apathy • Member lack of interest • Member lack of curiosity • Lack of recognition by members (such as for nascent messaging, such as for high-novel messaging, such as for messaging outside of accepted meta-narratives) • Cultural invisibilities	• High competition for human attention on socio-technical sites and social media platforms • Co-evolved engagement on social media platforms

continued on following page

Table 1. Continued

5. (Messaging) noticed but rejected from consideration (and / or continuance)	• End user license agreements (EULAs) for socio-technical systems • Enforcement of rules (through human and automated means)	• Social rejection of messages, messaging, and persons representing certain messaging	• Evolved and / or designed social norms and cultures
6. Misapprehended messaging	• Speed of message sharing	• Receptivity of members to particular messaging • Cognitive biases (systematic subjective misapprehensions of the world) • Perceptual limitations • Cultural exposures (and lack of cultural exposures) • Capability of members to identify nascent and weakly formed messaging (or realities related to the messaging) • Capabilities of members to read into their own subconscious and unconscious (both as individuals and as groups)	• Complex multimodal digital messaging
Electronic Hive Mind (EHM) silences and invisibilities	**Socio-technical technological reasons**	**Human reasons**	**Combined socio-technical technological and human reasons**
Part 3: Shadowed / Obfuscated Messaging			
7. (Messaging) hidden or suppressed	• Oversight or manipulation by owners and managers of socio-technical systems	• Suppression of information by leaders • Suppression of information by members	• Government censorship • Leadership censorship • Member censorship • Collaborative filtering (out)
8. (Messaging) skewed or manipulated	• Oversight or manipulation by owners and managers of socio-technical systems	• Reframing of information by leaders • Reframing of information by members • Sharing of inaccurate information (with or without the knowledge of the sharer) • Distribution of untruths and "deep fakes" for impression management (by deception) • The creation of sleeper egos and entities (including networks) through individuals and robots for particular aims	• Leader reframing of messaging • Member reframing of messaging
9. (Messaging) overshadowed by spectacle or misdirection	• Promotion of particular messaging (by automatic or human means, or a combination of means)	• Direction of mass attention or focus on a thing through agenda-setting • Focus on spectacle • Chasing misdirection	• Synergistic focuses on particular overshadowing phenomena

Figure 1. Information Processing in an Electronic Hive Mind

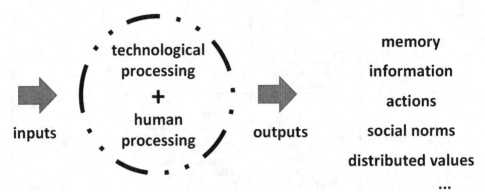

Information Processing in an Electronic Hive Mind

It may help to understand the focus of the EHM, based on keywords, #hashtags, social imagery, and formal documents (manifestos, rules, and other elements). Then, follow on with a "sanity check" about what information would be included if the EHM were fully engaged. What is missing, and why?

The leaders and other influentials in an EHM may be profiled to understand their filtering effects, based on their personalities, cognition, intellect, social connections, value systems, and other details. (Social network mapping methods may be applied here for part of this work.)

Perhaps the EHM membership may be studied to see who is at the table, and by contrast, who is not. What sorts of recruitment efforts are there, and how is membership retained? Those who are not participating will lose the potential power of their own voices.

It is important to see what is actively suppressed and what the members choose not to see (and how they go about this). It is important to see light visibilities, such as the long tails of content analyses (to see where the smaller conversations are occurring among individuals and dyads and motifs and smaller groups). It is important to identify subliminal messaging, where it exists.

On any general electronic hive mind, there will be a number of different individual members, all with different incentives and motivations. All will have realities and information that are invisible to others on social media platforms because of the technology (and their limited informational channels) and the social realities of limited sociality among strangers. Beyond known invisibilities like people's true selves and real lives (RLs)—and pretty much every else about them—there are lesser known and more unknown latencies and hidden interests that should be at the forefront of people's minds when they go online.

It may help to analyze the extant assumptions of the membership, to better understand what messages they are more prone to accepting. It may help to see what their collective assumptions may be to understand what their preferences are in terms of what they want to see vs. not. (Confirmation bias can be a powerful incentive to be selective of information and to stay in groups that have similar ideas.)

Perhaps during seminal events that have high impacts on the EHM, it is important to see how it functions and what revelatory information may leak.

Essentially, the work is to develop increased and more effective ways of seeing, through data mining, data analyses, analysis of social media platform affordances, knowledge of humans, and knowledge of the content space, among others. For those within EHMs, it would help to make these more resilient by raising topics for attention and to enhance the perceptions, learning, memory, and other aspects, through technological and social means. The membership would do well to be more aware of hidden hands in their midst to avoid the hiding or masking of relevant and accurate information.

DISCUSSION

It is reasonable to assume that all EHMs are incomplete, with various silences and invisibilities, for various reasons. Said another way, no EHM is fully informed knowledge-wise. No socio-technical systems or human groups will lack preferences for some information and act on information somewhat selectively. EHMs are about meeting particular human aims, and their general interests will follow accordingly. Between sparsity and comprehensiveness, social networks online focus on the first ("less is more") and not the latter (in most cases). And yet, there are benefits to understanding latency in EHMs because the implications of lack of memory and lack of understanding can be so harmful and negative. In other cases, it can be argued that what is latent may remain so, without undue harm, in which case, sleeping narratives can be let lie. Still, those who would engage EHMs should not take on the naïve assumption that EHMs have full information and awareness of that information. The "what you see is all there is" (WYSIATI) is a risky approach.

FUTURE RESEARCH DIRECTIONS

The practice of mapping latencies in EHMs is a fairly novel one. The methods suggested here for mapping the silences and invisibilities of EHMs are eminently achievable with available technologies and methods. These should be tested. Additional other methods should also be brought into play. For example, a sousveillance approach (from within a target EHM) may provide insights that are not directly attainable otherwise, from without.

CONCLUSION

Looking at EHMs as informational spaces can be rewarding, and understanding them by informational absences can be insightful about the membership, the purposes of the entity, and other aspects.

REFERENCES

Baños, R. A., Borge-Holthoefer, J., & Moreno, Y. (2013). The role of hidden influential in the diffusion of online information cascades. *EPJ Data Science*, *2*(6), 1–16.

Dunbar, R. (2010). *How many friends does one person need? Dunbar's Number and other evolutionary quirks*. Cambridge, MA: Harvard University Press.

Hai-Jew, S. (2009, Sept.). Exploring the immersive parasocial: Is it you or the thought of you? *Journal of Online Learning and Teaching*. Retrieved Oct. 15, 2018, from http://jolt.merlot.org/vol5no3/hai-jew_0909.htm

Hai-Jew, S. (2019). The electronic hive mind and cybersecurity: Mass-scale human cognitive limits to explain the 'weakest link' in cybersecurity. In *Global Cyber Security Labor Shortage and International Business Risk* (pp. 206–262). Hershey, PA: IGI Global. doi:10.4018/978-1-5225-5927-6.ch011

Injadat, M. N., Salo, F., & Nassif, A. B. (2016). Data mining techniques in social media: A survey. *Neurocomputing*, *214*, 654–670. doi:10.1016/j.neucom.2016.06.045

Kondracki, N.L., Wellman, N.S., & Amundson, D.R. (2002). *Content analysis: Review of methods and their applications in nutrition education*. Report.

O'Connor, K. M., & Gladstone, E. (2018). Beauty and social capital: Being attractive shapes social networks. *Social Networks, 52*, 42–47. doi:10.1016/j. socnet.2017.05.003

Preibusch, S. (2009). Establishing distributed hidden friendship relations (transcript of discussion). In B. Christianson, J.A. Malcolm, V. Matyáš, & M. Roe (Eds.), *Lecture Notes in Computer Science: Vol. 7028. Security Protocols XVII*. In the 17th International Workshop, Cambridge UK. Berlin: Springer.

Singer, P. W., & Brooking, E. T. (2018). *LikeWar: The Weaponization of Social Media*. Boston: Houghton Mifflin Harcourt.

KEY TERMS AND DEFINITIONS

Cognitive Bias: Systematic subjectivities in engaging the world (vs. more rationalist approaches).

Confirmation Bias: A human tendency to over-weight information that aligns with prior beliefs.

Deception: Purposeful misleading of others through the providing of untruths or misinformation.

Electronic Hive Mind: A synchronous temporal and informal patchwork of emergent shared social consciousness (held by geographically distributed people, cyborgs, and robots) enabled by online social connectivity (across a range of social media platforms on the web and internet), based around various dimensions of shared attractive interests.

Latency: Hiddenness.

Swarm Intelligence: Collective intelligence from decentralized egos and entities.

Chapter 3
Defining Collective Personalities, Dispositions, Temperaments, and Moods of Electronic Hive Minds

ABSTRACT

An electronic hive mind, a temporal shared consciousness (or massmind) of people interacting through online communications technologies and other means, may be thought of as having collective personalities, dispositions, and temperaments. These human-based features may be seen from various dimensions: the public (and private) messaging (textual, imagistic, audio, video, and multimodal elements), the collective culture(s) and practices, the human membership and member motivations, the group actions (virtual and in-world), the sociotechnical systems, and others. This early work explores some dimensions of collective and more stable personality, dispositions, and temperament that may be inferred form EHMs, as well as more transitory moods. These aspects of EHMs may inform on future actions and provide a predictive function.

DOI: 10.4018/978-1-5225-9369-0.ch003

INTRODUCTION

An electronic hive mind (EHM), the collective consciousness of a group of people interacting via online means (Hai-Jew, 2019), may be conceptualized as having a shared massmind (over a particular period of time), but also as having a collective personality or sense of personhood. A "folk" definition of personality involves the set of qualities that form a distinctive individual, and applied to a collective, a group personality involves the observed person-similar characteristics of the group. Personality is comprised of "a multitude of continuous and orthogonal constructs" (Akhtar, Winsborough, Ort, Johnson, & Chamorro-Premuzic, 2018, p. 91). Those who engage actively on social media and build vibrant social networks tend towards extraversion (Wehrli, 2008), based on their enjoyment in engaging socially with others. More recent research suggests that "increased social media use (SMU) has been linearly associated with increased real-life social isolation," but "extraversion and agreeableness were associated with lower odds of SI" (social isolation), and "neuroticism" was associated with higher odds of social isolation (Whaite, Shensa, Sidani, Colditz, & Primack, 2018, p. 45). So individuals engaging on social media may be extraverted but also subjectively and experientially socially isolated. Individual personality traits—"extraversion, emotional stability and openness to experiences—play a role in the uses of interactive social media" (Correa, Hinsley, & de Zúñga, H. G., 2010, p. 251). In the transient and semi-permanent collectives that form online, certain aspects of human personalities are valued, resourced, supported, and come through in the shared intercommunications and actions. An EHM, comprised of linked human consciousnesses, can be perceived as having a certain macro-level mindset, some shared values, motivations, impetuses for action (or non-action), and other patterned tendencies. If language and multimedia expressions are the repository for people's ideas, and their interactions represent the growing connectivity of people around shared interests, then it may be possible to collect and analyze some of the residual artifacts on social media around particular topics and interests and endeavors and reverse-extract a collective personality, disposition, and temperament around a particular electronic hive mind (EHM). The general abductive logic suggests that EHMs are made up of people empowered through sociotechnical technologies and those enablements and so may be seen to have a common shared state at various times that may be informative of personalities. In the same way, natural swarms of social insects may be seen to act as one based on shared interests—for various acts of hive interest, like survival, like foraging, like reproduction, like collective defense, like hive building, and others.

The initial analytical approach will draw on five main sources of information:

- The public (and private) messaging (textual, imagistic, audio, video, and multimodal elements)
- The collective culture(s) and practices
- The human membership and member motivations
- The group actions (virtual and in-world)
- The sociotechnical systems, and others.

This initial work explores some early methods at understanding EHM personalities, dispositions, and temperaments (as fairly stable features), as well as the more transient moods (as emotions, states of mind, feelings). One established EHM is analyzed based on digital residua from user-generated data, especially text (using computational text analysis) and scraped social imagery (using manual coding). This approach involves a remote psychological reading of a collective EHM, without data from direct interactions. This particular work takes an "etic" or "from outside" approach, instead of an "emic" or "from within / inside" or "sousveillance" (surveilling from within, from bottom up, per Steve Mann's term) approach.

Also, while the conceptualized sense of "personalities" is based on facets of people's distinctive features, the application is analogical to the application of the concept to brands ("brand personalities"), geographical destinations ("destination personalities"), and so on. The personality frame has been applied to "geographical personality" although the sizes of states may be too large of a geographical space for this approach to be effective (Elleman, Condon, Russin, & Revelle, 2018, p. 72). Still, this approach of using personality scores "aggregated by geographical regions" is seen as valuable for "exploring macro-level relationships between patterns of human behavior, environment, and social outcomes" (Elleman, Condon, Russin, & Revelle, 2018, p. 72).

To be more specific, a destination personality is defined as "the set of human characteristics associated with a destination" (Ekinci & Hosany, 2006, p. 128, as cited in Kim & Stepchenkova, 2017, p. 420); for example, the destination personality traits may include "sincerity, excitement, competence, sophistication, ruggedness, peacefulness, uniqueness, (and) traditionalism" as applied to one location (Kim & Stepchenkova, 2017, p. 420). Such destination personalities may help create a vacation state of mind and "that bright postcard world" (Atkinson, 2008, p. 104), for commercial ends.

Electronic hive minds, whether or not there are commercial interests, have an interest in recruiting members and particular behaviors from those members, in order to exist. Similarly, they have an interest in maintaining an attractive personality and communicating that personality to the larger world.

REVIEW OF THE LITERATURE

Over the years, various inventories have been created to map people's personalities. Some require formalized clinical testing, and others may be done at a distance through instrumentation, such as online surveys. These assessments may be used for acceptance/declination decisions for work places, sports teams, study programs, and other practical applications.

One common way to standardize the modeling of human personality is across five dimensions, based on the 5-Factor Model. The Big Five personality traits include conscientiousness, neuroticism, openness to experience, extraversion, and agreeableness. On continuums, the polar ends would be as follows:

- **Conscientiousness:** "Efficient / organized vs. easy-going / careless"
- **Neuroticism:** "Sensitive / nervous vs. secure / confident"
- **Openness to Experience:** "Inventive / curious vs. consistent / cautious"
- **Extraversion:** "Outgoing / energetic vs. solitary / reserved"
- **Agreeableness:** "Friendly / compassionate vs. challenging / detached" ("Big Five personality traits," Nov. 15, 2018)

Various personality inventories assess various dimensions of personhood. Many are built to be robust against attempts at deception. One study found the robustness of "the general factor of personality" under assigned faking conditions in experimental contexts (Schermer, Holden, & Krammer, 2019).

Within these large constructs, people's tendencies may also include various more unique quirks and idiosyncrasies. Certainly, other frameworks to understand individuals may be simultaneously applied, such as cross-cultural ones and others built on different or overlapping constructs.

On Digital Footprints and Remote Personality Reading

On social media, people perform socially for their respective imagined audiences, and in their strategic communications, they share both intentional information and unintentional reveals ("leaks"). This dynamic occurs at the individual level as well as at group levels, including web-scale groups.

On social media, personality plays important roles on personalized social networks, and different personalities build different types of observable social ties:

We show that neurotic persons have a tendency towards triad structures encompassing structural holes, whereas extroverted persons show a preference for networks with stronger ties. Moreover, our findings support the potential relationship between the three hitherto neglected personality traits—agreeableness, openness to experience, conscientiousness—with personal networks structures. (Rapp, Ingold, & Freitag, 2018, p. 1)

Those who engage on participatory media are thought to have positive personality traits:

In the increasingly user-generated Web, users' personality traits may be crucial factors leading them to engage in this participatory media. The literature suggests factors such as extraversion, emotional stability and openness to experience are related to users of social applications on the Internet. Using a national sample of US adults, this study investigated the relationship between these three dimensions of the Big Five model and social media use (defined as use of social networking sites and instant messages). It also examined whether gender and age played a role in that dynamic. Results revealed that while extraversion and openness to experiences were positively related to social media use, emotional stability was a negative predictor, controlling for socio-demographics and life satisfaction. These findings differed by gender and age. While extraverted men and women were both likely to be more frequent users of social media tools, only the men with greater degrees of emotional instability were more regular users. The relationship between extraversion and social media use was particularly important among the young adult cohort. Conversely, being open to new experiences emerged as an important personality predictor of social media use for the more mature segment of the sample. (Correa, Hinsley, & de Zúñga, H. G., 2010, p. 247)

People's "digital footprints" inform on their respective personality traits. One meta-analysis examined the ability to accurately infer the Big Five personality traits from social communications:

Results of analyses show that the predictive power of digital footprints over personality traits is in line with the standard 'correlational upper-limit' for behavior to predict personality, with correlations ranging from 0.29 (Agreeableness) to 0.40 (Extraversion). Overall, our findings indicate that accuracy of predictions is consistent across Big 5 traits, and that accuracy improves when analyses include demographics and multiple types of digital footprints. (Azucar, Margengo, & Settanni, 2018, p. 150)

Emojis, small images that communicate ideas or emotions as social communications, may be indicative of some personality traits. For example, 36 of 91 examined emojis from the Apple Color Emoji font set "significantly related with three of the Big-Five personality traits—emotional stability, extraversion, and agreeableness" (Marengo, Giannotta, & Settanni, 2017, p. 74).

Social media profiles may be assessed for how influence-able those individuals are by others. One research team examined the relationships between personality profiles and "susceptibility to persuasion" in various forms:

Latent profile analysis identified three distinct profiles which were labelled Socially Apt, Fearful and Malevolent. These profiles were correlated with scores on the persuasion subscales—authority, commitment, liking, scarcity, reciprocity, consensus—and a number of interesting associations were identified. The malevolent profile self-reported as more susceptible to a higher use of scarcity relative to the other principles of persuasion, and was least susceptible to reciprocity and authority. The socially apt profile appear to be more inclined to be persuaded to do something if it is consistent with their beliefs or a prior act whereas individuals in the Fearful profile were more likely to report obeying those in authority and going along with a crowd. (Wall, Campbell, Kaye, Levy, & Bhullar, 2019, p. 69)

Delusions or idiosyncratic beliefs unsupported by facts may come from both individuals and groups. A "complex interplay between specific emotional and paranoid dispositions within personality" affect individual proneness to delusional ideations and beliefs (Tonna, Paglia, Ottoni, Ossola, De Panfilis,

& Marchesi, 2018, p. 78). For example, those with "dark personalities" (narcissism, Machiavellianism, psychopathy) have been found to correlate positively with "outgroup threat perceptions" (Hodson, Hogg, & MacInnis, 2009, p. 686). These personality states may result in inaccurate or over-sized senses of threat from others and resulting over-reactions.

Personality informs how individuals and groups engage the world. In terms of the "echo chambers" found on the Web and Internet, researchers have found common personality traits for those who end up in these social spaces of reinforcing convergent ideas, in the study of a science-based echo chamber and a conspiracy-based echo chamber:

Our results show that such personality traits are similarly distributed within the polarized communities, with the exception of the emotional stability, which is higher in users supporting the conspiracy-like narrative. Moreover, we find very similar and significant correlations between personality traits within different echo chambers. Furthermore, we show that the prevalent personality model is the same in both the observed echo chambers. In particular, the most common supporters of Science and Conspiracy tend to enjoy interactions with close friends (low extraversion), are emotionally stable (high emotional stability), are suspicious and antagonistic towards others (low agreeableness), engage in anti-social behavior (low conscientiousness), and have unconventional interests (high openness). (Bessi, 2016, p. 323)

In an experimental study, research participants used their knowledge of "personality pathology" (described in the experimental condition as "the avoidant, histrionic, antisocial, narcissistic, schizotypal, dependent, and borderline vignette") to inform their bargaining strategies (Reed, Harrison, Best, & Hooley, 2018, p. 1). People will read each other and try to use that information for their own advantage and gain, in strategic conditions. There is no reason to assume that this does not occur at group and even more macro levels.

Personality attributes may be associated with "pleasurable emotions" including "tranquility, contentment, interest, cheerfulness, and vigor":

Extraversion was strongly associated with cheerfulness and vigor, openness to experience was associated with interest, and neuroticism was negatively associated with most of the pleasurable emotions. Contentment, but not tranquility, was consistently associated with conscientiousness and extraversion. (Berenbaum, Chow, Schoenleber, & Flores, 2016, p. 400)

This study offers observations of various intensities (and directions) of personality dimensions and their self-identified "pleasurable activities" [such as "social, nurturant, entertainment, physical, basic needs, intellectual, mastery, spiritual, vigor, cheerfulness, contentment, tranquility, (and) interest"] (Berenbaum, Chow, Schoenleber, & Flores, 2016, p. 405). Personality traits may be understood as providing some impetuses to "drive behaviors and influence attitudes" (Jonason & Zeigler-Hill, 2018, p. 98). Personality traits may relate to virtues ["wisdom and knowledge, courage, humanity, justice, temperance, (and) transcendence"] and related character strengths ["creativity, curiosity, open-mindedness, love of learning, perspective, bravery, persistence, integrity, vitality, love, kindness, social intelligence, citizenship, fairness, leadership, forgiveness and mercy, humility/modesty, prudence, self-control, appreciation of beauty, gratitude, hope, humour, (and) spirituality"], per Peterson and Seligman's (2004) classification (Macdonald, Bore, & Munro, 2008, p. 788). Higher traits like "Positivity, Intellect, Conscientiousness and Niceness" have salutary effects (Macdonald, Bore, & Munro, 2008, p. 798). Personality informs on long-term well-being. For example, "high neuroticism, low conscientiousness, low extraversion, low openness and low agreeableness" were found to be related to "higher frailty across samples" in older adults (Stephan, Sutin, Canada, & Terracciano, 2017, p. 46).

Personality also has associations with both "psychological resilience and ego-resilience" (Oshio, Taku, Hirano, & Saeed, 2018, p. 54), which suggest abilities to handle unexpected challenges. Among the Big Five personality traits, neuroticism (emotional sensitivity) has a negative association with resilience, extraversion a positive association, openness a positive association, agreeableness a positive association, and conscientiousness a positive association. (Oshio, Taku, Hirano, & Saeed, 2018)

One more point: thinking style is different from measurable known personality dimensions. Recent research suggests that "thinking styles are distinct from, rather than subordinate to, personality traits" (Fan, Zhang, & Chen, 2018, p. 50).

The understanding of personality is not without value judgments. The "Dark Triad" personality includes three personality traits: narcissism (high sense of self-importance), Machiavellianism (immorally self-interested and manipulative), and psychopathy (antisocial and remorseless). In combination, these may inform a person who is uncaring of others and manipulative, and potentially "malevolent" ("Dark triad," Nov. 15, 2018). Those who embody the Dark Triad personality may engage in either narcissistic impulsivity or psychopathic impulsivity:

Based on regression analyses, psychopathy was most closely associated with dysfunctional impulsivity whereas narcissism was associated with functional impulsivity. It appears that narcissistic impulsivity involves venturesome social engagement whereas psychopathic impulsivity stems from poor self-regulation. (Jones & Paulhus, 2011, p. 679)

The first impulsivity is seen as more adaptive than the latter. "Impulsivity" is a personality feature that plays a role in individuals with "high extraversion and low conscientiousness" (Jones & Paulhus, 2011, p. 679).

The HEXACO personality inventory is a six-dimensional model based on the following elements: Honesty-Humility, Emotionality, eXtraversion, Agreeableness (versus Anger), Conscientiousness, and Openness to Experience. The Honesty-Humility measure is used as a way to understand the person's willingness to exploit others (and potential malevolence).

Finally, personality is thought to inform on passion and high investments in exploring that passion through learning and exploration and skills acquisition. Of two types of passion—harmonious passion and obsessive passions—the first is thought to be positive and the latter potentially negative. The authors observe:

The Dualistic Model of Passion (DMP; Vallerand, 2015; Vallerand et al., 2003) defines passion as a strong inclination toward a self-defining activity that one loves, values and considers important, and in which one invests considerable time and energy. The DMP also distinguishes two types of passion. Harmonious passion (HP) refers to a strong yet controllable desire to engage in the activity that one loves. The passionate activity is a significant part of the person's identity but is coherent and well-integrated with other life domains. (Dalpé, Demers, Verner-Filion, & Vallerand, 2019, p. 280)

Obsessive passions come about based on individuals internalizing a passion based on "intra and / or interpersonal pressure" and tends to lead to "less adaptive outcomes" ("Dualistic Model of Passion (DMP), n.d."). Electronic hive minds may involve mass groups pursuing shared aims and passions of both positive and negative types, based on collective psychological needs as form in and expressed in an environment.

Research Approaches on Social Media

Remote psychological reads on people based on their user-shared contents may be achieved through computational analysis of language use. In terms of computational analytics, the Linguistic Inquiry and Word Count (LIWC) tool has long been used to analyze various types of human speech and writing (Pennebaker, Boyd, Jordan, & Blackburn, 2015), with validated applications to remotely read the psychology of the respective speakers and writers. Two authors who both contributed to the co-creation of the tool write:

Beyond self-reports and biological markers, recent research has demonstrated that a powerful reflection of personality can be gleaned from the words people use in everyday life. As an increasing number of studies demonstrate, the ways in which people use words is reliable over time, internally consistent, predictive of a wide range of behaviors and even biological activity, and varies considerably from person to person. Language, then, is yet another fundamental dimension of personality. Of great benefit to researchers, and unlike other standard personality markers, people do not need to complete questionnaires or submit to invasive blood or genetic tests in order to provide useful personality data in the form of language (Boyd & Pennebaker, 2017, p. 63).

Other researchers observe that "the full spectrum of dysfunctional dispositions can be measured using online language" in an inferential way using multiple tools, including LIWC (Akhtar, Winsborough, Ort, Johnson, & Chamorro-Premuzic, 2018, p. 90). This work involves the analysis of contents beyond words and will include social imagery.

In a study of user personality traits from social media, one research team studied three main areas of personality traits: Big 5, "Basic Values," and "Needs." They defined Basic Values as the following: "self-transcendence" ("showing concern for the welfare and interests of others"), "conservation" ("emphasizing conformity, tradition, security"), "self-enhancement" ("seeking personal success for oneself"), "openness-to-change" ("emphasizing stimulation, self-direction"), and "hedonism" ("seeking pleasure and sensuous gratification for oneself"). They defined Needs as the following: "ideals" ("a desire for perfection"), "harmony" ("appreciating other people, their feelings"), "closeness" ("being connected to family and setting up home"), "self-expression" ("discovering and asserting one's own identity"), "excitement" ("upbeat emotions, and having fun"), and "curiosity" ("a desire to discover and grow") (Gou, Zhou, & Yang, 2014, p. 956). This work used constructs from a well-known personality inventory as well as other defined elements in concert.

In the multimodal online space, analyses may be applied to imagery, video, audio, emoticons/emojis, and multimodal contents.

DISCERNING MASS PERSONALITIES, DISPOSITIONS, TEMPERAMENTS, AND MOODS OF ELECTRONIC HIVE MINDS

In people, personality is conceptualized as stemming from the individual's lived experiences and their engagement with the world around them. It is shaped by core influential individuals during the individual's growing up. It is shaped by their socially-informed and individual choices. It is shaped by their culture and language. Personality is also informed by the brain and its underlying structure and capabilities. Analogically, the electronic hive mind's personality (as a pattern) is partially a product of its human membership and the structural enablements by the underlying sociotechnical spaces that underpin the mind. How the group forms, intercommunicates and interacts, acts in the world, all inform how the social personality(ies) of the EHM evolves and develops. The above is not a clean analogy per se, but it is not meant to be.

This work is based around three related hypotheses:

Hypothesis 1: Electronic hive minds (EHM), distributed massminds enabled through social media platforms and ICT, have collective personalities, dispositions, temperaments, and moods.
Hypothesis 2: The personalities of EHM may be discerned and understood (in part) through remote analysis of member messaging, culture and practices, human membership, group actions, and related sociotechnical systems (and understructures).
Hypothesis 3: The personalities of EHM may inform on predictive aspects, including capabilities, interests, motivations, attractiveness/aversiveness, and current future actions.

To Hypothesis 1, a "collective personality" is a unique combination of fairly stable qualities that form a coherent identity, based on human personality attributes. A "collective disposition" is conceptualized as inherent aspects of a group character. A "collective temperament" is based on a foundational nature, with effects on the entity's attitudes and behaviors. A "collective mood" is a temporary and transient state of feeling or emotion. This work does not assume that the moods pervade the whole EHM but only larger parts and only for particular lengths of time.

For this work, data will be sampled to understand the outlines of an electronic hive mind, and then that data and additional data will be sampled for observable "signals" about these aspects of personality in an EHM. The five general sources of information are listed below not as a comprehensive list but as places to start:

- The public (and private) messaging (textual, imagistic, audio, video, and multimodal elements)
- The collective culture(s) and practices
- The human membership and member motivations
- The group actions (virtual and in-world)
- The sociotechnical systems

An initial coding table captures these elements (Table 1).

A TRIAL RUN: EXPLORING A 4CHAN PERSONALITY

Against the trend towards perfect memory, 4chan occupies an oddly forgetful space. - Vyshali Manivannan (Oct. 10, 2012)

To see how this might work, a community which has been in continuous existence since October 1, 2003 was selected. This community is an imageboard website that is known for its core feature of being "anonymous, and it has no memory" (Poole, February 2010), according to its 15-year-old founder. The site maintains no archives, no registration, and "no barrier" (Poole, February 2010). 4chan ("4channel") was inspired by a Japanese-based imageboard. In the 15 years since its inception, 4chan has built a reputation as a "raw" and "unfiltered" space, which has output various memes or "units of cultural

Table 1. Identifying Observable Signals to Understand EHM Personalities, Dispositions, Temperaments, and Moods

	Observable Signals
Collective Personality(ies) **(a collective person-based identity)**	Messaging: Collective Cultures and Practices: Human Membership: Group Actions: Sociotechnical Systems:
Collective Disposition(s) **(a group character)**	Messaging: Collective Cultures and Practices: Human Membership: Group Actions: Sociotechnical Systems:
Collective Temperament(s) **(attitudes and behaviors)**	Messaging: Collective Cultures and Practices: Human Membership: Group Actions: Sociotechnical Systems:
Collective Mood(s) **(state of feeling or emotion)**	Messaging: Collective Cultures and Practices: Human Membership: Group Actions: Sociotechnical Systems:

information" (like the pervasive LOLcats), NSFW (not safe for work) imagery, various political speech, pranking, group sleuthing exploits, and dark expressions (such as "child pornography," "racist," "hate," and "misogynistic" expressions). The lack of persistent identity is both a feature (not a bug) and a risk and part of the spectacle that makes the site a destination one. It has an earned reputation for "underground influence" and is considered a core destination on the Internet. The site itself has a number of boards (threads), and it claims some 20 million users a month.

On a Google Search, "4chan" results in 25 million results. On Google Correlate, the 4chan search does not result in any co-search terms, which suggests that the term does not reach a particular threshold in mainstream awareness. On Google Books Ngram Viewer, there are also no hits, which suggests that "4chan" is not sufficiently institutionalized in the book literature (of course, it was only founded in 2003). On Flickr, no related tags were found when trying to map the related tags network around "4chan." On Google Scholar, a search for "4chan" resulted in 4,980 results (in 0.04 sec), but the downloadable links fast devolve to citations of news articles with a handful of citations each.

The point of this exercise in exploring 4chan is not to actually profile the personality as an electronic hive mind but to capture some initial insights about how this analytical process might work, how to improve the research approach, and some strengths and weaknesses of the approach.

A one-degree article-article network around "4chan" on Wikipedia, the crowd-sourced encyclopedia, shows the concept and practice's broad reach and also some of its darker connections to darker aspects of people's thinking. (Figure 1 and Table 2)

A #4chan hashtag network on Twitter shows 28 groups conversing around this space in small group conversations (motifs and subgroups). Identities of social media accounts may be observed, and actual personally identifiable information (PII) may be ultimately extrapolated (Figure 2 and Table 3).

At the time of this work, there were dozens of boards on 4chan, under the main categories: Japanese Culture, Video Games, Interests, Creative, Other, Misc, (and) Adult. For this exploration, several days' worth of messaging on two boards on 4chan were downloaded fully for text analysis (including "Technology" and "Science and Math"), and over 1000 images linked to 4chan were downloaded from Flickr using Flickr Downloadr, and perused

Figure 1. 4chan article-article network on Wikipedia (1 deg.) in a Harel-Koren Fast Multiscale Network Graph

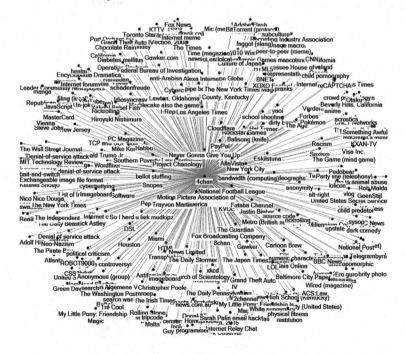

Table 2. 4chan article-article network on Wikipedia (1 deg.)

Graph Metric	Value
Graph Type	Directed
Vertices	284
Unique Edges	282
Edges With Duplicates	2
Total Edges	284
Self-Loops	0
Reciprocated Vertex Pair Ratio	0
Reciprocated Edge Ratio	0
Connected Components	1
Single-Vertex Connected Components	0
Maximum Vertices in a Connected Component	284
Maximum Edges in a Connected Component	284
Maximum Geodesic Distance (Diameter)	2
Average Geodesic Distance	1.98594
Graph Density	0.003521127
Modularity	Not Applicable
NodeXL Version	1.0.1.336

Figure 2. #4chan hashtag network on Twitter (basic network)

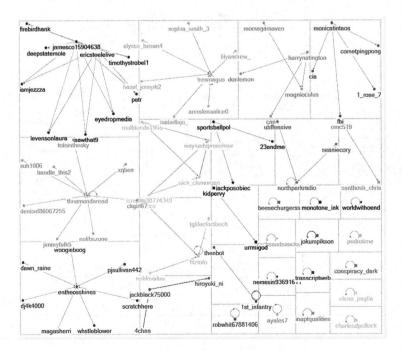

Table 3. #4chan hashtag network on Twitter

Graph Metric	Value
Graph Type	Directed
Vertices	81
Unique Edges	77
Edges With Duplicates	24
Total Edges	101
Self-Loops	25
Reciprocated Vertex Pair Ratio	0
Reciprocated Edge Ratio	0
Connected Components	28
Single-Vertex Connected Components	14
Maximum Vertices in a Connected Component	10
Maximum Edges in a Connected Component	17
Maximum Geodesic Distance (Diameter)	3
Average Geodesic Distance	1.337995
Graph Density	0.009722222
Modularity	Not Applicable
NodeXL Version	1.0.1.336

for some themes. From these, a few observations were made, with the main focus on analyzing electronic hive minds for personality features.

A close-in reading of the messages of 988 expired messages on Technology (/g/) (http://boards.4channel.org/g/archive) and 213 expired messages on Science and Math (/sci/) (http://boards.4channel.org/sci/archive) show a dynamic of assertions and counter-assertions. Some of the postings are clearly commercial ones, to sell particular items.

What was more interesting came from analyses using LIWC. The textual features of the two datasets were fairly close in terms of scoring against other public natural language data sets. Specifically, the writing tends to be high on Analytic features, fairly high on Clout (power, influence), low in terms of emotional warmth and human connection (Authentic), and negative in terms of sentiment (Tone) (Figure 3). This suggests that the personality on 4chan is a pungent and sour one…an assertive and knowing one…and somewhat skeptical and caustic. The delivery is often acerbic. The contents are not particularly well informed but more second-hand and from other sources.

Figure 3. Scored textual features of the messaging on collections of 3-5 days of archived messages on two 4chan boards

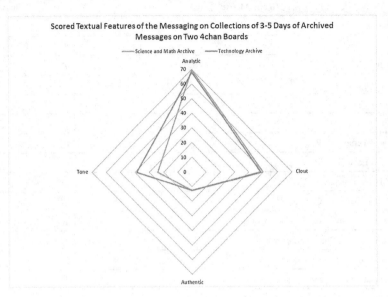

Anger, a form of hostility, is a main feature in the writing as compared to anxiety and sadness. In other words, for both sets, the language is forward and aggressive (Figure 4).

In terms of the sociality in the language, the writing trends more male; regardless, both sets seem to pace each other on these features (Figure 5).

A fair amount of the language is "cognitive," so the members are engaging around ideas and thinking (Figure 6).

In terms of perceptual language, a major focus is on words indicating sight and visuals, with much less from hearing and feeling (Figure 7).

In terms of references to biology, there are focuses on various bodily functions (Figure 8). In the image set, the "sexual" references come to the fore (in a pretty juvenile way).

Human drives are also addressed, with a main focus on power and reward (Figure 9).

In terms of time references, both sets are firmly ensconced in the present in terms of language (Figure 10).

In terms of references to relativity, motion, space, and time, the focus is on space, time, and motion, in that order (Figure 11).

Figure 4. Emotional features of messaging on collections of 3-5 days of archived messages on two 4chan boards

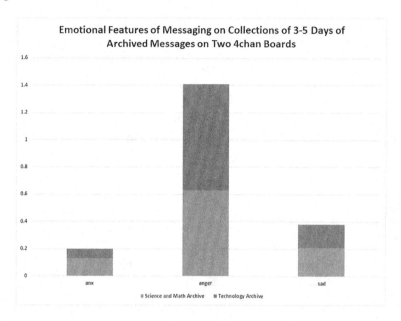

Figure 5. Social language features of messaging on collections of 3-5 Days of archived messages on two 4chan boards

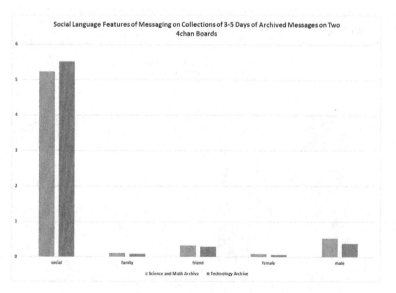

Figure 6. Cognitive language features of messaging on collections of 3-5 days of archived messages on two 4chan boards

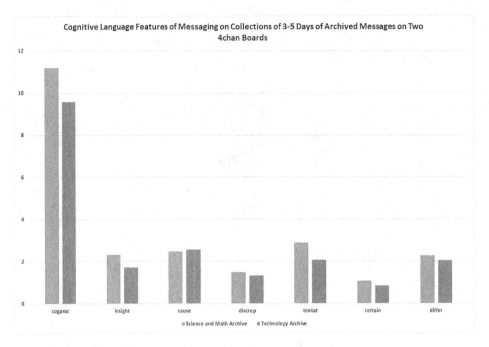

Figure 7. Perceptual language features of the messaging on collections of 3-5 days of archived messages on two 4chan boards

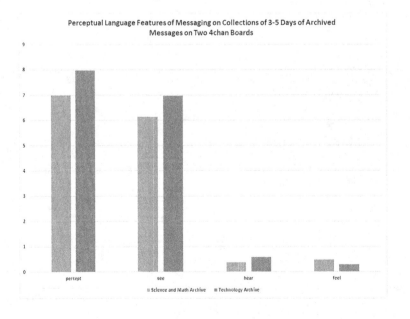

Figure 8. Biological language features of the messaging on collections of 3-5 Days of archived messages on two 4chan boards

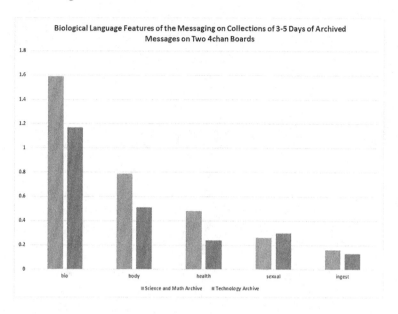

Figure 9. Human drives language features of the messaging on collections of 3-5 days of archived messages on two 4chan boards

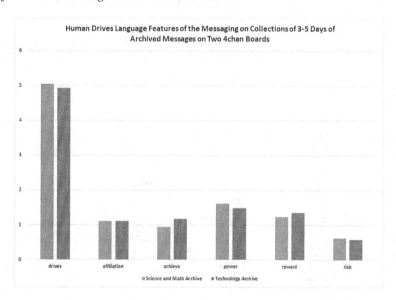

Figure 10. Time focus orientation language features of the messaging on collections of 3-5 days of archived messages on Two 4chan boards

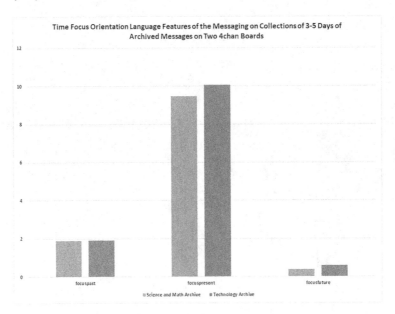

Figure 11. Relativity, motion, space, and time language features of the messaging on collections of 3-5 days of archived messages on two 4chan boards

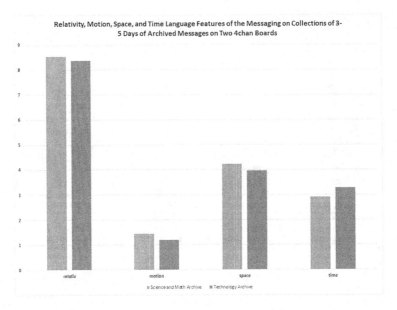

The lifestyle language features show some divergences between the two sets. Both archives show a major emphasis on Work. And the Technology archive shows more of a focus on Money and Leisure than the Science and Math one. (Figure 12)

Finally, in terms of alternate language usage, "informal" and "netspeak" and "swear" words predominated for both sets (Figure 13).

The psychometric analysis of the archived messages from two recent 4chan imageboards shows one approach, but a more insightful one may involve close-in readings over time and inculcation into the anonymous cultures of the respective boards, given the "discursive practices dependent on its synchronicity, anonymity, and ephemerality" (Manivannan, Oct. 10, 2012). The ephemerality is fairly extreme: "We find that most threads spend just five seconds on the first page and less than five minutes on the site before expiring" (Bernstein, Monroy-Hernández, Harry, André, Panovich, & Vargas, 2011, p. 50).

Figure 12. Lifestyle language features of the messaging on collections of 3-5 days of archived messages on two 4chan boards

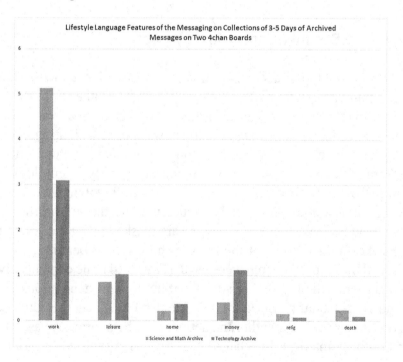

Figure 13. Alternate language features of the messaging on collections of 3-5 days of archived messages on two 4chan boards

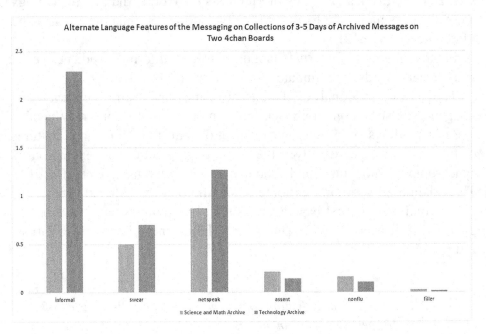

Analysis of Social Images Around 4chan

A walk-through of the scraped 4chan image set from Flickr showed a number of visual puns and jokes, many involving cats and other animals. There were fandom efforts at praising "awesomeness" such as Star Wars and other mainstream media contents. One photo shows squirrels fighting with light sabers. There were mocking memes about people making stupid mistakes. There were critiques of religious systems and particularly Scientology. There are images of real-life events involving cosplay, involving technologies, involving demonstrations and social critiques; in some, the high profile founder of 4chan may be seen. Some participants are masked using the Anonymous (Guy Fawkes mask). Some of the images show gender bending, and some that slipped through the search were lewd. (Figure 14) The contents give the sense that users will outgrow the site, and if not for new generations of those who find the personality appealing, the site itself may become outdated and banal (even as juvenile thoughts and actions may be a forever phase for each generation of humanity). In other words, the EHM typified by 4chan may live on with or without 4chan.

Figure 14. 4chan Flickr social image set (1095 Images)

Research into 4chan suggests that even anonymized members police each other's postings and co-define "acceptable" postings (Trammell, Feb. 2 – 3, 2014), with a social forcing function that limits the freeing effects of advertised anonymity. 4chan's "culture of anonymity" and standing for "alterity" has been described as "haphazard" and "s a discordant bricolage of humour, geek cultures, fierce debates, pornography, in–jokes, hyperbolic opinions and general offensiveness" (Knuttila, Oct. 3, 2011). Its value lies in the breadth of its messaging and its dedicated membership, almost in spite of the "repugnant" messaging for which it is known (Knuttila, Oct. 3, 2011). Researchers suggest that sites like 4chan can be harnessed for atypical uses, such as in the aftermath of the Boston Marathon bombings, with communities activated to sleuthing behaviors (Potts & Harrison, 2013).

Validating or Invalidating EHM Personalities, Dispositions, Temperaments, and Moods

Profiling the personalities of an EHM is inexact—from the initial step of identifying an EHM through reading its messaging, collective cultures and practices, its human membership, its group actions (online and offline), and its harnessed technologies, among others. Strengthening the initial personality profiling may be done through the following means:

- Engaging a wider range of data

- From a wider time span, and
- Applying a greater variety of research and analytical methods (including both human- and computational approaches), with controls against over-reaching and over-inferring, and
- Documenting the approaches with precision and care.

In terms of wider ranges of data, analysis of leadership in EHMs may be informative, given the outsized influence of the few who can move the masses based on ideas, charisma, talent, vision, and leverage. [The Pareto principle or 80/20 rule or "law of the vital few" or "principle of factor sparsity" suggests that 80% of the effects come from 20% of the causes (Juran, 1951, as cited in Craft & Leake, 2002). This idea of the Pareto principle was created by Joseph Juran. This idea suggests that a few can have an outsized effect.] The "immersive parasocial" dynamic of virtual worlds (Hai-Jew, Sept. 2009) may expand to social media, with its charismatic personalities and hordes of followers.

Depending on the size of the EHM, the explorations may include a variety of EHM compartments and social media and other technologies. If an EHM may be understood to have various disparate parts and sub-communities, those aspects may be explored in more depth. If particular social media platforms and / or sociotechnical functionalities affect EHMs, those may be studied as well.

Or if the modes of information were mostly textual and social image-based, as it was for the example in this chapter, perhaps video and multimodal data and memes may be studied in addition.

If outside observer approaches were taken, perhaps inside observer approaches should also be harnessed, or vice versa. Or both "etic" and "emic" approaches may be applied, for outsider and insider perspectives...both analytic and experienced senses of the EHM. Or different analytical frameworks may be applied, given the high dimensionality of social data in EHMs.

Still, depending on the analytical lenses, the theoretical frameworks, the coding hands, the coding methods, and other approaches, an EHM may be understood in diverse (and contradictory) ways. This begs the question of how to test the respective analytical impressions of personality. Is there convergence around massmind personality characteristics or divergence? How can the polysemous understandings be understood together, and if needed, reconciled? Also, if predictions are made for the near-future (as well as mid-term future, and long-term future) of the EHM, how well do these play out, and how accurately? And if researchers themselves are engaging in an EHM, how informative are the respective personality profiles in informing their actions and in attaining their objectives? Of these approaches, which parts are reproducible and efficient and accurate, and which are more idiosyncratic and subjective?

One way that such interpretations may **not** be validated is by testing the evaluation against the experiences of insiders (per se). First, there are differences between external and internal perspectives and subjectivities. Insiders may not have the perspective of the whole, of which they are a part. They may not be aware of the particular transient "state" of the group or its history. They may not have background trainings on the "etic" analytic methods. Second, observed "personalities" of EHMs should be built on the available evidence from the naturalistic observations; the research should be based on empirics (and should be falsifiable).

Also, even though these analyses are built off a formal literature on personality, this is not to constrain the analyses to formalized methods and codebooks. There should always be room for "telling details" (observations that may be revelatory in an outsized way) and bottom-up grounded theory-inspired coding.

Finally, massmind personality profiling is by definition an over-simplification. There may not be a final, definitive, or rigorous way to validate findings. Multiple frameworks and interpretations and understandings may be applicable simultaneously. It may be that more "fuzzy" or inexact understandings is the general aim, with observations of tendencies and ranges, instead of something absolutely discrete or precise. The signal and noise (static) may be enmeshed, and it may be that both types inform in their own ways.

DISCUSSION

The hypotheses were as follows:

Hypothesis 1: Electronic hive minds (EHM), distributed massminds enabled through social media platforms and ICT, have collective personalities, dispositions, temperaments, and moods.

Hypothesis 2: The personalities of EHM may be discerned and understood (in part) through remote analysis of member messaging, culture and practices, human membership, group actions, and related sociotechnical systems (and understructures).

Hypothesis 3: The personalities of EHM may inform on predictive aspects, including capabilities, interests, motivations, attractiveness/aversiveness, and current future actions.

So what was found in this work? In terms of the hypotheses, there are senses of collective personalities that may be extracted from electronic hive minds. If longer observations were made, different moods would likely be observable (as it seems clear that particular in-world events may trigger different responses among those in this EHM). There are states of excitement and calm. There are observable emotional states. [Robert Plutchik's Wheel of Emotions suggests that humans may experience—at core, eight types of emotions. These include ecstasy, admiration, terror, amazement, grief, loathing, rage, and vigilance (at high intensity); joy, trust, fear, surprise, sadness, disgust, anger, and anticipation in the next step out; and then serenity, acceptance, apprehension, distraction, pensiveness, boredom, annoyance, and interest (in the third ring from the center (with dissipating potency of the emotions the farther one moves from the center). (Donaldson, Apr. 27, 2017). In the work, it is possible to observe the coloring of human emotions across EHMs at different phases. (Hypothesis 1)

Second-hand reportage of the membership, culture, and actions can be informative of personality. (In this case, the members of 4chan apparently share images of their own events and exploits, so sousveillance content is available along with surveillance contents.) The sociotechnical means by which the group connects publicly is simple: bulletin boards, video sharing sites, social media platforms, and others. These enable connectivity…and some identity leakage (for all the fanfare of the anonymity of the original platform). (Hypothesis 2)

As to predictivity, it would stand to reason that some predictivity is possible. A 4chan EHM is focused on self-defined particular issues of interest, and based on their membership and resources, they will act on those interests online and in-world as they have in the past. (Hypothesis 3) A. Maslow's concept that people's psychological needs inform their goals and focuses and that they perceive psychological threats from any barriers to their "basic human goals" (1943, p. 388) may apply to this space.

For this particular case, the general five sources were harnessed, albeit incompletely. The five elements include the following:

- The public (and private) messaging (textual, imagistic, audio, video, and multimodal elements)

- The collective culture(s) and practices
- The human membership and member motivations
- The group actions (virtual and in-world)
- The sociotechnical systems, and others

The messaging, in this case, involved a small sample of mostly public messaging. Observations of the collective culture and practices were induced from the messaging and also second-hand by hearsay and published accounts. The human membership and member motivations were backwards inferred from actions and from messaging, given the anonymity of the membership. The group actions are the stuff of Internet lore and generally not denied by the organization. The sociotechnical system studied was a basic bulletin board.

About Messaging

What was learned about these respective sources? First, in terms of messaging, understanding the min-max ranges of the expressed ideas and their coherence / incoherence is helpful to illuminate the diversity of the EHM. Themes can generally be identified even for very diverse EHMs, but analyzing for "long tail" topics is also valuable even if the topics are only of interest to a few members or parts of the EHM. In terms of language, visuals, symbolism, humor, there seems to be a fair amount of convergence as a predicate for participation and membership. From such interactions, there are meta-narratives that may be identified. These grand level themes may be inferred from the sub messaging.

About Collective Cultures and Practices

Attention, resources, energy, and other group "powers" are limited, and given these real-world limitations, EHMs have to pick and choose what they will focus on.

About Human Membership and Member Motivations

Even when members are trying to be anonymous and to hide their hand, they give themselves away by their selectivity about what to message and how to message. In this case, those who would aspire to expertise show their hand when they make comments and assertions in-the-world, which includes objectively testable assertions. Leadership—in form and in figure—may affect how much enthusiasm there is among the membership and how much persistence there is among the members.

About Group Actions (Virtual and In-World)

Electronic hive minds that exist online have spillovers into the real world and real life (RL). The passions of an EHM require actions.

About Sociotechnical Systems

Sociotechnical systems offer a range of enablements, but even with some fairly simple interfaces, whole EHMs may form and be fairly persistent in time.

FUTURE RESEARCH DIRECTIONS

Personalities of EHMs are thought to be somewhat self-organizing and emergent, based in part on the membership of the participants and their shared messaging. It is thought that dominant personalities and those in leadership may also play a role. The sociotechnical spaces and technological enablements may also have an effect. Also, the extant group "personality" is thought to interact with in-world occurrences, with resulting and transient "moods" and intensifications of interests (and some reactance).

As a nascent work in this space, this chapter provided an initial approach to mapping the personalities of EHMs, based on messaging, inferred culture, human membership, group actions, and sociotechnical systems. The data collected was partial and not even random. As such, a number of extant questions exist:

- What is a typical developmental sequence for the creation of personality on EHMs? What are the time frames for the development of personality on EHMs? Are there crucial formative periods when particular personalities emerge, and when personality may "freeze" for a time?
- When understanding EHM personalities, which aspects are "core" vs. "peripheral" ones? Why?
- What is a typical vs. atypical EHM personality?

- What are the mechanisms for the emergence of an EHM personality? Social ones? Technological ones? Sociotechnical ones?
- What is the relationship between an EHM personality and its group identity online? What psychic needs are met for the group members in the particular EHM?
  - Is there an association between a collective EHM personality and its human membership? If so, what? If not, why not?
- Are there associations between types of personalities of EHMs and motivations to expression and motivations to action? EHM personality types and capabilities? Are there associations between EHM personalities and actions taken?
  - Do EHMs have values and principles that serve as behavioral guideposts? Why or why not?
- How fixed or malleable are EHM personalities? What factors affect these personalities, and how are they changed? What about for dispositions? Temperaments? Moods?
  - How do various historical events affect EHMs?
  - How does leadership affect EHMs?
  - How do technologies affect EHMs?
  - What are ways to incentivize particular types of changes in EHMs?
- How could an EHM personality be considered "ordered" vs. "disordered"? "Efficient" or "inefficient"? "Healthy" or "unhealthy"? "Resilient" or "non-resilient"? "Transient" or "enduring"? "Adaptive" or "non-adaptive"? "Social" or "non-social" or "a-social"? "Benevolent" or "malevolent"?
- What are features of EHM personalities considered attractive? Aversive?
  - What aspects of EHM personalities engage with newcomers, and how?
  - What sorts of affective engagements are present? Sensory engagements? Experiences? Intellectual challenges?
- What does the EHM "alert to"? How does it "alert to" particular issues? How does it respond? Is the EHM excitable or not, in relation to particular signals? Does the response move from the conceptual side to the action side (where the physical membership "body" is activated)? What arouses particular EHMs?
- Based on EHM personality, what may be predicted from the available information, and with what degree of certitude?

- In the same way that there are studies that associate individual personalities with long-term outcomes, are there long-term outcomes that may be predicted for EHM personalities? (Personality can affect long-term outcomes for people, with longitudinal studies showing associations between personality types and career achievements, financial well-being, health, and other aspects.

- What are the common moods to particular EHMs? What are its most common affective states? How can these moods be influenced—sparked? Maintained? How metacognitively aware is the EHM of its own moods?

Earlier in this work, it was suggested that the understood personalities of electronic hive minds may be studied to understand additional information: the potential appeal of an EHM to particular populations, the types of interactions among its members, the potential capabilities that may be co-evolved, the types of future actions that may be taken on by the members of the EHM, how reactive the EHM may be to particular triggers and messages and incentives, how the target EHM personalities may evolve, and others.

While personality inventories of people touch on whether some personality types are benevolent or malevolent, prosocial or antisocial, this consideration has not been advanced per se for collective personalities on EHMs. Considering the effects of an EHM on general life, on contributions to society, on experiences for its users, and other intended and unintended effects, may be relevant in considering the ethics of EHMs. There may be practical considerations, too, about whether an EHM is maladaptive or disordered: Does information processing in the EHM lead to erroneous ideas, decision making, and practices? Are parts of the EHM taken advantage of for the benefit of others; are there manipulative and deceptive agents (wolves) taking advantage of the others (sheep)?

While Freudian concepts have slipped out of favor, the "split mind" approach of studying EHMs as ids, egos, and super egos may have value, to capture EHMs in different angles and even states. [Separately, 4chan has been characterized as "the Id of the Internet" (Chen, Spring 2012, p. 7).]

Also, there is interest in how various EHMs—as personalities—interact with others. What happens when multiple EHMs interact? What are collaborative possibilities? How do discrete cultures enmesh? How do members interact and engage?

CONCLUSION

From the research angle, as an early work, this case-based chapter does suggest that it is possible to infer a collective personality from electronic hive minds from the messaging, membership, group actions, and sociotechnical technologies related to an EHM. The described approach is somewhat reproducible (in terms of the computational text analysis), but other interpretations are subjective and affected by the lens of the analyst. While there are some computational efficiencies, there are some aspects that are custom and boutique—although some early tools for analysis have been shared here as well.

At the heart of this chapter is a simple idea—that conglomerations of people connected on the Web and Internet—may form larger entities that have emergent personalities. These personalities may be in formative stages, or they may be in more settled stages, depending on the evolution of the electronic hive minds (EHMs). Based on the members, their messaging, their interactions, and their actions, certain tendencies come to the fore that influence how the group communicates, acts, and engages the world. These penchants form a distinct group personality, disposition, temperament, and moods. These tendencies may evolve with or without the memberships' awareness. In a sense, this larger entity is greater than the sum of its parts. This work focused on more stable aspects of collective personhood (personality, disposition, temperament) and more transitory affective states (mood); the first aspects are thought to be more internal and membership-based and the latter maybe more influenced by the social ecosystem or external contextual factors. These aspects of EHM personhood are thought to be both elements of the EHM membership (internal) and the larger social ecosystem (external), in some complex and interactive combination. The respective lifespans of EHMs also vary, and the collective personalities may vary based on how developed they are and what influences inform them.

The evolved and emergent personality can motivate its members as individuals, motifs, small groups, and large entities to certain world views and certain actions; the EHM leadership may direct its members, or the direction may be much less concentrated and more dispersed and distributed. The personalities of the respective EHMs may be positive or negative in its effects on its members and others and the world. It is hypothesized that such personalities can be affected to some degree by its membership and by others and even by the sociotechnical technologies used. These aspects of EHMs may inform on future actions and provide a predictive function.

REFERENCES

Ahktar, R., Winsborough, D., Ort, U., Johnson, A., & Chamorro-Premuzic, T. (2018). Detecting the dark side of personality using social media status updates. *Personality and Individual Differences*, *132*, 90–97. doi:10.1016/j.paid.2018.05.026

Atkinson, K. (2008). *When Will There be Good News?* New York: Little, Brown and Company.

Azucar, D., Marengo, D., & Settanni, M. (2018). Predicting the Big 5 personality traits from digital footprints on social media: A meta-analysis. *Personality and Individual Differences*, *124*, 150–159. doi:10.1016/j.paid.2017.12.018

Berenbaum, H., Chow, P. I., Schoenleber, M., & Flores, L. E. Jr. (2016). Personality and pleasurable emotions. *Personality and Individual Differences*, *101*, 400–406. doi:10.1016/j.paid.2016.06.023

Bernstein, M. S., & Monroy-Hernández, A. (2011). 4chan and /b/: An analysis of anonymity and ephemerality in a large online community. In *Proceedings of the Fifth International AAAI Conference on Weblogs and Social Media*. Association for the Advancement of Artificial Intelligence.

Bessi, A. (2016). Personality traits and echo chambers in Facebook. *Computers in Human Behavior*, *65*, 319–324. doi:10.1016/j.chb.2016.08.016

Big Five personality traits. (2018, Nov. 15). In *Wikipedia*. Retrieved Nov. 23, 2018, from https://en.wikipedia.org/wiki/Big_Five_personality_traits

Boyd, R. L., & Pennebaker, J. W. (2017). Language-based personality: A new approach to personality in a digital world. *Behavioral Science*, *18*, 63–68.

Chen, C. (2012, Spring). The creation and meaning of Internet memes in 4chan: Popular Internet culture in the age of online digital reproduction. *Institutions*, 6–19.

Correa, T., Hinsley, A. W., & de Zúñiga, H. G. (2010). Who interacts on the Web? The intersection of users' personality and social media use. *Computers in Human Behavior*, *26*(2), 247–253. doi:10.1016/j.chb.2009.09.003

Craft, R. C., & Leake, C. (2002). The Pareto principle in organizational decision making. *Management Decision*, *40*(8), 729–733. doi:10.1108/00251740210437699

Dalpé, J., Demers, M., Verner-Filion, J., & Vallerand, R. J. (2019). From personality to passion: The role of the Big Five factors. *Personality and Individual Differences*, *138*, 280–285. doi:10.1016/j.paid.2018.10.021

Dark triad. (2018, Nov. 15). In *Wikipedia*. Retrieved Nov. 24, 2018, from https://en.wikipedia.org/wiki/Dark_triad

Donaldson, M. (2017, Apr. 27). Plutchik's Wheel of Emotions – 2017 Update. *Six Seconds*. Retrieved Jan. 1, 2019, from https://www.6seconds.org/2017/04/27/plutchiks-model-of-emotions/

Dualistic Model of Passion (DMP). (n.d.). Laboratoire de Recherche sur la Comportment Social. Retrieved Nov. 23, 2018, from https://www.lrcs.uqam.ca/en/results/dualistic-model-of-passion-dmp/

Elleman, L. G., Condon, D. M., Russin, S. E., & Revelle, W. (2018). The personality of U.S. states: Stability from 1999 to 2015. *Journal of Research in Personality*, *72*, 64–72. doi:10.1016/j.jrp.2016.06.022

Fan, J., Zhang, L., & Chen, C. (2018). Thinking styles: Distinct from personality? *Personality and Individual Differences*, *125*, 50–55. doi:10.1016/j.paid.2017.12.026

Gou, L., Zhou, M. X., & Yang, H. (2014). KnowMe and ShareMe: Understanding automatically discovered personality traits from social media and user sharing preferences. CHI 2014, One of a CHInd, 955 – 964.

Hai-Jew, S. (2009, Sept.). Exploring the immersive parasocial: Is it you or the thought of you? *Journal of Online Learning and Teaching*. Retrieved Oct. 15, 2018, from http://jolt.merlot.org/vol5no3/hai-jew_0909.htm

Hai-Jew, S. (2019). The electronic hive mind and cybersecurity: Mass-scale human cognitive limits to explain the 'weakest link' in cybersecurity. In *Global Cyber Security Labor Shortage and International Business Risk* (pp. 206–262). Hershey, PA: IGI Global. doi:10.4018/978-1-5225-5927-6.ch011

Hodson, G., Hogg, S. M., & MacInnish, C. C. (2009). The role of 'dark personalities' (narcissism, Machiavellianism, psychopathy), Big Five personality factors, and ideology in explaining prejudice. *Journal of Research in Personality*, *43*(4), 686–690. doi:10.1016/j.jrp.2009.02.005

Jonason, P. K., & Zeigler-Hill, V. (2018). The fundamental social motives that characterize dark personality traits. *Personality and Individual Differences*, *132*, 98–107. doi:10.1016/j.paid.2018.05.031

Jones, D. N., & Paulhus, D. L. (2011). The role of impulsivity in the Dark Triad of personality. *Personality and Individual Differences, 51*(5), 679–682. doi:10.1016/j.paid.2011.04.011

Kim, H., & Stepchenkova, S. (2017). Understanding destination personality through visitors' experience: A cross-cultural perspective. *Journal of Destination Marketing & Management, 6*(4), 416–425. doi:10.1016/j.jdmm.2016.06.010

Knuttila, L. (2011, October 3). User unknown: 4chan, anonymity and contingency. *First Monday, 16*(10). doi:10.5210/fm.v16i10.3665

Macdonald, C., Bore, M., & Munro, D. (2008). Values in action scale and the Big 5: An empirical indication of structure. *Journal of Research in Personality, 42*(4), 878–799. doi:10.1016/j.jrp.2007.10.003

Manivannan, V. (2012, Oct. 10). Attaining the ninth square: Cybertextuality, gamification, and institutional memory on 4chan. *Enculturation Net*. Retrieved from http://www.enculturation_net/attaining-the-ninth-square

Marengo, D., Giannotta, F., & Settanni, M. (2017). Assessing personality using emoji: An exploratory study. *Personality and Individual Differences, 112*, 74–78. doi:10.1016/j.paid.2017.02.037

Maslow, A. H. (1943). A theory of human motivation. *Psychological Review, 50*(4), 370–396. doi:10.1037/h0054346

Oshio, A., Taku, K., Hirano, M., & Saeed, G. (2018). Resilience and Big Five personality traits: A meta-analysis. *Personality and Individual Differences, 127*, 54–60. doi:10.1016/j.paid.2018.01.048

Pennebaker, J. W., Boyd, R. L., Jordan, K., & Blackburn, K. (2015). *The development and psychometric properties of LIWC2015*. Austin, TX: University of Texas at Austin.

Poole, C. (2010). The case for anonymity online. *TED2010*. Retrieved Nov. 23, 2018, from https://www.ted.com/talks/christopher_m00t_poole_the_case_for_anonymity_online#t-69368

Potts, L., & Harrison, A. (2013). Interfaces as rhetorical constructions: reddit and 4chan during the Boston Marathon bombings. *SIGDOC'13*, 1 – 9.

Rapp, C., Ingold, K., & Freitag, M. (2018). Personalized networks? How the Big Five personality traits influence the structure of egocentric networks. *Social Science Research,* 1 – 13. (in press)

Reed, L. I., Harrison, E. G., Best, C. K., & Hooley, J. M. (2018). Bargaining with characters: How personality pathology affects behavior in the ultimatum and dictator games [Preprint]. *Personality and Individual Differences*, 1–5.

Schermer, J. A., Holden, R. R., & Krammer, G. (2019). The general factor of personality is very robust under faking conditions. *Personality and Individual Differences, 13,* 63–68. doi:10.1016/j.paid.2018.09.025

Stephan, Y., Sutin, A. R., Canada, B., & Terracciano, A. (2017). Personality and frailty: Evidence from four samples. *Journal of Research in Personality, 66,* 46–53. doi:10.1016/j.jrp.2016.12.006 PMID:28649150

Tonna, M., Paglia, F., Ottoni, R., Ossola, P., De Panfilis, C., & Marchesi, C. (2018). Delusional disorder: The role of personality and emotions on delusional ideation. *Comprehensive Psychiatry, 85,* 78–83. doi:10.1016/j.comppsych.2018.07.002 PMID:30005180

Trammell, M. (2014, Feb. 2 – 3). User investment and behavior policing on 4chan. *First Monday,* 19.

Wehrli, S. (2008). *Personality on social network sites: an application of the Five Factor Model.* ETH Zurich Sociology Working Paper No. 7.

Whaite, E. O., Shensa, A., Sidani, J. E., Colditz, J. B., & Primack, B. A. (2018). Social media use, personality characteristics, and social isolation among young adults in the United States. *Personality and Individual Differences, 124,* 45–50. doi:10.1016/j.paid.2017.10.030

KEY TERMS AND DEFINITIONS

Big Five Personality Traits: The so-called "big 5" personality traits from the 5-Factor Model include openness to experience, conscientiousness, extraversion, agreeableness, and neuroticism.

Collective Disposition: Inherent group mind and character.

Collective Mood: Group feeling, as a temporary and transient affective state (including states of contemplation, excitement, frustration, engagement, and others).

Collective Personality: Distinctive combination of group dimensions (characteristics) that coalesce as an identity (with the dimensions aligning with aspects of human personality).

Collective Temperament: Foundational group nature, which affects group behavior.

Electronic Hive Mind: A synchronous temporal and informal patchwork of emergent shared social consciousness (held by geographically distributed people, cyborgs, and robots) enabled by online social connectivity (across a range of social media platforms on the web and internet), based around various dimensions of shared attractive interests.

Mass Mind: Collective consciousness.

Sousveillance: Observation from below, from within (as compared to "surveillance" or observation from above, as in "eye in the sky").

Chapter 4

Frugal Living for Our Collective and Mutual #Bestlife on a Distributed and Global Electronic Hive Mind

ABSTRACT

What is not as commonly identified as an optimal life #bestlife is living #frugal, and yet, there is a global electronic hive mind about how to live sparingly based on highly variant local realities. There are blogs about living on a shoestring, stretching funds, cooking in, engaging in a DIY economy (bartering with like-minded others), living off the grid, taking low-cost and simple vacations, maintaining a food garden, raising food animals, and forgoing the more spendy aspects of modern living. The narrative goes that saving up and retiring early enables low-pressure and intentional lifestyles (and an ability to focus on family and friends), low-carbon footprints (with low impacts on the environment), and the embodiment of a frugal virtue. This chapter explores what a #frugal living EHM looks like and how it brings together people around shared values and lifestyle practices for personal peace of mind, social justice, and long-term sustainability.

DOI: 10.4018/978-1-5225-9369-0.ch004

INTRODUCTION

Without frugality none can be rich, and with it very few would be poor. - Samuel Johnson

Many people take no care of their money till they come nearly to the end of it, and others do just the same with their time. - Johann Wolfgang von Goethe

In terms of most people's #bestlife (that leads to others' jealousy and plenty of FOMO) in the materialistic West, there are various sorts of selfie-shared (or paparazzi-captured) depicted acts:

- The pursuit of ostentatious and expensive pleasure (jets, parties, high fashion, luxury bling, spa vacations, and shopping sprees),
- Having the perfect family (well set and not a hair out of place),
- Dating up (and often),
- Experiencing various acts of daring (jumping out of planes, buildering, bungee jumping, and other risk-taking),
- Hanging out with friends in various exotic locations, and
- Simply being famous, among others.

And yet, there is a narrative of frugal living on social media that has attracted adherents from around he world. Some human behaviors involve personal decisions and actions at a ground level that taken together have a larger impact on the environment and on others. There is an "emergent" aspect to individual actions taken collectively and writ large. Sometimes, the individual actions are merely individual choices, and others are somewhat coordinated. Some electronic hive minds (EHMs) can speak into such collective spaces and encourage collective awarenesses and behaviors of various types (Hai-Jew, 2019). "Frugality" or a kind of resourcefulness and avoidance of waste (of money or material resources) is one of these phenomena. People choose how they want to use their moneys and resources, and their consumption affects others' livelihoods, the respective product and service supply chains, the natural environment, and other outcomes.

Being frugal (or frugal living) goes against some of the core assumptions of economics: that people's appetites are insatiable and unlimited in a resource-constrained environment. No amount fully satisfies people's appetites, so some constraints have to be applied—such as people's financial wherewithal.

There are some "stars" (personalities) and "models" in this space:

- A "zero-waste" young woman becomes well known for apparently being able to condense all her garbage for four years in a small glass jar (East, July 6, 2016). Everything else, she says, has been composted or recycled. She is working hard on maintaining a light "carbon footprint." Her achievements have sparked a "zero-waste" movement with others working towards similar goals.
- Two young men host a podcast about frugal living in the finance realm. (They advertise themselves as "frugal dudes.")
- Several different families share on social media about their living off-the-grid and simply, while raising children. For some of the families, they have a rental that they use for funding; others have a retirement fund, built up during years of intense and often lucrative careers (and ensuing burnout). Their stories are similar in that they live in nature, raise their own food, hunt in-season, and provide for themselves through sparse resources.
- Some have stories of leaving high-powered careers in order to live off savings in urban environments, with some traveling globally and sharing their adventures.
- Others are living carefully off of their social media presences. They use advertising funds and company-provided funds for their travels and then provide reviews and evaluations to their huge populations of followers. Various world travelers visit different locales, and they share photos of their travels and low-cost adventures. They further share stories of those who are running taxi, tourist, food, and other scams.
- A farmer buys a used truck for $100, and he video records other people wanting to sell their used trucks for a lot more money and calls them out for daring to ask for more moneys. He has clearly gotten a deal, but subsequent tales of truck breakdowns and other challenges fill his video channel.

How people present on social media may be part of a social performance. It may be "cheap talk" vs. "costly signaling," the latter of which requires actual commitments and actual sacrifices. Certainly, there has been no shortage of "reveals" of people's fictions shared widely on social media. Superficially, a simple walk-through on social media provides some snapshots of frugality, via stories that people tell about themselves (in a form of *sousveillance*):

- **People will not let usable goods go to waste. (They will somewhat make up for some of their less frugal compatriots.)**
  - ○ A search of "dumpster diving" (as a seeding term) on Google Images shows intrepid individuals hip deep in discarded contents looking for valuables. There are people with boxes of fruits and vegetables, print goods, canned goods, plastic wrapped foods, and other resources. There are signs advertising an art to dumpster diving. On Google Scholar, "dumpster diving for food" results in some 5,470 results. In mass media, there are articles that share the art to dumpster diving: in order to track what goods are dumped when and the best times to collect them (and which dumpsters are locked and which are accessible) and how to stay safe while collecting others' undesirables. Dumpster diving is now not just a practice of starving college students but of organized groups that collect goods for distribution to the hungry through food banks and other organizations.
  - ○ Second hand shopping (thrift shopping) in second hand stores and garage sales and yard sales is a global phenomenon. Social videos share various shopping adventures and finds. Some social videos unwrap the finds in others' storage units, which are auctioned off after non-paying customers stop paying rent on their storage units. Mainstream media shares stories of treasures found. Some mainline television shows feature experts who evaluate various used and antique objects for their market value to collectors.
- **They work to have small carbon footprints, and they can make do with less than others.**
  - ○ Individuals and sometimes families live in micro houses, which are just a portion of the sizes of mainstream houses. These are portable, and they have many of the affordances of other houses, but in miniature.
  - ○ Major news outlets have carried stories of landfills and the multi-generational persistence of plastics and other discarded items. There are stories of electronic goods graveyards where computers and electronic equipment is retired and salvaged for anything usable. A pioneering family who is living "plastic-free" is spotlighted and lauded. Anything left over (most of the device) is left to leach toxins into the soil and environment.
  - ○ People develop skills to grow their own food, repair their own homes and cars, cook home meals, and engage the world differently

than in the mainstream. They sew their own clothes. They create their own soaps and toothpaste.

° They engage in trade with like-minded individuals. They learn to keep their bills to a bare minimum. They are creating an alternative lifestyle to the material-driven ones. Some work intense careers and then choose to retire in their late 20s, their 30s, their 40s… and show how they can guarantee sufficient funds skimmed off of their savings.

- **They will manage finances and invest with care.** Frugal people will have a working budget that makes sense in relation to their earnings. They will have a financial plan and follow through on their savings. They will be aware of the compounding expenses of even small fees by their investors.

Frugality is not quite a coalesced movement or even really a trend yet. It reads like a general drifting phenomenon that has captured the interest of some on the periphery. The effort feels counter-cultural (because of the focus on non-materialism), and frugality is certainly not in the mainstream. In terms of people's spending, at least in the U.S., people are mostly at the limits of what their earnings enable (and beyond, for many, living on debt).

In many senses, the frugality endeavor is told from a Western point of view, and for many, the lifestyle is somewhat by choice and by purposeful expression of preferred values and behaviors (of non-wastage of material and other resources). As a construct, "frugality" is seen as more of a composite of various values than an entity alone except as a "lifestyle choice" (Todd & Lawson, 2003, p. 8). [A quote attributed to Cicero reads: "Frugality includes all the other virtues."]

As an EHM, "frugality" thinking and its thinkers seem distributed (geographically dispersed) with a mix of local interests and local realities. As a consumer phenomenon, it is studied by companies that want to know how to market to "frugal" individuals and to encourage them to spend. Some of the social imagery captured as part of this work show businesses that have arisen around "frugal" but with the idea of low-cost and discounts. Frugality is also studied by environmentalists who have an interest in encouraging people to live differently and more sustainably. One other aspect of interest with the frugality EHM is that it evokes private individual choices that have an emergent collective quality, with theoretically measurable impacts on expenditures and the natural ecosystem.

REVIEW OF THE LITERATURE

A core assumption of the "frugal living" EHM is that "endless growth" to meet insatiable human needs is infeasible. There is an ethos of "de-growth" that practitioners share, with the "politics of scarcity," so people may live in "responsible togetherness" (Natale, Di Martino, Procentese, & Arcidiaconom, 2016, p. 50). The authors explain:

The degrowth paradigm offers a possible solution to the negative effects of capitalistic and consumeristic culture. This lies in curbing the unbridled production and consumption of commodities—along with the values attached to them—and downshift towards what Latouche (2011) has named 'frugal abundance', that is, a relational and economic system freed from the myth of endless growth (Natale, Di Martino, Procentese, & Arcidiacono, 2016, p. 49).

Those who pursue "voluntary simplicity" avoid "clutter" (Gregg, 1936, as cited in Leonard-Barton, Dec. 1981, p. 243). A draft behavioral index to measure individuals' tendencies towards voluntary simplicity "characterized by ecological awareness, attempts to become more self-sufficient, and efforts to decrease personal consumption of goods" (Leonard-Barton, Dec. 1981, p. 243) includes elements like making gifts instead of purchasing them, riding bicycles for exercise and commuting, recycling (newspapers, jars, cans, and others), doing oil changes at home, developing skills "in carpentry, car tune-up and repair, or plumbing" for self-reliance, eating "meatless main meals," buying clothes from second hand stores, setting up a compost pile, making "furniture or clothing for the family," and bartering "with others in lieu of payment with money" (Leonard-Barton, Dec. 1981, pp. 250 - 251).

These values are often translated to actions, with frugality as a "pervasive consumer trait" (Lastovicka, Bettencourt, Hughner, & Kuntze, 1999, p. 85). Such approaches have been a part of "day-to-day American life" beginning in colonial times (Witkowski, 1989, as cited in Lastovicka, Bettencourt, Hughner, & Kuntze, 1999, p. 85). What are some basic observed traits of people who are frugal?

Empirically, the frugal are less susceptible to interpersonal influence, less materialistic, less compulsive in buying, and more price and value conscious. Being frugal does not correspond with being ecocentric nor with being prone to using coupons. A motivation to save the planet and being frugal are found unrelated. Further, it seems, being frugal means no necessary interest in the coupons used so often to promote convenience goods. Frugality consistently explains consumer usage behaviors. The data show the frugal use products and services resourcefully; this ranges from timing their showers to eating leftovers for lunch at work. Being frugal empirically affects purchasing. In a mental accounting experiment examining how the source of income influences spending, only the less frugal are manipulated into spending more. Scale norms from a general population survey, combined with data from Tightwad Gazette subscribers, show Gazette subscribers are on average at the top two deciles on the frugality scale. (Lastovicka, Bettencourt, Hughner, & Kuntze, 1999, p. 96)

Frugality is a part of social movements. As a "social innovation," defined broadly as "new ideas that address unmet social needs—and that work" (Mulgan, Tucker, Ali, & Sanders, 2007, p. 2, as cited in Nicholls, Simon, & Gabriel, 2015, p. 2), frugal living may lead to individual-level (micro), group level (meso), and societal and global level (macro) changes.

World-scale religious ideas and philosophies have also been harnessed for the avoidance of over-consumption through frugality, including Eastern philosophies of Confucianism, Jainism, Buddhism, Daoism, and other traditions (Roiland, 2016). Various world religious systems (including "American Indian, Buddhist, Christian/Jewish, Taoist, (and) Hindu") speak to frugality and its importance (Lastovicka, Bettencourt, Hughner, & Kuntze, 1999, p. 86). These evocations speak to spiritual dimensions in electronic hive minds, a Zen aspect with particular balanced decisions and practices.

There are arguments against lifestyles in "industrial societies and people (who) spend too much in goods and items when a majority only tries to survive" (Roiland, 2016, p. 571). And yet, frugality has to be balanced against practical considerations: "Frugality is a concept that forces (us) to redefine our priorities in life, in economy in a global system. An Ethic of frugality on different levels appears essential to face the actual challenges. However frugality cannot be presented in opposition with creativity and economic growth." (Roiland, 2016, p. 583)

Other research has focused on the various types of "food wasters" (non-frugals, meant in a derogatory sense). A study conducted in Italy described this group of "food wasters" with seven profiles.

Out of seven profiles identified, four are the most representative ones in terms of size: the conscious-fussy type, who wastes because food doesn't smell or look good; the conscious-forgetful type, who forgets what is in the fridge or on the shelves; the frugal consumer who tends not to consume fruits and vegetables and declares to waste nothing (or almost nothing); and the exaggerated cook, who overbuys and overcooks (Gaiani, Caldeira, Adorno, Segrè, & Vittuari, 2018, p. 17)

The additional profiles are "the unskilled cook," "the confused type" [who is "confused about (food) labelling"], and "the exaggerated shopper" who overbuys (Gaiani, Caldeira, Adorno, Segrè, & Vittuari, 2018, p. 23). In a sense this and other works call out those who misuse available resources. Indeed, in developed countries, when food is wasted, it is usually at the "consumption stage of the food supply chain" (Gaiani, Caldeira, Adorno, Segrè, & Vittuari, 2018, p. 17).

Thrift in terms of energy usage has been associated with consumer motivations based on "multiple self-identities" with self-concepts of the self as "environmentally friendly and a frugal person" (Thøgersen, 2018, p. 1528) as contrasted against a "green" (pro-environmental) motivation in terms of engaging in energy-saving behaviors in the home (p. 1521). Research does suggest a positive correlation between the "frugal" and "green" self-identities.

One core concept in the consumption debate is that of fairness: Which populations in the world have rights to consume outsized shares of the Earth's resources? Sustainable consumption is debated at both local and more global scales.

Socially conscious consumer behavior, like its ecological counterpart, appears to be an expression of pro-social values. In contrast, frugal consumer behavior relates primarily to low personal materialism and income constraints. As such, it does not yet represent a fully developed moral challenge to consumerism. (Pepper, Jackson, & Uzzell, 2009, p. 126)

Even if the challenge is not direct to the retail-industrial complex (so to speak), the idea of living with basic necessities alone without excess may have impacts on consumption. Marketers of firms with B-to-C (business to consumer) businesses have an interest in studying "non-consumption" (Gould, Houston, & Mundt, 1997, as cited in Todd & Lawson, 2003, p. 8). Retailers trying to find the right formula to encourage more spending among the frugal who nevertheless have the means to buy and spend more. Multiple researchers have observed that "frugal consumers feel more independent than average" (Lastovicka, Bettencourt, Hughner, & Kuntze, 1999, p. 87), which may suggest that they are less suggestible to advertising. People who are frugal are thought to be "resistant to social influences" but may be induced to spend more if they are with their "high-spending networks of friends vs. low-spending networks of friends"…in "strong-tie networks" (Lee, 2016, p. 1). A countermove for frugal consumers is to avoid such social situations (Lee, 2016, p. 5). This is also not to say that there are not industries that have arisen around the concept of "frugal," as in low-cost products and services.

There is also push-back from the "politics and geographies of scarcity" as a meta-narrative that sustains "elite and capitalist power" (Mehta, Huff, & Allouche, 2018, p. 1) and enables the denial of fuller lives for many (goes the narrative).

Some research focuses on "alternative measures of frugality" (Mowen, 2000, p. 187). For example, "tightwadism" has been studied "in conjunction with impulsiveness, bargaining proneness, materialism (negative relationship), and emotional instability" (Mowen, 2000, p. 187). As a construct, frugality was found to have "poor internal reliability" as compared to "care in spending," which did have "good internal reliability" (Mowen, 2000, p. 187). Other insights were discovered:

The only construct predictive of care in spending was the need for arousal (negative relationship). Tightwadism was inversely related to a measure of materialism and positively related to the need for arousal, the need for body resources, and present orientation. (Mowen, 2000, p. 187)

Those who do not have a high need for excitement tend to be able to show "care in spending," and those who were less materialistic tend to be able to engage in "tightwadism," among other observations.

At more macro levels, "frugal innovations" enable better meeting the needs of those "low-income consumers who live on an income that is less than $5 a day" (Vadakkepat, Garg, Loh, & Tham, 2015, p. 1) as compared to the expensive products and services designed for those "at the top of the economic pyramid" (Vadakkepat, Garg, Loh, & Tham, 2015, p. 1).

While there is a not-unfounded fear of mass-scale "digital wildfires" sparking online and wreaking havoc (Webb, et al., Sept. 2015), social media also enables the spread of constructive and prosocial ideas, including for frugal living. Several studies inform this research work.

On social media, topic communities are those "created on-the-fly by people that post messages about a particular topic (i.e., topic communities)" (Kardara, Papadakis, Papaoikonomou, Tserpes, & Varvarigou, 2012, p. 1). The messages may be informational, advocacy-based, call-to-action, and other types. In topic communities, there are often "core influencers" or members who have outsized influences on the other members; these are "users who produce original content that is frequently retweeted" (Kardara, Papadakis, Papaoikonomou, Tserpes, & Varvarigou, 2012, p. 12). An empirical study of core influencers in a topic community found the following dimensions:

Although they are highly mentioned by other users, they avoid getting into discussions or reproducing others' opinions. When they actually do so, they mainly refer to or cite other influential members. Their messages are mostly factual, with just a negligible part of them explicitly expressing strong sentiments about the community's topic. Nevertheless, they precede their peers in expressing their feelings towards the topic in question, thus playing a major role in shaping the dominant opinion in each community. This explains the extremely high levels of correlation they exhibit with the community's aggregate sentiment. Their high levels of influence can be attributed to their specialized activity, as they are typically focused on few, similar topics. Our large-scale experimental analysis over real-world data verified that these patterns apply particularly to core groups of size k = 50 that are defined by the Mentions influence criterion (Kardara, Papadakis, Papaoikonomou, Tserpes, & Varvarigou, 2012, p. 12)

The core influencers play important leadership roles for the distributed online community. In terms of leadership on social media, "message content, social behavior, and (social) network structure" affect followership links on Twitter over time (Hutto, Yardi, & Gilbert, 2013, p. 821), and as such, they serve as "follow predictors" (Hutto, Yardi, & Gilbert, 2013, p. 821). Given the tendency for negative messages to be shared faster and more frequently than neutral messages or positive ones (Tsugawa & Ohsaki, 2015), those shepherding social movements may have to apply messaging finesse to avoid damage to the respective causes.

Researchers also identified image patterns on "image-based social media websites" used to support social movements (Cornet, Hall, Cafaro, & Brady, 2017, p. 2473). This work also suggests the importance of identifying image patterns around image-sharing sites harnessed for particular social movements (as in the frugal living EHM).

These research works suggest the importance of identifying leaders in electronic hive minds and studying social imagery patterns, among others. Common research methods on social media include "social network analysis, sentiment analysis, trend analysis and collaborative recommendation"

(Sapountzi & Psannis, 2018, p. 893), and some of these approaches will be used here as well.

"FRUGAL LIVING" AND #BESTLIFE LIFESTYLES AND DECISION MAKING IN A DISPERSED AND GLOBAL ELECTRONIC HIVE MIND

The dispersed frugal living EHM reads as a personalized space where people commit to living simply, without clutter, in green ways. These are people who are "woke" about the need to live intentionally and in ways that preserve financial and material resources. They are not obviously political, without ties to environmental activist organizations or other entities, and they are not obviously anti- the retail-industrial complex (if you will). So from the Social Web and various social media platforms, what does this EHM look like?

On Reddit

On social media, frugality as a "thing." One of the top subreddits "about personal or domestic advice" is a thread about the "frugal use of resources" with 41,911 members in the online community and identified gendered differences in the topic (Thelwall & Stuart, 2018, p. 12). This particular subreddit ranked 100 in the "subreddits about personal or domestic advice" (Thelwall & Stuart, 2018, p. 12).

On Google Search's Autocomplete

A search for "frugal" on Google Search has some insights in the autocomplete, in this order: frugal, frugal meaning, frugality, frugal house, frugal house topeka, frugalwoods, frugal male fashion, frugal house topeka ks, frugal inc, (and) frugality definition. The autocomplete does show some sensitivity to the physical location of the author during the search. (Figure 1)

On YouTube Video Sharing Site's Autocomplete

In terms of the autocomplete on the Google YouTube platform's search, they include the following (in descending order): "frugal aesthetic, frugal living, frugal, frugal crafter, frugal gourmet, frugalwoods, frugalnista, frugal finds, frugal chic life, (and) frugal fit mom" (Figure 2).

Figure 1. "Frugal" auto complete in Google search

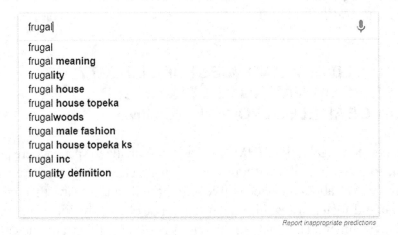

Figure 2. "Frugal" auto complete on YouTube

On Google Correlate

In terms of mass-scale search terms that co-occur with a search for "frugal" (on a weekly basis in the U.S.), there are some evocative aspects related to shopping, couponing, lower cost services, free services, and some how-to directions—but not a full coalescence of the idea of frugality. (Table 1)

Table 1. "Frugal" on Google correlate (in the U.S., weekly mass search data)

0.7991	the frugal
0.6815	free sheet music for piano
0.6694	docs to go
0.6653	download free
0.6546	eyebrow piercing
0.6545	celexa
0.654	safeway coupons
0.6537	supras
0.6527	network password
0.6515	attract women
0.6513	wow robot
0.6496	serial number mac
0.6491	jill cataldo
0.6489	shop blog
0.6485	coupon mom
0.6485	washington state unemployment
0.646	melt my heart to stone lyrics
0.6457	computer repair
0.6451	where can i download
0.6445	m1100
0.6438	instant watch netflix
0.6437	r910
0.6427	.zip
0.6421	verizonwireless.com/backupassistant
0.6417	dock app
0.6416	dragon care
0.6413	album list

continued on following page

Table 1. Continued

0.6413	pc free
0.6412	number mac
0.641	westell 7500
0.64	pixdrop
0.6396	fupa games
0.63953	.5 character sheet
0.6394	hats online
0.6373	go2ui
0.6371	design your own shoes
0.6364	eastwestworldwide
0.636	reviews for kids
0.6358	can i download
0.6358	adele melt my heart to stone lyrics
0.6355	by email
0.6355	speeddate.com
0.6355	download mac
0.635	download free music
0.6349	filmicity
0.6347	self shooters
0.6342	safe web
0.6342	missouri career source
0.6341	screenium
0.634	how to pierce
0.6339	domo games
0.6337	how to attract women
0.6333	youtube partners
0.6331	download cnet
0.6329	ipod touch is frozen
0.6327	texts online
0.6326	a2z scrabble
0.6323	canadian pharmacy
0.6322	funniest facebook status
0.6318	melt my heart to stone
0.6314	netflix instant play
0.6306	texting signatures
0.6302	subimg

continued on following page

Table 1. Continued

0.6301	yimmy yayo
0.63	facebook for lg
0.63	enlarge
0.6299	cheat o matic
0.6299	new @ 2
0.6298	goodyear eagle gt
0.6296	o_o
0.6294	missouricareersource
0.6292	netflix watch instantly
0.6291	bearded dragon care
0.6291	adele melt my heart to stone
0.6291	shepherd rescue
0.6288	first federal savings bank
0.6288	phone cover
0.6285	how to erase hard drive
0.6285	instant watch
0.6284	best facebook status
0.6283	free printable coupons
0.6283	sir pizza miami
0.6281	smart balance coupon
0.6278	esn repair
0.6276	good sites
0.6275	blowback
0.6274	eagle gt
0.6273	rock the keys
0.6272	workforce services
0.6271	gas blowback

On Google Books Ngram Viewer

An exploration of "frugal" in the formal book archives from the 1800s to 2000 show a general dropping trendline over time into the present. This is not an idea gaining traction per se at least in the formal literature. Over longitudinal time, "frugal" has become less popular. (Figure 3)

A one-degree related tags network on Flickr for "frugal" shows connections to activities like shopping and cooking. There are references to homemade

Figure 3. "Frugal" trending over 200 years in the Google books ngram viewer

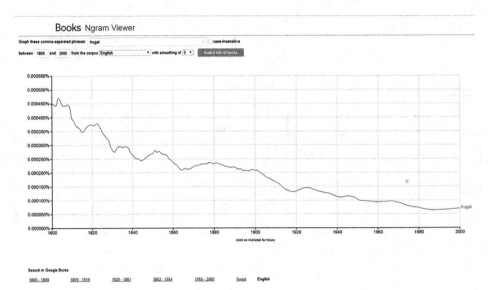

and cheapfoods, recipes and vegetarianism, groceries and pasta, and DIY. (Figure 4). This network graph was laid out using the Fruchterman-Reingold Force-Based Layout Algorithm.

A 1.5 degree network graph of the "frugal" related tags network on Flickr resolves into two general groups. Group 1 at the left is more about various aspects of the frugal lifestyle, and the group to the right is more about food consumption. (Figure 5)

On Flickr Image Sharing Site

A Flickr image set (1947 items) was extracted around the seeding term "frugal." (Figure 6). The images were run through manual coding, and some themes were extracted.

Frugal living involves living close to the earth, with photos of freshly dug carrots from the ground laid side-by-side. Some photos show various fruits growing on a branch. (There is something here about knowing where one's food actually comes from.) One image shows sparsely-flowering cauliflower, which might have illustrated a story of a garden #fail. One photo shows seedlings in paper pots. Self-grown objects need not be lower quality. There are images of prize-winning flowers, prize-winning onions, and other plants entered into contests.

Figure 4. "Frugal" related tags network on Flickr (1 deg.)

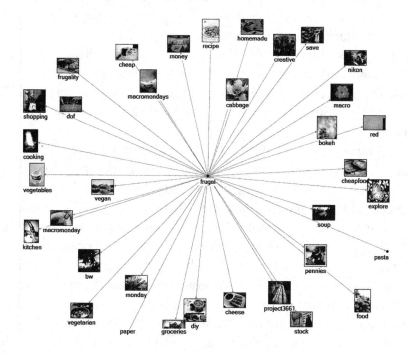

Figure 5. "Frugal" related tags network on Flickr (1.5 deg.)

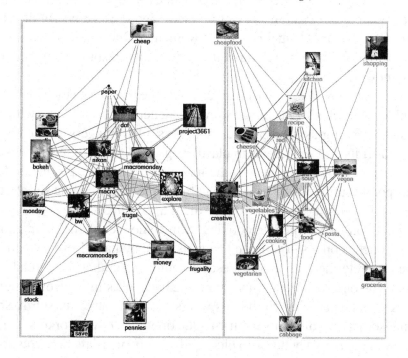

There are raw vegetables highlighted in the image set, such as a close-up of garden vegetables without ends trimmed. Several images show raw chicken, with one raw chicken covered in spices.

Food displays figure prominently in this image set, with servings mostly for individuals and groups. A few close-up images show single-bite food morsels. There are cut vegetables and fruits in single serve containers. There is a soup with various leafy greens. Another soup features beans and leftover foodstuffs.

Some images show grilled fruit. There are all sorts of baked foods: roasted vegetables, baked stuffed peppers, roasted yellow squash, Brussel sprouts topped with cheese, a vegetable lasagna, and others. There is a closeup of a hand-prepared baked pie (it looks hand-shaped with its edge pressed with a fork). Some of the foods look hearty and high-carb: spaghetti and bread, a cheese pasta dish, and others. Different meals are depicted: one of miso soup, fruit and yogurt, raw carrots with dip, and a grain with vegetables mixed in. Another shows a lunch of grapes and cherries, carrots and snap peas, crackers and cheese, and an undressed green salad with carrot slices. This latter one looks like a child's packed lunch. Another several show sushi. One shows a meal of bread, cheese, and a drink in a glass (Water? Wine?). Some of the meals are suggestive of self-reportage, maybe about how closely one is adhering to a planned diet. Portion sizes seem on the smaller side, at least compared to restaurant servings. One image shows a box of dry foods.

One sign claims "frugalfoodie" movements. One question is posed in an image: "What's the one thing you can do easily to start eating better and saving money?"

One image shows home-jarred sauces and other preserved foodstuffs (with natural preservatives). One image shows a kitchen in a microhome with basic dry foodstuffs in glass and plastic containers. One image shows consumer packaged fruits and vegetables in plastic bags, and whole grains; this seems to be about healthy eating even if the foods are from mass producing farms and corporate suppliers. In one photo with people in it, a couple sits at a table side-by-side, with the food in front of them untouched.

Some photos show people cooking. Some show cookbooks. In another, a man crouches on a sidewalk and eats his meal by hand from a small plate on the concrete; he is in a non-Western country. Another far-abroad photo shows a wok on a rock stand—as if pointing back to a simpler (romanticized) time. A woman carrying cloth bags walks down the street in sturdy shoes, evoking something of a universalism. One drawing shows workers in a long line walking over to a window to pick up their food in a cafeteria; this speaks to workplaces and communal eating. Some images show different types of street food.

The "bare minimums" concept is depicted as applied to cooking (a set of cooking utensils, pots and pans, a knife set, and some electric-powered cookers), gardening tools (hand trowels and paint brushes hung on a wall), and others. Another photo shows a Canon professional camera kit, with all basic elements included.

Method comes into play, with a formalized diagrammed flowchart for a "year of living frugally," with major decision points highlighted.

"Travel hacks" come into play. One photo shows a traveler traveling light, with an image of a magazine about travel to a town in France, some bread, a bottle of Evian water, all on a plastic bag on a rock. An apparent selfie shows a man is standing on a white sand beach against a blue sky (the camera is angled upwards from the sand).

Some imagery are expressions of "splurges" and "guilty pleasures." One shows a group of musicians and the text: "I know it's ridiculously pathetic that stupid frugal things like clothes and celebrities make me happy but they do! Heck yes, they do" (in this case, the Jonas brothers). The b/w treatment gives the prior meme a retro feel. Then, there is a stacked pile of golden brownies with nuts and marshmallows, a layered cake, sweets and desserts, which also read like extravagances.

Companionship also comes into play. One photo shows two young people sitting outside on the side of a building and holding hands. This suggests appreciation for the simpler things in life. ("All the best things in life are free.") Two joggers run together, in an image about friendship and mutual health. A miniature horse as a pet is depicted in another image. There are also farm animals, like pigs in a quadtych. Toddlers and children figure in some of the photos, often in custom handmade clothing.

One theme involves low-gasoline transportation: micro cars, scooters, and others. In one, a motorcycle is parked next to a mini car. There are bicycles and two-wheeled scooters (one used for commuting for a woman in business dress). One image shows a double-decker bus. By contrast, one photo shows a stretch recreational vehicle (RV).

Some of the images tell a story; they make a statement. One photo shows a paper price tag with a 2D barcode. The printed price is $49.50, and the "sale" price added on is $49.99 or 49 cents more than the original price. This shows the fungibility of pricing and suggests the importance of paying attention and of not getting taken price-wise. Another messaging image shows a Visa credit card next to a machine button with three settings: reverse, off, auto.

One can reverse usage of the credit card, turn it off, and use it automatically and without thinking. Another photo shows a closeup of a wrinkled plastic Walmart bag with the logo and the tagline "Save money. Live better." The camera is zoomed in on the first part of the tagline "Save money." Another series of multiple images shows the back panel of an electronic console, with the imprint of the location where it was assembled (Norway, in this case). This is suggestive of the importance of being aware of supply chains. Another shows various engineering blueprints for a device. A black chalkboard reads: "Make art not war," evoking a 1960s vibe. There is a photo of an empty shopping cart (except for a paper shopping circular) with a name on the cart "Mac Frugal's." Another message reads: "Our dreams and imaginations are smothered" (under the weight of monetary pursuit). A road sign reads: "SAVINGS AHEAD." Some messages contain advice: "Try to be plain in the best ways: plain truthful, plain frugal, and just plain caring." (There is an implied value system.) One image depicts a receipt, two paper bags, napkins, and an empty plastic cup to show how much wastage there is in terms of "to go" food packaging. Two images show political ads with politicians asserting that they will prevent or limit "wasteful spending." One image is a play on sparsity with words in a parking garage next to arrows, with a sign for "up" and a sign for "dn." A Snoopy cartoon shows Snoopy lying on the roof of his red dog house with Charlie Brown seated on the grass beside him with a broad smile: "The less you want, the more you love." One visual advertises "extreme couponing." A road sign reads: "Tough Decision Ahead." There are solutions promised for "Hard water stain, tips & tricks" and "RV Traveling Tips and Tricks." There is an encouraging message for living frugal, maybe even a rallying cry: "I'll go to someone cheaper."

One image shows homemade toothpaste with a highly liquid consistency in a plastic bag. A young man is using the toothpaste to brush. One photo shows a closeup of a woman receiving professional dental care (an exam). Another image shows human-made face cream. One photo shows what looks to be self-made fingernail polish, with a lumpy texture.

Another work shows an antique frog, possibly a keepsake, possibly a knick-knack. This is part of images that show antique objects. Appreciating older things is an act against a disposable economy, one in which new things are most desirable and prevail. A young boy examines an old tractor parked next to a new John Deere one. (The younger generation is bridging the two machines.) There are related photos of a wooden box and its personal contents. One photo shows an old-style instant camera. One photo shows a rusted iron handle on a wooden surface (A wooden box? A wooden drawer?), suggesting a sense of appreciation for aged objects. Old-style vintage aircraft from a prior time are shown in several "frugal" social images.

By contrast, a modern smart phone is shown with an "eco" app pulled up. In other visual depictions, there are smart phones depicted with shopping apps pulled up.

There are expressions of enthusiasm for particular elements of modern life. One image shows a bike rack with a knit "coat" with a button. Another shows an image of a low-energy long-lived spiral CFL (compact fluorescent) lightbulb.

Frugal expressions in living spaces may involve various quilts, curtains, and blankets. There are decorated dining spaces (a white kitchen table with pops of red color in the décor). There are handmade dresses and children's clothes. There are handmade shoulder bags. There are leather boots which have been hand-decorated.

Certainly, there are do-it-yourself (DIY) scenes: a table with tape and cardboard wrapped around parts of it; projects in various stages of development; some clay projects, and others. Creative expression is important. Various images depict handmade jewelry, beadwork, embroidery, knitting, crocheting, painting, and other creative endeavors. There are handmade toys. A child holds up a Lego toy creation.

There are examples of gifts wrapped in brown paper bags and tied with red yarn, depicting gifting or re-gifting. One image shows a latte on a counter in a restaurant; the drink is served in a handmade mug, giving the sense of an artisanal feel. Some photos show close-ups of hand stitching—even and skilled.

One photo shows the interior of a church. Another shows a teacher in a classroom. One visual shows a female avatar in Second Life, which open the possibility of the "immersive parasocial" and celebrity following in immersive virtual worlds (Hai-Jew, Sept. 2009).

There are examples of mutual supports—through events such as clothing swaps. There are calls for "frugal, healthy recipes" and "menu planning tips" to share. A "dumpster diving angel" preens next to a dumpster (such diving is for both individual selves and for others). Fellow home schoolers share expertise and pool their resources. Several visuals suggest the importance of frugal friends, so that there is a supportive social network.

Some of the "frugal" social imagery are commercial in nature. One business promises "coffer budget friendly portraits at an affordance price." Another touts Craigslist to "successfully sell." Various mom-and-pop business seem to be piggy-backing on this meta-narrative.

There are visual messages of engaging the public. One photo shows a man seated at a piano and performing for the public, in a park space. In several, people show off their face painted faces.

There are a miscellany of imagery, which are part of a narrative (elsewhere). There are photos of tourist sites, such as historical train cars, one showing one painted well, and another with peeling paint. There seem to be self-decoration themes, with handmade artworks (like decorative wall panels), fractal imagery (found art?), and colored pencils, fountain pens, and paint brushes. One photo shows a hand-made photo album. Craftiness is highlighted, such as with a knitted handmade Christmas ornament, homemade neckties, hand-made paper decorations. A woman has highlights put into her hair at a salon (as part of a personal narrative). A woman sitting in a car shows off a toe ring. A cat lies on its back and looks toward the camera. There are several older model cars with UK license plates. One sits in a field of hay stubble against a backdrop of scattered hay bales. One photo shows a cross in front of some older stone buildings. There is a screenshot of a website with discount sales items. One photo depicts green spaces in a city where people exercise. One shows a magazine layout of an article related to frugal living. Another image shows library books in a stack (why buy when you can borrow?).

Certainly, social imagery is multi-meaninged and can be interpreted in different ways, especially when the images are de-contextualized and analyzed separately from their original contexts. Many images are also somewhat designed to be understood in a stand-alone way. Some messages are spelled out in words, which are also potentially polysemous. This is to say that such interpretations should be understood within the limits of the manual image analysis.

On Wikipedia

"Frugality" is an article on the crowd-sourced Wikipedia encyclopedia. An extraction of the article network around "Frugality" shows ties to a range of other values, people, concepts, and lifestyles. (Figure 7). The one-degree network graph was laid out using the Harel-Koren Fast Multiscale Layout algorithm.

A 1.5 degree article-article network around "Frugality" on Wikipedia results in 3,957 vertices (unique article pages) and 4,530 unique edges, in a network graph with a maximum geodesic distance (graph diameter) of four. An extraction of clustering using the Clauset-Newman-Moore cluster

Figure 6. "Frugal" social imagery from Flickr

Figure 7. "Frugality" article-article network on Wikipedia (1 deg.)

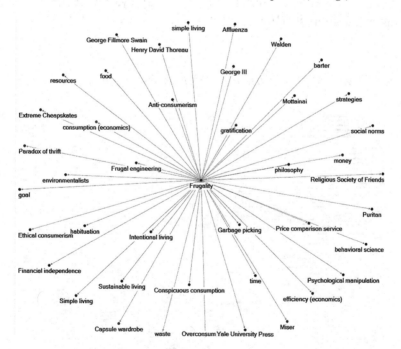

algorithm results in 19 groups. The extended article-article network graph (including article transitivity) shows links to environmental, philosophical, stewardship, faith, and nature-based implications, among others. (Figure 8)

Microblogging Site

On the Twitter microblogging site, a half-dozen accounts were explored around issues of frugality. The most recent Tweets were extracted from each, excluding retweets. At the time of the data capture, here were the basic details of the respective accounts. (Table 2)

These frugal social accounts on Twitter are both local and global (Figure 9).

A word cloud of the "frugal" account Tweetstreams show a focus on gratefulness (Figure 10). There are references to public personalities and to news sites. Days of the week also figure into the messaging, suggesting some time sensitive information.

At the top level, the most popular autocoded (machine-coded) topics include deals, frugal deals, https, things, and today, which suggests a focus on commercial interests (Figure 11).

Figure 8. "Frugality" article-article network on Wikipedia (1.5 deg.)

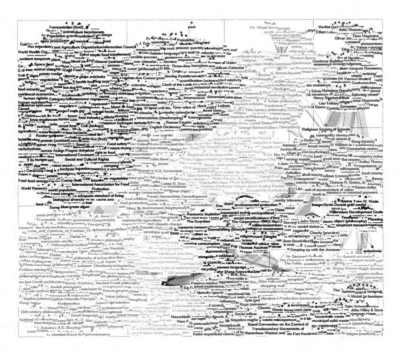

Table 2. Features of the "frugal" Twitter accounts mapped for analysis

	Tweets	Following	Followers	Likes	Lists	Start Date	Account Location
@frugalfamily https://twitter.com/frugalfamily	50,014	8,650	14,172	25,374	3	July 2009	North East, England
@TheFrugalGirl https://twitter.com/ TheFrugalGirl	8,165	39	2,059	532	0	May 2009	(not shared)
@frugaldealsuk https://twitter.com/ frugaldealsuk	8,007	1,378	4,538	31	1	February 2013	United Kingdom
@frugal_living1 https://twitter.com/frugal_ living1	630	49	58	82	0	January 2015	United Kingdom
@frugal_Rob https://twitter.com/frugal_Rob	1,021	31	4	108	0	March 2011	(not shared)

Figure 9. Local and global social networks around "frugal" on Twitter microblogging site

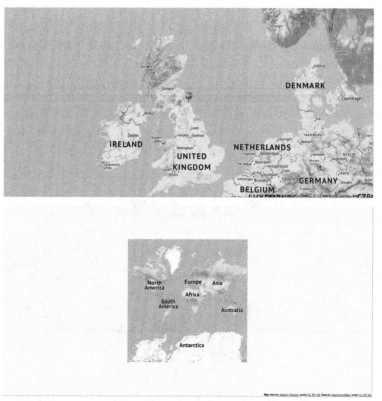

Local and Global Social Networks around "Frugal" on Twitter Microblogging Site

Figure 10. Word Cloud of tweetstreams from multiple "frugal" social accounts on Twitter microblogging site

Figure 11. Autocoded topics from mixed "frugal" social account tweetstreams on a microblogging site

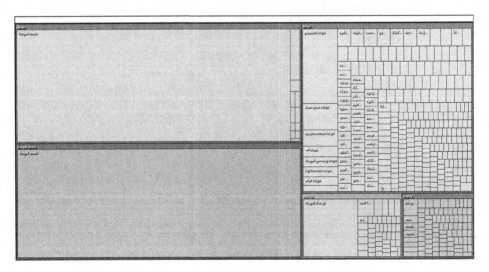

The sentiment on the Tweetstreams of the "Frugal" social accounts on Twitter show little in the way of sentiment except for one account, which shows a high level of "Very Positive" sentiment (Figure 12).

An extracted word tree around "frugal" as the seeding term shows a lot of outlinking, which suggests the usage of Twitter to drive traffic to other websites (Figure 13).

To integrate the idea of a #bestlife and to show that that may either complement or contrast the idea of a frugal lifestyle, a single Twitter account built around the concept of "bestlife" was trawled.

On a Single Twitter Account About a #bestlife

In contrast to a frugal life, a "best life" may be somewhat understood from a Twitter account (@bestlifeonline at https://twitter.com/bestlifeonline), with 2,190 Tweets, 28 following, and 6,612 followers. This account joined Twitter in January 2016. From this account, 2,145 messages were extracted, without retweets included. The social map for this account shows a global network (Figure 14).

The mapping of tweetstreams from @BestLifeOnline on Twitter shows the following word cloud on Figure 15.

Figure 12. Autocoded sentiments from "frugal" social account tweetstreams

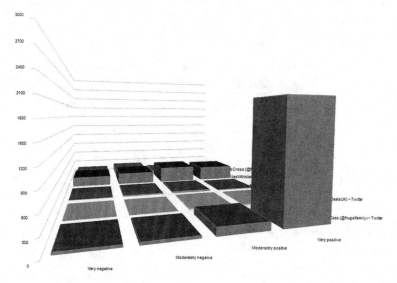

Figure 13. A "frugal" word tree from mixed frugal social account tweetstreams

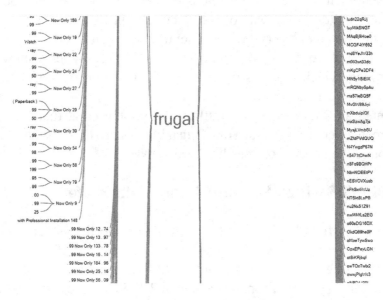

Figure 14. @Bestlifeonline Social network map on the twitter microblogging site

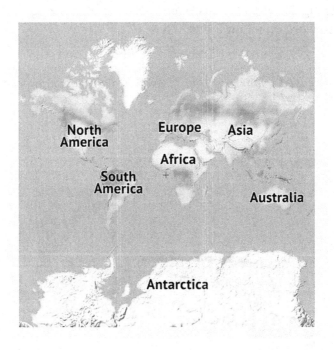

Figure 15. A Mixed sense of a #bestlife from a Twitter account

The sentiment of the messaging on the @bestlifeonline account does show a tendency towards moderate sentiment, both negative and positive, but more trending towards positive (Figure 16).

In terms of auto-extracted themes, a #bestlife involves lives that induce FOMO or "fear of missing out." There is royalty, the British royal family, and American Meghan Markle. There is Hollywood glamor and references to the Oscars. There is health, weddings, dating, happiness, welcoming a baby, and exercise. A subtopic is "sex life sizzle." (Figures 17 and 18) Much of social media focuses on conspicuous consumption and over-the-top lifestyles, to stand out from crowds. Very little here would be suggestive of "frugality," and yet, the general assertion in some sectors is that a "frugal" life may actually be the real #bestlife: long-lived, fulfilling, non-excessive, non-selfish, and respectful of the environment.

On a Google Social Imagery Set

A social imagery set from Google Images resulted in 486 images (Figure 19), using an older version of Picture Downloader Professional on Google Chrome. The image tags include the following: "living, cheap, infographic, define, money, rich, cartoon, icon, word, minimalist, clip art, scotsman, life,

Figure 16. Sentiment related to "bestlifeonline," from a Twitter account

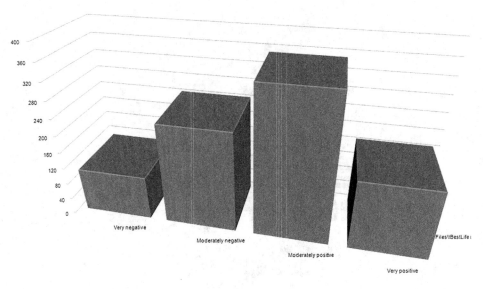

Figure 17. Autocoded themes related to "Bestlifeonline," from a Twitter account

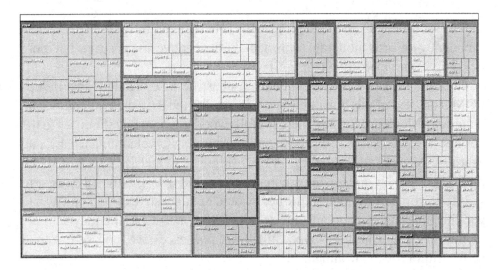

quote, family, family food, kids, family fun, homemaking, economides, texas, frugal living, saving, family meals, youtube, saving tips, save money, budget, activities, expenses, (and) big family." (Is the inclusion of "scotsman" a negative stereotype?) If the Flickr social image set around "frugal" focused more on image-based messaging, the Google Imagery set seems to include much more

Figure 18. Auto-Extracted themes from a "Bestlifeonline" account on Twitter (pareto chart)

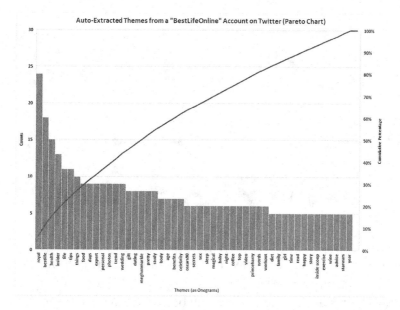

text and more "how-to's." This set was about a fourth the size of the Flickr set but seems to offer more unique and different extractable themes. Both image sets do show a bright and attractive sheen, with "join us" messaging. [Frugality is not inherently attractive to most. Communicators walk a fine line of engaging in "costly signaling" to show their commitment to a frugal lifestyle, but they risk losing their audience if they come across as too skilled, too elitist, too smug, too proselytizing, too superior, too critical, too blaming, and so on. Calling out others and casting aspersions are fast ways to alienate and lose an audience. Something that is too extreme will make it difficult for people to assume that they can make the sufficient changes. (Can you get by on $5 a day?" is a non-starter in the West.) "Frugalistas," "frugals," and their adherents are preaching to the choir in part but also engaging others considering the lifestyles and choices. Imagine how far conversations get if the conversation starters are: "So how little can you live on?" "How wasteful are you in your daily life consumption?"]

The images show gifts, foods, clothing, makeup, household cleaners, and furniture created by skilled craft-y individuals and do-it-yourself-ers (DIYers). There are explicit messages about saving money with calculators, piggy banks, glass jars of U.S. coins, a padlock atop a man's leather wallet,

Figure 19. "Frugal" social imagery from Google images

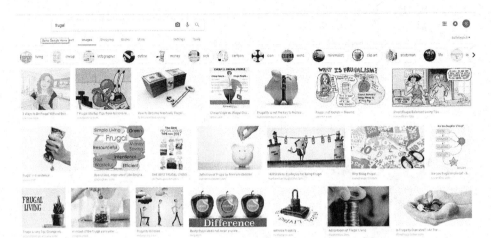

and cut-up credit cards. The past is used as a basis for present living: "12 frugal lessons from the Great Depression," and "22 frugal living tips from the Great Depression." There are throwback messages and senses of retro time periods: "10 old fashioned frugal recipes from Grandma."

Some visuals show methods for saving money (and using less electricity or gas or energy). In one, a finger lowers the temperature on a thermostat, from 66 degrees to 62 degrees.

There are redefinitions of entertainment and simple pleasures. A gray-haired couple sits together companionably on a bench each reading, with something that might be suggestive of #relationshipgoals. A different older couple is seated at a round kitchen table clipping coupons together, in an indication of maybe a fixed budget and maybe working together for frugal aims.

Some of the social images tout a frugal "new you," and some suggest remorse from overspending and a lack of self-control. One image shows "6 simple ways for spenders to finally become frugal," which suggests people in transition. There are guides for "beginners." Some of the imagery indicates an awareness of the difficulty of staying disciplined. One visual advertises "ways to stay frugal" and to maintain. Another advertises "what to eat every day: a month of frugal meals" for people who prefer a more structured approach to discipline. There are "frugal living tips" calendars that may have the same effect.

Some of the language used in the visuals suggest religious motivations. One visual reads: "The frugal homeschooling mom living an abundant life on a not-so-abundant budget." Another reads: "the spiritual discipline of being frugal." Another one reads: "12 easy frugal ways to be a blessing to others." Another visual points to the desirability of "debt free living" shown with a pair of scissors being used to cut up a credit card; such living without debt is a goal described by various Christian organizations.

A particular segment of the social imagery involves messaging about how to engage with holidays (Valentine's Day, Christmas, July 4 / Independence Day, Halloween) and seasons (Fall, Autumn), with big life events (weddings, family gatherings), celebrations (parties), activities (vacations, home staycations, trips, backpacking, camping), in equivalent ways to the mainstream but with adjustments for frugality. There are directions for "12 frugal days of Christmas" and "DIY stocking stuffers." There are frugal gifts for men. (Quite a few of the gifts seem to be for the self.) There are décor ideas and decorating projects for the various holidays and seasons of the year. One visual promises an "ultimate guide to a romantic and frugal Valentine's Day." There are low-cost costume ideas for Halloween. There are "50 frugal ways to celebrate fall." A frugal wedding can involve homemade dresses for the bride and her bridal party, and there can be savings on food and photos. People who "travel at home" can practice "frugal food tips" ("For travel at home: frugal food tips"). There are "frugal gift ideas for kids." There are suggested ideas for hosting a "frugal fondue party." "Frugal backpackers" are exhorted to "spend less (and) play more," and there are even specific "frugal tips for the solo female backpacker."

A stack of gold foiled covered chocolate coins with the words "10 Frugal Living Goals You Should be Making This Year." An ambition is to be "fabulessly (sic) frugal healthy wealthy wise," reads one word mark. There are everyday ways to live frugally, such as saving money on "household expenses," "extreme couponing," building a "frugal pantry," engaging "frugal self-care tips," using "frugal living tips for single mothers," and working to "save money" without self-deprivation. Large families have "frugal living tips for large families." Eating on a budget is a common theme: "10 easy & delicious frugal dinner recipes," "family approved dinner recipes," "10 frugal weeknight dinners to make when you're broke," "10 frugal weeknight dinners to make when money's tight," "frugal Paleo" diets, and others. There are "10 frugal foods to eat for a healthy pregnancy."

Household concerns account for another tranche of social imagery from the "frugal" seeding term: "10 simple + frugal ideas to clean and organize your home…5 weeks to an organized home," different "hacks, tips & tricks" for your home, tips for "frugal homemakers," "7 ways a large family can be frugal," and others. There are creative ideas for snacks, for making low-cost ice packs, for making anti-bacterial wipes—on a budget. There are lists for "everything you need in a frugal kitchen."

There is a branch related to financial decisions: "Frugal Living: Smart Financial Decisions to Thrive!" Fashion lovers have strategies on "how to wear designer brands when you're on a budget: sale, sale, sale." Crafters can engage in "frugal crafting: how I get craft supplies and fabric for free or cheap." For basic health needs, there are low-cost options, such as for "cracked heel remedies."

"Frugal gardening" is a way to provide for a family, with potentially limited inputs, and outsized outputs. Some photos show chickens in a coop. There are idyllic images of farmhouses. Some messages advertise "eating clean" via "healthy and budget friendly meal ideas." There are descriptions of "frugal vegan" cooking, a flavor for every type of eater.

There is "frugal landscaping," which can offer lower-cost options for yard work. People can apply frugal "laundry strategies." Some of the visuals are flyers advertising frugal workshops for how to gain "frugal living skills."

Children seem to figure centrally as an important area of focus. There are "20 kids activities you wouldn't spend a dime on." There are tips on children's lunches. There are hand-sewn baby and toddler and child clothes. For those who may be anxious about frugal living, there is a visual sign that asks: "does frugal living harm kids?" Those who need to store toys have "over 15 super frugal toy storage ideas." One image shows three boys (brothers?) sitting at a counter in front of their food and ready to share a meal. All three are smiling broadly at the camera. There are "frugal family fun ideas," frugal "first birthday parties," and "frugal food favorites."

While much of the focus in the social imagery is about doing more with less ("slash spending"), some also suggest money-making from blogs and other forms of social media.

A meta-narrative "frugal millionaires" suggests that frugality has a value even for those who could choose to live otherwise. Another visual touts the "frugal habits of the super rich," by capturing single tips from globally recognizable wealthy individuals based on their life experiences. Another visual touts "frugal NBA athletes." The approach seems to be: Who do you respect, and who will you listen to, in order to promote frugal living? (It is notable that this information of wealthy frugals is second hand and broadcast by third parties. In terms of actual direct spokespeople for frugal living, most are young Caucasians and a few Asians—at least in this initial trawl of social communications data. There are mainstream media stories of billionaires who do not carry billfolds, but their reputations are sufficient that businesses will extend services and products on credit or on the promise of payment.)

Several visuals (usually Venn diagrams) compare a frugal family with a spendy one. A "frugal family" interacts with family and friends; they go hiking; they play board games; they engage in DIY; they buy index funds. A "spendy family," by contrast, has debt; they live in a McMansion; they pay for a bottle service; they care about image; they go to malls; they buy purses and shoes there. And in terms of the overlap between the spendy and frugal family, they each "breathe air, eat, go potty, (and) sleep." The visual suggests that the differences are not that extensive. Another visual (a vertical Venn diagram) suggests that frugal families drink wheat beer or India pale ale, buy Charmin, buy Honda and Toyota, shop Kirkland brands; outdoors, they engage in cooking, building and using DIY skills; use manual transmissions; invest; engage in "travel hacking" and engage in "MMM" (unclear meaning). The visual suggests that the lives of frugal families are rich. There are "frugal hacks for single living." There are frugal gifts "for new moms" and "kid-friendly autumn craft projects." There are warnings against profligate spending, such as "15 things frugal people don't pay for," "21 things frugal people don't do," and "10 habits of HIGHLY FRUGAL people that you NEED to know."

In terms of technologies, one informational graphic differentiates between "homegrown" tech and "high tech, and others suggest luddite-approaches to technologies vs. technologically savvy ones.

People need conduct their "financial affairs" with "ethics & etiquette" suggests an image, with a risqué play on the idea of "affairs." A lack of financial management skills leads to suffering. One cartoon shows a man hunched over at an ATM (automated teller machine), and one of two women observing him quips, "Withdrawal symptoms."

Another comparative informational graphic contrasts a "cheap" person vs. a "frugal" one. One data visualization asks: "Frugal vs. Cheap: Which are You?" Frugal people "care about value"; they will buy necessities at reasonable prices; they save up for things that they care about; they splurge occasionally as a reward; they "maintain good personal relationships despite their thrift." On the negative side, "cheap" individuals "care only about price" and "save money for the sake of saving money" and eschew splurging; they offend people with their cheapness. Several images warn about not being "rude" to friends because of frugality. Others visual messages warn against "being boring" in "how to be frugal without being boring." A different visual (overlapping circles on a white board or paper) addresses "frugal friends," described as "Optimists! Happy! Fun! Smart!"

Another opinion-laden visual shows "frugal" as somewhere between "miser" and "cheap," with the idea that people should not be out there shorting others or taking advantage of others. For social human beings, there are "10 frugal gift ideas." Those with children who want to impress teachers can engage "100 free or frugal teacher gift ideas" and consider "frugal & diy teacher gifts."

People not only have to engage in a social ecosystem but an environmental one. One visual shows how "frugal innovation" can increase the multiple uses of water (including gray water), to extend the life cycle uses of water, and to enhance its management as a resource. Multiple images suggest that frugality contributes to environmental conservation efforts and lessen environmental degradation.

A mind map on social media puts "frugal theory" at the center of a graph, with direct links to "food," "DIY, "shopping," "reuse / repurpose," "finance," "lifestyle," (and) "efficiency & sustainability." Another degree out are related phenomena, including "small filling meals, cheap ingredients, (and) healthy" for food; "home products, repairs, (and) home projects" for DIY, "buy it for life" for shopping, and so on. There is a network of behaviors that have implications for the individual and for the larger society. A frugal life is one that is driven by "goals & purpose."

In terms of businesses mentioned under the "frugal" label, there are book promoters, restaurants, carpenters, photography studios, and others. There is a whole other literature that deals with frugal innovations by businesses to ensure that the costs of their respective products and services are as low-cost as possible (based on smart and efficient designs). On social media, there are "frugal favorites" in terms of discount stores: Aldi's, Dollar Tree, Dollar General, and "Frugal MacDoogal beverage warehouse." There is a Frugal Kitchens & Cabinets (as a business name). Some antiques stores' storefront and internal images are also shared. Online, Craigslist is a destination site. (Some of the images show laptops being used to earn and save money.)

There are "best books" lists for those who subscribe to frugality. There are frugal bookstores. There is a free downloadable and printable resource for how to feed "a family of 7 for just $75 a week!" Some books provide angles on how to engage in "frugal innovation." Some data visualizations show book covers about frugality. There are lists of the "12 best books on budgeting, saving money, frugal living & climbing out of debt."

Some shared images seem to be "found images," such as a street sign reading "Village of Frugality." (There are faux "found images," too, with street signs made to read other messaging.)

Hunger is a real phenomenon, and it is no joke. Some headings suggest real-world challenges, such as "frugal shopping tips for when times are tight" and frugal tips "for feeding your family." For many this is about survival. One paneled illustrated work shows "handy tips for living in your car," including what essential items to have, safe places to park at night, how to keep a low profile in a neighborhood, how to maintain personal hygiene, and how to live the "mobile life." Some works offer tips on "epic frugality."

For others, there is a built-in resistance. Those who tend towards pleasure-seeking may be attracted to "frugal hedonism." There is a young woman who is a "frugal model." Frugal vagabonds live by the motto: "Life is short. Save hard. Travel far." Those who are pregnant select "10 frugal foods to eat for a healthy pregnancy," so there are mixes of considerations. There are visuals about "living well with less $$$" and "fake-it-frugal," which suggests less than full engagement. Some come-ons tease using the appeal of "secrets": "6 frugal secrets no one has told you" (with an image of a young woman whispering in another's ear). There are "9 frugal tips to finally lose 10 pounds)," for those interested in some weight loss. One image shows a crockpot; cans of beans, corn, and broth; seasonings and spices…for one-pot taco soup. There are "easy recipes from the frugal girls kitchen!" potentially building on a television comedy show about broke young women. There are ideas for "how to live frugally without feeling deprived." Those who are online socialites may engage the meme of "how to deal with the fear of missing out (FOMO) when you must live frugally." (Social media, with its focus on glamor and social brags, can be an especially hard space for those who want to be frugal. They have to give up the social one-up-manship, social comparisons, and acquisatory lifestyles portrayed on much of social media. The counter-messaging in the frugal EHM does provide an "authorizing environment" to practitioners and makes the lifestyle more appealing than it may seem on the face of things. Such encouragements may be sufficient to encourage some commitment to this path. For others, sharing on social media—impressing others—may also provide some support. Certainly, the practical information about how to maintain a family budget, how to avoid debt, how to control against financial binging, how to prepare foods in frugal ways, how to invest financially (and relatively safely), and how to avoid outsized negative impacts on the environment, are all life skills aspects of modern life.

Human nature, with its darker sides of easy jealousies and striving and judgmentalness, has to be suppressed for longer-term frugal commitments. Most people will not be satisfied with less than those around them.)

A number of the social images address issues of identity. There is a "frugal fanatic" referring to a committed individual There are frugal people and non-frugal people, based on "20 things frugal people never ever do." "Frugal entrepreneurs" engage in "low cost marketing and promotional" outreaches. Some frugal people are "minimalists," who have a preference for sparsity and simplicity. There are "tests" to assess "how frugal are you?" and "Here's how frugal you are, according to your personality type."

Counter-Messaging

In the Google image set of some 486 images, there were a few that were explicitly counter message. One read: "10 signs you're taking frugality too far and how to stop," apparently for the extremists and the obsessives. One piece of advice reads: "Be frugal with your time, not your money." Another counter viewpoint reads: "No one ever gets rich by being frugal." A meme shows an intense actor in a scene, and this reads: "One does not simply stop buying lattes"

The "frugal" electronic hive mind membership seems to draw from the conservative to the liberal continuum, from the religious to the non-religious, from the environmentally minded to the non-environmentally minded. Core impetuses range from the personal to the social. Their commitments seem to range in intensity. Some basic role types in this EHM may be understood in Table 3, from drop-in visitor to the EHM to lurker to engaged member / user-generated content contributor, and influencer. Individuals can certainly move between role types and can change their levels of commitment.

DISCUSSION

The frugal living movement has attracted participants from different walks of life, and it has attracted the attention of people in different verticals interested in reaching a more resistant market. The idea of living more conscientiously and mindfully and without waste is an alluring one, and the constant thinking and constant improvement approach may enable swaths of humanity to live in the world in more sustainable ways. This non-threatening approach may be

Table 3. Behavior-based role types in the "frugal" electronic hive mind

Roles	Target objectives
Drop-in visitor to EHM	• Find information • Find occasional support • Discover what the "frugal" EHM is about
Lurker to EHM	• Learn new strategies • Learn new tactics • Learn new tips • Identify new resources • Explore the online communities
Engaged member (and) User-generated content contributor in the EHM	• Create an online persona and public reputation • Interact with a virtual community • Make acquaintances, maintain relationships • Make friends, maintain relationships • Interact with community members in RL • Elicit support for self-discipline • Elicit support for problem-solving • Co-lead the EHM • Share self-generated information with others • Share other-generated information with others • Share self-generated digital contents with others • Share other-generated digital contents with others • Help in problem-solving issues raised by others • Earn moneys • Gain non-monetary resources • Build a public following • Contribute to the strength and resilience of the EHM • Create value for the community
Influencer (leader) in the EHM	• Share ideas, resources, connections, and other resources • Recognize and support others • Recruit new members • Raise the profile of the EHM • Interact with others • Engage (and occasionally change) social norms • Co-lead the EHM • Create value for the community • Create aspirational goals • Maintain an earned and outsized influence on the EHM

appealing to many and may enable speaking into people's personal decisions and spaces in meaningful ways, peer-to-peer, friend-to-friend, given people's receptivity to close and trusted others. If people are to internalize particular values and practices, working through people's personal trust networks seems to be a winning strategy. Practical approaches at the lived level enable "small wins" and help avoid the paralysis of facing large-scale challenges (like environmental degradation). The support of an online community may enable greater encouragement of individual and small group commitments. Individual choices made individually can have widespread (even global- or planet-scale) impacts, with potential implications on human survival. What is an alternative lifestyle today can gain wider adoption and become more mainstream.

The meta-narratives are about fiscal survival, ethical living, living closer to nature, having a slower pace of modern life, non-wastage of resources, religious commitments, and environmental protections.

This research work showed only a few spokespersons—individuals, duos, and families—for this value system and lifestyle. For this effort to advance, a larger number of spokespersons and models would be needed, and more diverse spokespersons may be needed. The inventiveness of the members of this EHM seem to have been applied at low-hanging fruit (home cooking, growing vegetables, applying craftiness, sharing resources, building furniture, and so on), and it is possible that there are many other endeavors that may be adopted at micro-to-macro levels.

This work offered an early effort at modeling electronically-enabled social membership. It showed more of a cyber-physical confluence. If nothing else, this work shows that studying EHMs is not just an academic exercise but engages real-world implications.

FUTURE RESEARCH DIRECTIONS

How transferable this mix of appeals is to those in other cultures and social contexts may vary. It may well be that this lifestyle will be appealing but for a whole different set of other messaging, around community or other values. It is likely that frugality in other contexts likely will involve different sets of human-to-human innovations, given the differing cultures and contexts. Some of the social imagery are suggestive of non-Western approaches, such as "rickshaw banks" and "easy paisa" mobile banking and Grameen Bank microloans (with relatively high interest rates), and others. Some images show mini clay refrigerators (which do not require electricity) used on the African subcontinent.

This work can be built on in various ways. The main research methods here involve using publicly available data from social media platforms. These were captured at macro levels (mass search data, mass book data), meso levels (Wikipedia article networks), and at micro levels (various social media accounts based on frugality and #bestlife). Certainly, there are more direct ways to elicit responses, such as by direct online surveying. It may be interesting to map the membership of the "frugal" EHMs based on user motivations, based on self-reportage. It may be helpful to evaluate the outcomes of people's EHMs in terms of measurable behaviors and outcomes.

CONCLUSION

The meta-narrative of "frugality" is a dispersed one which does not seem to be an important challenge to mainstream material-based living. It seems to be something simultaneously aspirational as it is practical. And yet, the subjectivities of people and their intersubjectivities in interactions enable mutual encouragement in this space—for engaging with difficult challenges of living frugally in the present days. The frugal EHM does inform a range of endeavors that affect people's sparser and more mindful lifestyles, in many ways. On social media platforms, the frugality EHM involves the sharing of creative crowd-sourced ideas for living a form of a #bestlife and being in harmony with the self, with others, and with the environment. Some may be read as "trial balloons" to see how well others may accept those grassroots bottom-up approaches.

Some of the social messaging suggests extremes, with common searches for how long expired food may be consumed without severe adverse health effects. There are stories of making do on a shoestring, such as living out-of-cars and being homeless…and even travels abroad on a shoestring (hitchhiking, trading work for food, and other endeavors). Equipment, like microwaves, may be used long after their integrity has been compromised.

Perhaps Benjamin Franklin said it best in two quotes that suggests a balanced approach: "Waste neither time nor money, but make the best use of both" and "Wealth is not his that has it, but his that enjoys it." A more modern take is a quote from American industrialist Owen D. Young, who said:

We are not to judge thrift solely by the test of saving or spending. If one spends what he should prudently save, that certainly is to be deplored. But if one saves what he should prudently spend, that is not necessarily to be commended. A wise balance between the two is the desired end.

And finally, the idea of frugal living should not take away from the need for livable wages, social security nets, school nutrition programs, affordable healthcare, and policies and programs to address homelessness. Subsistence, no matter how it is dressed up and even glamorized, can be brutal and with long-term detrimental effects.

REFERENCES

Cornet, V. P., Hall, N. K., Cafaro, F., & Brady, E. (2017). How image-based social media websites support social movements. *Proceedings of the 2017 CHI Conference Extended Abstracts on Human Factors in Computing Systems*, 2473 – 2479. 10.1145/3027063.3053257

East, S. (2016, July 6). Four years' trash, one jar…zero waste. *CNN*. Retrieved Dec. 6, 2018, from https://www.cnn.com/2016/07/04/us/lauren-singer-zero-waste-blogger-plastic/index.html

Gaiani, S., Caldeira, S., Adorno, V., Segrè, S., & Vittuari, M. (2018). Food wasters: Profiling consumers' attitude to waste food in Italy. *Waste Management (New York, N.Y.)*, *72*, 17–24. doi:10.1016/j.wasman.2017.11.012 PMID:29174684

Hai-Jew, S. (2009, Sept.). Exploring the immersive parasocial: Is it you or the thought of you? *Journal of Online Learning and Teaching*. Retrieved Oct. 15, 2018, from http://jolt.merlot.org/vol5no3/hai-jew_0909.htm

Hai-Jew, S. (2019). The electronic hive mind and cybersecurity: Mass-scale human cognitive limits to explain the 'weakest link' in cybersecurity. In *Global Cyber Security Labor Shortage and International Business Risk* (pp. 206–262). Hershey, PA: IGI Global. doi:10.4018/978-1-5225-5927-6.ch011

Hutto, C. J., Yardi, S., & Gilbert, E. (2013). A longitudinal study of follow predictors on Twitter. *Proceedings of CHI 2013*, 821 – 831. 10.1145/2470654.2470771

Kardara, M., Papadakis, G., Papaoikonomou, T., Tserpes, K., & Varvarigou, T. (2012). Influence patterns in topic communities of social media. *Proceedings of the 2nd International Conference on Web Intelligence, Mining, and Semantics (WIMS '12)*, 1 – 12. 10.1145/2254129.2254144

Lastovicka, J. L., Bettencourt, L. A., Hughner, R. S., & Kuntze, R. J. (1999). Lifestyle of the tight and frugal: Theory and measurement. *The Journal of Consumer Research*, *26*(1), 85–98. doi:10.1086/209552

Lee, S.H. (M.). (. (2016). When are frugal consumers not frugal? The influence of personal networks. *Journal of Retailing and Consumer Services*, *30*, 1–7. doi:10.1016/j.jretconser.2015.12.005

Leonard-Barton, D. (1981, December). Voluntary simplicity lifestyles and energy conservation. *The Journal of Consumer Research, 8*(3), 243–252. doi:10.1086/208861

Mehta, L., Huff, A., & Allouche, J. (2018). The new politics and geographies of scarcity. *Geoforum,* 1-9. (in press)

Mowen, J. C. (2000). *From frugality to modest living. In 3M Model of Motivation and Personality* (pp. 187–203). Boston, MA: Springer. doi:10.1007/978-1-4757-6708-7_14

Natale, A., Di Martino, S., Procentese, F., & Arcidiacono, C. (2016). Degrowth and critical community psychology: Contributions towards individual and social well-being. *Futures,* 78 – 79, 47 – 56.

Nicholls, A., Simon, J., & Gabriel, M. (2015). Introduction: Dimensions of social innovation. In *New Frontiers in Social Innovation Research.* Basingstoke, UK: Palgrave Macmillan. doi:10.1057/9781137506801_1

Pepper, M., Jackson, T., & Uzzell, D. (2009). An examination of the values that motivate socially conscious and frugal consumer behaviours. *International Journal of Consumer Studies, 33*(2), 126–136. doi:10.1111/j.1470-6431.2009.00753.x

Roiland, D. (2016). Frugality, a positive principle to promote sustainable development. *Journal of Agricultural & Environmental Ethics, 29*(4), 571–585. doi:10.100710806-016-9619-6

Sapountzi, A., & Psannis, K. E. (2018). Social networking data analysis tools & challenges. *Future Generation Computer Systems, 86,* 893–913. doi:10.1016/j.future.2016.10.019

Thelwall, M. & Stuart, E. (2018). She's Reddit: A source of statistically significant gendered interest information? *Information Processing and Management,* 1 – 16. (in press)

Thøgersen, J. (2018). Frugal or green? Basic drivers of energy saving in European households. *Journal of Cleaner Production, 197,* 1521–1530. doi:10.1016/j.jclepro.2018.06.282

Todd, S. & Lawson, R. (2003). Towards an understanding of frugal consumers. *Australasian Marketing Journal, 11*(30), 8 – 18.

Tsugawa, S., & Ohsaki, H. (2015). Negative messages spread rapidly and widely on social media. *Proceedings of COSN '15*, 151 – 160. 10.1145/2817946.2817962

Vadakkepat, P., Garg, H. K., Loh, A. P., & Tham, M. P. (2015). Inclusive innovation: Getting more from less for more. *Journal of Frugal Innovation*, *1*(2), 1–2. doi:10.118640669-015-0002-6

Webb, H., Burnap, P., Procter, R., Rana, O., Stahl, B. C., Williams, M., ... Jirotka, M. (2016). Digital wildfires: Propagation, verification, regulation, and responsible innovation. *ACM Transactions on Information Systems*, *34*(3), 15. doi:10.1145/2893478

KEY TERMS AND DEFINITIONS

Autocoding: The coding of information through computational or machine means.

Electronic Hive Mind: A synchronous temporal and informal patchwork of emergent shared social consciousness (held by geographically distributed people, cyborgs, and robots) enabled by online social connectivity (across a range of social media platforms on the web and internet), based around various dimensions of shared attractive interests.

Frugality: Thrift, resourcefulness, making do with less.

Micro House: A smaller-than-regular-sized home, built often as part of the tiny house movement.

Sentiment Analysis: The analysis of language for positive or negative sentiment (without neutrality).

Zero-Waste Lifestyle: A process of making decisions and consuming in ways with as little waste as possible.

Chapter 5
Buy/Hold/Trade or Sell/Divest/Disengage:
Using Executive Functions in Electronic Hive Minds for Decision Making Around Cryptocurrencies

ABSTRACT

An electronic hive mind (EHM) can be a distributed virtual community and a mental space for information-gathering, analysis, and ultimately, decision making; it can play the role of executive functioning (in the same way a frontal lobe does for a human brain) and inform real-world actions. To see how this might function, the EHM around cryptocurrencies was explored from multiple social media platforms. This topic addresses an issue that is not fully defined and is of broad-scale mainstream interests. Cryptocurrencies may be everything from virtual ephemera and hot promises to a life-changing innovation. As a phenomenon, it has instantiated in different ways around the world, with cryptocurrency "farming" centers, nation-state-issued cryptocurrencies, government efforts at regulating such exchanges, and volatile gains and losses for cryptocurrency speculators and investors. How people engage with cryptocurrencies can affect their real-world net worth as well as other aspects of their lives, so this is not merely a theoretical issue but one with real-world impacts. This work explores three hypotheses around social messaging, the general membership of the target electronic hive mind, and mass virtual executive functioning and discovers a mind hyped on seductive promise.

DOI: 10.4018/978-1-5225-9369-0.ch005

INTRODUCTION

People use their mental processes to understand the world, pay attention to what is relevant, problem-solve, and act, to engage effectively within it. This engagement requires intelligence and strategy, and it requires self-control. Collectively, groups may be thought of as having some leadership and applied rules and bureaucratic structures that enable people to collaborate and cooperate. A core question in this chapter is whether an electronic hive mind, defined as "a sentient and potent mass entity with potential for various types of concentrated mass action as well as dispersed smaller-unit actions, among others" (Hai-Jew, 2019, p. 210). The thinking is that socio-technological connectivity enables people to share ideas and enable particular temporal mind-melds and understandings around topics of shared interest, which may lead to in-world actions. More specifically, this work explores precursors to action—based around cognitive executive functions (such as information gathering, sense making, and planning). These functions are considered analogous to some of the capabilities in the human mind's frontal lobe and its application for learning, decision making, and action taking. The frontal lobe is also critical in applying "theory of mind," or understanding others' thinking and anticipating others' actions (Stone, Baron-Cohen, & Knight, 1998).

A general assumption is that people may engage the world in a learning way: they gather information, ask family and friends, make decisions (rationally and irrationally, emotionally and unemotionally), test their decision making in the world, gather more data, and repeat.

Analogically, the electronic hive mind (EHM) involves information processing and some decision making. An earlier work showed the importance of having (informed and benevolent) experts in the EHM space to inform the larger publics of complex issues, like cybersecurity (Hai-Jew, 2019). This work explores what the executive function of an EHM may look like:

- What does executive functioning look like an in EHM? What are reliable indicators of the executive functioning? What does executive functioning look like when it is centralized or decentralized?
- How is collective virtual working memory maintained, with certain issues kept top-of-mind? (Through memes? Through stories? Through repetition? Through symbolism?) How is selective history kept alive? How is group identity affirmed?

- Are there cognitive biases in this executive functioning, and where does it come from? How can cognitive biases in EHMs be mitigated?
  - How are disparate threads of information handled in a way to create coherence?
  - How are some types of information privileged over others?
- Is there an actual "command and control" that affects how the EHM gathers information, processes it, plans from it, organizes around it, makes decisions from it, and acts on it (and if so, what is the command and control comprised of, and who are the members that exert the most control, and why)?
  - Is there coherent goal setting, whether explicitly or implicitly? Does the particular EHM enable control over impulsivity (Of its members? Of subgroups? Of the overall entity?)?
- How does the EHM activate the distinct agencies of individual members and groups of members (acting as the "body" of the mind)? What are enthusiasms and excitements that may drive members of an EHM to actions? How are member individual and sub-group and whole-group collective actions understood and evaluated? If there are incentives to actions, what are these, and how are these funded and distributed?
- If there are resources owned by members and sub-groups, how are these managed? What sorts of record-keeping (if any) occurs around communal resources?
- Do EHMs self-regulate (particularly in the diffuse and pseudo-anonymized / pseudonymized social media spaces), and if so, how?
- Does the executive function change over the lifespan of the EHM? If so, why and how? Is there framing such as with an "authorizing environment" (that gives its membership permission and cover for certain actions)?
- Is there a wide disparity between expert opinions and those of the public imagination in the EHM?
- What are aspects of an EHM and other endeavors that may interfere with its executive functioning?
- How relevant is this concept of concentrated (or semi-concentrated) control and focus given the ephemerality and loosely-connected aspects of many online EHMs? Or can it be conceptualized that executive functions are multitudinous and distributed within an online EHM, with individuals, dyads, triads, and other motifs and subgroups acting as decision making functions?

The topic around which an EHM coalesces requires something relevant and timely and contested, without a broad mainstream consensus. The topic also should enable some discovery learning for the researcher, so the researcher can relate to that learning mindset of the EHM members. It should relate to some decision or action that may be taken. An EHM coalesced around "cryptocurrencies," a new asset class which emerged in 2009 and popularized in 2014, would seem to be particularly engaging for considering executive functions, based around a simple binary: (1) buy, hold, trade, or (2) sell, divest, disengage. With a market capitalization of some $210 billion (according to the latest information by CoinMarketCap) and some 1,658 cryptocurrencies in existence (Frankel, Mar. 16, 2018), cryptocurrencies have been the new hot thing. One research team considers 2014-onwards as the age of competition between cryptocurrencies (Iwamura, Kitamura, & Matsumoto, 2014). The various altcoins have a variety of target constituencies, features (such as being "the first audible cryptocurrency" coin, which begs the question of "sound money"), raising moneys for charity, supporting a sports team, and others. Some have derivative names of others even without any legal relationship with the other.

If alternate coins are in competition if more are in the market, sopping up fiat currencies, then it would stand to reason that existing coin owners may want to discourage other market entrants. One researcher suggests that actual competition cannot exist without some preconditions:

First, the proliferation of copycat currencies (altcoins) cannot be inflationary unless any protocol is a perfect substitute for any other. Whether they are substitutable in some technical sense or not, entrenched network benefits mean that copycat protocols will not displace or rival existing protocols without clear feature advantages. Where physical notes from one bank or another may fit equally well in a wallet (and both of which might even be dollars), holding multiple cryptocurrencies involves the technical inconvenience of operating on multiple disjunct protocols, plus the additional calculational inconvenience that the currencies float against one another in value. (Harwick, Spring 2016, p. 572)

Further, once a cryptocurrency is defined, "it cannot be changed arbitrarily once created. Once a protocol comes into use, the control of its constitution depends entirely on continued trust in the developers" (Harwick, Spring 2016, p. 572). If technologies "fork" in untrustworthy ways, Harwick suggests that the update will not be accepted.

Competing with existing cryptocurrencies is not as simple as setting up shop and advertising. The early comers in the space may actually have the "first mover" advantage. In order of market capitalization, the top five major cryptocurrencies are Bitcoin, Ethereum, Ripple, Bitcoin Cash, and Litecoin, worth a total of around $156 billion (Gkillas & Katsiampa, 2018, p. 109).

Yet, for all the captured funds, there is a sense that such "coinage" is a mirage, a gigantic and expanding asset bubble, and underlying "assets" with no intrinsic value. A forced scarcity (e.g. an artificial limit to the issuance of cryptocurrency coinage) also contributes to the "value." One team notes: "With a limited supply and with no underlying fundamentals, speculation and trends, which can be seen as a reflection of market attention, seem to significantly affect Bitcoin price changes. Therefore, investors in Bitcoin markets can benefit from Google data for their investment decisions" (Dastgir, Demir, Downing, Gozgor, & Lau, 2018, p. 5). (As a side note: The technological effort of issuing more currency is likely not more complex than a line or two of code.)

Market capitalization of 000,000,000,000 also seems somewhat extreme, even though these assets are really only 1's and 0's without intrinsic value, but buoyed only by hype and belief. As Howard Wang (cofounder of Convoy Investments) is quoted as observing, "The 'only source of value' that bitcoin has 'is other people's perception of its value'" (Vlastelica, Dec. 14, 2017, n.p). Others may be enamored of cryptocurrency "blockchain," defined as a public electronic ledger that records cryptocurrency transactions. One researcher suggests that a blockchain is "a 20-year-old technology that somehow causes idiots to throw money at it" (Illing, Apr. 11, 2018). Another appeal may be the ability to write "permanent messages" (in text format) into the blockchain (Sward, Vecna, & Stonedahl, 2018, p. 1). [Various businesses are looking to apply blockchain technologies into other areas, such as "notary publics, manual vote recounts, and the way banks manage transactions" (Plansky, O'Donnell, & Richards, Spring 2016, p. 2). Other sources mention application in biometrics. These applications also feature centrally in various advertisements from information technology companies who point to these records to assure various types of quality standards for imports and exports.]

The question is how does a loosely-coupled online "collective" acquire information about unprecedented global efforts at creating "private" currencies? Where do people seek information when it is unclear where trustworthy information may be found or how it should be vetted? In an environment of volatility and uncertainty and risk, and the cryptocurrency market meets all three requirements, how do people decide on what to risk and with whom to risk and with whom to partner for pooling funds for investments and other endeavors?

This work posits three main hypotheses, about the social messaging, the membership (participants), and the state of executive functioning of this target EHM.

H1: In the electronic hive mind (EHM) surrounding cryptocurrencies, the **social messaging** around such currencies will be strategic and tactical, sometimes baldly and sometimes subtly.

H1a: A majority of the multimodal social messages will be in support of cryptocurrencies (as a reflection of communicator interests).

H1b: In formal mass media, a majority of the messages will be skeptical of and questioning of cryptocurrencies because of the lack of intrinsic value and its volatility.

H1c: In the academic research space, the respective works will show strengths and weaknesses to cryptocurrencies, based on available and discoverable information.

H2: The **general membership** of the cryptocurrencies EHM may be sussed out inferentially from the social messaging based on stakeholder interests.

H2a: A portion of the cryptocurrency EHM will be comprised of individuals who have little to no background on cryptocurrencies but who are seeking advice and direction as potential investors.

H3: The EHM around cryptocurrencies demonstrates some **executive functioning** in part based on real-world interests.

This work involves the capture of naturalistic data from the online ecosystem related to cryptocurrencies, and abductive logic is applied to the found information. Bottom-up coding is applied to the data to understand some aspects of the executive function of an EHM created around cryptocurrencies. The EHM will be understood based on data from multiple socio-technical platforms (Wikipedia, Flickr, Reddit, Facebook, and Twitter), mass-scale analytics sites (Google Books Ngram Viewer and Google Correlate) and different methods of data analysis. The information used is publicly available data only, nothing from private channels. The data are a recent sample in many cases, and nothing even close to an N = all. Also, for all the ambitious objectives of the questions above, the findings will likely only offer some light insights and nothing definitive.

REVIEW OF THE LITERATURE

The origin story for cryptocurrencies is somewhat hazy, maybe purposefully so. "Satoshi Nakamoto," who has not yet been identified to a real-world person or a group, first published a white paper in October 2008 about a peer-to-peer electronic cash system for "bitcoin," and the software was released as open source on SourceForge in January 2009 ("Satoshi Nakamoto," Oct. 25, 2018). The paper itself describes the technological specifications of the novel system, cites a few sources, and is written as "we" in both the abstract and the paper (Nakamoto, Oct. 2008), potentially suggestive of a group. This work describes a "proof-of-work" mining protocol by which double-counting of currencies is avoided and the blockchain financial ledger is maintained, with some micropayment in cryptocurrency is given to the crowd-sourced miners. A technological precursor of this currency (known as "bitcoin," with the "bit" in reference to "binary" and "digit" and "coin" referring to stamped metal used as money) and is credited to Adam Back's "development of the hashcash proof of work (POW) function in 1997" and Hal Finney's application of that function "to develop a reusable proof of work (RPOW) as a form of money, which was used in Wei Dai's B-Money Proposal, Nick Szabo's Bit Gold proposal, and finally, Satoshi Nakamoto's Bitcoin proposal" (Roth, 2015, p. 528). Nakamoto's work describes technological means to avoid "double-spending" of moneys and the power of having "nodes that are not cooperating to attack the network…to outpace attackers" (Nakamoto, Oct. 2008, p. 1). So what is bitcoin? Bitcoin is "a digital currency and payment system" (Bouri, Molnár, Azzi, Roubaud, & Hagfors, 2017, p. 192) although it is "mainly used as an asset rather than a currency" (Glaser et al., 2014; Baek and Elbeck, 2015; Dyhrberg, 2016a, as cited in Katsiampa, 2017, p. 3) Bitcoin as a "homogeneous, virtual good" (Pieters & Vivanco, 2017, p. 1). It is part of an emerging asset class of cryptocurrencies. "The cryptocurrency market is "a market of competing private irredeemable monies (or would-be monies) (White, Spring/Summer 2015, p. 383). It is a "private money" (Srokosz & Kopyściański, 2015, p. 619). Bitcoin has been compared to "a speculative commodity rather than a currency" (Selgin, 2015; Baeck & Elbeck, 2015, as cited in Wei, 2018, p. 21).

Even though Bitcoin has been the focus of much research, there is a sense that there is a "lack of comprehensive research on Bitcoin" (Sauer, Oct. 2015, p. 285). Owners of the cryptocurrency may remain anonymized within the system (but their identities may be known depending on the exchanges that handle the cryptocurrency). In general, there is the sense that current cryptocurrencies are "extremely opaque by design" (Goertzel, Goertzel, & Goertzel, 2017, p. 68).

While the "first mover" may be Bitcoin (in 2009), a lot of other emulative altcoins has followed with the same technological understructure (Halaburda, 2016, p. 7) but also a range of different selling points and differentiators. Generally, encryption is used to "generate units and regulate the transactions associated with those units" without ties to a central bank (Marshall, 2018, p. 1). In a sense, this design of a cryptocurrency emerged from the financial stresses of the U.S. (in recession after a financial crash) and the global system (North, Apr. 23, 2018, p. 14). [With the passage of time, it has become clear that cryptocurrencies do not exist in an unregulated or ungoverned space. They do not exist in gray sectors that are informal. National and global governance regimes are developing to ensure national government controls and oversight and the protection of citizens.]

An online "ledger" (record of financial accounting) of purchases and spends of the currency is maintained "forever" in online collective memory based on (crowd-sourced) "miners" who apply computing power to calculate "hashes" to ensure that coinage is not spent more than once and write to the blockchain. One author explains:

Blocks are secured by a hash function, preventing new blocks from being added to an invalid block, as each new block would also contain an invalid hash. Hash functions link a key to a specific hash value, which is often associated with access to a certain element that a user may be looking for, so if the correct key is provided, the hash function will produce a valid hash, validating a specific block. The hash for each block essentially acts as a lock for that block. The ledger is accessed by a network of servers that maintain the blockchain, using mathematical models to create a consensus for the network, which allows incorrect hashes to be flagged (Marshall, 2018, p. 2).

Owners of the currency are "anonymized" and must prove ownership with the proper unique code to access funds to spend. Those defining features inform the term "cryptocurrency": "Bitcoin's ingenious use of cryptographic tools gave rise to the name of 'cryptocurrency,' now shared by hundreds of digital currencies that utilize similar technology" (Halaburda, 2016, p. 1). (The glamorous aspect of "crypto" may be part of the allure to invest in these financial instruments.) Active trade in Bitcoin only started in 2013 even though it was created in 2009 (Caporale, Gil-Alana, & Plastun, Dec. 2017, p. 2).

The conceptual precursor for "digital cash" or "digicash" is credited to David Chaum in the 1980s. The cypherpunk movement, described as activism advocating "strong cryptography and privacy-enhancing technologies as a route to social and political change" ("Cypherpunk," Sept. 18, 2018), is also thought to support digital cash (Roth, 2015, p. 528). This libertarian movement focuses on a decentralization of government and more power to self-organizing peoples. In Eric Hughes' "A Cypherpunk's Manifesto," he wrote:

Cypherpunks write code. We know that someone has to write software to defend privacy, and since we can't get privacy unless we all do, we're going to write it. We publish our code so that our fellow Cypherpunks may practice and play with it. Our code is free for all to use, worldwide. We don't much care if you don't approve of the software we write. We know that software can't be destroyed and that a widely dispersed system can't be shut down. (Mar. 9, 1993)

The open release of the software to implement a cryptocurrency may reflect that value of publishing code openly. It may indicate an idealism, a utopianism, instead of pursuing personal material interests and maintaining intellectual property ownership over the designed system.

Understanding Some Basics of the Cryptocurrency Space and Markets

The cryptocurrency market is thought to have popularized beginning in 2014. As of October 2017, there were more than 1,000 cryptocurrencies available (Gkillas & Katsiampa, 2018, p. 109), with many essentially printing digital money. Part of the widespread interest in cryptocurrencies has to do with social promotion through Pied Piper effects. There is also the "fear of missing out" (FOMO) (Marshall, 2018, p. 3) and the "fear of missing deals" (FOMD) even in the environment of volatile valuations, hacking and theft, pump and dump schemes, poor or absent government regulation, and other challenges. This nascent stage of cryptocurrency deployment manifests in different ways in different locales, often with a sense of hidden hands and mixed motives. In one locale, there are "shadowy lenders…putting ads on Georgian Facebook pages offering $10,000 to buy bitcoin or mining equipment—with interest rates starting at 18 percent" (North, Apr. 23, 2018, p. 15). Bitcoin miners are individuals who purchase particular hardware and software in order to be able to write and record transactions to the blockchain. It is described as follows:

Think of it like a lottery, where computers linked across the Internet compete to solve complex mathematical puzzles, with the number of players constantly rising. The owner of the computer that finds the right solution is rewarded with a 'block' of bitcoin or other cryptocurrency, which is then registered and verified on a decentralized database system known as the blockchain (North, Apr. 23, 2018, p. 3)

In terms of the *status quo*, a majority of moneys exchanged in the world today is digital, with a small amount in print or "physical" form (estimated at some 8%). The Money Project suggests that "the total value of the world's money is $90.4 trillion" and includes "coins, banknotes, money market accounts, as well as saving, checking, and time deposits (DesJardins, Oct. 26, 2017). Bitcoin was valued at $100 billion, the other altcoins at $45 billion, and Ethereum at $28 billion, with the comment: "The world's fastest growing asset class is cryptocurrency—but even Bitcoin looks tiny in the grand scheme of things, when compared to other global markets" (DesJardins, Oct. 26, 2017).

In capitalist systems, there are cyclical booms and busts, based on economic expansion and contraction. Stock markets, based on conventional wisdom, are driven by human greed (buy) and human fear (sell), with tradeoffs between the two. Currency value, generally speaking, is affected by a mix of economic and financial factors and government (central bank) policies. One visual approach to understanding what cryptocurrency is in relation to more traditional moneys is via the "the money flower, a taxonomy of money"; in this explanatory visual, cryptocurrency is a peer-to-peer currency that is "universally accessible" (Bech & Garratt, Sept. 2017, p. 60). Historically, currencies have been represented by precious metals (silver, gold, copper, bronze, and combinations of metals), banknotes (paper), shells, record-keeping on stones, and other ways to enable trade and transactions (with some understood base value). In contrast to fiat currencies, cryptocurrencies are not backstopped by government power but are of the people only (peer to peer), and their value depends on how other investors value the online financial ledger record-keeping (0s and 1s). The initial enthusiasms for creating people-maintained cryptocurrencies occurred in 2007 – 2008, during the global financial crisis when trust in governments was low. Cryptocurrencies were conceptualized "in response to the perceived failures of government and central banks during the 2008 crash (Weber, 2014a, as cited in Fry & Cheah, 2016, p. 344). As with all new systems, the cryptocurrency technology and concept solved some challenges but created others. Removing government and its ability to "manipulate" currencies was seen as a desirable feature, not a bug. (Government ability to create moneys for liquidity and to retract moneys to control for inflation is seen as a net positive in general.) One author explains the thinking behind the cryptography-enabled electronic money system:

A cryptocurrency uses cryptographic controls to eliminate the need for a central authority's involvement in transactions, which removes the risk that they might manipulate the supply of currency, or feel compelled to mediate on disputes. The upper bound on the amount of cryptocurrency units is known and carefully controlled to mimic a scarce resource, such as gold (Roth, 2015, p. 528).

Another author explains this security feature. Fighting "counterfeiting of bitcoins (also known as the problem of 'double spending') is prevented not through police work and legal prosecution by any central authority, but quite elegantly by the decentralized verification process that prevents the transfer of any coin of unattested provenance from being accepted onto the public ledger" (White, Spring/Summer 2015, p. 395). [Note: Just prior to this chapter's being published, a news article came out in which "chain reorganization" resulted in a double-spend of Ethereum classic in what was termed a "confidence-breaking attack" (Kharpal, Jan. 8, 2019). In other words, a core tenet at the heart of the value and security of cryptocurrencies was found not to hold in the real world. Further, hundreds of millions of value in cryptocurrencies seem to have been lost with the death of a 30-year-old CEO of a cryptocurrency wallet company (Alexander, Feb. 4, 2019).]

For cryptocurrencies, for which there are not direct historical precursors, many often turn to other "assets," anything that people consider of value. Often in the same breath, they point to "asset bubbles," which occur when the price of an asset rises too quickly in a way that is not supported by intrinsic valuations. Such bubbles may occur when large groups of people experience enthusiasm for a particular resource, and they "bid up" a value because they are acting *en masse*. (Housing prices may be bid up when there is a shortage of housing in particular locations. The rarity of the resource is one factor in higher valuations. Artificial scarcities may create a sense of value, such as the producers of Beanie Babies only releasing particular limited editions of the toys. Hype can also feed into the creation of asset bubbles, with people believing messaging about a particular asset or class of assets.) Historically, asset bubbles have built up around tulips (1619 – 1622), US stocks, real estate, gold, technologies, oil, and others (depicted in a line graph visualization by Convoy Investments (and Elliott Wave International, Yale SOM, St. Louis FRED, GlobalFin, and Convoy Investments, as cited in Vlastelica, Feb. 13, 2018). The Beanie Babies craze occurred in the 1990s. In this visual, the selected asset bubbles lasted between some three to 23 years. The asset bubble trajectories follow a pattern, with a rapid (or somewhat graduated) buildup to a peak value and then sharp drops or graduated drops back to a low baseline when the asset bubble breaks. At some point, the irrational exuberance ends, the asset bubble bursts, and prices fall to more accurate levels of valuation. The hard part is to "time" the particular market to anticipate when peak values might be occurring without room for rise left and to know when to sell (to minimize losses). The general rule is that "what goes up must come down" (the laws of gravity), but sitting on the sidelines may mean missed opportunities (to make out like a bandit); divesting too early may mean leaving money on the table, and mistiming the cryptocurrencies market may mean a complete loss (not to mention the instability of exchanges, susceptible to hacking and unscrupulous business people). As a general rule, irrational exuberance leads to heady valuations which will not hold up over time, when in-world conditions change. Depending on their stance on the asset class (cryptocurrency) and particular "coins" (by brand), some see asset bubbles with the feverish rises (crypto-craze) in value and volatility, and others see opportunity (and both can be true simultaneously). For example, there was a 20-fold value rise in bitcoin from its $1000 value in January to $20,000 in December (2017) (Wren, Jan. 25, 2018, p. 2).

While proponents of the digital currency bitcoin argue that its massive price appreciation over the course of 2017 is only the latest step in a rally that will see it multiply several times over from its current levels, another analyst has a far different take: Not only is bitcoin a bubble, it is the biggest bubble of all time" (Vlastelica, Dec. 14, 2017, n.p)

Cryptocurrency, as an asset class, has been called a "dangerous speculative bubble by any shadow or stretch of the imagination" and a "toxic concept for investors" (Meyer, Dec. 5, 2017, p. 1). The vertical pattern of its value rise (at some 22,000% of one cryptocurrency) suggests a fast expansion of an asset bubble. Stephen Roach, Chief Economist of Morgan Stanley, is quoted as saying, "Bitcoin is a dangerous speculative bubble with a lack of underlying intrinsic value to the concept" (Bjordal & Opdahl, Autumn 2017, p. 60).

Other features of the coinage create concerns. The "irreversibility of Bitcoin payments" is seen as heightening transaction risks (Böhme, Christin, Edelman, & Moore, Spring 2015, p. 227). The risks do not only come from the coin, but the related currency exchanges may be a site of risk:

45 percent of the Bitcoin currency exchanges studied by Moore and Christin (2013) ultimately ceased operation. High-volume exchanges were more likely to close because of a security breach, while operators of low-volume exchanges were more likely to abscond without explanation. Of the exchanges that closed, 46 percent did not reimburse their customers after shutting down. If users avoid holding their bitcoins in an exchange and instead use a digital wallet service, other risks arise, as these firms have become a lucrative target for cybercriminals. (Böhme, Christin, Edelman, & Moore, Spring 2015, pp. 226 – 227)

Nearly $400 million in investor losses have occurred from "botched ICOs," according to Ernst & Young (Wren, Mar. 1, 2018, p. 3). There have been tens of billions of losses for cryptocurrency investors (Comm, June 28, 2018). The names of the top two market leaders with "the highest information share" for the trade in Bitcoins (Brandvold, Molnár, & Vagstad, 2015) with one of them already in bankruptcy proceedings a year prior to the article's publication ("Mt. Gox," Sept. 13, 2018) and the other seized by the U.S. government for illegal financial activities ("BTC-e," Oct. 23, 2018).

And if the volatile valuations were not enough, there are dedicated hackers in the space. People have created dedicated malware to attack alternative currencies, with "annual thefts probably measure in the billions of dollars" ("Alternative currencies fall prey to hackers and malware," Mar. 2014) or tens of millions of dollars worth of cryptocurrencies (Kimmelman, Sept. 20, 2018). In the first half of 2018, an estimated $1.1 billion in cryptocurrency was stolen, much of it with low-cost malware from the Dark Web (Rooney, June 7, 2018). People have also conducted distributed denial of service (DDOS) attacks on bitcoin services (Vasek, Thornton, & Moore, 2014, as cited in Böhme, Christin, Edelman, & Moore, Spring 2015, pp. 226 – 227), which interrupt service provision (unless effectively defended against). Cryptocurrency mining machines have also been the target of "crypto-jacking malware" ("Fortinet Threat Landscape Report," June 2018). A confluence of simultaneous factors has enabled observable vulnerabilities: "Cryptocurrencies present opportunities for *fraud*. Because the cryptocurrency market is still opaque and the regulatory framework still in the process of development, cryptocurrencies present opportunities for scams including the theft of units of cryptocurrency through fraud or hacking." (Leckow, 2017, p. 135) Pump and dump schemes, similar to those with penny stocks, are not unheard of. Cryptocurrency holdings are not insured, and they do not have the backing of any government agency.

There are those calling for the creation of an index for the cryptocurrency market segment (Trimborn & Härdle, May 20, 2016). Some argue that cryptocurrencies are the future and do not represent bubbles by pointing to the fact that futures markets are being created around cryptocurrencies; a retort: "As we know, the Dutch market issued futures for tulips just before the crash" (Bjordal & Opdahl, Autumn 2017, pp. 61 - 62). The authors observe:

Like tulips, cryptocurrency has no rate of return. Stocks have the dividend, real-estate has rent, bonds have coupons, but cryptocurrency has nothing, the coins have zero intrinsic value, creating zero income, but are based on the expectation of adaption. A zero rate of return implies that if a potential bubble burst, nothing supports cryptocurrencies, and they can drop to a value of zero. (Bjordal & Opdahl, Autumn 2017, p. 62)

Said another way: "cryptocurrencies are mostly speculative tools and it remains unknown for how long that may last" (Leclair, Apr. 17, 2018, p. 3). Those who "create" cryptocurrencies have a "cost of production (that) is zero" (DeLong, 2013, as cited in White, Spring/Summer 2015, p. 397). The fundamentals do not suggest inherent value.

Others have suggested different analogies for cryptocurrencies, such as to gaming (gambling), playing lotteries, with wins at vanishingly small odds, but with fueling of such behaviors by fantasy and storytelling and glitter. Or another analogy could be with the virtual moneys from immersive games that turn out to have real-world value Castronova (2005). Concomitant with the earlier concept is the concern of many that cryptocurrencies are virtual, and they generally have to be converted back to mainline fiat currencies to be spent (only some entities are willing to be paid in cryptocurrencies). The notional value of bitcoins has to be made real with others accepting it as legal tender (Hayes, 2017, p. 1308).

Setting Values for Cryptocurrencies

00:23:23: *Crypto currencies don't provide benefit to society. They don't provide benefit to all of us who aren't interested in committing crimes. But they do enable these problems, and I think it is important to speak out. Another thing is is just the amount of scams in the space are just incredible. So effectively every initial coin offering these days should be called a scam because it is an unregistered security, and wouldn't even pass the laugh test at a Shark Tank show. - Dr. Nicholas Weaver in Gary McGraw's Silver Bullet Security Podcast (June 2018)*

Initial coin offerings (ICOs) are ways for new crypto-currency companies to raise capital for start-up funding. There are features that make ICOs more attractive: "if the code source is available, when a token presale is organized, and when tokens allow contributors to access a specific service (or to share profits)" (Adhami, Giudici, & Martinazzi, 2018, p. 1).

The success of the ICO directly affects "the viability of the currency as a medium of exchange" (Sockin & Xiong, March 2018, p. 28). The nature of the cryptocurrency market leaves it open to "manipulation from large investors" (Sockin & Xiong, March 2018, p. 28), known as "whales" in the jargon. In terms of ICO valuation, the authors explain their thinking:

What determines the fundamental value of a cryptocurrency? How would market trading interact with its fundamentals in an uncertain and opaque environment? In our model, a cryptocurrency constitutes membership in a platform developed to facilitate transactions of certain goods or services. The complementarity in the households' participation in the platform acts as an endogenous, yet fragile, fundamental of the cryptocurrency. There exist either two or no equilibria, and the two equilibria, when they exist, have disparate properties. When the transaction demand for the platform is unobservable, the trading price and volume of the cryptocurrency serve as important channels for not only aggregating private information about its fundamental, but also facilitating coordination on a certain equilibrium (Sockin & Xiong, March 2018, p. 1).

A simple assertion about the value of cryptocurrencies is what the market will bear, what people will pay for them (at the risk of over-relying on the state of the world as the benchmark). The jury is still out on "their value and adoption" (Böhme, Christin, Edelman, & Moore, Spring 2015, p. 235). Empirically, "the fundamental price of Bitcoin is zero" (Cheah & Fry, 2015, p. 32), and there are questions about the "long-term viability" of Bitcoin (Cheah & Fry, 2015, p. 35). What affects cryptocurrency prices? One argument is the supply-and-demand, with the supply artificially controlled by cryptocurrency providers.

In a study of weekly cryptocurrency data from 2010 – 2018 for Bitcoin, Ehereum, Dash, Litecoin, and Monero, researchers found various factors that affected their respective prices over time:

First, cryptomarket-related factors such as market beta, trading volume, and volatility appear to be significant determinant for all five cryptocurrencies both in short- and long-run. Second, attractiveness of cryptocurrencies also matters in terms of their price determination, but only in long-run...Third, SP500 index seems to have weak positive long-run impact on Bitcoin, Ethereum, and Litcoin (sic), while its sign turns to negative losing significance in short-run, except Bitcoin that generates an estimate of -0.20 at 10% significance level (Sovbetov, 2018, p. 1).

There are both internal and external factors that affect cryptocurrency prices. The internal factors involve factors that affect supply and demand, including "transaction cost..., reward system, mining difficulty (hash rate), coins circulation (and) forks (rule changes)" in the code (Sovbetov, 2018, p. 7). There are external factors, too, including the cryptomarket ["attractiveness (popularity), market trend, speculations"], macro-financial factors ("stock markets, exchange rate, gold price, interest rate, others"], (and) political ["legalization (adaptation), restrictions (ban), others"] (Sovbetov, 2018, p. 7).

However, there is no clear consensus yet on how such cryptocurrencies should be rationally valued and benchmarked. Different researchers find different ways to approach their notional value. One researcher suggests three main drivers of cryptocurrency value: "the level of competition in the network of producers, the rate of unit production, and the difficulty of algorithm use to 'mine' for the cryptocurrency" (Hayes, 2017, p. 1308).

Regardless, there are some who are arguing for the need for cryptocurrencies to diversify and balance investment portfolios (Anyfantaki, Arvanitis, & Topaloglou, April 2018). Another asserts that investing in bitcoin may be appropriate for "risk averse investors in anticipation of negative shocks to the market" because "bitcoin has a place on the financial markets and in portfolio management as it can be classified as something in between gold and the American dollar on a scale from pure medium of exchange advantages to pure store of value advantages." (Dyhrberg, Bitcoin, gold…, 2016, p. 85) One research study explored how to optimize an investment portfolio with cryptocurrencies and found that a "passive buy-and-hold" approach is more effective than "active strategies" (Bjordal & Opdahl, Autumn 2017, p. 2). They also found that "including a portion of cryptocurrency in a portfolio with more traditional assets will improve the risk-adjusted return" (Bjordal & Opdahl, Autumn 2017, p. 2). Contrary to diversification theory, others found that the "highly disordered and risky" nature of Bitcoin markets make them unsuitable for hedging purposes (Lahmiri, Bekiros, & Salvi, 2018). A different team suggests that Bitcoin is "a poor hedge and is suitable for diversification purposes only" (Bouri, Molnár, Azzi, Roubaud, & Hagfors, 2017, p. 192). However, there are those who suggest that cryptocurrencies may serve "as a hedge against stocks" and against "the American dollar in the short-term" (Dyhrberg, Hedging capabilities…, 2016, p. 139) and that Bitcoin can "act as a hedge and safe haven for major world stock indices, bonds, oil, gold, the general commodity index and the US dollar index" (Bouri, Molnár, Azzi, Roubaud, & Hagfors, 2017, p. 192). These latter bets suggest that more formal and historical financial instruments may go through severe pressures that would not affect cryptocurrencies negatively. ["A diversifier is an asset that has a weak positive correlation with another asset on average. A weak (strong) hedge is an asset that is uncorrelated (negatively correlated) with another asset *on average*. A weak (strong) safe haven is an asset that is uncorrelated (negatively correlated) with another asset on average during times of stress. As gold has been traditionally considered a hedge and a safe haven, these concepts have previously been applied mostly to gold…and credit default swaps…" (Bouri, Molnár, Azzi, Roubaud, & Hagfors, 2017, p. 193)] A challenge is that "Bitcoin investments are far less liquid that conventional assets" (Bouri, Molnár, Azzi, Roubaud, & Hagfors, 2017, p. 197). For another, Bitcoin is "a complement to emerging market currencies" and may be used to "add balance to emerging market currency portfolios" (Carrick, 2016, p. 13).

In a study of seen top cryptocurrencies (BTC, ETH, XRP, LTC, DASH, XEM, and XMR), researchers found the level of volatility around cryptocurrencies to be unprecedented:

Even compared to the volatility of stocks during the financial crisis of 2008, the volatility of cryptocurrency is enormous. Equity and fiat currency volatility only reached volatilities in the 60 – 70% range over short periods during the peak of the crisis (Schwert, 2010)…we can observe from the 30-day rolling volatility, that there are periods where the cryptocurrencies exhibit substantially higher volatility than 60-70% (Bjordal & Opdahl, Autumn 2017, pp. 37 – 38, p. 39).

Volatility of the cryptocurrency suggests that "the diversification ability of Bitcoin is not constant over time" (Bouri, Molnár, Azzi, Roubaud, & Hagfors, 2017, p. 197). A further challenge is that the signals about cryptocurrency valuations are not sufficiently transparent or clear given inefficiencies in the cryptocurrency market. Some researchers have tried to identify a "trading signal based on shifts in momentum" (Bjordal & Opdahl, Autumn 2017, p. 37).

Others have studied what affects cryptocurrency exchange rates including technological and economic determinants (Li & Wang, 2017). Some have tried to use machine learning to try to time trading in the cryptocurrency market (Alessandretti, ElBahrawy, Aiello, & Baronchelli, May 23, 2018). Agent-based models have been built, depicting "Random Traders" and "Chartists") to better understand the system (Cocco, Concas, & Marchesi, 2014). Artificial neural networks have been harnessed to explore the available cryptocurrency market data (Gullapalli, 2018). Others use machine learning to enable short-term predictions of Bitcoin values using machine learning (Guo & Antulov-Fantulin, 2018). Another group looked to publicly expressed sentiment to understand price fluctuations of an alternate cryptocurrency (Li, Chamrajnagar, Fong, Rizik, & Fu, 2018). Some researchers are developing algorithms to trade in cryptocurrency markets, with Twitter sentiment to understand public chatter to inform the trades (Colianni, Rosales, & Signorotti, 2015). Others have tapped social media and mined texts from those platforms to capture "cryptocurrency market intelligence" (Laskowski & Kim, 2016). A research team uses predictive modeling to try to understand Bitcoin prices (Indera, Yassin, Zabidi, & Rizman, 2017). A major challenge for investors is to identify relevant signals from noise in the cryptocurrency market.

And while large amounts of moneys are expended into the cryptocurrency markets, these are currencies that "appear and disappear continuously" (ElBahrawy, Alessandretti, Kandler, Pastor-Satorras, & Baronchelli, 2017, p. 1). Between April 2013 and June 2017, some 1,469 cryptocurrencies were introduced; as an asset class, these had a market capitalization of over $100 billion in June 2017. An analysis of this space found that some statistical properties have remained stable, including "the number of active cryptocurrencies, the market share distribution and the turnover of cryptocurrencies" (ElBahrawy, Alessandretti, Kandler, Pastor-Satorras, & Baronchelli, 2017, p. 1).

Less rational information to inform whether or not to engage in the cryptocurrency market and how…involves "herding behaviors," the taking on of others' beliefs as one's own and emulating them. In the cryptocurrency market, such behaviors may include making trading behaviors based on others' choices often based on insufficient objective information and a lack of "consensual agreement on the asset's value, which makes investors' beliefs unstable and subject to the herd behavior" (Leclair, Apr. 17, 2018, p. 2). Such herding actions may lead to under- or over-valuation of assets and lead to distortions in market information. A research study found that investors in cryptocurrency markets are susceptible to others' buy activities (even those of robots). In this study, the researchers used scripted agents / robots that "executed over one hundred thousand trades costing less than a penny each in 217 cryptocurrencies over the course of six months" (Krafft, Penna, & Pentland, 2018, p. 1) and found copy-cat behaviors. Market herding, mass behavior in terms of "market consensus" could "simultaneously be a result of the uncertainty about cryptocurrencies' value as financial assets, and explain the extreme volatility in the market" (Leclair, Apr. 17, 2018, pp. 3-4). One researcher writes:

Both in the weighted and non-weighted models, there appear to be a positive trend in herding since the start of the sample period. This can be interpreted as market participants being less and less confident about the financial value of cryptocurrencies and suggests an increase in uncertainty, which may be consistent with my initial hypothesis of new market participants being less informed. This is relevant because this type of uncertainty is characterized by a specific type of behavior, which is not the case with other metrics for uncertainty.

Interestingly, the herding pattern is very similar for both the weighted and the unweighted models. This means that what is happening with the most popular cryptocurrencies such as Bitcoin (BTC) and Ethereum (ETH) is also translating itself into smaller assets. (Leclair, Apr. 17, 2018, p. 14)

The challenges with herding become worse when others harness this tendency in people and engage in price manipulation of cryptocurrencies, with various suspicious behaviors observed in different platforms, including both human and bot actors (Gandal, Hamrick, Moore, & Oberman, 2018). Other researchers have also found "significant herding behavior, which varies over time," with increases when "uncertainty increases" (Bouri, Gupta, & Roubaud, June 2018, p. 2). This suggests that when people are fearful, they are more pliable and vulnerable to others' messaging and behaviors. The outreaches to people through social media are also constant and barely moderated, if at all, so those who are particularly suggestible may be influenced through the amplification of social media. Cryptocurrencies are mentioned in memes (Benaim, 2018).

Aligned with the idea of herding, researchers have found a "causal relationship between Bitcoin attention and Bitcoin returns" using the "Copula-based Granger causality test" (Dastgir, Demir, Downing, Gozgor, & Lau, 2018). The authors compared "Google Trends search queries" and Bitcoin returns...from Jan. 1, 2013 to Dec. 31, 2017, and they found a "bi-directional causal relationship between Bitcoin attention and Bitcoin returns with the except of the central distributions from 40% to 80%"; in other words, "the bidirectional causality mainly exists in the left tail (poor performance) and the right tail (superior performance) of the distribution" (Dastgir, Demir, Downing, Gozgor, & Lau, 2018, p. 1). Finally, if the social intercommunications is an important aspect of these currencies, researchers suggest that based on the social network around Bitcoin that this currency will predominate (Gandal & Halaburda, 2016). The interrelationships between the users of a cryptocurrency define in part its strength. (The social exchange in the usage of currencies as recognized and legal tender is an important factor.) As the first cryptocurrency with wide-spread adoption, Bitcoin accounts for "41% of the total estimated cryptocurrency capitalization at present (coinmarketcap.com accessed on Jun 12th 2017)." (Katsiampa, 2017, p. 3). A different study found "winner-take-all effect" dominant in the early Bitcoin market but an evolution to more features conducive to its usage as an asset over time (Gandal & Halaburda, 2014, p. 3). There may be some zero-sumness in terms of gains for Bitcoin as some losses for other cryptocurrencies (Halaburda, 2016, p. 10).

Game theory methods have been applied to understand cryptocurrency markets, and the researchers found that the equilibria could be affected by a "sovereign" or "whale" (a large holder of crypto coins). They explain:

We analyze two settings, differing in whether the households' aggregate goods endowment is observable, which captures the demand fundamental for the platform. In the first setting, where the platform fundamental is publicly observable, there exist either two or no cutoff equilibria. When there are two equilibria, they exhibit opposing behavior. One of the equilibria has a higher cryptocurrency price and a lower equilibrium cutoff for each household's cryptocurrency purchase decision, and the other has a lower price and a higher equilibrium cutoff. These two equilibria are self-enforcing as a result of the complementarity among the households' trading needs—if more households join the platform by choosing a lower cutoff strategy, they all benefit more from trading goods in the platform, and are therefore willing to pay a high cryptocurrency price. On the other hand, if each household chooses a higher cutoff strategy, there will be less households in the platform, making the platform less desirable, and lowering the price of the cryptocurrency. The presence of these two opposing equilibria suggest that one may observe entirely different dynamics of cryptocurrencies in practice, simply as a result of the endogenous and fragile nature of their business model, without necessarily involving any reckless speculation, abuse, or manipulation. In the absence of a sovereign to provide guidance and support the platform, cryptocurrencies are vulnerable to these large price swings, and large investors may act as cryptocurrency whales to help coordinate participant expectations (Sockin & Xiong, March 2018, p. 3).

A lack of transparency and information can lead to coordination failure (and market failure). Poor information can also lead to volatility in the cryptocurrency market, with "price overreactions":

This paper examines price overreactions in the case of the following cryptocurrencies: BitCoin, LiteCoin, Ripple and Dash. A number of parametric (t-test, ANOVA, regression analysis with dummy variables) and non-parametric (Mann-Whitney U test) tests confirm the presence of price patterns after overreactions: the next-day price changes in both directions are bigger than after 'normal' days. A trading robot approach is then used to establish whether these statistical anomalies can be exploited to generate profits. The results suggest that a strategy based on counter-movements after overreactions is not profitable, whilst one based on inertia appears to be profitable but produces outcomes not statistically different from the random ones. Therefore the overreactions detected in the cryptocurrency market do not give rise to exploitable profit opportunities (possibly because of transaction costs) and cannot be seen as evidence against the Efficient Market Hypothesis (EMH). (Caporale & Plastun, Jan. 2018, n.p.)

Researchers have explored how to create a system for cryptocurrencies to arrive at a positive valuation (Dwyer, 2015). They have worked to estimate "the two major tail risk measures of Value-at-Risk (VaR) and Expected Shortfall (ES) as extreme quantiles of the GPD" (generalized Pareto distribution) (Gkillas & Katsiampa, 2018, p. 110). Their findings: "We found that Bitcoin Cash has the highest potential gain and loss and is thus the riskiest cryptocurrency, while Bitcoin and Litecoin were found to be the least risky, and hence position in those can be viewed safer than in the other cryptocurrencies considered in this study" (Gkillas & Katsiampa, 2018, p. 110) Using econophysics models (from "statistical physics and mathematical finance"), researchers have considered what would happen if cryptocurrency markets were exposed to "an unpredictable shock" and modeling the aftermath (Fry & Cheah, 2016, p. 347). The current market capitalization of the cryptocurrencies are, in descending order, as follows: Bitcoin, Ethereum, Ripples, NEM, and Dash (Phillip, Chan, & Peiris, 2018). In terms of predictivity, they could all survive, but will there be a particular cryptocurrency that dominates? (Halaburda, 2016, p. 9) Will cryptocurrencies integrate with the real world economies and people's lives?

Research Studies of the Cryptocurrency Marketplace

The widespread public interest in cryptocurrencies is paralleled by interest by academic researchers. Observations of the cryptocurrency markets have been studied, and models have been created from the data based on "best fit" to the observations (Katsiampa, 2017, p. 3).

An efficient market is one in which "all pertinent information is available to all participants at the same time, and where prices respond immediately to available information" ("efficient market," 2018). The function of a market is to enable people to engage in trades and actions that serve their respective interests, without hidden hand manipulations. Researchers have approached the study of cryptocurrency markets with that understanding. A study of the volume of trades and the prices of coins showed Bitcoin as inefficient but potentially moving towards efficiency (Urquhart, 2016); a follow-on study to the prior work found some weak efficiencies in Bitcoin (Nadarajah & Chu,

2017). According to the Efficient Market Hypothesis, "prices should follow a random walk" (Fama, 1970, as cited in Caporale, Gil-Alana, & Plastun, Dec. 2017, p. 2) and not display residual effects from "memory." A research team applied "long memory techniques" to study this phenomenon (R/S analysis and fractional integration) on cryptocurrency valuation data from 2013 – 2017. The idea is that the market is efficient if it reflects informed real-world values of the assets but inefficient if it is taking its cues from non-relevant sources. More established cryptocurrencies perform better:

We find that efficiency is stronger, and volatility lower, in liquid markets as active traders are more likely to arbitrage away signs of return predictability. Higher transaction costs in markets where turnover is low impacts the ability for traders to act quickly and readily, resulting in market inefficiency. We also find that illiquid cryptocurrencies exhibit strong return anti-persistence in the form of a low Hurst exponent. Our findings suggest that whilst established cryptocurrencies are improving in terms of market efficiency, fledgling new altcoins with limited liquidity continue to struggle (Wei, 2018, p. 24).

In the lowest quintile cryptocurrencies, there is less efficiency and more signs of "mini boom-bust cycles as speculators sway from being overly optimistic to pessimistic" (Wei, 2018, p. 24). In general, the different cryptocurrency exchanges should all reflect the so-called "law of one price" (LOOP) for the costs of the same coins and fees; "identical goods should sell for identical prices after trade costs are taken into considerations" (Pieters & Vivanco, 2017, p. 1). Other researchers suggest that the Bitcoin market is efficient with the exception of some periods, such as April-August 2013 and August-November, 2016 (Tiwari, Jana, Das, & Roubaud, 2018), albeit without more explanatory information. Another study found that market efficiency increased during cooling down periods after price surges in two Bitcoin markets. The researcher found the two studied Bitcoin markets ("with respect to the US dollar and Chinese yuan") were "mostly inefficient between 2010 and 2017 with exceptions of several periods directly connected to cooling down after the bubble-like price surges" (Kristoufek, 2018, p. 257). The efficiency of the markets also vary based on context. Researchers discovered the following:

Existence of behavioral bias and creation of events can change efficiency. The unanimity in findings from the methods employed signifies the robustness of this study. It suggests that speculators and arbitrageurs can exploit extra returns, but not always (Khuntia & Pattanayak, 2018, p. 28).

Some cryptocurrency market patterns are suggestive of "complex underlying dynamics" (but these were not explained in this particular work) based on a sliding windows approach to understanding "synthetic currency market(s)" and volatility clustering (Bariviera, 2017, p. 3). Researchers have explored identifying properties of cryptocurrencies that enhance their "instability" (Phillip, Chan, & Peiris, 2018).

The "long memory effect" (Hosking, 1981; Bariviera, 2017, as cited in Phillip, Chan, & Peiris, 2018, p. 6) has long been studied as one indicator of potential market inefficiency. Any predictable patterns can be "used as a basis for trading strategies aimed at making abnormal profits in the cryptocurrency market" (Caporale, Gil-Alana, & Plastun, Dec. 2017, p. 2). These researchers selected four cryptocurrencies to study, those "with the highest market capitalization and longest span of data" (BitCoin, LiteCoin, Ripple and Dash). They measured for the Hurst exponent, a measure of long-term memory (various autocorrelations) of time series data (such as whether the data either regresses to the mean or clusters directionally). A "random walk" would be 0.5 or as close to this as possible.:

A value H in the range 0.5–1 indicates a time series with long-term positive autocorrelation, meaning both that a high value in the series will probably be followed by another high value and that the values a long time into the future will also tend to be high. A value in the range 0 – 0.5 indicates a time series with long-term switching between high and low values in adjacent pairs, meaning that a single high value will probably be followed by a low value and that the value after that will tend to be high, with this tendency to switch between high and low values lasting a long time into the future. A value of H=0.5 can indicate a completely uncorrelated series, but in fact it is the value applicable to series for which the autocorrelations at small time lags can be positive or negative but where the absolute values of the autocorrelations decay exponentially quickly to zero. ("Hurst exponent," Aug. 8, 2018)

Researchers found that the cryptocurrency valuation "series do not follow a random walk, and are persistent, which is inconsistent with market efficiency" (Caporale, Gil-Alana, & Plastun, Dec. 2017, p. 7). Of the studied cryptocurrencies, the most efficient one was Bitcoin, "which is the oldest and most commonly used, as well as the most liquid" (Caporale, Gil-Alana, & Plastun, Dec. 2017, p. 7). They did find that the maturing of the cryptocurrency in the market seems to lead to increasing efficiencies (Caporale, Gil-Alana,

& Plastun, Dec. 2017, p. 9). These findings were echoed in a later today that found that while Bitcoin returns showed "signs of efficiency, numerous cryptocurrencies still exhibit signs of autocorrelation and non-independence" (Wei, 2018, p. 21). There is a relationship between "the Hurst exponent and liquidity on a cross-sectional basis," with liquidity as a critical factor on market efficiency and "return predictability" of new cryptocurrencies (Wei, 2018, p. 21).

In terms of valuation patterning, one team used statistical techniques and identified a "day of the week effect" for one of the cryptocurrencies: "Most crypto currencies (LiteCoin, Ripple, Dash) are found not to exhibit this anomaly. The only exception is BitCoin, for which returns on Mondays are significantly higher than those on the other days of the week" (Caporale & Plastun, Oct. 2017, n.p.).

The general public does apparently engage rationally in some ways, by going to mass media for relevant information. Bitcoin is "inherently tied to the dynamics of the real economic system" and regulatory effects may affect Bitcoin markets (Cheah, Mishra, Pari, & Zhang, 2018, p. 25), and the market values are sensitive to "stochastic shock." Researchers have observed that "impactful news, such as regulations and bans on cryptocurrency services, affects the cryptocurrency market" (Bjordal & Opdahl, Autumn 2017, p. 37). Whether cryptocurrencies have a direct effect on financial markets is contested. One researcher suggests that the lack of direct connections between Bitcoin and other markets means minimal effects, although they did find "a large spike in spillovers to gold after a price crash on markets for Bitcoin" (Kurka, 2017, p. 12). Researchers have observed user exposure to "significant legal and economic risk" due to the lack of no central issuer with actual responsibility for cryptocurrency valuations (Srokosz & Kopyściański, 2015, p. 619), and such risks may have an effect on the stability of the financial system. They clarify that cryptocurrencies should not be conflated with virtual currencies (Srokosz & Kopyściański, 2015, p. 620) because the latter is backstopped by legally responsible issuers, which the first lacks.

If Bitcoin is a "disruptive innovation" beyond criminal activity, what might it disrupt? Bitcoin "displays the characteristics of both Low End and New Market Disruptive Innovations" and does "have the potential to disrupt the payment processor market and the organisations operating within the industry" (McDougall, Aug. 2014, p. 7), according to one researcher. Specific coin-based factors also affect their valuation:

It is also natural to assume that coin specific factors will drive the price in the long run. An investment in a coin is exposure to the qualities and factors behind the development of the coin, as well as exposure to the cryptocurrency market. Some of the unique qualities could be underlying technology, the market sentiment, and the development team behind the cryptocurrency. (Bjordal & Opdahl, Autumn 2017, p. 37)

Regulators

There is no global oversight or global regulatory framework over cryptocurrency markets at present (Pieters & Vivanco, 2017, p. 1), and there is only a patchwork of national ones. Some countries have decided to enter the fray and issue national cryptocurrencies (Wren, Feb. 22, 2018), including Venezuela with their "petro" coins and Iran, among others. Some nations have issued a "blanket ban on anything related to cryptocurrencies" (Wren, Mar. 14, 2018, p. 5). Some countries are even bad actors in this space, engaging in hacking and theft. If parallel currency systems exist, with a majority regulated and the crypto one unregulated, cross-border payments may occur that may affect national governance; as yet, it is unclear what a central regulation regime may look like with multiple systems at play (Sauer, Oct. 2015).

While early years of cryptocurrency rollouts seemed fairly unregulated, over time, there have been signs that respective governments have started stepping into this space to ensure that they can properly enforce taxes on gains and transactions. For example, the U.S. Securities and Exchange Commission (SEC) has taken steps to warn consumers of some of the risks in the space. They created a website mimicking those with initial coin offerings (ICOs) to show how easy it is to set up a fake storefront and mislead potential investors (Wren, May 16, 2018). The HoweyCoins.com site "mirrors marketing materials published by actual cryptocurrency promoters" replete with "a countdown timer, promises of outsized investment returns, and even a 'Meet the Team' section with SEC employees posing as cryptocurrency developers" (Wren, May 16, 2018, p. 2). "The name 'HoweyCoins' is a reference to the HoweyTest, a four-part legal test issued by the Supreme Court in 1946 for determining whether an investment counts as a 'security.' Generally, if something passes the Howey test, and is therefore considered a security, it is subject to SEC regulation" (Wren, May 16, 2018, p. 3). Those who would launch cryptocurrencies are subject to SEC enforcement actions. However, there is nothing to protect investors against the total loss of their invested funds.

Cryptocurrencies have been used in various criminal endeavors, with illicit purchases on the Dark Web and in online drug markets (Van Hout & Bingham, 2013), including the Silk Road, which existed from 2011 – 2013. Those who deploy ransomware often request that their victims pay in cryptocurrencies to anonymized accounts (Cohen & Nissim, 2018, p. 161). The interests of law enforcement and agencies related to consumer protection have long had an interest in regulating cryptocurrencies (Böhme, Christin, Edelman, & Moore, Spring 2015, pp. 229 – 230). There is interest in enforcement of "know-your-customer" (KYC) policies to control against terrorist financing (Pieters & Vivanco, 2017, p. 1). The "unregulated" and "speculative" nature of the financial products pose risks to users (Wren, Mar. 14, 2018, p. 3). Indeed, "cryptocurrency relations" may involve "administrative, criminal and civil liability" (Drozd, Lazur, & Serbin, 2017, p. 221), given the semi-regulated features of the space. There are limits to "private innovation in monetary and payment systems" (Beer & Weber, 2015).

While governments are exploring their roles in this space, citizens in democracies are engaging with their leaders using cryptocurrencies. For example, political donations have been made through Bitcoin (Hernández, Oct. 26, 2018).

Detractors

Detractors of cryptocurrencies ask what the basis is for trust in these private moneys when there are no governing authorities (the buck stops where?). Weaver, a leading computer scientist, comments:

The rationale for these things is that there's no central authority, which means no one can block or undo a transaction. And so far at least, it's true that transactions aren't blocked. But why do you need such a system? Because you're doing a transaction that a central authority would otherwise block, like paying off a hitman or buying drugs. If that's what you need money for, the cryptocurrencies are the only game in town. But if you don't need to buy drugs or hitmen, the cryptocurrencies are vastly less efficient. (Weaver, 2018, as cited in Illing, Apr. 11, 2018)

Others also suggest that it is not only an issue of questionable value but environmental harms from the electricity required for "mining" cryptocurrencies using computers. Spyros Foteinis, in his famous letter to *Nature*, posed this question about Bitcoin's technology with a challenging carbon footprint, suggesting that these are inherently wasteful (Foteinis, Feb. 7, 2018), without really adding value. Another author observes:

In practice, it involves a kind of constant digital bombardment to find these solutions, 24 hours a day, consuming huge amounts of electricity. And thanks to its cheap hydropower and low regulation, Georgia is now ranked second in the world for cryptocurrency mining—behind only China. (North, Apr. 23, 2018, p. 3)

For all the disparities between how people valuate cryptocurrencies, it may be valuable to explore the electronic hive mind around this phenomenon over a multi-day period in late 2018. What seems to be the public mind around this issue? What information is shared, by whom, why, and in what ways?

ONLINE LEARNERS AND COMMUNITIES AROUND CRYPTOCURRENCIES

This work explores three interrelated hypotheses, focused around a target electronic hive mind (EHM) through social media residua: social messaging, general membership, and executive functioning.

H1: In the electronic hive mind (EHM) surrounding cryptocurrencies, the **social messaging** around such currencies will be strategic and tactical, sometimes baldly and sometimes subtly.

    H1a: A majority of the multimodal social messages will be in support of cryptocurrencies (as a reflection of communicator interests).

    H1b: In formal mass media, a majority of the messages will be skeptical of and questioning of cryptocurrencies because of the lack of intrinsic value and its volatility.

    H1c: In the academic research space, the respective works will show strengths and weaknesses to cryptocurrencies, based on available and discoverable information.

H2: The **general membership** of the cryptocurrencies EHM may be sussed out inferentially from the social messaging based on stakeholder interests.

H2a: A portion of the cryptocurrency EHM will be comprised of individuals who have little to no background on cryptocurrencies but who are seeking advice and direction as potential investors.

H3: The EHM around cryptocurrencies demonstrates some **executive functioning** in part based on real-world interests.

These three main hypotheses will be explored based on real-world information from various social media platforms to understand the affordances and constraints of online communal electronic hive minds for executive functioning.

MASSTHINK AROUND CRYPTOCURRENCIES?

There are several ways to get at how the public imagination approaches cryptocurrencies. One is through the exploration of mass search data through Google. The Google Correlate tool online enables the identification of search terms correlated by time. In an exploration of "cryptocurrency" (Table 1) and "bitcoin" searches (Table 2), both have a coherent set of understandings. For search terms which are not coherently understood, the search term associations tend to be disparate and non-aligned and unrelated topically. The references show some tie also to consumer goods.

Another approach may be to examine references in scanned books, based on the Google Books Ngram Viewer. While "currency" has been a term long in use, "crypto" has been less so, and "crypto currency" and "cryptocurrency" do not show up at all in the hundreds of years of book data, captured at mass scale. The terms have not yet seeped in the public lexicon in the formalization of books.

Related tags networks may offer ways to understanding mass mind around a particular topic, too. Related tags to "crypto" (at 1 degree) bring in technology references and war-time breaking of encryptions, on the Flickr image-sharing site (Table 3 and Figure 2).

A "currency" related tags network on Flickr (at 1.5 degrees) brings up references to a global economy (Table 4 and Figure 3).

A popular account on Facebook, a predominant social networking site, focused on common mainstream topics (Figure 4). This @ cryptocurrenciesupdates community had over 144,500 subscribers at the time of this data capture. A close-in reading of the poststream shows a very active community engaging around a range of topics. Research on online

Table 1. "Cryptocurrency" search time patterns on Google correlate (weekly, in U.S., January 2003 – present)

0.9779	cryptocurrencies
0.9623	best cryptocurrency
0.9608	cryptocurrency market
0.9604	cryptocurrency exchange
0.9537	altcoin
0.9529	new cryptocurrency
0.9439	coinmarket
0.9348	cryptocurrency mining
0.9285	altcoins
0.9285	something meaning
0.9247	what is cryptocurrency
0.9239	coinmarketcap
0.9232	crypto market cap
0.9218	matrix mastercard
0.9218	altcoin mining
0.9202	cryptocurrency market cap
0.9202	let her go ukulele chords
0.9197	mining cryptocurrency
0.9196	crypto mining
0.9179	let her go ukulele
0.9177	coinbase bitcoin
0.917	bitcoin news
0.9161	rocktape knee
0.9148	crypto market
0.9139	say something ukulele
0.9131	coinbase
0.9108	crypto exchange
0.9104	bitcoin reddit
0.91	the wallace culver city
0.9095	say something ukulele chords
0.9094	let her go piano
0.907	rust servers
0.907	value of bitcoin
0.9057	bitcoin coinbase
0.9048	liquid libs

continued on following page

Table 1. Continued

0.9046	bitcoin today
0.9042	cex.io
0.9041	activation locked
0.9037	district donuts new orleans
0.9027	row 34 boston
0.9027	putlocker.to
0.9025	best cryptocurrency to mine
0.9018	wallace culver city
0.9018	container park las vegas
0.9018	ward 8 boston
0.9013	cryptocoin
0.901	brickell heights
0.9009	p90x3 workouts
0.9007	crypto coins
0.9005	planet fitness jacksonville nc
0.9001	stone bowl milwaukee
0.8998	charter app
0.8987	play timber
0.8985	stbyop.com
0.8984	what does the cat
0.8983	hashrate
0.8976	rust server
0.8974	lagu bara
0.8973	texas roadhouse fredericksburg
0.8972	bitcoin worth
0.8969	about time full movie
0.8967	say something piano
0.8962	what is bitcoin worth
0.8958	best dmr
0.8956	how to make a rust server
0.8955	say something karaoke
0.895	miami valley gaming
0.8949	th/s
0.894	drink a beer chords
0.8929	coin bitcoin
0.8922	cryptocurrency news

continued on following page

Table 1. Continued

0.8921	ride on you baby
0.8914	valley gaming
0.8913	buffalo wild wings riverhead
0.8909	let her go guitar
0.8898	dell active stylus
0.8896	coin market cap
0.8894	current price of bitcoin
0.88922	jeep cherokee limited
0.8882	jordan 12 cleats
0.8881	pho nomenon
0.888	bitcoin blockchain
0.888	jim n nicks cullman
0.8879	borgata online casino
0.8879	yellow claw dj turn it up
0.8878	dosa royale
0.8876	doge the dog
0.8867	hyatt place bayamon
0.8866	accept bitcoin
0.8863	play say something

Table 2. "bitcoin" search time patterns on Google Correlate (weekly, in U.S., January 2003 – present)

0.9779	cryptocurrencies
0.9623	best cryptocurrency
0.9608	cryptocurrency market
0.9604	cryptocurrency exchange
0.9537	altcoin
0.9529	new cryptocurrency
0.9439	coinmarket
0.9348	cryptocurrency mining
0.9285	altcoins
0.9285	something meaning
0.9247	what is cryptocurrency
0.9239	coinmarketcap
0.9232	crypto market cap

continued on following page

Table 2. Continued

0.9218	matrix mastercard
0.9218	altcoin mining
0.9202	cryptocurrency market cap
0.9202	let her go ukelele chords
0.9197	mining cryptocurrency
0.9196	crypto mining
0.9179	let her go ukelele
0.9177	coinbase bitcoin
0.917	bitcoin news
0.9161	rocktape knee
0.9148	crypto market
0.9139	say something ukelele
0.9131	coinbase
0.9108	crypto exchange
0.9104	bitcoin reddit
0.91	the wallace culver city
0.9095	say something ukelele chords
0.9094	let her go piano
0.907	rust servers
0.907	value of bitcoin
0.9057	bitcoin coinbase
0.9048	liquid libs
0.9046	bitcoin today
0.9042	cex.io
0.9041	activation locked
0.9037	district donuts new orleans
0.9027	row 34 boston
0.9027	putlocker.to
0.9025	best cryptocurrency to mine
0.9018	wallace culver city
0.9018	container park las vegas
0.9018	ward 8 boston
0.9013	cryptocoin
0.901	brickell heights
0.9009	p90x3 workouts
0.9007	crypto coins

continued on following page

Table 2. Continued

0.9005	planet fitness jacksonville nc
0.9001	stone bowl milwaukee
0.8998	charter app
0.8987	play timber
0.8985	stbyop.com
0.8984	what does the cat
0.8983	hashrate
0.8976	rust server
0.8974	lagu bara
0.8973	texas roadhouse fredericksburg
0.8972	bitcoin worth
0.8969	about time full movie
0.8967	say something piano
0.8962	what is bitcoin worth
0.8958	best dmr
0.8956	how to make a rust server
0.8955	say something karaoke
0.895	miami valley gaming
0.8949	th/s
0.894	drink a beer chords
0.8929	coin bitcoin
0.8922	cryptocurrency news
0.8921	ride on you baby
0.8914	valley gaming
0.8913	buffalo wild wings riverhead
0.8909	let her go guitar
0.8898	dell active stylus
0.8896	coin market cap
0.8894	current price of bitcoin
0.8892	2014 jeep cherokee limited
0.8882	jordan 12 cleats
0.8881	pho nomenon
0.888	bitcoin blockchain
0.888	jim n nicks cullman
0.8879	borgata online casino

continued on following page

Table 2. Continued

0.8879	yellow claw dj turn it up
0.8878	dosa royale
0.8876	doge the dog
0.8867	hyatt place bayamon
0.8866	accept bitcoin
0.8863	play say something

Figure 1. "Crypto," "currency," "crypto currency," "cryptocurrency" in Google books ngram viewer

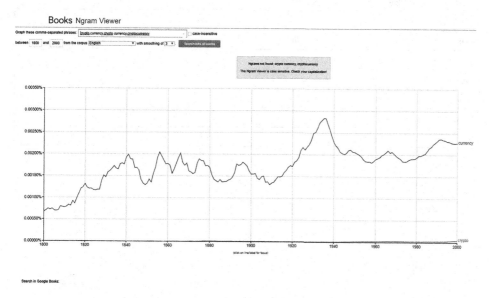

social networks show that trust may be somewhat transitive, with information moving through trust relationships—for a de facto "collaborative filtering" of trust-based information (vetted through subjective logics) (Bhuiyan, Josang, & Xu, 2010).

Two accounts on the microblogging site, Twitter, were analyzed based on a scraping of about a week's worth of messaging from each [https://twitter.com/cryptocurrency and https://twitter.com/cryptoboomnews] The focuses here seem somewhat more idiosyncratic and with an over-focus on local interests (Figure 5).

Table 3. "Crypto" related tags network on Flickr (1.5 deg)

Graph Metric	Value
Graph Type	Directed
Vertices	6
Unique Edges	23
Edges With Duplicates	0
Total Edges	23
Self-Loops	0
Reciprocated Vertex Pair Ratio	0.642857143
Reciprocated Edge Ratio	0.782608696
Connected Components	1
Single-Vertex Connected Components	0
Maximum Vertices in a Connected Component	6
Maximum Edges in a Connected Component	23
Maximum Geodesic Distance (Diameter)	2
Average Geodesic Distance	0.888889
Graph Density	0.766666667
Modularity	Not Applicable
NodeXL Version	1.0.1.336

Figure 2. Placeholder

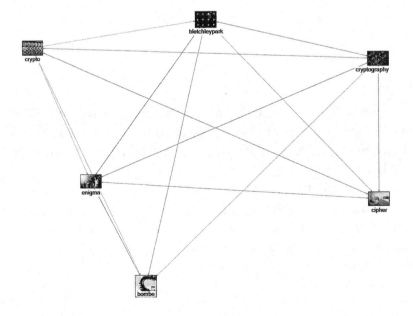

Table 4. "Currency" related tags network on Flickr (1.5 deg)

Graph Metric	Value
Graph Type	Directed
Vertices	67
Unique Edges	1172
Edges With Duplicates	0
Total Edges	1172
Self-Loops	0
Reciprocated Vertex Pair Ratio	0.260215054
Reciprocated Edge Ratio	0.412969283
Connected Components	1
Single-Vertex Connected Components	0
Maximum Vertices in a Connected Component	67
Maximum Edges in a Connected Component	1172
Maximum Geodesic Distance (Diameter)	2
Average Geodesic Distance	1.555803
Graph Density	0.265038444
Modularity	Not Applicable
NodeXL Version	1.0.1.336

Figure 3. "Currency" related tags network on Flickr (1.5 deg)

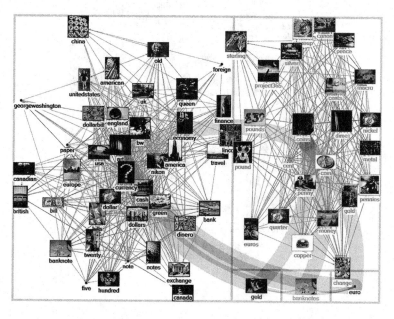

Figure 4. @Cryptocurrencyupdates poststream from Facebook account (https://www.facebook.com/cryptocurrencyupdates/)

Figure 5. "Cryptocurrency" and "cryptoboomnews" from Twitter accounts [https://twitter.com/cryptocurrency]

Then, in the Tweetstream for one particular cryptocoin brand, the messaging seems focused around the commercial aspects of the coin (Figure 6).

In terms of the social networking account, and three microblogging accounts, the top level messaging may be seen in Figure 7 as a treemap diagram and the same data in Figure 8 as a pareto chart.

In terms of the autocoded sentiment analyses of the respective Facebook account, combined two Twitter sets, and stand-alone coin-based Twitter account, the sentiment tends to trend Moderately Positive and "Very Positive" (Figure 9).

ON A NEWS SHARING SITE

Reddit is one of the predominant news sharing sites on the Internet. It hosts a number of moderated sub-reddits on a number of topics. On this site, people can share information, links to articles and videos and podcasts, and they can comment on the shared news and vote them up or down for others' attention. Two subreddit threads were analyzed: https://www.reddit.com/r/CryptoCurrencies/ and https://www.reddit.com/r/CryptoMarkets/. A close-in reading of the 3- 6 days of postings in each list showed outlinks to

Figure 6. Tweetstream messaging from one coin-focused site on Twitter

Figure 7. Auto-Extracted top-level themes from four disparate cryptocurrency-focused accounts on Twitter and Facebook (as a Treemap diagram)

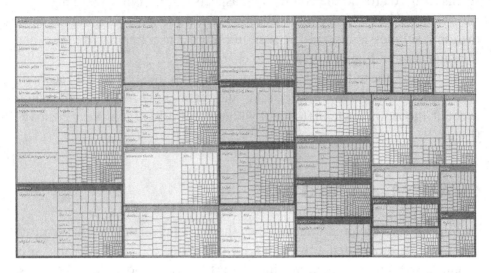

Figure 8. Auto-Extracted top-level themes from four disparate cryptocurrency-focused accounts on Twitter and Facebook (as a pareto chart)

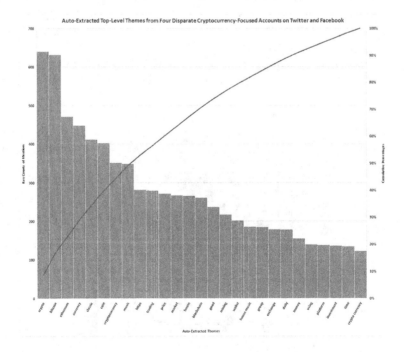

Figure 9. Trending "moderately positive" and "very positive" on combined cryptocurrency-focused accounts on Twitter and Facebook

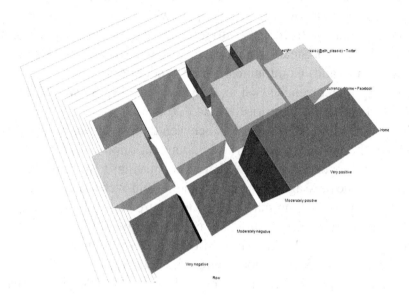

promotional messages and very succinct messaging otherwise. Interactions in which there was a human-created reply and some sort of interaction were rare, with a majority of messaging as broadcast ones (one-to-many). Most of the messages were in English, with an occasional one in Russian or Korean. The social chatter was not socially warm but more aligned with sell and advocacy. Some messages invited going straight to the encrypted messaging app Telegram for private advisement on logistics of cryptocurrency buys (which adds to the atmospherics of secrecy and crypto-appeal).

At the time of the data collection, r/CryptoCurrencies had 57.2k subscribers and 295 online, and r/CryptoMarkets had 164k subscribers and 1.2k online. r/CryptoCurrencies advertised as "The Internet's #1 place to follow cryptocurrencies," and the profile for r/CryptoMarkets read as follows:

FOREX community for cryptocurrencies. Tags: mt gox bitcoin, long term potential, open source exchange, low inflation rate, demand and price, technical analysis, fundamentals, Bitcoin, Ethereum, Litecoin, Monero, Dash, Augur, token, volume, oscillator, RSI, stochastic, trend, sentiment, strategy, scam, coin, coinmarketcap, altcoin, Peercoin, script, blockchain, PoW, PoS, Proof of Work,

The focus of this latter subreddit is about standards setting and support. The ten posted rules for the r/CryptoMarkets subreddit reads: "Obey the Golden Rule & Maintain Decorum, No Spam, No Manipulation, No Low Quality Content, Do Not Incite Illegal Activities or Beg, Do Not Reveal Personal Information, Do Not Steal Content, Keep Discussions o Topic, Use Suitable Titles & Flairs, (and) Communicate With Moderators."

The r/Crypto/Currencies/ set is comprised of 111,883 words, and the r/CryptoMarkets/ one is comprised of 34,320 words.

There were some crossover posts between the two news sharing lists. On the whole, the messages were mostly about sell, and only a rare message addressed cryptocurrency scams. There were outlinks to multiple videos and one podcast. The messaging was mostly global and Web scale. The combined summary-level messaging may be seen in Figures 10 and 11.

To see how each of the subreddits fared in terms of top-level topics, the linegraph in Figure 12 shows the differences. For comparison, in one, r/CryptoCurrencies/ focused more shares on "android," "game," and "users" in one, and r/CryptoMarkets/ had more talk of "assets," "crypto," "market," "price," and "token."

In terms of autocoded sentiment, both showed bumps on "Moderately Positive." (Figure 13)

The first subreddit had more focus on sell, and the latter had more of an objective information focus.

Figure 10. Auto-extracted themes and related subthemes from the two cryptocurrency news sharing subreddits (on Reddit) (treemap diagram)

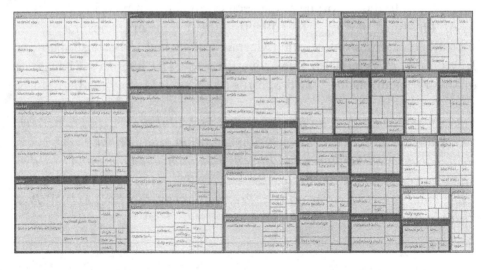

Figure 11. Auto-extracted themes from the two cryptocurrency news sharing subreddits (on Reddit) (pareto chart)

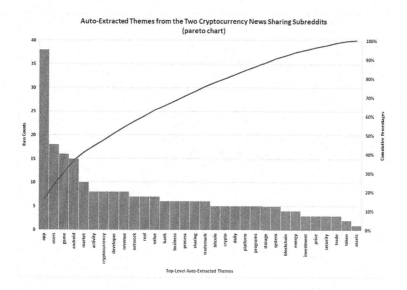

Figure 12. Auto-Extracted Themes from the two cryptocurrency news sharing subreddits (on Reddit) (line graph)

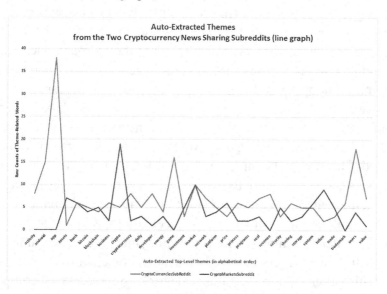

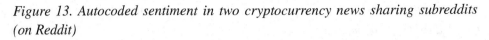

Figure 13. Autocoded sentiment in two cryptocurrency news sharing subreddits (on Reddit)

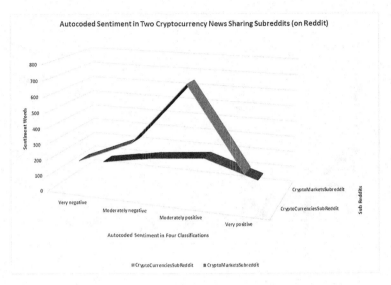

CRYPTOCURRENCY EHM IN SOCIAL IMAGERY

Social imagery may also be informative in this cryptocurrency space. A search for "cryptocurrency" on Google Images resulted in the following image tags: blockchain; top, christmas, cake; portfolio, regulation, name, design, bank, art; periodic table; app, comic, fact, poster, facebook, news; ico; volatility; mining, trade, shopping; price, graph, logo, symbol, icon, market; brochure, usage, investing, rating, education, template; business card, banner; bitcoin price; infographic, quote, cartoon; forex; cheat sheet; use case, mind map, flow chart; road map; profit; landing page; website, illustration, trend, transaction, security, definition; dashboard; coin, gold; happy new year; introduction, risk, payment, feature, brand; exchange; wallpaper; stock, market cap; word cloud; apa itu; wallet; google; nem; arbitrage; india, china, malaysia, africa, australia, russia; legality; process, flyer, technology, setup, statistics, book; hack; altcoin; ticker; rainmeter; ledger; mining machine; zcash; aureus; sign, characteristic, platform, conference, event, development; broker; pepe; dollar; urdue; ripple, ethereum; crash; moon; category, growth, history, comparison, timeline, benefit; verge; physical; atc; bill gates, Richard branson; token; disadvantage; humor; litecoin, digital currency, dogecoin; decentralized, money, network, architecture; lcf; millionaire; revolution; different; mobile, game, collage, training; background image, clipart; popular; animated gif;

vector, algorithm; bubble; desktop background; explained; cover photo; cat; pro con; black, green; advantage disadvantage; overview; onecoin; code; ecosystem; header; work top volume; top ten; dummy; node; global; future, landscape, universe; king; anonymous.

A screenshot of some of the scraped images may be seen in Figures 14 and 15. The first figure is shown with an older version of the clustered tags, and the tags above are from the latter image set. Figure 16 shows a zoomed-out view of the more recent image set.

The initial image set capture is comprised of 432 images, which were manually coded for messaging about cryptocurrencies. This set contained images of coins burnished to a digital sheen, futuristic images of outer space, floating digital locks to convey security, images of bulging bags of money and money falling from the sky, and images of branded cryptocurrency coins. Part of the image set may be seen in Figure 17. This set was scraped based on the algorithms that Google uses for returning images based on a text search. Of the 432, 25 were shown as not directly related to the topic and were not coded.

Social Image Messaging Around Cryptocurrencies

A vast majority of the decontextualized images convey optimistic messages about cryptocurrencies (Figure 18).

Figure 14. Screenshot of the Google image search for "cryptocurrency"

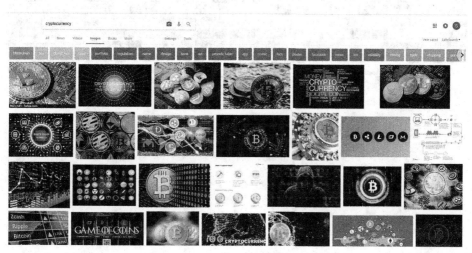

Figure 15. Updated "cryptocurrency" search on Google search

Figure 16. Zoomed-Out view screenshot of the Google image search for "cryptocurrency"

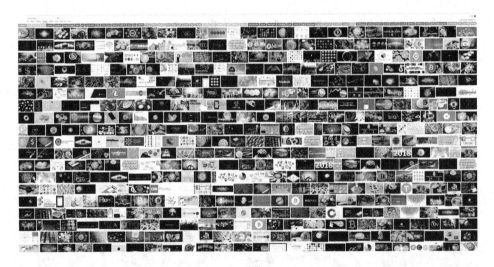

Figure 17. Social imagery related to cryptocurrency (432 Images)

Figure 18. Direct and indirect messaging about cryptocurrencies in social image set

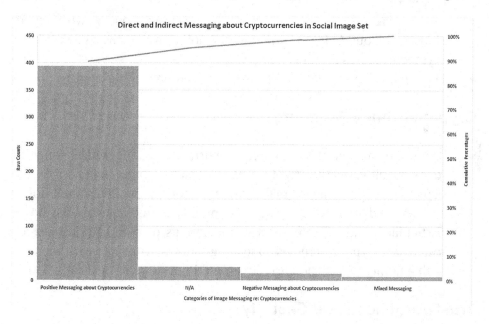

- **Positive Messaging:** In terms of positive messaging, they include the following:

Wealth and Plenty

- A common message is of wealth (115): cryptocurrency coins and coinage in gleaming piles, floating in the air, flowing out of wallets, posed on computer keyboards, posed next to a gold-plated microchip, a Bitcoin as a moon in a night sky, and a "one hundred trillion" bill from an imaginary reserve bank. A laptop spits out bright yellow (gold) cryptocurrency coins in two images.
- A common motif is comprised of rising line graphs (with arrows pointed off to the right) to show growing value, with time on the x-axis. Sometimes the rising value line is depicted in the design background (7).
- Several images show bags of money with coins (multiple types or one type) (3).
- Some images depict digital wallet s(or physical ones), with crypto coins flying out. One is a clipart one. Another wallet shows a variety of cryptocurrencies in it. (5)
- One image shows a pile of cooked bacon (representing money) (1).

Cryptocurrency Branding

- There are images of various cryptocurrency brands with a range of logos to indicate the cryptocurrency space. Some brand logos are depicted as personages making the victory sign. Individual logos are depicted to promote particular brands or indicate discussion of particular brands. There are also indications of competition between respective cryptocurrencies. One image shows a man facing the camera with a number of cryptocurrency brand logos around his head. (79)

Trustworthiness and Security

- Other messages show how closely cryptocurrencies are linked to the larger financial ecosystem, with multiple stock ticker motifs, in the background usually. Another image shows virtual values in futuristic boards (5)

- Informational graphics and illustrations with text convey a message of understanding for viewers and affirms that they understand how the cryptocurrency system works with public and private keys. Another image is of a money tree to differentiate different forms of moneys, including cryptocurrencies (6).
- One photo shows a handshake between two people (to signify trust), and overlaid over this image is depiction of the cryptocurrency market (1).
- Several images use the visual motif of glowing padlocks (signifying security) floating in a digital environment. Various lock motifs are used. (3)
- One image depicts a related application (app) (1).

Government Regulation

- One image shows cryptocurrencies in the foreground and representations of government in the background (U.S. flags) and also American business (Wall Street street sign) (1).
- Two images show institutions that have roles in regulating securities (the U.S. SEC) and a Thai bank (2).
- Two images show business office scenes, with a message of business as usual (2).

Modernity and Technologies

- Three of the images showed server farms. Another showed a user's high tech work space to "mine" bitcoins in another. One shows computer racks with computer cabling. (7)
- Technologies are celebrated, with images showing various related technologies, cyber, high tech, a digital chain of 0s and 1s to indicate the blockchain; one a mix of phone and digital wallet and a mix of coins (how the pieces and parts might look altogether); algorithms; hacker-sorcerers; node-link diagrams, and others (22).
- There are images of smart phones (with digital wallets pulled up and / or valuations of cryptocurrencies on-screen) (7).

Data Driven

- If data can be a fetish, it is fetishized here, with various common data visualizations (pie charts, bar graphs, line graphs, doughnut graphs, area charts). There are data tables, mixed data tables, common "business intelligence" visualizations, and other suggestion of a data heavy field. Statistics are mentioned in some images, and raw counts in others. Accompanying the data are stock ticker screens. One shows a data table with valuations. (24)
- Two images directly communicate a tie between technologies and data (2). One is an onscreen valuation of various cryptocurrencies on a computer screen.

The Marketplace

- There are screenshots of websites to provide service to cryptocurrency investors, consultancies, legal advisers. There are some screenshots of sites with announced prices. One shows a cursor as an unseen individual clicks on a link (13).
- Some images show a general label for a service or product, sometimes with a brand name and photo (5).
- There are advertisements for wallets, for low fees in cryptocurrency exchanges, an app promising low prices; lots of features for a particular cryptocurrency service; advisement on how to invest in cryptocurrencies, and a sales announcement (6).

Community

- Some images celebrate cryptocurrency miners, as drawn cartoon figures, some represented also with a pick (3).
- Some images show messaging against those who are leery of investing, by labeling them negatively (2). One specifically calls out non-investors as "haters" (defined as "having anger towards everyone reaching success"). Belonging is about investing.
- One image shows a coin linked to a social networking site and the highly recognizable company founder with it and a coin by his head, using personality (possibly building on the billionaire's cult of personality) (1). There is a depiction of a sentient or intelligent coin (one a cartoon

one with arms and legs and holding a candle) (1). The personification makes the coins more approachable and potentially more buyable.

- Multiple photos convey the sense of a large number of users of particular coinage. One reads "more than one million users" (for an apparent bandwagon effect). (21)
- In terms of images with human focuses, there are some: silhouetted figures dancing with talk bubbles of them talking about Bitcoin; human hands (male) forging gold coins from a fire (agency and power and wealth); people in the space (a guy holding up two bitcoins of different types, his face in the background), sort of a vote of confidence; a hand holding a particular cryptocurrency (4). This is not just about inert money but about people engaging.
- There is a photo of a person holding up a hand as if advising or teaching (in the cryptocurrency space) (1).

Global Standing

- There is global inclusiveness through multilingual messaging (in Russian, Korean, Chinese, Thai, and others) (6).
- There are recognizable cityscapes and locations. There are depictions of the urban landscape at dusk. (5)
- One photo shows the Earth and then an earth-sized cryptocurrency coin next to it to suggest global-ness (1).
- Some images indicate particular nations. Several show recognizable flags in the background behind cryptocurrencies (for Iran, for China) (2).

Cryptocurrencies in Action (in Animated Gifs)

- In the set, there were two animated gifs: one showed a bitcoin used to buy a bubble-gum ball from a machine; one showed a bitcoin in the middle with links out to a home, a RIP headstone, a baby, a checkmark and $ (so the bitcoin is at the center of a life for a lifespan). (2)
- Some images show book covers (a guide for beginners, two of an investing bible, one about BTC and crypto technos, a step-by-step guide to cryptocurrencies, one about the cryptocurrency age), which gives a sense of "how to" and information about how these work. (6) These are one of many offers by cryptocurrency sherpas who offer to

help investors achieve valuation heights by selecting the appropriate cryptocurrencies.

- One image showed an apparently posed smart phone with a photo of cryptocurrency coins in front of rolls of USD bills. The phone is on top of real bills in $20 denominations on a red carpet (1).

Cryptocurrencies as Social Crazes

- There are images showing paraphernalia linked to cryptocurrencies, like keychains (1).
- Some photos show various mixes of cryptocurrencies (3), against lush velvety black backgrounds or floating in high-reflectance blue computer screens.
- Some images seem to be from initial coin offerings, such as particular brand-specific types being introduced (like a petro-based cryptocurrency) (3).

Cryptocurrencies as the Future

- There are futuristic depictions of humans and glowing coins, with pictures of horizons, and a futuristic illustration with the word "security" forefronted (5). There are photos of the world as digitally connected, with the sun rising on the horizon.

Cryptocurrency Storytelling

- One image seemed to convey a kind of back story (it showed a robot hand putting a bitcoin into a house, affecting people's lives, in front of a glowing sun, in an idyllic depiction); one showed a montage of a cryptocurrency coin riding into a scene, with images of men huddled around an older model Mac, and a feel of something of a visual origin story (2).
- In some cases, the images were comprised mostly of words or text alone. These include communications about how systems work; questions to answer; explanatory information (cryptocurrency vs. digital currency); "cryptocurrency: advantages and disadvantages explained; "how to tell if cryptocurrency is undervalued" (how to be strategic, how to find a deal, how to get rich); several how to create your

own cryptocurrency notices; "safest cryptocurrency bets"; a statement of values ("cooperation, focus on quality, long-term planning, well-aligned incentives, real usefulness"); "10 things you should know about its bright future"; references to "consortiums" and "certification consortiums" (to feel authoritative—and to "certify" what?); one a text-only identifier for a named exchange; full of promises like "2018 Best Crypto Currencies: 100% Long Term Winners" (assertions that lead to nothing); an invitation to a government-backed initial coin offering (ICO); "easy-breezy ways to create your own cryptocurrency"; labels for articles and blogs and wikis; marketing brochures; "trading strategies"; a security standard reference; "the future of kids and cryptocurrency" (future focus, something with value even for future generations); "cryptodiversification" (to encourage people to buy more of different kinds, to expand the space); "gold-backed" cryptocurrency, and so on. (21) In terms of word-heavy imagery, there are also word clouds (10), indicating the high-dimensionality of the cryptocurrency space.

NEGATIVE MESSAGING

In terms of negative messaging, they include the following.

Untrustworthiness

- In one image, a crypto coin is broken, with sharp edges. In another, a red "x" is drawn over the cryptocoin to suggest it is forbidden or ineffectual. Another has "BANNED" written over a bitcoin. (4)
- Hackers appear in multiple images as well as robbers making off with bitcoin, both indicating risk (2).
- One image shows a thumbs down in terms of cryptocurrencies, apparently suggesting that cryptocurrencies are difficult to turn back into cash or cash into cryptocurrencies. (Decontextualized social images are somewhat ambiguous.) (1)
- One image shows a number of different branded cryptocurrency coins sinking into a whirlpool of water (1).
- Another shows a dropping values linegraph in a side-by-side picture with a cryptocurrency coin depicted to the right (1).

- There are downward sloping lines indicating values loss (but surprisingly little about price volatility) (1).
- In another image, cryptocurrencies are personified as characters gambling (engaging in redistributing market share?) (1).
- In one image, a cryptocurrency miner has an "x" written over him (1).
- A sign reads: "Sorry we are closed" (1).

The images may appear "negative" though, but the messaging may be more objective and neutral in context. For example, the banning of the cryptocurrency miner may be a reflection of a government decision that is being shared on social media.

- **Mixed Messaging**: In terms of mixed messaging, they include the following. These include line charts going up and down, text claiming focuses on both "advantages" and "disadvantages" of cryptocurrencies, bitcoins compared with gaming chips (depends on how one views gaming), puppeteer hands controlling cryptocurrencies (depends on how one thinks of issuers or whomever the hands represent, and shelves of cryptocurrency coins as physical analog objects (to show their realness) but also conveying their actual ephemerality by contrast, and others.

Entities and Egos in the Social Imagery

Examining visuals based on entities (groups) and egos (individuals) can sometimes bring insights to the fore, with social imagery. (Hai-Jew, 2018) In terms of some patterns, the majority of genders portrayed was male vs. female, with a 2:1 ratio. In general, most representations of people were as individuals (12 males, 3 females), and occasional groups (four images with more than one male within and three of mixed groups with both males and females present), with min-max ranges from two to about two dozen. In terms of non—human animals, a few were depicted with unspecified genders: including two chickens, a whale, a shark, a tiger, a monkey, a bird. In terms of inanimate depictions, there was a robot and a smiley face. There was a visual of a deity in another depiction. Visual synecdoche, in which parts of bodies represent the whole, these were mostly hands holding coins or engaged in particular cryptocurrency-related activities, with nine males and one unspecified gender. In terms of depicted actions, people were buying something, holding something, teaching, dancing and talking about cryptocurrencies, and sitting in an office chair with money falling all around. If anything, the messaging seems generally abstract and not particularly focused on people or animals, whether entities or egos.

Mixes of Cryptocurrencies in Representation

A review of the social imagery suggests that two main focuses exist in the image set. One involves engagement with the cryptocurrency space (based on the high number of branded cryptocurrency coinage shown…and also those in which the cryptocurrency coin is a generic unlabeled one). The other most common depiction is of one branded coin, which suggests promotion of a brand; that said, Bitcoin (BTC) is often used as a stand-in for the larger cryptocurrency market in the visuals. When two coins are shown, it is often to show combat or competition. When there are three different branded coins in an image, it is often to suggest a mix of investments. Sometimes, one is forefronted, and the other two are in the background (one "golden" and the other two grayed out). Other brands appear, too, such as those referring to exchanges and wallets. (Table 5 and Figure 19)

MACRO, MESO, AND MICRO PHYSICAL LOCATIONS IN THE SOCIAL IMAGERY

In terms of physical spatial indicators, a majority of the social images did not indicate any particular sociocultural physical location. The next largest category involved the depictions of virtual space, cyberspace, and the cloud, with images of node-link diagrams, glowing high-tech depictions, and cloud depictions in night skies over city-scapes. The next most common sense of spatiality refers to a state/province or city, most typically, urban areas.

Table 5. Numbers of cryptocurrency coinage in each social image

	Cryptocurrencies in General with a Mix of Branded Coins / Tokens (4 or more)	Three Branded Coins or Coin Brands / Tokens (as the main focus	Two Branded Coins or Coin Brands (as the main focus)	One Branded Coin or Coin Brand (as the main focus)	One Unbranded or Generic Coin (as the main focus) / no specified brand
Social Image Set	100	13	10	165	29

Figure 19. Numbers of cryptocurrency coinage in each social image (pie chart)

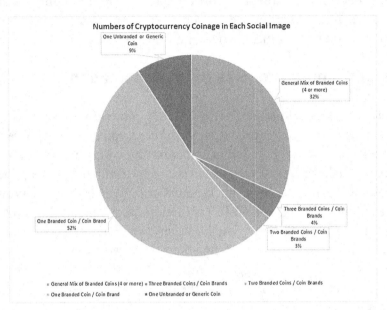

Following that are galactic and even universe depictions of outer space, which is often used as a visual indicator of the abstract future and far horizons. Next, there are globalist and Earth-related sense of space, with satellite pictures of Earth, the edge of space and the Earth's atmosphere, and digital connectivity between spaces on Earth. Then, there is a sliver of references to nation-states, often communicated by the uses of flags or maps in the background behind cryptocurrency coinage or iconic buildings representing federal government. The locational issue communicates messages, and they are of particular welcome to individuals from the physical there depicted. (Rollouts of cryptocurrencies often target particular buyers from particular locales based on targeted messaging and exchange- and wallet- services. As such, cultural and geographical spaces are not just incidental sorts of visual information.) (Figure 20)

DISCUSSION

This work explored three hypotheses:

Figure 20. Macro, meso, and micro physical locations in the cryptocurrency social images

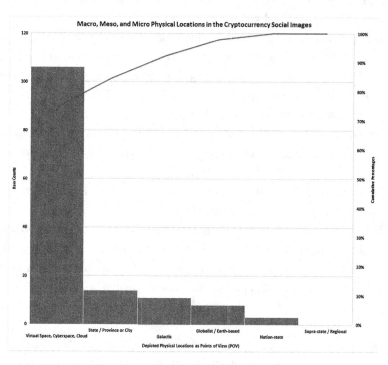

Figure 21. No physical spatial indicators vs. some in the cryptocurrency social image set

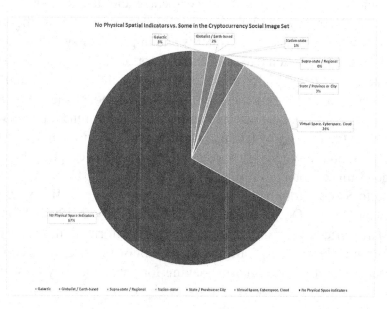

H1: In the electronic hive mind (EHM) surrounding cryptocurrencies, the **social messaging** around such currencies will be strategic and tactical, sometimes baldly and sometimes subtly.

> **H1a:** A majority of the multimodal social messages will be in support of cryptocurrencies (as a reflection of communicator interests).
>
> **H1b:** In formal mass media, a majority of the messages will be skeptical of and questioning of cryptocurrencies because of the lack of intrinsic value and its volatility.
>
> **H1c:** In the academic research space, the respective works will show strengths and weaknesses to cryptocurrencies, based on available and discoverable information.

H2: The **general membership** of the cryptocurrencies EHM may be sussed out inferentially from the social messaging based on stakeholder interests.

> **H2a:** A portion of the cryptocurrency EHM will be comprised of individuals who have little to no background on cryptocurrencies but who are seeking advice and direction as potential investors.

H3: The EHM around cryptocurrencies demonstrates some **executive functioning** in part based on real-world interests.

Hypothesis 1 was generally supported, with the observation of a range of strategic messages around cryptocurrencies, often with a commercial angle (and limited dissident voices).

Hypothesis 1a was also supported, with social news sharing sites showing a leaning towards the promotion of cryptocurrencies and similar findings in scraped social imagery. The latter set showed plenty of glitter and messages of value and future promise, both explicitly and implicitly. Psychology research suggests that people often make decisions emotionally first and then provide a rational "cover story" for having taken that particular action, though, which may suggest that the alluring messaging may or may not be the initial impetus (Harris, Jan. 26, 2015). The social messaging is not deterministic per se, without recipients of the messaging taking on unthinking behavioral roles. There are hurdles to action, including the costs of entry of some cryptocurrencies [at the time of this chapter's writing, BTCUSDs were $6,514 per coin, but had dropped to $4,600, totally a 70% drop from the start of 2018, with a peak value of $19,000 in December 2017 (La Monica, Nov. 20, 2018)] Certainly, people have different thresholds for responding to information, and the glittery come-ons may leave many indifferent and unmoved. After all, people have been recipients of commercial messaging for years and may be somewhat inured and even inoculated.

Hypothesis 1b was also supported with quite a few expressions of skepticism related to cryptocurrencies because of questionable fundamentals (such as a lack of intrinsic value). Running a financial ledger on distributed computers by itself does not make wealth unless people imbue the records with some sort of understood and redeemable value.

Hypothesis 1c, which asserted that the research literature would have both pro and con stances regarding cryptocurrencies, was generally borne out. One of the more dire observations came in a professional podcast with a leading computer science professor:

00:21:22: *…In the recent run-up, I've come to the conclusion that it's no longer harm-limited to a small population of self-inflicted believers. It is spilling out into the regular public… (Weaver, June 2018, as cited in McGraw, June 2018)*

There is research showing skepticism but also the rare wildly enthusiastic paper on the future possibilities of cryptocurrencies within the existing regulatory environment (Dibrova, 2016) and the unbreakability of code and the "completely safe" aspects of the currency? (Milutinović, Jan. – Mar. 2018, p. 108). Various interest groups have other hopes for such cryptocurrencies, such as farmers, who may save on the cost of doing business with "cashless" customers who use credit cards for purchases, in their "high-volume, low-profit business" (Gustafson, Nov. 12, 2013, p. 3). Having less costly "cash for the digital marketplace" (in lieu of credit cards) is another rationale for cryptocurrencies (Halaburda, 2016, p. 1). Some suggest that economic drivers point to a natural evolution to cryptocurrencies (Halaburda, 2016).

Hypothesis 2 was also supported, with a sense of the interests of those in the cryptocurrency space on social media. The main groups seemed to comprise a marketplace: expressive sellers (by a wide margin) and more silent potential buyers (more as a lurking audience). Based on some of the questions posted and responded to, some proportion of individuals do seem to be in the early stages of exploring cryptocurrencies and their potential as possible investors. In terms of indicators of "leaders" and "followers," that dynamic may be seen as informed sellers trying to reach out to potential buyers. There were not signs that people went online to foster relationships and experience camaraderie, except for business ones. In terms of actual named individuals, though, the broad uses of handles and lack of verified personally identifiable information (PII) made that hard to discern. If social network analysis might suggest the possibility of identifying large nodes with high influence (high degree), that network positionality was also not particularly apparent because of the slice-in-time nature of the data (and the fact that leadership often takes time to manifest).

Hypothesis 3 was also lightly supported, with a sense of some executive functioning based on real world interests. The social media posts would be a starting point only to explore, but they should not be the end point of the research. Confirmation biases towards cryptocurrencies (and the resulting digital filter bubbles and human cognitive biases) can be dangerous. A WYSIATI ("what you see is all there is") approach may reflect a naïve mind angle that may quiet counterfactuals and other points of view. For many, the glamor of something "crypto," something they can "own," something that is written into some "permanent" ledger, something that may be a get-rich-quick scheme, may be too much to resist. Even those prone to fact-checking may end up with a set of facts that may not support a clear approach. The varied interpretive lenses of those engaging the information may also affect how information is interpreted or framed. Or the amounts of complexity may be overwhelming and too complicated to engage. The idea of future value is elusive to engage for most. The mainstream population has not been trained nor disciplined to vet investments and so are at risk of uninformed or manipulated messaging. (There are invitations to leave public spaces to communicate on encrypted applications, where various propositions for buying in are made.)

In none of these explorations were there fully formed informal online learning communities. Rather, there seemed to be ways for people to push information in a one-to-many way (broadcasting) and little in the way of actual relating. The discussions on the news sharing sites were rare, maybe with a handful of interchanges more than two or three levels deep. The substance of the communications seemed limited.

In terms of novel and high-value information, none was apparent in the multimodal scraped data from social media platforms. Some of the academic research and the journalism (with the support of fact checkers, in many cases) did reveal some fresh insights. If anything, social media pointed to these various journalistic articles in some cases, and to advertising and commercial messaging most commonly.

While some may think that cryptocurrencies are just an idea whose time has come, the social media messaging suggests a sophisticated approach with outreaches to potential investors based on the glamor of high technology and science fiction utopias, the allure of language ("blockchain," "cryptocurrency," and anonymized ownership, among others), the notional and elusive glitter of extreme wealth and get-rich-quick, and the attraction of feeling like part of a new movement (instead of sitting it out on the sidelines) and a risk-taking mindset.

More important than if cryptocurrencies lose all value or implode from one day to the next is the idea of the power of executive functions in electronic hive minds. Indeed, there may be those that are self-serving, inept, manipulative, and malevolent. Are there checks and balances against such dynamics? Can members be sufficiently aware of what the executive functions in their respective EHMs are speaking into the world? Are there ways to head off such dynamics? Are there ways to detect #fakenews and deceptions and impression management? Are there ways to promote "watchdogs" and "regulators" in such spaces, who would protect the public interest and provide some vetting and oversight in meaningful ways? (Moderators of groups seem to take a stand-back role and protect against personal attacks but not the factuality of posted assertions. If they take on too much of an editing role, they become legally liable for what is posted on forums, based on media law.) Are there types of EHM acculturation that lead its members to be more suggestible and vulnerable to particular messaging?

And even if EHM-level changes aren't made to increase the safety of its members, individual participants may have to take responsibility for their own well being and their own beliefs. However, in this context, a sophisticated bundle of understandings and disciplines will be required. These would include the following:

- A sophisticated foundational understanding of the topic;
- The ability to seek relevant information and separate wheat from chaff;
- The ability to learn from others' mistakes and to see how these lessons and patterns might apply to them in their own contexts;
- Knowledge of human cognitive biases and limits, including their own vulnerabilities ("vulns");
- The understanding of the numerous ways to create "deep fakes" through various digital modalities online (faked videos, faked messaging, faked social media accounts, faked imagery, faked backstopped stories, and others);
- The risks of "filter bubbles" and only learning from limited informational channels with desirable stories that may align with one's desired belief systems;
- Understanding the individuals in the social ecosystems and their interests, intentions, and methods;

- The ability to inure against manipulation by identifying these and resisting them;
- A willingness to hypothesize and test beliefs in the world, with a search for disconfirming information to one's ideas;
- Ruthless self discipline to follow through on what he / she knows to be true even if there are alluring in-world bedazzlements and allurements, and
- Other efforts…in a world with high competition for attention and effort.

It would be unreasonable to expect people to acquire these skills and understandings for all issues that may affect their lives, or actually, even for a few small issues that may affect their lives. The world is a complex place, and people often fail to register that they are Ground Zero for relevancies in their world, and they have a deep responsibility to themselves and to others to make the best decisions and to not compromise themselves.

As noted in a caveat earlier, this work is an exploratory one, with some suggestive findings, only, given the limits of the amounts of data collection and methods. While the author had initially conceptualized more of a sense of community around these issues, those aspects did not come to the fore. There was not much in the way of people's social presences or personalities or backgrounds. There was bald outreaches to sell but not even a semblance of care for others. The messaging seemed to be broadcast and less so narrowcast (few-to-few or one-to-one), except maybe offlist or on private channels. Social networking sites seemed to have a little more of a sense of relating, but not much.

FUTURE RESEARCH DIRECTIONS

Online, any number of narratives about cryptocurrencies proliferate. At present, it is unclear what the main impetuses are driving the popularization of cryptocurrencies for the mass publics except some combination of "greed and fear." Digital gold seems to mesmerize with the faux shimmer. Does the buying / holding / trading / selling of cryptocurrencies vary based on the shared messaging of electronic hive minds? Do EHMs have a macro-level influence on various financial markets? At any one time, multiple meta-narratives are being engaged, and what consumers of information choose to perceive and believe depends in large part on who there are and what they perceive their interests to be. [As a side note, it does seem that people will explore online to answer questions they have about their lives (sometimes like consulting a magic 8 ball toy). Indeed, there are online oracle sites for people's decision making (by some algorithm or pseudo-random answer generator)]. Perhaps such personal financial decisions may be better addressed with professional advisors with formal training and professional ethics to guide advisement.

To recap, the "executive function" of an electronic hive mind deals with the aspects of learning, decision making, and action taking. This involves knowing the following:

- How information is collected, processed, and vetted,
- How choices are made singly, in small groups, and as a whole,
- How related actions are taken, and
- How those actions are understood and vetted

It is generally thought that different EHMs evolve different executive functioning, including those that may be quite different than what was seen here in a lightly explored cryptocurrency EHM. Exploring how these various executive functions emerge, develop, change (and improve), decay, and so on, would be of research interest. In the one example explored here, the EHM around cryptocurrencies based on several social media platforms, the executive function seemed diffuse and informed by stakeholders with varying self-interests. The information shared did not seem particularly objective but more based on self-interest.

An Informational Executive Function?

Of course, there are other ways to conceptualize an executive function of a collective. Researchers have applied the cognitive load theory to human thinking, and they suggest that what has been encoded into long-term memory informs the working memory, and the schemata may act as a "central executive" that organizes ideas in the working memory. This concept has applications to electronic hive minds as a kind of latent historical executive function. First:

Working memory has no known limitations when dealing with information retrieved from long-term memory (Ericsson and Kintsch, 1995; Sweller, 2003, 2004). In effect, long-term memory alters the characteristics of working memory. Long-term memory holds cognitive schemata that vary in their degree of complexity and automation...In this sense, schemata can act as a central executive, organizing information or knowledge that needs to be processed in working memory (van Merriënboer & Sweller, June 2005, pp. 148 - 149)

In a collective EHM, the cognitive focus of the EHM may depend on what is seen as selectively sufficiently important to be remembered and therefore organized as relevant into working memory (e.g. what the EHM pays attention to as a live issue). This idea of an executive function from what has been encoded into long-term memory is more indirect and latent, and this depends on historically valued ideas and collective memories. This also depends on what the respective social platforms enable as "memory."

Over time, such historical influences may become invisible, even while influencing working memory focuses (what is top-of-mind), inherited worldviews, heuristics or rules-of-thumb, values, habits, practices, and other hand-me-downs. The history will inform culture. It will inform the "authorizing environment" about what actions members should or should not take; it will suggest some actions as being preferable over others. That "memory" will define which members are desirable and what features of the membership are desirable. In some cases, that sense of history may define in-groups (belongingness) and out-groups (others). This history may inform on the types of leaders that would be followed and respected and raised up. It may inform which types of spinoff groups are encouraged and supported. Some of the prior are encoded formally into memes and rules; most are passed along in the ether in informal and even subconscious ways. In many cases, the past may be mythologized, informed by fictions and imaginations more than facts.

The evolved and semi-directed histories of the EHM will likely result in certain selection of information sourcing and resultant non-sourcing in other ways. In the transmission (think "serial reproduction" or the "phone game" between individuals and groups, even via ICT-enabled intercommunications), many of the details and nuances, the luster and shimmer, disappear. Mistakes are introduced and reproduced, particularly in public spaces where there may not be a focus on accuracy or fidelity but on convenience and speed and social agreement. Simplicity replaces complexity. Newcomers who come into the EHM at a particular time—especially if they are ahistorical, incurious, and non-exploratory—will assume that that's just how things are, without considering origins and without considering history (and continuing history).

[The existence of histories depends in part on how much information is made available on the respective social media platforms, the Social Web, and the other information and communications technology (ICT) systems. It also depends on selectivity of information and how that history is interpreted and remembered.] They may experience the EHM as it is at those slice-in-time moments based on a number of influences, mostly not visible to them. All to say, the selective history of the EHMs serve as a forcing function, with potential far-reaching implications. In many cases, where people are mostly self-dealing and transactional in their relationships, the collective history is not remembered and not formally codified, and it may drift. Perhaps a few members may step forward to offer their interpretations, and their voices may carry outsized weight and be influenced by their own subjectivities.

Massthink

A lesser assumption has been that individuals in an EHM may fall into massthink, unthinkingness, and suspension of disbelief. Without engaging a critical mind and a cool state for learning and decision making, individuals may be more open to taking on risks. They may engage in irrational exuberance in ways that prior asset bubble manias involved. They may let down their guard and be dazzled by the promise of a gold-filled future and collect points like in virtual games. They may put real resources on the line for a chance at some get-rich-quick scheme or to have a vote in a social experiment in currency. If potential investors and investors take an ahistorical approach to this phenomenon (this time will be different), these decisions may have real-world implications on their lives on the downside. A disaster scenario could go down like past asset bubbles, with an event or revelation that shakes confidence in the cryptocurrency edifice (like a hack or a fraud or insider dealing), and the loss of confidence may cascade, and values may plummet. Mass sell-offs may occur if the bottom hasn't fallen out right away, and many will be left with cryptocoins with 0 value, in the rush to the exits. The value will dissipate into the ether, on a permanent digital chain, for all to see. This review of the messaging on multiple social media platforms around this topic suggests that the majority of the messaging is positive toward cryptocurrencies, and not without ulterior motives. Those who need counter-balancing messages against the crypto-craze will have to look to some investigative journalistic pieces and some academic analyses.

About Research Methods

The research method applied here involved selecting a topic that is contemporaneous, time-relevant, and high-effect in the world, but also not fully defined or understood or known, so existing in a context of uncertainty. It involved drawing information from the academic literature and journalism to set a baseline of understanding about the topic. Then multiple types of data were extracted from social media platforms: text, image, and multimodal data, and these were analyzed in a bottom-up coded way through both manual coding and autocoding. The content analysis involved using the topic as a frame from which to understand the contents. The focus was on "actionable" information shared online, to spark people to particular desirable behaviors. It was assumed that all social actors (egos) in the space were "biased" (in a non-judgmental social networking sense) and had preferred outcomes in the space. There is room to advance the research methods for understanding EHMs, by extending data collection to N = all (for particular time periods) and capturing other data beyond "convenience sample" social media residua (such as going with elicited information, such as through surveys, interviews, focus groups, and others). It may help to elicit some feedback information from those who may have used information from an EHM to make investment decisions and to better understand their experiences and outcomes, in an ego-based way. This question of executive functioning in EHMs may also be extended through the study of other seeding topics, beyond cryptocurrencies.

This work begs the question of how designed socio-technical spaces may be built to support the EHM's executive function and in ways that benefit the people who comprise that hive mind. Are there ways to promote accurate information and mitigate potential filter bubbles (and cognitive biases), especially in environments of uncertainty? (Valuations are partially subjective based on the available information the valuator has. There may be a range of potentially "right answers" based in part on political-economic-fiscal future-confidence.) The uses of collective intelligence to understand reality suggests an underpinning of facts which may be accessed against which disinformation may be compared (Chessen, Sept. 7, 2017). Are there ways to encourage cool analytical state decision making? Are there ways to encourage understandings of uncertainty and risk that better align with reality and baselines? Are there ways to encourage community and other-care and not just the promotion of self-interest? Are there ways to bring to light the EHM's meta-narratives and the resultant blind spots (the unspeakable messages that the community will not accept or even consider)? If charismatic personality appeals are in play, are there ways to help members avoid the trap of the "immersive parasocial" and one-directional faux relationships Hai-Jew, S. (Sept. 2009) that may result in various forms of advantage-taking? (Think "catfishing," think "ghosting.") Are there ways to maintain awareness even when coverage by mainstream medias do not enable continuing coverage of relevant issues? Are there ways to encourage real-world thinking while understanding the value of people's imaginations and abilities to conjure possible futures?

Finally, it may help to consider some early theorizing. It may be that different EHMs manifest in different ways for different topics. It is also assumed that different social media platforms and their incentives will affect how people use them and how they present socially (and perform socially) on them.

CONCLUSION

People socialize and collaborate around shared topical interests (not individual self-interests), and they tend to be purposeful when engaging in social ways. They co-create or co-evolve norms and shared cultures, around which they engage thinkingly or unthinkingly. They have implied social contracts in their interactions. In these interactions, they express various individual and shared values. Some will rise to leadership and promote a sense of executive functioning. Or a sense of executive functioning may emerge from the inter-communications and the affordances of the socio-technical tools. Or executive functioning may arise from other factors and mixes of factors. The residua from social media, the digital desiderata, may be suggestive of hidden hands (*sub rosa* influencers), but they alone cannot really settle the questions sensibly because there is noise, and there are allurements.

Socially, in marketplaces, people collaborate around shared understandings of value. This occurs around coherent currencies. In a more volatile sense, this occurs around cryptocurrencies (digital claims of value), around which there may be no objective stable markers of value. [As a case in point, the author was in a computer lab during part of the writing of this work, and she struck up a conversation with a graduate student in the same lab on a weekend. The student started talking about cryptocurrencies he was buying and how much money he had made in his "day-trading" approach. This was in a year that BTC values fell approximately 70 – 80%. In early 2019, Bitcoin was "no longer worth the mining cost" (Gibson, Jan. 25, 2019).

However, other news suggested some more stable governments were getting into cryptocurrencies and were regulating different wallets.] When it comes to markets (especially cryptocurrency ones), where items of values may be traded, people's executive functioning may be dazzled by faux shininess and the prospect of "easy money" and claims of stratospheric gains. For some, it looks like a game of timing, fast in, fast out, and richer for it and someone else holding the risk. In some cases, it is swapping the real for the fake, the actual value for the valueless.

This work is about how executive functions may become and manifest in electronic hive minds on social media. And while this work is not directly about cryptocurrencies, the seeding topic for this EHM, one of the perennial truisms is that all that glitters…is not gold, and "worst case scenarios" and "black swan events" can and do happen all the time, even if they are not always trumpeted in the press. In any social context, there is a plethora of broken beliefs, hallucinations, false inferences, and delusions. There are manipulations of others based on varying levers of untruths, partial truths, and full truths. On social media, social accounts are virtually costless to create and maintain, as well as videos, flyers, visuals, and other content, to create the sense of cryptocurrency value. Investments into this space may involve in a range of outcomes, but lost funds or mis-invested funds may involve opportunity costs (the money could have been better invested elsewhere). Few would disagree that cryptocurrencies are high-risk investment vehicles, but it is hard to grasp the broad faith in cryptocurrencies even though the technologies are not fully tested, and there is no intrinsic value, and the networks are run by pseudonymous individuals (with no one to be responsible if such currencies tank in value or are stolen). Beyond the insights of executive functions in EHMs, it is *caveat emptor* in all aspects—the sense making and decision making, and the various entrancing attractions online and offline.

REFERENCES

Adhami, S., Giudici, G., & Martinazzi, S. (2018). Why do businesses go crypto? An empirical analysis of initial coin offerings. *Journal of Economics and Business*, 1–12. (in press)

Alessandretti, L., ElBahrawy, A., Aiello, L.M., & Baronchelli, A. (2018, May 23). *Machine learning the cryptocurrency market*. arXiv. 1 – 20.

Alexander, D. (2019, Feb. 4). Technology: Crypto CEO dies holding only passwords that can unlock millions in customer coins. *Bloomberg*. Retrieved Feb. 11, 2019, from https://www.bloomberg.com/news/articles/2019-02-04/crypto-exchange-founder-dies-leaves-behind-200-million-problem

Alternative currencies fall prey to hackers and malware. (2014, Mar.). In *Computer Fraud & Security*. Elsevier.

Anyfantaki, S., Arvanitis, S., & Topaloglou, N. (2018, Apr.). *Diversification, integration and cryptocurrency market.* Working paper 244. Bank of Greece. Eurosystem.

Bariviera, A. F. (2017). The inefficiency of Bitcoin revisited: A dynamic approach. *Economics Letters, 161,* 1–4. doi:10.1016/j.econlet.2017.09.013

Bech, M. L., & Garratt, R. (2017, Sept.). Central bank cryptocurrencies. *BIS Quarterly Review,* 55 - 70. Retrieved Nov. 1, 2018, from https://www.bis.org/publ/qtrpdf/r_qt1709f.htm

Beer, C., & Weber, B. (2015). Bitcoin—the promise and limits of private innovation in monetary and payment systems. *Monetary Policy and the Economy,* 53 – 66. Retrieved Oct. 27, 2018, from https://papers.ssrn.com/sol3/papers.cfm?abstract_id=2556800

Benaim, M. (2018). From symbolic values to symbolic innovation: Internet-memes and innovation. *Research Policy, 47*(5), 901–910. doi:10.1016/j.respol.2018.02.014

Bhuiyan, T., Josang, A., & Xu, Y. (2010). Managing trust in online social networks. In B. Furht (Ed.), Handbook of Social Network Technologies and Applications (pp. 471 – 496). Academic Press. doi:10.1007/978-1-4419-7142-5_22

Bjordal, A. & Opdahl, E. (2017, Autumn). *Portfolio optimization in the cryptocurrency market.* Norwegian School of Economics.

Böhme, R., Christin, N., Edelman, B., & Moore, T. (2015, Spring). Bitcoin: Economics, technology, and governance. *The Journal of Economic Perspectives, 29*(2), 213–238. doi:10.1257/jep.29.2.213

Bouri, E., Gupta, R., & Roubaud, D. (2018, June). *Herding behaviour in the cryptocurrency market.* University of Pretoria. Department of Economics Working Paper Series.

Bouri, E., Molnár, P., Azzi, G., Roubaud, D., & Hagfors, L. I. (2017). On the hedge and safe haven properties of Bitcoin: Is it really more than a diversifier? *Finance Research Letters, 20*, 192–198. doi:10.1016/j.frl.2016.09.025

Brandvold, M., Molnár, P., Vagstad, K., & Valstad, O. C. A. (2015). Price discovery on Bitcoin exchanges. *Journal of International Financial Markets, Institutions and Money, 36*, 18–35. doi:10.1016/j.intfin.2015.02.010

BTC-e. (2018, Oct. 23). In *Wikipedia*. Retrieved Oct. 25, 2018, from https://en.wikipedia.org/wiki/BTC-e

Caporale, G., & Plastun, A. (2018, Jan.). *Price overreactions in the cryptocurrency market*. German Institute for Economic Research (DIW Berlin). Discussion Papers. 1718. Retrieved from www.econstor.eu

Caporale, G. M., Gil-Alana, L., & Plastun, A. (2017, Dec.). *Persistence in the cryptocurrency market*. Discussion Paper 1703. Deutsches Institut für Wirtschaftsforschung (DIW), Berlin.

Caporale, G. M., & Plastun, A. (2017). *The day of the week effect in the crypto currency market. DIW Discussion Papers, No. 1694. Deutsches Institut für Wirtschaftsforschung*. Berlin: DIW.

Carrick, J. (2016). Bitcoin as a complement to emerging market currencies. *Emerging Markets Finance & Trade*, 1–14.

Castronova, E. (2005). *Synthetic Worlds: The Business and Culture of Online Games*. Chicago: The University of Chicago Press.

Cheah, E.-T., & Fry, J. (2015). Speculative bubbles in Bitcoin markets? An empirical investigation into the fundamental value of Bitcoin. *Economics Letters, 130*, 32–36. doi:10.1016/j.econlet.2015.02.029

Cheah, E.-T., Mishra, T., Parhi, M., & Zhang, Z. (2018). Long memory interdependency and inefficiency in Bitcoin Markets. *Economics Letters, 167*, 18–25. doi:10.1016/j.econlet.2018.02.010

Chessen, M. (2017, Sept. 7). Collective intelligence: Fighting online propaganda with a new, 21st century institution of democracy. *Medium*. Retrieved Feb. 25, 2019, from https://medium.com/artificial-intelligence-policy-laws-and-ethics/collective-intelligence-90b55e160cf2

Cocco, L., Concas, G., & Marchesi, M. (2014). *Using an artificial financial market for studying a cryptocurrency market*. arXiv. 1 – 13.

Cohen, A., & Nissim, N. (2018). Trusted detection of ransomware in a private cloud using machine learning methods leveraging meta-features from volatile memory. *Expert Systems with Applications, 102,* 158–178. doi:10.1016/j. eswa.2018.02.039

Colianni, S., Rosales, S., & Signorotti, M. (2015). *Algorithmic trading of cryptocurrency based on Twitter sentiment analysis.* CS229 Project.

Comm, J. (2018, June 28). What are the worst Bitcoin losses ever? Cautionary tales of Bitcoin losses. *Inc.* Retrieved Oct. 30, 2018, from https://www.inc. com/joel-comm/who-is-bitcoins-biggest-loser.html

Cypherpunk. (2018, Sept. 18). In *Wikipedia.* Retrieved Oct. 31, 2018, from https://en.wikipedia.org/wiki/Cypherpunk

Dastgir, S., Demir, E., Downing, G., Gozgor, G., & Lau, C.K.M. (2018). The causal relationship between Bitcoin attention and Bitcoin returns: Evidence from the Copula-based Granger causality test. *Finance Research Letters,* 1 – 5. (in press)

DesJardins, J. (2017, Oct. 26). *All of the world's money and markets in one visualization.* Retrieved Oct. 31, 2018, from http://money.visualcapitalist. com/worlds-money-markets-one-visualization-2017/

Dibrova, A. (2016). Virtual currency: New step in monetary development. *Procedia: Social and Behavioral Sciences, 229,* 42–49. doi:10.1016/j. sbspro.2016.07.112

Drozd, O., Lazur, Y., & Serbin, R. (2017). Theoretical and legal perspective on certain types of legal liability in cryptocurrency relations. *Baltic Journal of Economic Studies, 3*(5), 221–228. doi:10.30525/2256-0742/2017-3-5-221-228

Dwyer, G. P. (2015). The economics of Bitcoin and similar private digital currencies. *Journal of Financial Stability, 17,* 81–91. doi:10.1016/j. jfs.2014.11.006

Dyhrberg, A. H. (2016). Bitcoin, gold and the dollar—A GARCH volatility analysis. *Finance Research Letters, 16,* 85–92. doi:10.1016/j.frl.2015.10.008

Dyhrberg, A. H. (2016). Hedging capabilities of bitcoin. Is it the virtual gold? *Finance Research Letters, 16,* 139–144. doi:10.1016/j.frl.2015.10.025

Efficient market. (2018). In *Business Dictionary.* Retrieved Nov. 3, 2018, from http://www.businessdictionary.com/definition/efficient-market.html

ElBahrawy, A., Alessandretti, L., Kandler, A., Pastor-Satorras, R., & Baronchelli, A. (2017). *Evolutionary dynamics of the cryptocurrency market.* arXiv. 1 – 16.

Fortinet Threat Landscape Report. (2018, June). *Computer Fraud & Security,* 4.

Foteinis, S. (2018, Feb. 7). Bitcoin's alarming carbon footprint. Correspondence. *Nature.* Retrieved Oct. 30, 2018, from https://www.nature.com/articles/d41586-018-01625-x

Frankel, M. (2018, Mar. 16). How many cryptocurrencies are there? Bitcoin, Ethereum, and Ripple are just the beginning. *The Motley Fool.* Retrieved Nov. 3, 2018, from https://www.fool.com/investing/2018/03/16/how-many-cryptocurrencies-are-there.aspx

Fry, J., & Cheah, E.-T. (2016). Negative bubbles and shocks in cryptocurrency markets. *International Review of Financial Analysis,* 47, 343–352. doi:10.1016/j.irfa.2016.02.008

Gandal, N., & Halaburda, H. (2014). *Competition in the cryptocurrency market.* Bank of Canada Working Paper, No. 2014-33. Ottawa: Bank of Canada.

Gandal, N., & Halaburda, H. (2016). *Can we predict the winner in a market with network effects? Competition in cryptocurrency market.* MDPI.

Gandal, N., Hamrick, J. T., Moore, T., & Oberman, T. (2018). Price manipulation in the Bitcoin ecosystem. *Journal of Monetary Economics,* 95, 86–96. doi:10.1016/j.jmoneco.2017.12.004

Gibson, K. (2019, Jan. 25). Bitcoin no longer worth the mining cost, JPMorgan says. *CBS News.* Retrieved Jan. 26, 2019, from https://www.cbsnews.com/news/bitcoin-worth-less-than-it-costs-to-mine-jpmorgan/

Gkillas, K., & Katsiampa, P. (2018). An application of extreme value theory to cryptocurrencies. *Economics Letters,* 164, 109–111. doi:10.1016/j.econlet.2018.01.020

Goertzel, B., Goertzel, T., & Goertzel, Z. (2017). The global brain and the emerging economy of abundance: Mutualism, open collaboration, exchange networks and the automated commons. *Technological Forecasting and Social Change,* 114, 65–73. doi:10.1016/j.techfore.2016.03.022

Gullapalli, S. (2018). *Learning to predict cryptocurrency price using artificial neural network models of time series.* Manhattan, KS: Kansas State University.

Guo, T. & Antulov-Fantulin, N. (2018). *An experimental study of Bitcoin fluctuation using machine learning methods.* arXiv preprint: 1802.04065.

Gustafson, T. A. (2013, Nov. 12). *Have Bitcoin to burn? Next stop could be the farm.* National Public Radio (NPR). Retrieved Oct. 23, 2018, from https://www.npr.org/sections/thesalt/2013/11/08/243970494/have-bitcoin-to-burn-next-stop-could-be-the-farm

Hai-Jew, S. (2009, Sept.). Exploring the immersive parasocial: Is it you or the thought of you? *Journal of Online Learning and Teaching.* Retrieved Oct. 15, 2018, from http://jolt.merlot.org/vol5no3/hai-jew_0909.htm

Hai-Jew, S. (2018). *Techniques for Coding Imagery and Multimedia: Emerging Research and Opportunities.* Hershey, PA: IGI Global. doi:10.4018/978-1-5225-2679-7

Hai-Jew, S. (2019). The electronic hive mind and cybersecurity: Mass-scale human cognitive limits to explain the 'weakest link' in cybersecurity. In *Global Cyber Security Labor Shortage and International Business Risk* (pp. 206–262). Hershey, PA: IGI Global. doi:10.4018/978-1-5225-5927-6.ch011

Halaburda, H. (2016). *Digital currencies: Beyond Bitcoin.* Retrieved Oct. 24, 2018, from https://papers.ssrn.com/sol3/papers.cfm?abstract_id=2865004

Harris, M. D. (2015, Jan. 26). When to sell with facts and figures, and when to appeal to emotions. *Harvard Business Review.* Retrieved Nov. 3, 2018, from https://hbr.org/2015/01/when-to-sell-with-facts-and-figures-and-when-to-appeal-to-emotions

Harwick, C. (2016, Spring). Cryptocurrency and the problem of intermediation. *Independent Review*, *20*(4), 569–588.

Hayes, A. S. (2016). Cryptocurrency value formation: An empirical study leading to a cost of production model for valuing bitcoin. *Telematics and Informatics*, *34*(7), 1308–1321. doi:10.1016/j.tele.2016.05.005

Hernández, K. (2018, Oct. 26). Is Bitcoin secretly messing with the midterms? *Politico.* Retrieved Oct. 26, 2018, from https://www.politico.com/magazine/story/2018/10/26/is-bitcoin-secretly-messing-with-the-midterms-221915

Hughes, E. (1993, Mar. 9). *A Cypherpunk's Manifesto.* Retrieved Nov. 1, 2018, from https://www.activism.net/cypherpunk/manifesto.html

Hurst exponent. (2018, Aug. 8). In *Wikipedia*. Retrieved Nov. 3, 2018, from https://en.wikipedia.org/wiki/Hurst_exponent

Illing, S. (2018, Apr. 11). Why Bitcoin is bullshit, explained by an expert. *Vox*. Retrieved Oct. 23, 2018, from https://www.vox.com/conversations/2018/4/11/17206018/bitcoin-blockchain-cryptocurrency-weaver

Indera, N. I., Yassin, I. M., Zabidi, A., & Rizman, Z. I. (2017). Non-linear autoregressive with exogeneous (sic) input (NARX) Bitcoin price prediction model using PSO-optimized parameters and moving average technical indicators. *Journal of Fundamental and Applied Sciences*, *9*(3S), 791–808. doi:10.4314/jfas.v9i3s.61

Iwamura, M., Kitamura, Y., & Matsumoto, T. (2014). *Is Bitcoin the only cryptocurrency in town? Economics of cryptocurrency and Friedrich A. Hayek*. Discussion Paper Series A. No. 602. Institute of Economic Research, Hitotsubashi University.

Katsiampa, P. (2017). Volatility estimation for Bitcoin: A comparison of GARCH models. *Economics Letters*, *158*, 3–6. doi:10.1016/j.econlet.2017.06.023

Kharpal, A. (2019, Jan. 8). A well-known cryptocurrency may have suffered a confidence-breaking attack. *CNBC*. Retrieved Jan. 8, 2019, from https://www.nbcnews.com/tech/tech-news/well-known-cryptocurrency-may-have-suffered-confidence-breaking-attack-n956046

Khuntia, S., & Pattanayak, J. K. (2018). Adaptive market hypothesis and evolving predictability of bitcoin. *Economics Letters*, *167*, 26–28. doi:10.1016/j.econlet.2018.03.005

Kimmelman, R. (2018, Sept. 20). Hackers steal $59 million in cryptocurrency from Japanese exchange. *National Public Radio (NPR)*. Retrieved Oct. 23, 2018, from https://www.npr.org/2018/09/20/650079273/hackers-steal-59-million-in-cryptocurrency-from-japanese-exchange

Krafft, P.M., Penna, N.D., & Pentland, A.S. (2018). *An experimental study of cryptocurrency market dynamics*. arXiv. 1 – 13.

Kristoufek, L. (2018). On Bitcoin markets (in)efficiency and its evolution. *Physica A*, *503*, 257–262. doi:10.1016/j.physa.2018.02.161

Kurka, J. (2017). *Do cryptocurrencies and traditional asset classes influence each other?* IES Working Paper, No. 29/2017. Charles University in Prague, Institute of Economic Studies (IES), Prague. Retrieved from http://hdl.handle.net/10419/174222

La Monica, P. R. (2018, Nov. 20). Bitcoin prices keeps (sic) plunging. When will they hit bottom? *CNN Business*. Retrieved Nov. 20, 2018, from https://www.cnn.com/2018/11/20/investing/bitcoin-prices-plunging/index.html

Lahmiri, S., Bekiros, S., & Salvi, A. (2018). Long-range memory, distributional variation and randomness of bitcoin volatility. *Chaos, Solitons, and Fractals, 107*, 43–48. doi:10.1016/j.chaos.2017.12.018

Laskowski, M., & Kim, H. M. (2016). Rapid prototyping of a text mining application for cryptocurrency market intelligence. *IEEE 17th International Conference on Information Reuse and Integration*. Retrieved Oct. 25, 2018, from https://ieeexplore.ieee.org/document/7785775

Leckow, R. (2017). Virtual currencies—the regulatory challenges. *Yale Journal on Regulations: Notice & Comment, 36*. Retrieved Oct. 27, 2018, from http://yalejreg.com/nc/virtual-currencies-the-regulatory-challenges-by-ross-leckow/

Leclair, E.M. (2018, Apr. 17). *Herding in the cryptocurrency market*. ECON 5029 Final Research. Carleton University.

Li, T. R., Chamrajnagar, A. S., Fong, X. R., Rizik, N. R., & Fu, F. (2018). Sentiment-based prediction of alternative cryptocurrency price fluctuations using gradient boosting tree model. *Applied Mathematics of Computation*, 1–9. (submitted)

Li, X., & Wang, C. A. (2017). The technology and economic determinants of cryptocurrency exchange rates: The case of Bitcoin. *Decision Support Systems, 95*, 49–60. doi:10.1016/j.dss.2016.12.001

Marshall, J. (2018, Apr. 12). A nescient investment. Department: *The Texas Orator. Vox Populi*. The University of Texas at Austin. Texas ScholarWorks. University of Texas Libraries. Retrieved Oct. 22, 2018, from https://repositories.lib.utexas.edu/handle/2152/64968

McDougall, M. (2014, Aug.). *An investigation of the theory of disruptive innovation: Does the cryptocurrency Bitcoin have the potential to be a disruptive innovation relative to an existing market?* (Master's Thesis). Edinburgh Napier University.

McGraw, G. (2018, June). Show 146: Nicholas Weaver discusses network security, botnets, and cryptocurrency. *Silver Bullet Security Podcast. Synopsis.* Retrieved from https://www.synopsys.com/software-integrity/resources/podcasts/show-146.html

Meyer, D. (2017, Dec. 5). Bitcoin is a 'toxic concept for investors,' Yale economist warns. *Fortune.* Retrieved Oct. 30, 2018, from http://fortune.com/2017/12/05/bitcoin-dangerous-bubble-stephen-roach/

Milutinović, M. (2018). Cryptocurrency. *Ekonomika (Nis), 64*(1), 95–104. doi:10.5937/ekonomika1801105M

Mt. Gox. (2018, Sept. 13). In *Wikipedia.* Retrieved Oct. 25, 2018, from https://en.wikipedia.org/wiki/Mt._Gox

Nadarajah, S., & Chu, J. (2017). On the inefficiency of Bitcoin. *Economics Letters, 150*, 6–9. doi:10.1016/j.econlet.2016.10.033

Nakamoto, S. (2008, Oct.). *Bitcoin: A peer-to-peer electronic cash system.* Academic Press.

North, A. (2018, Apr. 23). How the tiny nation of Georgia became a Bitcoin behemoth. *National Public Radio (NPR).* Retrieved Oct. 23, 2018, from https://www.npr.org/sections/parallels/2018/04/23/597780405/how-the-tiny-nation-of-georgia-became-a-bitcoin-behemoth

Phillip, A., Chan, J. S. K., & Peiris, S. (2018). A new look at cryptocurrencies. *Economics Letters, 163*, 6–9. doi:10.1016/j.econlet.2017.11.020

Pieters, G., & Vivanco, S. (2017). Financial regulations and price inconsistencies across Bitcoin markets. *Information Economics and Policy, 39*, 1–14. doi:10.1016/j.infoecopol.2017.02.002

Plansky, J., O'Donnell, T., & Richards, K. (2016, Spring). A strategist's guide to blockchain. *Strategy+Business, 82*, 1 – 10.

Rooney, K. (2018, June 7). $1.1 billion in cryptocurrency has been stolen this year, and it was apparently easy to do. *CNBC*. Retrieved Nov. 3, 2018, from https://www.cnbc.com/2018/06/07/1-point-1b-in-cryptocurrency-was-stolen-this-year-and-it-was-easy-to-do.html

Roth, N. (2015). An architectural assessment of Bitcoin using the Systems Modeling Language. *Procedia Computer Science, 44,* 527–536. doi:10.1016/j.procs.2015.03.066

Satoshi Nakamoto. (2018, Oct. 25). In *Wikipedia*. Retrieved Oct. 31, 2018, from https://en.wikipedia.org/wiki/Satoshi_Nakamoto

Sauer, B. (2015, Oct.). Central bank behaviour concerning the level of Bitcoin regulation as a policy variable. *Athens Journal of Business and Economics,* 273 – 286.

Sockin, M., & Xiong, W. (2018, Mar.). *A model of cryptocurrencies*. Working paper.

Sovbetov, Y. (2018). Factors influencing cryptocurrency prices: Evidence from Bitcoin, Ethereum, Dash, Litcoin(sic), and Monero. *Journal of Economic and Financial Analysis, 2*(2), 1–27.

Srokosz, W., & Kopyściański, T. (2015). Legal and economic analysis of the cryptocurrencies impact on the financial system stability. *Journal of Teacher Education, 4*(2), 619–627.

Sward, A., Vecna, I., & Stonedahl, F. (2018). Data insertion in Bitcoin's blockchain. *Ledger Journal,* 1 – 23.

Tiwari, A. K., Jana, R. K., Das, D., & Roubard, D. (2018). Informational efficiency of Bitcoin—An extension. *Economics Letters, 163,* 106–109. doi:10.1016/j.econlet.2017.12.006

Trimborn, S., & Härdle, W. K. (2016, May 20). *CRIX or evaluating blockchain based currencies*. SFB 649 Discussion Paper, No. 2016-021, SFB 649. Economic Risk. Berlin. Retrieved from http://hdl.handle.net/10419/14619

Urquhart, A. (2016). The inefficiency of Bitcoin. *Economics Letters, 148,* 80–82. doi:10.1016/j.econlet.2016.09.019

Van Hout, M. C., & Bingham, T. (2013). 'Surfing the Silk Road': A study of users' experiences. *The International Journal on Drug Policy, 24*(6), 524–529. doi:10.1016/j.drugpo.2013.08.011 PMID:24075939

van Merriënboer, J. J. G., & Sweller, J. (2005, June). Cognitive Load Theory and complex learning: Recent developments and future directions. *Educational Psychology Review, 17*(2), 147–177. doi:10.100710648-005-3951-0

Vlastelica, R. (2017, Dec. 14). Why bitcoin is now the biggest bubble in history, in one chart. *MarketWatch*. Retrieved Oct. 29, 2018, from https://www.marketwatch.com/story/why-bitcoin-is-now-the-biggest-bubble-in-history-in-one-chart-2017-12-13

Wei, W. C. (2018). Liquidity and market efficiency in cryptocurrencies. *Economics Letters, 168*, 21–24. doi:10.1016/j.econlet.2018.04.003

White, L. H. (2015, Spring/Summer). The market for cryptocurrencies. *The Cato Journal, 35*(2), 383–402.

Wren, I. (2018, Jan. 25). *Amid Bitcoin frenzy, SEC warns against risky cryptocurrency products*. Retrieved Oct. 23, 2018, from https://www.npr.org/2018/01/25/580439589/amid-bitcoin-frenzy-sec-warns-against-risky-cryptocurrency-products

Wren, I. (2018, Feb. 22). Iran may follow Venezuela in launching its own cryptocurrency. *National Public Radio (NPR)*. Retrieved Oct. 23, 2018, from https://www.npr.org/sections/thetwo-way/2018/02/22/588080130/iran-may-follow-venezuela-in-launching-its-own-cryptocurrency

Wren, I. (2018, Mar. 1). SEC investigates cryptocurrency offerings. *National Public Radio*. Retrieved Oct. 23, 2018, from https://www.npr.org/sections/thetwo-way/2018/03/01/590076973/sec-investigates-cryptocurrency-offerings

Wren, I. (2018, Mar. 14). Google follows Facebook in banning cryptocurrency ads. *National Public Radio (NPR)*. Retrieved Oct. 23, 2018, from https://www.npr.org/sections/thetwo-way/2018/03/14/593553255/google-follows-facebook-in-banning-cryptocurrency-ads

Wren, I. (2018, May 16). SEC creates spoof cryptocurrency website to warn investors. *National Public Radio*. Retrieved Oct. 23, 2018, from https://www.npr.org/2018/05/16/611742303/sec-creates-spoof-cryptocurrency-website-to-warn-investors

ADDITIONAL READING

Hai-Jew, S. (2018). *Techniques for Coding Imagery and Multimedia: Emerging Research and Opportunities*. Hershey, PA: IGI Global. doi:10.4018/978-1-5225-2679-7

Top 100 cryptocurrencies by market capitalization. (n.d.). Retrieved from https://coinmarketcap.com/

KEY TERMS AND DEFINITIONS

Altcoin: Non-Bitcoin cryptocurrencies considered "alternate" to the main one.

Asset Bubble: The situation arising from a fast rise in asset valuations beyond that justified by fundamentals.

Blockchain: A public digital ledger secured through cryptography.

Crypto-Jacking: The theft of cryptocurrencies through various means, especially malware.

Cryptocurrency: A digital money secured through encryption and other processes.

Cryptocurrency Exchange: A business that enables the buying and selling of cryptocurrencies.

Electronic Hive Mind: A synchronous temporal and informal patchwork of emergent shared social consciousness (held by geographically distributed people, cyborgs, and robots) enabled by online social connectivity (across a range of social media platforms on the web and internet), based around various dimensions of shared attractive interests.

Executive Function: The directing of mental skills for learning, decision making, and action taking.

Fiat Currency: Legal tender with its value backed up by a government (with its resources and capabilities).

Filter Bubble: An isolated mental state which results from being exposed only to ideas that one prefers to hear (enabled by social media that helps filter informational content).

Frontal Lobe: The front part of the human brain where learning, personality, and actions are based.

Hash Function: A compression of data into a shorter format.

Hedging: An action to limit risk.

Herding Behaviors: The individual or mass emulation of others' thoughts and behaviors, often without analysis.

Immersive Parasocial: The illusion of having a relationship with another human being, often a public figure, in multi-perception-information-rich virtual world spaces; a one-way follower relationship that is mistaken for a two-way relationship.

Initial Coin Offering (ICO): The initial public offering and rollout of a cryptocurrency to investors.

Irrational Exuberance: Investor enthusiasm for particular assets that may raise valuations beyond what the fundamentals and facts would justify.

Mania: Obsessive enthusiasms, often on a mass scale.

Massthink: A consensus of opinion among a large population with its individual members not critically assessing the thinking.

Portfolio Diversification: Including a range of financial products in an investment portfolio in order to control for risk.

Pump and Dump Scheme: Artificially raising the value of an asset by sharing false information about the asset and then divesting of the asset once its value rises (and leaving other shareholders to experience the future drop in value).

Serial Reproduction: The passing of information from one person to another (often with misunderstandings and mistakes introduced and passed on).

Social Imagery: Images from the Social Web.

Spillover Effect: Positive or negative effects from one economic context to another, usually in unpredicted or unforeseen ways.

APPENDIX

The appendices contain the various tables used for the coding of the social imagery.

Social Image Messaging Around Cryptocurrencies

See Table 6.

Entities and Egos in the Social Imagery

See Table 7.

Mixes of Cryptocurrencies in Image Representation

See Table 8.

Table 6. Coding messaging about cryptocurrency solidity and trustworthiness

Cryptocurrencies have value (solid and trustworthy)	Cryptocurrencies do not have value (ephemeral and untrusted)	Mixed messaging: Cryptocurrencies have value but these have yet to be fully realized	Neutral on cryptocurrency and trust; focus elsewhere

Table 7. Entity and ego representations in cryptocurrency-related social imagery

	Groups (Entities)	Individuals (Egos)
Animate	Humans: Males: Females: Indeterminate: Mix of genders in group: Non-human animals:	Humans: Males: Females: Indeterminate: Non-human animals:
Inanimate	(entities with personalities which are inanimate) (in groups)	(entities with personalities which are inanimate) (singletons)
Mixed Animate / Inanimate	(like cyborgs in groups)	(like cyborgs as individuals)

Table 8. Numbers of cryptocurrency coinage in each social image

	Cryptocurrencies in General with a Mix of Branded Coins / Tokens (4 or more)	Three Branded Coins or Coin Brands / Tokens (as the main focus	Two Branded Coins or Coin Brands (as the main focus)	One Branded Coin or Coin Brands (as the main focus)	One Unbranded or Generic Coin (as the main focus)
Social Image Set					

Macro, Meso, and Micro Physical Locations in the Social Imagery

See Table 9.

Table 9. Macro, meso, and micro physical locations in the cryptocurrency social images

	A galactic and universe point of view (POV)	A globalist / Earth-based (POV)	Supra-nation-state or regional POV	A national POV	A local (state or province, or city) POV	Unspaced culturally, including cyber as a space, including cloud
Social Image Set						

Chapter 6

Being and a Trolling State of Electronic Hive Mind:
(1) Organically Emergent/Evolved Troll Groups and (2) Created/ Instrumented Troll "Armies"

ABSTRACT

Trolling others, broadly defined as communicating provocative messages (and even threats) online, has been a pervasive part of the web and internet and even information and communications technology (ICT). While many consider trolling a net negative, some do suggest that it provides counter-viewpoints, encourages caution in mainstream participants online, and broadens conversations. This chapter studies trolling as a state of electronic hive mind and being in two main forms: (1) organically emergent, decentralized, and organically evolved troll coalitions for both personal member and group interests; and (2) created, instrumented, centrally supported/funded "troll armies" created for political and other purposes. Through the prism of "trolling," a part of the electronic hive mind will be explored, the pathologically aggressive, angry, aggrieved, and vengeance-seeking side.

DOI: 10.4018/978-1-5225-9369-0.ch006

INTRODUCTION

Mundus vult decipi (The world wants to be deceived) - Sebastian Franck, Paradoxa Ducenta Octoginta (1542)

Trolling is "one of the most talked about issue(s) in relation to the internet in the second decade of the 21st century to date" (Bishop, 2013, p. 28), and it has been seen as an element of the dark side of cyberspace and the Internet along with "cyberbullying, addictive use,…online witch hunts, fake news, and privacy abuse" (Baccarella, Wagner, Kietzmann, & McCarthy, 2018, p. 431). "Trolling" refers to quarrelsome and upsetting behaviors by "trolls" who aim to "distract and sow discord by posting inflammatory and digressive, extraneous, or off-topic messages in an online community (such as a newsroom, forum, chat room, or blog) with the intent of provoking readers into displaying emotional responses and normalizing tangential discussion, whether for the troll's amusement or a specific gain" ("Internet troll," Oct. 15, 2018). Trolling may include "offensive communications, social shaming, cyberbullying, flaming…and other harassing exchanges via the Internet" (Ransbotham et al. 2016, as cited in Bacile, Wolter, Allen, & Xu, 2018, p. 61). These behaviors are in part a result of personality (with "extraversion, agreeableness, and emotional stability" predicting "proactive aggression" and "agreeableness and emotional stability" predicting "reactive aggression") and "aggressive fantasy" (McCreery & Krach, 2018, p. 91).

The term itself comes from a practice in fishing. One research group explains:

Trolling, in fishing, is a method where one moves the fishing lines slowly back and forth, dragging the bait through the water and hoping for a bite. Trolling on social media is much the same—so-called trolls bait others by posting inflammatory lines (messages in the conversations block) or sharing inappropriate content (in the sharing block) and then wait for a bite on the line. The intent is to provoke members of an online community (groups block) and to disrupt normal, on-topic discussions, relationships, or reputations. The motivation for trolling is not to stimulate thought-provoking discussions but to sow discord on the Internet and get a rise out of people simply for the amusement of the troll. (Baccarella, Wagner, Kietzmann, & McCarthy, 2018, p. 435)

A "troll" as "a pejorative term for a disruptor or provocateur" (Meyer & McNeal, 2011, p. 118). Individuals and groups may be labeled based on the types of trolling they engage in, such as the term "misogynistic trolls" (Shaw, Sept. 2014), who harass females. Another description of trolls is as "keyboard warriors heavy on typing and tiny on feelings, they get a zing out of online aggression and what makes it attractive to trolls is the anonymity" (Mali, Jan. 2015, p. 36). The underlying motivation of trolls seems to be malice, with the intention "to aggravate, annoy or otherwise disrupt online interactions and communication" (Binns, 2012; Bishop, 2012a, as cited in Coles & West, Trolling the Trolls..., 2016, P. 233). Traditional forms of trolling suggest that most trolls act "primarily independent of each other, with no guidelines on 'proper ways to troll'" (Klempka & Stimson, 2014, p. 3). Regardless, public online social spaces like the microblogging site Twitter are seen to be "unsafe" and "rife with misogyny and racial violence" and "cyber-violence" (Nagle, 2018, p. 86).

Troll messaging is often targeted to individuals and small groups (narrowcasting) and more broadly to the larger community and publics (broadcasting). Trolls themselves may work as individuals or as larger groups ("packs" or "armies"), with many individual trolls calling for their peers to directly "troll" a target as a way of extending their power. Others will buy access to robots (scripted agents or "bots") to magnify the impact of their trolling and to create a sense of a trolling crowd to the target.

In the same way that tricksterism (cunning deception used against other people) may be observed as a universal in various forms of literature, "trolling" is applied not only to messaging but a range of behaviors that are considered inappropriate on a range of dedicated socio-technical platforms, including dating sites, news sharing sites, gaming sites, immersive virtual worlds, data sharing sites, crowd-sourced encyclopedias, and others. Trolling "can be found in almost every discussion that includes emotionally appealing topics" (Paavola, Helo, Jalonen, Sartonen, & Huhtinen, 2016, p. 100). Trolls are a pervasive presence in online media, and their actions manifest in different ways. Trolling may be subtle or unsubtle (Coles & West, Trolling the trolls..., 2016, p. 234). Online, people can be highly perceptive to the tone in others' messaging (Anderson, Brossard, Scheufele, Xenos, & Ladwig, 2014). The tone in intercommunications may be softened with emoticons for more harmonious and non-conflictual interactivity (Kavanagh, 2016).

The ability to engage online in anonymized and pseudonymous ways is seen as one of the core enablements for people to troll others without direct potential blowback or repercussions (Klempka & Stimson, 2014, p. 5; (Sparby, 2017, p. 86) or accountability. The de-individuation of the self and others may lead to a lack of empathy with others, and without practice "net etiquette" (netiquette), people may feel disrespected and harmed. The culture of "lulz" (or "lols" or "laugh out louds"), the celebration of "transgressive humor" and morally ambiguous humor, encourages social performances online for others' amusement through one's wit and critique and unboundedness by rules(Klempka & Stimson, 2014, p. 10). Some trolling taps into a culture of the "lulz" ("lols" or "laugh out louds" or amusement, including at others' expense) and engages issues through "irony and critique," which may be constructive if it is wielded in an inclusive way with all having voice (Milner, 2013). Certainly, trash talk has long been a part of online culture, along with disses, fighting words, name calling, and threats. Internet trolls are part of an "online subculture" (Klempka & Stimson, 2014, p. 2). They "provoke inflammatory debate for their own enjoyment, aiming to disrupt genuine online dialogue" (Donath, 1999; Herring et al., 2002), as cited in Megarry, 2014, p. 51), and oftentimes, in the same way that people gather around a street fight, other users are very welling to serve as audience members, with some jumping into the virtual fray. Snarkiness may be seen as an expression of wit, for example. On the other hand, the accusation of being a troll is "a severe insult in digital culture" (Gredel, 2017, p. 109). Trolls are seen in a negative light (Coles & West, Trolling the trolls..., 2016, p. 243).

The decentralized "rhizomatic" structure of information networks makes trolling "easy to implement" because "it has no central head or decision-maker...no central command or hierarchies to quell undesired behaviour" (Paavola, Helo, Jalonen, Sartonen, & Huhtinen, 2016, p. 101). The "an oversaturation of incivility in media" leads to the so-called "nasty effect," known as the polarizing effect among online users around issues of risk perception, resulting in less openness to new practices and more reliance of existing heuristics for the respective individuals (Anderson, Brossard, Scheufele, Xenos, & Ladwig, 2014, pp. 375 and 381). To strengthen hardiness against the fear-inducing effects of trolling, individuals need to build up cognitive stores of information about a topic (Anderson, Brossard, Scheufele, Xenos, & Ladwig, 2014, p. 382). The separation of people based on their respective opinions and senses of interests can have very real world effects, such as the inability to collaborate and cooperate or come to consensus.

The trolling actions, including "sexist/homophobic slurs, physical violence, poor grammar, profanity, rude to other commenters/readers, sarcastic or silly, (and) nonsensical/off topic" approaches, were found to lead to various responses, including "humor, approval, surprise, confusion, none, disapproval, (and) anger" (Klempka & Stimson, 2014).

A Contrarian Sense of Online Trolling

An atypical counterfactual approach suggests that online trolling (also cybertrolling) may be considered in a judgment free way (Merritt, 2012, p. 6) to make social commentary. The author writes about the powerful affordances of online anonymity for people to create various identities (Merritt, 2012, p. 112). She explains the potency of non-mainstream points of view enabled by behaviors labeled as "online trolling":

Trolling is not a unique genre of interaction, as humor is frequently used in poignant social criticism, and disruptive behaviors can be used to establish order. I am reminded of the Shakespearean fool, a character that invites laughs and derision, but who uses wordplay, feigned ignorance, and mockery to make insightful commentary and cause even the most intelligent characters to themselves seem foolish. Trolling is simply a new face to this kind of behavior, or perhaps better put, a new iteration of this kind of phenomenon, lacking a face and disguised in anonymity. As we continue to embed new communicative technologies and online communication into our lives, it will become increasingly necessary to understand these kinds of behaviors, their characteristics, and the functions they serve, rather than discount and attempt to abolish them. (Merritt, 2012, pp. 114 - 115)

Here is more of a relativist approach. Certainly, the space is sufficiently broad to argue that the "tenth man principle" (having someone play devil's advocate to think of unthinkable or "impossible" things) may have some validity, and disagreements alone should not be viewed as "trolling." Marginal or outlier opinions may be understood as so far outside the realm of the expected that they can alone cause social shocks and outrages. From a research point of view, though, opposing views may have relevance. "Contrarianism" has an important role in online spaces (Ludemann, 2018, p. 97). While there may be a Volksgeist or "spirit of the people," there is a very present "Trollgeist" or "spirit of the troll" as "a social fact of the Internet" (Ludemann, 2018, p. 98).

In one study, a quarter of the survey respondents had engaged in aggressive behaviors online:

More than a quarter of our study participants indicated that they have engaged in harmful online behaviors such as sending threats and insults in messages, posting aggressive comments in discussions and/or disseminating somebody's private information on social media (Bogolyubova, Panicheva, Tikhonov, Ivanov, & Ledovaya, 2018, p. 156).

They may help broaden thinking on an issue and to break up an artificial or close-minded consensus. Perhaps, the issue is sometimes not what is said but the tone of how it is said (dismissively, hurtfully).

A Continuum of Trollish EHMs?

As defined, an electronic hive mind is conceptualized as "a sentient and potent mass entity with potential for various types of concentrated mass action as well as dispersed smaller-unit actions, among others" (Hai-Jew, The Electronic Hive Mind…, 2019, p. 210), and it is "inclusive of all potential members, no matter what their level of expertise" on the particular topical focus (Hai-Jew, The Electronic Hive Mind…, 2019, p. 211). Electronic hive minds may also be of smaller masses, although sizing is relative anyway on connected communicators at a global scale.

To explore troll thinking and behaviors online, this work conceptualizes the respective troll-based electronic hive minds (EHM) as ranging from those that are emergent / evolved ones (without a central guiding organization or individual) to ones that are highly created / instrumented for particular purposes. An evolved hive mind may be one built up around sarcastic stances around topics of interest by diverse individuals with distributed geographical connections and motivated by both individuals (as social selves) and loosely coupled groups. A created / instrumented EHM is one that is funded and guided centrally, whether as a 'bot army employed for the trolling (and as artificial intelligence "minds") or as people activated by messaging controlled by a central individual or organization (or even government).

This continuum is somewhat suggestive of a timeline in terms of early generation trolling electronic hive minds emerging from collective behaviors (with decisions made at the unique individual levels) but evolving into much more created and instrumented ones, that may have affected whole systems (like voting in a major democratic country). (Figure 1) There is also a timeline aspect to the uses of technologies to advance trolling. The harnessing of robots and scripting to convey particular trolling messages is an advancement. The uses of faked websites and stolen data (from hacking and from phishing) are other advancements. It is hard to say what percentage of trolling EHMs are fully human, cyborgian (partially human, partially automated), or fully automated (scripted robots). At present, it seems like there are some of each, but the tendency is for emergent/evolved ones to be more human-based, and created/instrumented ones to be more cyborgian (with human direction but also some parts fully automated).

To study this phenomenon, several troll-based EHMs that have apparently emerged will be study, as compared to the findings of the predominant current example of a created troll army circa 2016, courtesy of the Russian government (Kremlin). If old school trolling involves purposeful posting of provocative messages "with no obvious instrumental goal" (Buckels, Trapnell, & Paulhus, 2014; Craker & March 2016, as cited in Bogolyubova, Panicheva, Tikhonov, Ivanov, & Ledovaya, 2018, p. 152), more modern constructed forms are not only to ruin reputations, disrupt societies, and throw elections but to change people's senses of reality ("gaslighting") and release broader-scale mayhem. This research involves computation-supported naturalistic observations of various online spaces.

Technologies

The software programs used in this chapter include NVivo 12 Plus, Network Overview, Discovery and Exploration for Excel (NodeXL), some third-party data exporting tools, and others. A range of social media platforms were harnessed as well.

Figure 1. A continuum of electronic hive minds from organically emergent/evolved to created/instrumented (for origination, for maintenance over time)

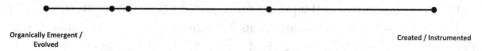

Organically Emergent /
Evolved

Created / Instrumented

A Continuum of Electronic Hive Minds from Emergent/Evolved to Created/Instrumented
(for Origination, for Maintenance over Time)

REVIEW OF THE LITERATURE

The origination of the term "trolling" in terms of disruptive and malicious online behavior is thought to stem from the 1980s, in the contexts of bulletin board systems (BBSes) and UseNet spaces ("Internet troll," Oct. 15, 2018). Internet trolls were thought to engage in unconstructive and even destructive behaviors "whether for the troll's amusement or a specific gain" ("Internet troll," Oct. 15, 2018). Others suggest that "trolling" originated in the 1990s in reference to "disrupting online conversations and communities "by posting incendiary statements or stupid questions onto a discussion board…for (the troll's) own amusement, or because he or she was a genuinely quarrelsome, abrasive personality" (Mantilla, 2013, p. 563). "Trolling" is seen to have become a "thing" starting around 2008, with case studies becoming more broadly public (Bishop, 2013, p. 28).

More Than Nastygrams

While trolling is about the posting of "offensive messages" (Bishop, 2013, p. 28), it goes beyond online incivility in discursive spaces. It includes "Internet abuse and data misuse" (Bishop, 2013, p. 28). It involves harassment ("Internet troll," Oct. 15, 2018). Some trolls engaging in sharing "fake news" and "hoaxes" and "hate comments" (Wagenknecht, Teubner, & Weinhardt, 2018, p. 10). Some impersonate others in order to harm the reputation of the individual. Trolling behaviors involve various forms of deception (Drouin, Miller, Wehle, & Hernandez, 2016), including identity concealment, scamming, information theft, catfishing, and others. Some use faked social media accounts to extend state power through information warfare and the spreading of propaganda (Aro, 2016). Many engage in off-topic messaging and spamming (spreading information widely in an untargeted way).

There are efforts to create false impressions of the world. Paid trolls spread messages to "astroturf" (pretend to be populist "grassroots" efforts) in order to bring certain topics to the public mind (Zelenkauskaite & Niezgoc, May 2017). Trolls are also paid to engage in the online harassment (Bogolyubova, Panicheva, Tikhonov, Ivanov, & Ledovaya, 2018, p. 152), to create a sense of threat or frustration. Another example involves the building of parody-based Facebook pages…"of both alternative information sources and online political activism. Their activities range from controversial comments and posting satirical content mimicking alternative news sources, to the fabrication of purely fictitious statements, heavily unrealistic and sarcastic. Not rarely, these memes become massively diffused and were used as evidence in online debates from political activists" (Ambrosetti, 2013, as cited in Mocanu, Rossi, Zhang, Karsai, & Quattrociocchi, 2015, p. 1199). Once information flows into the public online space, they may have lives of their own based on the uptake by other people and by robots.

In the formal literature, there are some tools by which to understand the intensities of various types of trolling. There is a sense of "Trolling Magnitude" based on four levels: playtime, tactical, strategic, and domination (four levels) (Bishop, Trolling for the…, 2014, p. 169; Bishop, 2012). In the online gaming space, there is a scale for grief play (Ladanyi & Doyle-Portillo, 2017). In terms of extremes, threats of violence and death threats are included in online trolling, and there are a number of news stories that describe spillovers of cyber behavior into the real.

Online harassment affects the targets and others with the "same psychological outcomes as harassment offline, including increased depression and lowered self-esteem" (Feinstein et al., 2013, as cited in March, Grieve, Marrington, & Jonason, 2017, p. 139). Those receiving negative message about themselves or their views tend to experience negative affective responses (Phillips & Smith, 2004, as cited in Anderson, Brossard, Scheufele, Xenos,. & Ladwig, 2014, p. 376). Further, when facing hostile language in online discussions, people may go with cognitive shortcuts and "be less receptive to new information" (Anderson, Brossard, Scheufele, Xenos, & Ladwig, 2014, p. 376).

While people may refer to actions online as "virtual" and therefore something different than "real," those targeted by trolls experience real harms, including "suicidal ideation and self harm among the victims of such behaviours" (Bauman, Toomey, & Walker, 2013; Hinduja & Patchin, 2010, as cited in Coles & West, 2016, p. 233). Online trolling can include "Net-based provocations of suicide" (Niezen, 2013, pp. 312 – 313); the communications can be lethal. Some trolls seek out high-profile cases in the news and take various stances on that issue, even in cases with real human lives at play and the inflicting of real harms, including the case of a missing child (Synnott, Coulias, & Ioannou, 2017). There are real harms from misinformation, public and private harassment, mocking, ridicule, and other forms of others' hostility. The harms go beyond those experienced by individuals. At the macro level, the incivility harms the social dynamics on socio-technical spaces. It lowers the sense of community among people who are sharing their ideas and experiences. It creates negative feelings.

Some Attributes of Trolls

Researchers have conducted various experiments to understand the psychology of those who engage in cyber aggressions. Many trollers are "narcissists, psychopaths and sadists" (Mali, Jan. 2015, p. 36). In a study of university students, those who engage in online trolling behavior tend to have a "sense of inferiority" and also tend to be more active on the respective platforms (Hong & Cheng, 2017, p. 397). Those identified with lower levels of "affective empathy predicted perpetration of trolling" (Sest & March, 2017, p. 69). Those with decreased senses of individuation and personalization may have a "lower level of self-control" and may decrease their sense of care about what others think of them and their actions (Bishop, 2013, p. 29). Those who engaging in trolling are seen to have "a number of similarities between the proposed anti-social personality disorder in DSM-V and flame trolling activities" (Bishop, 2013, p. 28).

While the motivations may come from within human "trolls," the social motivations include perceived effects on others. In the research, certain Dark Triad (narcissism, Machiavellianism, and psychopathy) or Dark Tetrad (the Dark Triad with sadism) personality types are seen as related to trolling behaviors because of the selfishness and lack of empathy for others. Based on established personality inventories, researchers found "trolling correlated positively with sadism, psychopathy, and Machiavellianism, using both enjoyment ratings and identity scores" (Buckels, Trapnell, & Paulhus, 2014, p. 97). As such, "cyber-trolling" may be seen as "an Internet manifestation of everyday sadism" (Buckels, Trapnell, & Paulhus, 2014, p. 97). There is enjoyment in "inflicting psychological pain and distress onto others through exerting negative social influence, power, and strength (Foulkes, Viding, et al., 2014, as cited in Craker & March, 2016, p. 79). For some, the social reward of "negative social potency" is aligned with the narcissism, Machiavellianism, psychopathy, and sadism; "trait psychopathy and sadism predict Facebook trolling" (Craker & March, 2016, p. 79). The "negative social reward motivation" motivates some trolls (Craker & March, 2016, p. 79), which is why the encouragement to not "feed" trolls is important. Sometimes, not giving trolls the "satisfaction" of responding is one way to discourage such behaviors. .

Different psychological traits contribute to different behaviors online:

Analyses revealed openness, agreeableness, and experience seeking as negative predictors of participants' intention to comment uncivilly, whereas attentional impulsivity, boredom susceptibility as well as intense Facebook use emerged as positive predictors (Koban, Stein, Eckhardt, Ohler, 2018, p. 9).

Personality affects different types of posting behaviors. One survey-based study found the following:

Trolls scored significantly higher on psychopathy, online acceptability of prejudiced comments, and lower on agreeableness; confessors scored significantly higher on neuroticism, Machiavellianism, feelings of reduced accountability online, and lower on social moral values. In contrast, lurkers scored significantly higher on conscientiousness and lower on Machiavellianism. (Siegfried-Spellar & Lankford, 2018, p. 54)

Those who tend to engage more pro-socially and constructively tend to be more altruistically motivated (Siegfried-Spellar & Lankford, 2018, p. 54). Personality traits also inform the writing, with particular linguistic features in the messaging by groups with different personality traits.

Some Types of Internet Troll "Triggers"

What people with a proclivity to trolling may respond to may vary. For some, it may be the sense of vulnerability (in the victimology). They may be motivated by ideologies (Zelenkauskaite & Niezgoc, May 2017) or political loyalties, such as state-sponsored trolls (of various nation-states and political identities and political stripes). Racial animus has also been a factor.

Other approaches suggest that anyone can turn trollish with the right conditions (Cheng, Danescu-Niculescu-Mizil, Leskovec, & Bernstein, May/Jun. 2017), not just so-called sociopaths (May/Jun. 2017, p. 152). The thinking is that people all have their cognitive biases and cognitive limits, their different experiences, their different value systems, and emotional triggers (with different levels of tolerances for stressors)—and beyond a certain point, their socialized restraints to rudeness may not hold. Or one person's justice is another person's injustice, seen through subjective (and myopic) lenses. In one experimental study, a person's mood affected their engagement in trolling (p. 152), defined as "name-calling, profanity, racism, or harassment" and as "oneoff, unintentional, or untargeted" (Cheng, Danescu-Niculescu-Mizil, Leskovec, & Bernstein, May/Jun. 2017, p. 153). Some common ideas support this idea, the idea that humans have aspects of their personalities and psyche that feed spitefulness: *schadenfreude* (pleasure from others' misfortune), *hong yan bing* ("red eye disease" or jealousy over others' fortune in Chinese culture), or the "green-eyed monster" (jealousy). People are not always agreeable in the presence of others. Or perhaps in some situations people are trying to practically address social issues and lose their temper and mishandle emotions. Some may be unable to understand other valid points-of-view on particular complex or personal or emotional issues.

Recent research suggests that individuals high in "psychopathy," a feature of human trolls, tend to target those who are popular "more so than of less popular individuals" (Lopes & Yu, 2017, p. 74). Those who are narcissistic, another psychological attribute of trolls, tend to target popular individuals because of their high profile, which may result in their being viewed as competition (Lopes & Yu, 2017, p. 74). The risks of being high profile online are real and may capture the attention of trolls.

Given the wide ranges of trolling behaviors, thinkers have identified trolls by various attributes. One involves the target of the trolling, such as "racist trolling" (Bliuc, Faulkner, Jakubowicz, & McGarty, 2018, p. 85) and "gendertrolling" (involving "coordinated participation of many, gender-based insults" and "including the widespread use of pejorative terms," "vicious language," "credible threats," "unusual intensity, scope, and longevity of attacks," reactions to "women speaking out" (Mantilla, 2013, pp. 564 - 565). Some gender trolling involves support for "rape culture" or attitudes that normalize sexual assault. Some of the trolling statements related to rape culture in social media forums include assertions about law and society suggesting "media reporting bias, discrediting rape culture, racial and cultural statements about rape, (and) gender differences" (Zaleski, Gundersen, Baes, Estupinian, & Vergara, 2016, p. 925). There are themes of victim blaming and questioning and support for perpetrators. There is incitement of hate and ridicule for victims (Zaleski, Gundersen, Baes, Estupinian, & Vergara, 2016, p. 925) and discrediting of rape culture (p. 922). Some research suggests that there is a gender angle to trolling:

Relative to women, men report more frequent engagement in Internet trolling behaviours and higher levels of trolling enjoyment (Buckels et al., 2014) – findings which have more recently been replicated specifically for the social networking site Facebook ® (Craker & March, 2016, as cited in March, Grieve, Marrington, & Jonason, 2017, p. 139).

Another research team observed: "Psychopathy and male gender were the unique predictors of engagement in harmful online behaviors" (Bogolyubova, Panicheva, Tikhonov, Ivanov, & Ledovaya, 2018, p. 151). In some research, the psychological traits (from the Dark Tetrad of narcissism, Machiavellianism, psychopathy, and sadism) were more revelatory:

Although there were no sex differences, the traits of psychopathy, sadism, and dysfunctional impulsivity were significantly associated with trolling behaviours. Subsequent moderation analysis revealed that dysfunctional impulsivity predicts perpetration of trolling, but only if the individual has medium or high levels of trait psychopathy. (March, Grieve, Marrington, & Jonason, 2017, p. 139)

Other types of online trolling may be based on respective technologies. For example, webcam trolling has been described as the "misuse of web cameras to attack other Internet service users" with risks to children of blackmail (Kopecký, 2016, p. 1). With the advent of the Internet of Things (IoT), the possibilities for malicious expression and widespread victimization multiply. There is some early conceptual work on "troller character types" (Bishop, Trolling for the…, 2014, p. 157), based on troll motivations and online behaviors.

These trolling behaviors may include various deceptions, such as taking on others' identities, manipulating others' personal data or "fraping" (from "Facebook + rape") ((Moncur, Orzech, & Neville, 2016, p. 126), spreading gossip, defaming others, sharing #fakenews, sharing disinformation, building pretend relationships ("catfishing" or using fake identities to start online relationships), providing purposefully bad or harmful advice, online vandalism and "griefing" (creating grief for an opponent in a competitive game context or virtual world context), and others. Spite and malice manifest in different ways in different online spaces. For multiplayer online games, "trolling" is defined as "intentionally making the game unpleasant for one's teammates" (Hughes, Griffin, & Worthington, 2017, p. 389). Businesses have experienced harassment through negative reviews from trolls (Salehi-Esfahani & Ozturk, 2018). In immersive virtual worlds, one-sided illusions of relationships with others (as parasocial followership connections) may magnify the impact of others based on the "immersive parasocial" (Hai-Jew, 2009).

Not Defenseless Against Trolls and Trolling

While trolling has captured much public attention in mass media, they do not go unchallenged—by law makers, by law enforcement, by companies hosting social media platforms, by online communities, and others. End User License Agreements (EULAs) of respective social media platforms forbid trolling and harassment. Human-moderated forums enable moderators to mute/ silence/ delete trollish messages. Moderators need to control for intragroup conflict sparked by trolls, especially in non-mainstream online discussion forums (Herring, Job-Sluder, Scheckler, & Barab, 2002). Indeed, "identifying trolls is not a simple and straight-forward task" (Coles & West, Trolling the trolls..., 2016, p. 233). In some online spaces, opinion leaders' perspectives are used to ferret out troll entities (Chiregi & Navimipour, 2016). Some level of peace has to be kept to maintain the functions of interactive spaces, which require cooperation and constructive interactivity. There are social standards for appropriate ways to express disagreement, without name-calling or disrespect.

The creation and maintenance of shared social norms may infuse participants with a sense of the shared values (Bishop, My Click..., 2014), in which their click is "their bond" and a restraint against anti-social actions. Social exclusion is practiced against those who subvert group identity (Ditrich & Sassenberg, 2017). De-friending and elements of gamification may be used to manage "lurking, trolling" (Bishop, Trolling..., 2014).

The communication of "imagined communities" has been harnessed to control for members' more negative impulses and behaviors. For example, the integration of user-generated contents (such as commenting) in online newspapers and other online platforms has enabled trolling, requiring social norms of politeness to be established and enforced (Coles & West, Weaving the internet..., 2016, p. 44). In some studies, trolls are defined as "outsiders" to a community, with the assumption that community members themselves would not engage in socially harmful behaviors. Indeed, banishment or social exclusion or "excommunications" are considered one of the most extremes sort of social enforcement in human communities.

There are clapback memes, such as an image-based meme of "soap for Internet trolls" in a green container. The tagline on the packaging reads: "SMELLS LIKE LIVING IN YOUR MOM'S BASEMENT" (in all caps). Below that, it reads (in sentence case): "Or so we imagine. Perhaps being a troll is a lucrative business? Nah." This meme points to the immaturity of trolls, unwashed and unsocial, and points to the fact that such behaviors are not particularly rewarding. Another shows a green troll in caveman garb, and the text reads: "TROLL MAKE INTERNET MAD. TROLL LIKE ANGER. TROLL WANT PEOPLE AS MISERABLE AS TROLL." Another meme asks, "What's a godly response to Internet trolls?"

The top image results in a search for "Internet troll" show many derogatory messages about them. (Figure 2) The applied tags for this search include the following, all in one category: "anatomy, confessions, hard knock, Michael nuccitelli, infographic, guide, Wikipedia, online, internet slang, psychopaths lucky, (and) social media." These images support the concept that Internet trolls are depicted in mostly negative light. Most of the trolls are visually depicted as male.

Moderators and social groups co-create social norms of expected behaviors, so members may interact in an environment of safety, emotional and otherwise. Some have called online communities to "disrupt negative memetic behaviors so that we can find, create, and seize more opportunities to open the kinds of productive, democratic discourses that online aggression tends to silence" (Sparby, 2017, p. 85).

Researchers have identified two basic types of aggressions online. "Proactive" aggression is considered a "cold" one, and "reactive" aggression is a "hot" one. The first type tends to be goal-based and intentional and instrumental, and the latter tends to be personal, emotion-based, and not directly instrumented. "Findings show that personality characteristics of extraversion, agreeableness, and emotional stability predicted proactive aggression, while

Figure 2. Top-level image search results for "internet troll" on Google image search

agreeableness and emotional stability predicted reactive aggression. Further, agreeableness, emotional stability and intellect predicted aggressive fantasies, and aggressive fantasies predicted both proactive and reactive aggression" (McCreery & Krach, 2018, p. 91). While the authors see cyberbullying and trolling as negative aspects, they also see some positive human features by those who engage in these behaviors. The authors write, "Individuals with Proactive Aggression consistently believe that their actions will result in a socially effective manner of achieving a desired outcome (Crick & Dodge, 1996; Dodge, 1991, as cited in McCreery & Krach, 2018, p. 91). "Reactive Aggression" may "manifest because the individual misjudges social cues after poorly interpreting ambiguous stimuli (Dodge & Coie, 1987; Miller & Lynam, 2006, Poulin & Boivin, 2000, as cited in McCreery & Krach, 2018, p. 91). Rehearsing aggressive thoughts (as aggressive fantasies) may normalize aggressive actions online (McCreery & Krach, 2018, p. 94). This research suggests that self-control is an important factor for restrained and civil behaviors online.

The academic literature depicts trolling in mostly a negative light, but this may not be seen with sentiment coding by machine. A review of the research literature around trolling does not show sentiment (either positive or negative) in the textual contents or in a proxemic word tree around the seeding term "troll." (Figure 3). This means that ratings of positivity or negativity in language were not extracted.

Also, an exploration of human-applied "folk" labels to uploaded images on the Flickr image-sharing social media platform shows a benign sense of "trolls" related to shred social images. (Figure 4)

Researchers have proposed technology systems to rank the trustworthiness and reputations of its users in relationship to their trolling (Ortega, Troyano, Cruz, Vallejo, Enríquez, 2012). There is a researcher-proposed troll detection system on the Twitter microblogging site (Fornacciari, Mordonini, Poggi, Sani, & Tomaiuolo, 2018). In other socio-technical systems, there is automated detection of trolling and the shutting down of some social media accounts. Technology protections are also critical to heading off such trolling behaviors and messaging and to protect users (Bishop, 2012). Socio-technical spaces for human interactions need to be comprised of "more sustaining infrastructure" for communities to grow to lessen trolling (Coles & West, Weaving the internet…, 2016, p. 52). Different "anonymity control mechanisms" were studied for their efficacy on a political news site; the policy-based one was found to not be particularly effective and to result in even increased flaming while the voluntary-based one significantly decreased inflammatory speech,

Figure 3. "Troll" word tree from research text set

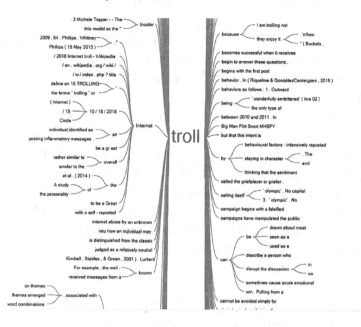

Figure 4. "Troll" related tags network on Flickr (1.5 deg.))

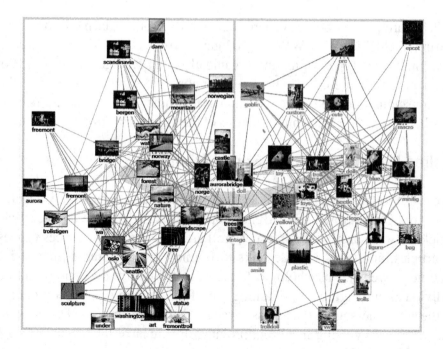

especially "among the moderate commentators" (Cho & Kwon, 2015, p. 363). The researchers studied both "policy-driven regulations, and promotion of voluntary disclosure of social cues" (Cho & Kwon, 2015, p. 365). They found that a policy approach might suppress discussion activities all around, not just trolling behaviors, and participants were more amenable to voluntary interventions (Cho & Kwon, 2015, p. 370).

A majority of mainline social media sites have mechanisms through which to report trollish behaviors, such as harassment. The service providers also have in-house methods to identify the validity/invalidity of respective accounts. A study of the online social climate suggests some main themes, including that "things will stay bad because to troll is human," that "tangible and intangible economic and political incentives support trolling," but also that some improvements may be made from "technical and human solutions" and "community moderation" (Rainie, Anderson, & Albright, Mar. 29, 2017).

ORGANICALLY EMERGENT/EVOLVED TROLLING ENTITIES VS. CREATED/ INSTRUMENTED TROLL "ARMIES"

This research uses publicly available information from social media platforms and the World Wide Web (WWW) and Internet to consider trolling as electronic hive minds, one type originating organically in an emergent way (based on topics of shared interest or other phenomenon) and another type originating in a consciously created way for particular instrumental outcomes. To start, it may help to capture some online senses of the main terms from social media.

Online Definitions From Social Media

The senses of an "Internet troll" are generally linked to some highly negative behaviors. On the crowd-sourced encyclopedia Wikipedia, a one-degree article-article network around the Internet_troll article shows 177 vertices (nodes) or articles, and these include links to flaming on the Internet, pejorative, fake news website, psychological harassment, identity deception, and de-individuation. (Figure 5) ["Flaming" or "flame-baiting" has been defined as the act of messaging the "message sender's hostile emotional expressions characterized by using insulting, profane, or offensive languages" (Cho & Kwon, 2015, p. 364).]

Figure 5. Internet_troll article-article network on Wikipedia (1 deg.)

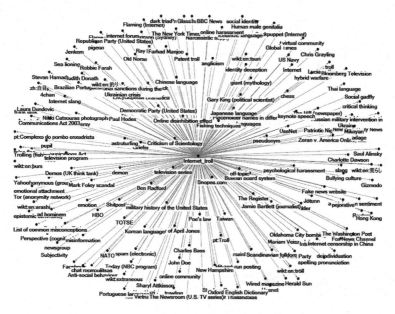

In Google Correlate, the term "troll" does not bring up much that evokes a coherent sense of the term except "fake people" (0.9416 correlate with the search for the term "troll") (Figure 6). The other terms relate to video sharing sites, mobile devices, dreams, social media platforms (by name), and other references. (Google Correlate enables the identification of macro-scale time patterns of text-based searches on Google Search from January 2003 to the present. For the cited data, the search was for within the U.S. in weekly time series.

One way to skim a sense of #troll in the specific conversations that are ongoing is to create a #hashtag network. This approach skims off the most recent messages related to #troll to enable the discussants using this folk tagging to label their interactions with each other. On the Twitter microblogging site, #troll resulted in 190 vertices (unique social media accounts) and 142 unique edges (replies and re-postings and forwardings). The were 64 groups identified, so the interactions around this term in this slice-in-time tend to be small-scale interactions (represented visually as motifs). That said, the largest connected component is 64 nodes, so there may be one large component that brought together some 64 interacting individuals around this term. (Figure 7 and Table 1). These show a range of conversations between the vertices (nodes), with a portion of the tweets showing on the edges (links). The

Figure 6. "Troll" on Google correlate from January 2003 – present in weekly time series in the U.S.

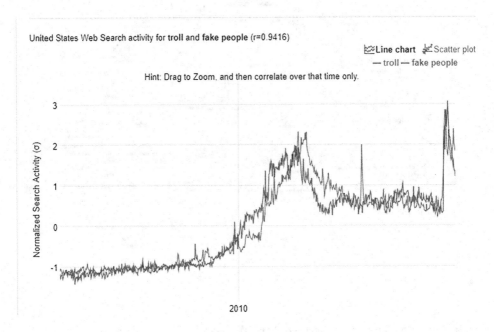

United States Web Search activity for **troll** and **fake people** (r=0.9416)

Hint: Drag to Zoom, and then correlate over that time only.

extracted data table contains the full messaging and other details about the respective involved social media accounts, based on the Twitter Application Programming Interface (API).

Another approach is to collect discussion threads and comment threads and other textual contents and use a mix of computational distant reading (such as for sentiment)…to narrow the search for trolling behaviors…and then human close reading may be engaged. Computational means may be used also to identify the topics around which people interact. Researchers do not have to look far to find textual contents on this topic, across a range of fields. An automated coding of the discussions around trolling on a Subreddit thread may be seen in Figure 8. The respective sentiment categories may be examined for the coded text, to see what is being discussed in the respective sentiment categories. The URL for this thread is https://www.reddit.com/r/trolling/.

Some of the light explorations above use a mix of full N = all sets in some cases and very partial data in others. It is possible through commercial companies to access full social media datasets (based on the privacy settings of the individual users). What is not available, though, is the back-end data maintained by the company about the respective accounts or about other data

Figure 7. #Troll hashtag network on Twitter microblogging site

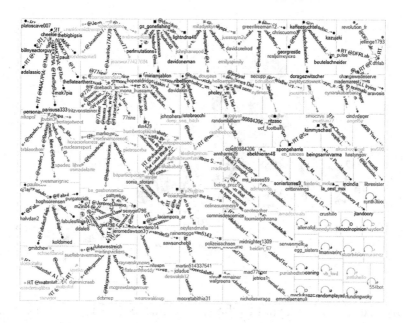

Table 1. #Troll hashtag network on Twitter (graph network metrics)

Graph Metric	Value
Graph Type	Directed
Vertices	190
Unique Edges	142
Edges With Duplicates	29
Total Edges	171
Self-Loops	21
Reciprocated Vertex Pair Ratio	0.007407407
Reciprocated Edge Ratio	0.014705882
Connected Components	64
Single-Vertex Connected Components	16
Maximum Vertices in a Connected Component	10
Maximum Edges in a Connected Component	14
Maximum Geodesic Distance (Diameter)	2
Average Geodesic Distance	1.199507
Graph Density	0.003787246
Modularity	Not Applicable
NodeXL Version	1.0.1.336

Figure 8. Automated sentiment coding of text from the trolling subreddit

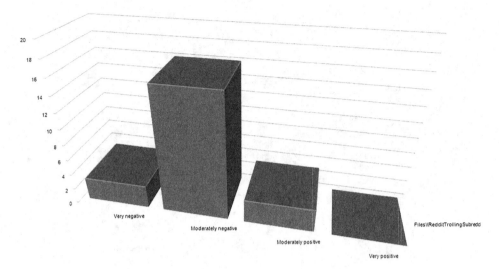

patterns that may be relevant to the exploration of trolling-based electronic hive minds.

DIFFERENTIATING BETWEEN EMERGENT AND CREATED ELECTRONIC HIVE MINDS

In theory, it would be possible to monitor when electronic hive minds spark and begin, in an organic way or a created way, and then how that "mind" evolves over time (whether it follows patterns of organic EHMs or created ones). In Figure 9, such phenomenon may spark and run in different ways. It is also wholly possible that such EHMs may not have clear start points, and that they may continue with influences that are both organic and created.

Some Ways to Differentiate Between Types of EHMs?

Some early exploration of ways to identify starts, continuances, and endings follow in Table 02. For example, do organic groups start slowly and catch on over time, and created ones sparked by collaborating members who step in and play support roles to the coordinated endeavor? Is the tell the purchase of particular services? Is the tell the sophistication of the launch in the messaging? In the technologies harnessed? And what of continuation of

Figure 9. A Continuum of electronic hive minds from organically emergent/evolved to created/instrumented (for origination, for maintenance over time) (as a 2x2 table plus)

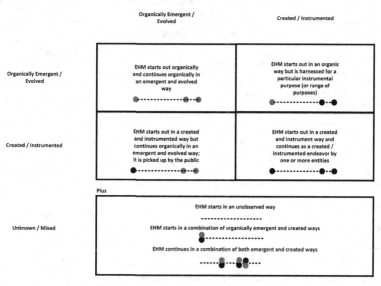

A Continuum of Electronic Hive Minds from Emergent/Evolved to Created/Instrumented
(for Origination, for Maintenance over Time) (as a 2x2 Table Plus)

the messaging? What differentiates one group from the other? Is there more coalescence of single-minded messaging for created and well-funded troll armies? How do organic hive minds sunset, vs. created ones? At what points are "hidden hands" seeable, and with how much confidence? The similarity of cells in the table might suggest that the issue of organic vs. created may be harder to differentiate than initially conceptualized.

If the 2016 attempt by the Russian government is a case in point, it has taken several years for the U.S. government, private companies, and others, to start to reveal the full scope of the effort, which included the stealing of private information, the creation of thousands of faked social media accounts across multiple social media platforms, servers stood up stateside, deep analytics of American voters and what might trigger their responses, and other insights. The costs to launch this endeavor is estimated in the millions, according to press accounts. Early work on trying to identify automated or cyborg accounts linked by media to this endeavor and still live (many accounts were shut down by the social media providers for months after the revelations) showed the difficulty of identifying 'bots and cyborg accounts using available tools because of the memetic nature of social accounts set

Table 2. Differentiating between (1) organically emergent / evolved troll groups and (2) created / instrumented troll "armies"

	(1) Organically Emergent, Evolved Troll Groups	(2) Created / Instrumented Troll "Armies"
Origination / Start (of EHM)		
Identifiable Start	Clear or Unclear Initial Messaging	Clear or Unclear Initial Messaging
Sophistication of Messaging	Sophisticated Not Sophisticated	Sophisticated Not Sophisticated
Others		
Continuance (of EHM)		
Instrumentation / Objectives	Coherence or Incoherence Stated or Unstated	Coherence or Incoherence Stated or Unstated
Deception	Present Not Present	Present Not Present
Messaging	Aligned or Diffuse Structured or Freeform Claiming or Disavowal	Aligned or Diffuse Structured or Freeform Claiming or Disavowal
Technologies Employed	Scripted Agents	Scripted Agents
Investments / Inputs / Costs	High Cost / Medium Cost / Low Cost / No Cost	High Cost / Medium Cost / Low Cost / No Cost
Membership	Decentralized Volunteer Members Self-borne Costs	Centralized Paid Members Other-borne Costs
Others		
Sunsetting (of EHM)		
Memory	Commemoration Mass Forgetting	Commemoration Mass Forgetting
Replacement	Substitution Change to a Proxemic Topic	Substitution Change to a Proxemic Topic
Concluding	Explicit and Marked Disappearance Gradual Steps	Explicit and Marked Disappearance Gradual Steps
Others		

up for information warfare (Hai-Jew, Multidimensional…, 2019). The speed of human adoption of these messages explain partly why identifying such endeavors from public data alone is near impossible, at least with any level of certitude. Humans may come across as bot-like, and bots may come across as very human-like. If 'bot armies may be set up by script, human-embodied armies may be triggered by messaging (activating a sense of self-righteousness and anger) and calls to action.

Discussion

This work focused on a particular type of EHM, those based on "trolling," conceptualized as representing a counter-viewpoint to those being shared on an online socio-technical platform, albeit in ways that are provocative and potentially offensive. A basic approach was suggested to identify both origination and continuing EHMs to see if start-points and continuing minds may be understood as organic vs. created, natural or artificial. While this early work suggests some ways to skim information to get at parts of a broader hive mind around a topic and incidences around the topic, the work is not conclusive one way or the other. In general, insider information and investigatory powers well beyond the public information available will be necessary to understand meddling in the creation and maintenance of EHMs.

There is a value for human participants online to be aware of troll armies—both those created by people in emergent ways and by nation-states and other well-funded entities for particular purposes. Maybe such awareness can lower the amounts of human hacking that is occurring in the public and private spheres and better enable human decision making with facts and logic (even as this sounds like wishful thinking). Maybe the "animal spirits" sparked by inflammatory messaging may be brought under control and prevent small- and large-scale social conflagrations. Maybe the collective consciousness around particular topics can be better informed and of calmer dispositions. Perhaps virtuous cycles of interactions may be promoted, and vicious ones prevented.

FUTURE RESEARCH DIRECTIONS

Meanwhile, there are questions of interest regarding electronic hive minds based on shared human thinking and practices. How do these form? How are the social norms created around these? How do these sunset, and why (if they do)?

For those that are conceptualized as ever-present and continuing, what makes some EHMs perpetual (in theory and likely in practice)? What are features of "continuous EHMs," such as the conceptualized ones around trolling (and resultant disruption, chaos, and mayhem)? What psychological aspects of people as individuals (social beings) and as groups encourage some of the continuous aspects of electronic hive minds? Are there technologies that encourage the creation of these types? [As to trolling, it is likely one of those persistent and ever-present aspects of electronic hive minds (in their many different instantiations) because trolling is an extension of aspects of human thinking and human social behaviors. Malice is part of human expression.] Are there ways to keep people from being swept up in mass-scale expressions of grievance through trolling?

Then, too, are there ways to head off the negativity and ugliness of trolling behaviors? Are there ways to help people better address their grievances in more prosocial and adaptive ways than to engage in trolling (and worse)? Are there ways to identify suggestive individuals who may be prone to become trollers and to continue as trollers? Broadly speaking, are there ways to increase a sense of empathy for others and to act in more caring ways? Are there ways to bring in those who may feel disenfranchised to meet their needs and acquire their full rights?

In a larger sense, are there ways to discourage nation-states and other macro-scale entities from using troll armies for their political ends? What are ways for modern societies to address such tendencies by other countries in order to protect their systems and citizens? (Such questions are being addressed at present.)

CONCLUSION

A core assumption of the magic of social media is the power of speaking into others' lives for mutual benefit. The widespread presence of trolling behaviors—malign, selfish, manipulative, non-constructively conflictual, and control-focused—requires those who would engage online to set up defenses and resistances against others' malign influences. It requires that people resist the allurements of the false warmth of others' expressed concerns ("cheap talk," designed emoticons) and superficial considerations in order to control for their own vulnerabilities ("vulns"). It requires that people strive against their own worst inclinations in relation to others and to discern the fake from the real, and vice versa. It requires that people put some thought into their actions for the entire possible scope of potential responses and outcomes and not clash for the sake of clashing alone.

In a prior work, the author wrote about the "health" of an electronic hive mind, to include "accurate long-term memory for relevant issues in the past" and with the ability to focus on the important things so as not to be distracted by irrelevances (Hai-Jew, The Electronic Hive Mind…, 2019, p. 239) and to be open-minded to a complex world but not be manipulated (Hai-Jew, The Electronic Hive Mind…, 2019, p. 240). She proposed the importance of discernment and acting on that discernment. These ideas seem quite idealistic in this light, but potentially, more important now than ever.

REFERENCES

Anderson, A. A., Brossard, D., Scheufele, D. A., Xenos, M. A., & Ladwig, P. (2014). The 'nasty effect': Online incivility and risk perceptions of emerging technologies. *Journal of Computer-Mediated Communication, 19*(3), 373–387. doi:10.1111/jcc4.12009

Aro, J. (2016). The cyberspace war: Propaganda and trolling as warfare tools. *European View, 15*(1), 121–132. doi:10.100712290-016-0395-5

Baccarella, C. V., Wagner, T. F., Kietzmann, J. H., & McCarthy, I. P. (2018). Social media? It's serious! Understanding the dark side of social media. *European Management Journal, 36*(4), 431–438. doi:10.1016/j.emj.2018.07.002

Bacile, T. J., Wolter, J. S., Allen, A. M., & Xu, P. (2018). The effects of online incivility and consumer-to-consumer interactional justice on complainants, observers, and service providers during social media service recovery. *Journal of Interactive Marketing, 44*, 60–81. doi:10.1016/j.intmar.2018.04.002

Bishop, J. (2012). Tackling Internet abuse in Great Britain: Towards a framework for classifying severities of 'flame trolling.' In *Proceedings of the International Conference on Security and Management (SAM)*. The Steering Committee of the World Congress in Computer Science, Computer Engineering and Applied Computing (WorldComp).

Bishop, J. (2012). The Persuasive and Assistive Interactive Extension (PAIX): A position paper on using gamified behavior management systems for reducing flame trolling in schools based on Classroom 2.0. In *Proceedings on the International Conference on Internet Computing (ICOMP)*. The Steering Committee of The World Congress in Computer Science, Computer Engineering and Applied Computing (WorldComp).

Bishop, J. (2012). The psychology of trolling and lurking: The role of defriending and gamification for increasing participation in online communities using seductive narratives. In *Virtual community participation and motivation: Cross-disciplinary theories*. Hershey, PA: IGI Global. doi:10.4018/978-1-4666-0312-7.ch010

Bishop, J. (2013). The effect of de-individuation of the Internet Troller on Criminal Procedure implementation: An interview with a Hater. *International Journal of Cyber Criminology, 28 – 48.*

Bishop, J. (2014). My click is my bond: The role of contracts, social proof, and gamification for sysops to reduce pseudo-activism and Internet trolling. In *Gamification for Human Factors Integration*. Hershey, PA: IGI Global. doi:10.4018/978-1-4666-5071-8.ch001

Bishop, J. (2014). Trolling for the lulz? Using media theory to understand transgressive humour and other internet trolling in online communities. In *Transforming politics and policy in the digital age* (pp. 155–172). IGI Global. doi:10.4018/978-1-4666-6038-0.ch011

Bliuc, A.-M., Faulkner, N., Jakubowicz, A., & McGarty, C. (2018). Online networks of racial hate: A systematic review of 10 years of research on cyber-racism. *Computers in Human Behavior, 87,* 75–86. doi:10.1016/j.chb.2018.05.026

Bogolyubova, O., Panicheva, P., Tikhonov, R., Ivanov, V., & Ledovaya, Y. (2018). Dark personalities on Facebook: Harmful online behaviors and language. *Computers in Human Behavior, 78,* 151–159. doi:10.1016/j.chb.2017.09.032

Buckels, E. E., Trapnell, P. D., & Paulhus, D. L. (2014). Trolls just want to have fun. *Personality and Individual Differences, 67,* 97–102. doi:10.1016/j.paid.2014.01.016

Cheng, J., Danescu-Niculescu-Mizil, C., Leskovec, J., & Bernstein, M. (2017, May/June). Anyone can become a troll. *American Scientist, 105*(3), 152–155. doi:10.1511/2017.126.152 PMID:29399664

Chiregi, M., & Navimipour, N. J. (2016). A new method for trust and reputation evaluation in the cloud environments using the recommendations of opinion leaders' entities and removing the effect of troll entities. *Computers in Human Behavior, 60,* 280–292. doi:10.1016/j.chb.2016.02.029

Cho, D., & Kwon, K. H. (2015). The impacts of identity verification and disclosure of social cues on flaming in online user comments. *Computers in Human Behavior, 51*, 363–372. doi:10.1016/j.chb.2015.04.046

Coles, B. A., & West, M. (2016). Trolling the trolls: Online forum users constructions of the nature and properties of trolling. *Computers in Human Behavior, 60*, 233–244. doi:10.1016/j.chb.2016.02.070

Coles, B. A., & West, M. (2016). Weaving the internet together: Imagined communities in newspaper comment threads. *Computers in Human Behavior, 60*, 44–53. doi:10.1016/j.chb.2016.02.049

Craker, N., & March, E. (2016). The dark side of Facebook®: The Dark Tetrad, negative social potency, and trolling behaviours. *Personality and Individual Differences, 102*, 79–84. doi:10.1016/j.paid.2016.06.043

Ditrich, L., & Sassenberg, K. (2017). Kicking out the trolls—Antecedents of social exclusion intentions in Facebook groups. *Computers in Human Behavior, 75*, 32–41. doi:10.1016/j.chb.2017.04.049

Drouin, M., Miller, D., Wehle, S. M. J., & Hernandez, E. (2016). Why do people lie online? 'Because everyone lies on the internet'. *Computers in Human Behavior, 64*, 134–142. doi:10.1016/j.chb.2016.06.052

Fornacciari, P., Mordonini, M., Poggi, A., Sani, L., & Tomaiuolo, M. (2018). A holistic system for troll detection on Twitter. *Computers in Human Behavior, 89*, 258–268. doi:10.1016/j.chb.2018.08.008

Google Books Ngram Viewer. (2018). *Google*. Retrieved Oct. 21, 2018, from: https://books.google.com/ngrams/info

Google Correlate. (2018). Retrieved on Oct. 21, 2018, from https://www.google.com/trends/correlate

Gredel, E. (2017). Digital discourse analysis and Wikipedia: Bridging the gap between Foucauldian discourse analysis and digital conversation analysis. *Journal of Pragmatics, 115*, 99–114. doi:10.1016/j.pragma.2017.02.010

Hai-Jew, S. (2009, Sept.) Exploring the immersive parasocial: Is it you or the thought of you? *Journal of Online Learning and Teaching*. Retrieved Oct. 15, 2018, from http://jolt.merlot.org/vol5no3/hai-jew_0909.htm

Hai-Jew, S. (2019). The electronic hive mind and cybersecurity: Mass-scale human cognitive limits to explain the 'weakest link' in cybersecurity. In *Global Cyber Security Labor Shortage and International Business Risk* (pp. 206–262). Hershey, PA: IGI Global. doi:10.4018/978-1-5225-5927-6.ch011

Hai-Jew, S. (2019). Multidimensional Mappings of Political Accounts for Malicious Political Socialbot Identification: Exploring Social Networks, Geographies, and Strategic Messaging. In *Global Cyber Security Labor Shortage and International Business Risk* (pp. 206–262). Hershey, PA: IGI Global. doi:10.4018/978-1-5225-5927-6.ch011

Herring, S., Job-Sluder, K., Scheckler, R., & Barab, S. (2002). Searching for safety online: Managing 'trolling' in a feminist forum. CSI Working Paper (WP-02-03). *The Information Society*, *13*(5), 371–384. doi:10.1080/01972240290108186

Hong, F.-Y., & Cheng, K.-T. (2018). Correlation between university students' online trolling behavior and online trolling victimization forms, current conditions, and personality traits. *Telematics and Informatics*, *35*(2), 397–405. doi:10.1016/j.tele.2017.12.016

Hughes, C. M., Griffin, B. J., & Worthington, E. L. Jr. (2017). A measure of social behavior in team-based multiplayer online games: The Sociality in Multiplayer Online Games (SMOG) scale. *Computers in Human Behavior*, *69*, 386–395. doi:10.1016/j.chb.2016.12.043

Internet troll. (2018, Oct. 15). In *Wikipedia*. Retrieved Oct. 18, 2018, from https://en.wikipedia.org/wiki/Internet_troll

Kavanagh, B. (2016). Emoticons as a medium for channeling politeness within American and Japanese online blogging communities. *Language & Communication*, *48*, 53–65. doi:10.1016/j.langcom.2016.03.003

Klempka, A., & Stimson, A. (2014). *Anonymous communication on the Internet and trolling. Concordia Journal of Communication Research*, 1–43.

Koban, K., Stein, J.-P., Eckhardt, V., & Ohler, P. (2018). Quid pro quo in Web 2.0. Connecting personality traits and Facebook usage intensity to uncivil commenting intentions in public online discussions. *Computers in Human Behavior*, *79*, 9–18. doi:10.1016/j.chb.2017.10.015

Kopecký, K. (2016). Misuse of web cameras to manipulate children within the so-called webcam trolling. *Telematics and Informatics, 33*(1), 1–7. doi:10.1016/j.tele.2015.06.005

Ladanyi, J., & Doyle-Portillo, S. (2017). The development and validation of the Grief Play Scale (GPS) in MMORPGs. *Personality and Individual Differences, 114,* 125–133. doi:10.1016/j.paid.2017.03.062

Lopes, B., & Yu, H. (2017). Who do you troll and Why: An investigation into the relationship between the Dark Triad Personalities and online trolling behaviours towards popular and less popular Facebook profiles. *Computers in Human Behavior, 77,* 69–76. doi:10.1016/j.chb.2017.08.036

Ludemann, D. (2018). pol/emics: Ambiguity, scales, and digital discourse on 4chan. *Discourse. Context & Media, 24,* 92–98. doi:10.1016/j.dcm.2018.01.010

Mali, P. (2015, January). IT Act 2000: Trolls, trolling, & cyber law. *CSI Communications,* 36–37.

Mantilla, K. (2013). Gendertrolling: Misogyny adapts to new media. *Feminist Studies, 39*(2), 563–570. Retrieved from https://www.jstor.org/stable/23719068

March, E., Grieve, R., Marrington, J., & Jonason, P. K. (2017). Trolling on Tinder® (and other dating apps): Examining the role of the Dark Tetrad and impulsivity. *Personality and Individual Differences, 110,* 139–143. doi:10.1016/j.paid.2017.01.025

McCreery, M. P., & Krach, S. K. (2018). How the human is the catalyst: Personality, aggressive fantasy, and proactive-reactive aggression among users of social media. *Personality and Individual Differences, 133,* 91–95. doi:10.1016/j.paid.2017.06.037

Megarry, J. (2014). Online incivility or sexual harassment? Conceptualising women's experiences in the digital age. *Women's Studies International Forum, 47,* 46–55. doi:10.1016/j.wsif.2014.07.012

Merritt, E. (2012). *An analysis of the discourse of Internet trolling: A case study of Reddit.com* (doctoral dissertation). Mount Holyoke College.

Meyer, K. A., & McNeal, L. (2011). Academics online: Their interests and foibles. *Internet and Higher Education, 14*(2), 113–120. doi:10.1016/j.iheduc.2010.09.002

Milner, R.M. (2013). FCJ-156 Hacking the social: Internet memes, identity antagonism, and the logic of lulz. *The Fibreculture Journal, 22.*

Mocanu, D., Rossi, L., Zhang, Q., Karsai, M., & Quattrociocchi, W. (2015). Collective attention in the age of (mis)information. *Computers in Human Behavior, 51,* 1198–1204. doi:10.1016/j.chb.2015.01.024

Moncur, W., Orzech, K. M., & Neville, F. G. (2016). Fraping, social norms and online representations of self. *Computers in Human Behavior, 63,* 125–131. doi:10.1016/j.chb.2016.05.042

Nagle, J. (2018). Twitter, cyber-violence, and the need for a critical social media literacy in teacher education: A review of the literature. *Teaching and Teacher Education, 76,* 86–94. doi:10.1016/j.tate.2018.08.014

Niezen, R. (2013). Internet suicide: Communities of affirmation and the lethality of communication. *Transcultural Psychiatry, 50*(2), 303–322. doi:10.1177/1363461512473733 PMID:23315147

Ortega, F. J., Troyano, J. A., Cruz, F. L., Vallejo, C. G., & Enríquez, F. (2012). Propagation of trust and distrust for the detection of trolls in a social network. *Computer Networks, 56*(12), 2884–2895. doi:10.1016/j.comnet.2012.05.002

Paavola, J., Helo, T., Jalonen, H., Sartonen, M., & Huhtinen, A.-M. (2016). Understanding the trolling phenomenon: The automated detection of bots and cyborgs in the social media. *Journal of Information Warfare, 15*(4), 100–V.

Rainie, L., Anderson, J., & Albright, J. (2017, Mar. 29). The future of free speech, trolls, anonymity and fake news online. *Pew Research Center.* Retrieved Oct. 20, 2018, from http://www.pewinternet.org/2017/03/29/the-future-of-free-speech-trolls-anonymity-and-fake-news-online/

Salehi-Esfahani, S., & Ozturk, A. B. (2018). Negative reviews: Formation, spread, and half of opportunistic behavior. *International Journal of Hospitality Management, 74,* 138–146. doi:10.1016/j.ijhm.2018.06.022

Seigfried-Spellar, K. C., & Lankford, C. M. (2018). Personality and online environment factors differ for posters, trolls, lurkers, and confessors on Yik Yak. *Personality and Individual Differences, 124,* 54–56. doi:10.1016/j.paid.2017.11.047

Sest, N., & March, E. (2017). Constructing the cyber-troll: Psychopathy, sadism, and empathy. *Personality and Individual Differences, 119,* 69–72. doi:10.1016/j.paid.2017.06.038

Shaw, A. (2014, September). The Internet is full of jerks, because the world is full of jerks: What feminist theory teaches us about the Internet. *Communication and Critical/Cultural Studies, 11*(3), 273–277. doi:10.108 0/14791420.2014.926245

Sparby, E. M. (2017). Digital social media and aggression: Memetic rhetoric in 4chan's collective identity. *Computers and Composition, 45*, 85–97. doi:10.1016/j.compcom.2017.06.006

Synnott, J., Coulias, A., & Ioannou, M. (2017). Online trolling: The case of Madeleine McCann. *Computers in Human Behavior, 71*, 70–78. doi:10.1016/j. chb.2017.01.053

Wagenknecht, T., Teubner, T., & Weinhardt, C. (2018). A Janus-Faced matter—The role of user anonymity for communication persuasiveness in online discussions. *Information & Management,* 1 – 14. (in press)

Zaleski, K. L., Gundersden, K. K., Baes, J., Estupinian, E., & Vergara, A. (2016). Exploring rape culture in social media forums. *Computers in Human Behavior, 63*, 922–927. doi:10.1016/j.chb.2016.06.036

Zelenkauskaite, A., & Niezgoc, B. (2017, May). 'Stop Kremlin trolls': Ideological trolling as calling out, rebuttal, and reactions on online news portal commenting. *First Monday, 22*(5). doi:10.5210/fm.v22i5.7795

KEY TERMS AND DEFINITIONS

Delusion: A belief that is generally debunked by evidence and/or rational argument.

Electronic Hive Mind: A synchronous temporal and informal patchwork of emergent shared social consciousness (held by geographically distributed people, cyborgs, and robots) enabled by online social connectivity (across a range of social media platforms on the web and internet), based around various dimensions of shared attractive interests.

Flaming (Flame-Baiting): The use of hostile expressions directed towards others as a criticism.

Folie à Deux: A delusion of two people in close relationship whose interactions inform and maintain the shared psychosis, means "madness of two" in French.

Fraping (Facebook + Rape): The act of co-opting another's social media presence and changing their personal data without their permission.

Gendertrolling: Uses of gender-based insults and pejorative terms against others based on their gender identity.

Griefing: Acts in order to cause trouble for opponents or others in immersive games or immersive virtual worlds (and other spaces).

Immersive Parasocial: The origination and maintenance of one-sided illusory followership (parasocial) relationships in perception-deep immersive virtual worlds and spaces.

Troll (Cyber Troll, Internet Troll): A person who engages in disruptive behaviors online for various purposes.

Trolling (Cybertrolling, Internet Trolling): The act of starting arguments in online social spaces by emotion-based messaging, such as calling out others, name-calling, sharing inaccurate information, posting off-topic messaging, and otherwise sharing disagreeable messages (including potentially threats).

Chapter 7

Consigned to Temporal or Permanent Oblivion?
Mass Remembering and Forgetting in Electronic Hive Minds

ABSTRACT

Mass and partial forgetting in electronic hive minds (shared consciousness enabled through socio-technical spaces, social media, and information and communications technology [ICT]) is conceptualized as something gradual and organic based on the functions of human memory and accelerated in other cases, depending on the adaptive needs of the EHM. How EHMs form, the proclivity to certain attitudes, favored meta-narratives, the exposure to a wide range of ideas (vs. filter bubbles), and other aspects affect what is retained and what is forgotten. This sheds some light on how some EHMs may coordinate to maintain memory on "critical issues" and "issues of facts" and the roles of those who act as "folk" historians and commemorators and the roles of technology as affordance/enablement and constraint. This work focuses on the hard effort of maintaining collective memory in the ephemera of transient EHMs. Methods for identifying blind spots and invisible spaces in memory in EHMs are suggested, and this method is applied in a walk-through of a portion of a star-based fandom and followership-based EHM. This chapter explores some of the nature of forgetting in EHMs.

DOI: 10.4018/978-1-5225-9369-0.ch007

INTRODUCTION

This was how people disappeared from history, wasn't it? They weren't erased, they were explained away. - Kate Atkinson, Transcription (2018, p. 235)

Paying attention is the cardinal sign of love. - Lea Carpenter, red white blue (2018, p. 75)

History, as nearly no one seems to know, is not merely something to be read. And it does not refer merely, or even principally, to the past. On the contrary, the great force of history comes from the fact that we carry it within us, are unconsciously controlled by it in many ways, and history is literally present in all that we do. - James Baldwin, 1965

A naïve approach to forgetting is understanding it as a failure of memory. An assumed ideal state is that people would remember everything, without fail. However, more recent research suggests that forgetting may well be an adaptive function; it helps people adjust to different realities without being unduly influenced by distractive information. The research also suggests that memory is highly influence-able by people's conversations with others, people's preferences, people's prior belief systems, and other factors.

In the individual mind, forgetting is both a gradual and normal phenomenon that occurs over time, based on how attentional resources are deployed and what is considered relevant, and an accelerated phenomenon based on how something was first learned and experienced, on experienced emotions, on human attention and intention, on health, on drug use, on situational physical or mental fatigue, on trauma, and other factors (and combinations of factors). Forgetting is also a factor of selectivity—what is not rehearsed vs. what is. The act of remembering selectively affects what is forgotten and how quickly, given memory's plasticity (malleability) and adaptivity. In group minds, what people value, how they interact, what they focus on, and other factors affect how remembering and forgetting occur *en masse*.

Electronic hive minds (EHM) are conceptualized as distributed mass consciousness around particular topics of shared interest built on the Web and Internet (Hai-Jew, 2019). As social populations, they exchange information, intercommunicate, and interact, and in so doing, they reinforce some aspects of knowledge and occlude others. For many groups, particularly those that are homophilous, there may be a common canon of understandings and shared values (and potential resulting "echo chambers"), which may bring people together but also prevent broader exploratory learning.

Virtual group minds, such as the electronic hive mind (Hai-Jew, 2019), combine the remembering and forgetting of people as individuals and as groups but with the added enablements of socio-technical systems, social media platforms, and information and communications technology (ICT). If the human default is forgetting over time, a technological reality is one in which remembrance is the default given "affordable storage, effortless retrieval and global access," and many so concerned that they are suggesting a return to "the default of forgetting our societies have experienced for millennia" (Mayer-Schönberger, April 2007, n.p.). If people are reminded to explore particular topics, the long memory of the Web and Internet may prove a powerful resource. There is a sense of "how relentless the iron memory of the Internet can be, and how suddenly data from the past can re-emerge in unexpected contexts," with implications of shared personal information available in an "indeterminate future" (Koops, Dec. 2011, p. 230). The risks of *sousveillance* (participant recording of an event in which he or she is a part) have arisen with pervasive computing and people's creations of life-logs that reveal their internal lives (an "interior panopticon"), with the need for computational forgetting as an emancipatory process (Dodge & Kitchin, 2007, p. 431). Cyber technologies may enable an "end of forgetting" where erasure is not possible (Rosen, July 25, 2010). Multiple researchers and groups have suggested ways that personal information may be controlled or erased. A new law in the European Union, known as the General Data Protection Regulation, enables a greater "right to be forgotten" or "right to erasure" for people who want their personal data removed from various data stores on social media and other online spaces (EU GDPR.org, 2018). On another more abstract layer, in technology systems, memory is not always desirable and may hinder some types of data processing and data analysis and machine-based decision making (and the converse may be true in other contexts). Remembering occurs in social ways, "dynamically entangled in conversations" and form "social binding" (Hirst & Echterhoff, 2018). In this space of hyper-sociality, social contagion affects people's memories (Koppel, Wohl, Meksin, & Hirst, 2014). Induced social forgetting (forgetting stemming from human interactions and intercommunications) has been found to propagate through social networks and subsequent conversations (Coman & Hirst, 2012, as cited in Echterhoff, 2014, p. 106). On social media, there are hot moments when "animal spirits" of people seem to affect awareness and decision making. Here is a space replete with voices and memes (memetic objects that enable people to emulate each other and which push certain ideas to be top-of-mind).

What happens in electronic hive minds (EHM), which are enabled by socio-technologies that enable theoretical and practical non-forgetting (permanent encoding of memories in digital form) and the propagation of social effects on memory? What are ways to understand blind spots of various EHMs, and why? (If EHMs are mostly enabled through social media and ICT, do the "filter bubbles" exacerbate some meta narratives and enable other types of mass forgetting? Are inhomogeneous social networks in EHMs more healthy than homogeneous ones? Are those that have commemorators expressing in the online space more broadly remembering than those that do not?) This early work provides a look at the nature of EHMs and how forgetting may occur on them. An early walk-through of a target EHM is done through the lens of star worship and fandom. This work suggests important implications of social tuning and individual responsibility around social forgetting in EHMs.

A Disclaimer: This work is an early one in exploring social forgetting and social remembering in electronic hive minds. The research techniques are tentative and early, without the depth and specificity and provability of forensic analyses.

REVIEW OF THE LITERATURE

A review of the research literature around human forgetting shows multiple approaches: physiological, neurological, chemical, and psycho-social, among others. Forgetting is conceptualized as something that is organic, natural, and gradual, as a feature of aging. The "forgetting curve" (by Hermann Ebbinghaus in 1885) shows a line graph with a decline in memory over time with differing levels of steepness of the drop-off in memory and different durations of memory retention. An initial drop-off in memory is fast, within a few days of the new learning, and then the forgetting levels off. His idea was that memory is retained due in part to the relative strength of that memory over time, in the absence of memory or learning refreshers (Ebbinghaus, 1885). The ultimate "fate of memories" has long been debated, with some hypothesizing that they are ultimately forgotten unless practiced and others suggesting that some make it into long term permanent memory (Averell & Heathcote, 2011), including instances of "quite brief study" resulting in "storage of some memories (that) was effectively permanent" (Averell

& Heathcote, 2011, p. 25). The focus has not always been on the optimal ways to learn for forever; even from antiquity, there has been the pursuit of "lethotechnics" to learn and practice forgetting (Esposito, 2008, p. 181). Forgetting is "not a unitary phenomenon" and it exists in various types and can have constructive usages (Connerton, 2008, p. 59).

While Ebbinghaus suggested that practice and training might refresh memories, a later researcher suggests that "the law of disuse" as not a primary cause of forgetting but "important only in that it so often gives the primary conditions an opportunity to act" (McGeoch, 1932, p. 370). Forgetting itself is "pervasive and systematically important" (McGeoch, 1932, p. 369):

In another sense forgetting is present in learning, in the alteration or loss which occurs in the parts, not only in those which are intrinsic and necessary, but also in those which are extrinsic and adventitious, of a total learning material such as a poem, a maze, or any other material, during the repetition of other parts. It is well known that as practice at any learning material goes on not only are 'wrong' acts and associations lost, and often those which are not wrong but only less effective than others, but a multitude of extrinsic associations and acts which are present earlier in the learning. As a result of these losses the total act is changed until it resembles only in its final outcome the act with which the learner started. This change is a result, to a significant extent, of the loss or forgetting of certain part-acts (McGeoch, 1932, p. 353).

Some refer to this as a virtuous or adaptive forgetting to avoid "remembering too much" but also to eliminate clutter for more efficient functioning (Michaelian, 2011, p. 399). A human learner is also, in part, a result of what he or she has forgotten. The complimentary colloquialism that a particular person "has forgotten more than most of us will ever know" captures this idea. Said more formally: "Perception, reasoning, emotional sensitivity, action are, in any general sense, a product of what the organism has forgotten as well as of what it has learned and retained." (McGeoch, 1932, p. 353). More recent research has updated on this idea, that information stored in memory may be "irrevocably destroyed" (forgotten in an irrecoverable way) (Loftus & Loftus, May 1980, p. 409). Non-human animals themselves also engage in adaptive forgetting, which enables them to engage in "behavioral plasticity" in the face of "conflicting information" (Kraemer & Golding, 1997, p. 483).

Some Factors in Human Remembering and Forgetting

Brain science studies and neuroscience suggests that brains, as they age, will lose some functions, even as some memories can last over a lifetime. Forgetting is assumed to occur as a general assumption even for those who are in the normal range of health and healthy lifestyles. Human forgetting is also conceptualized as something that occurs in accelerated ways based on health factors, lifestyle issues, accidents, and other factors. Forgetting is seen as a part of human learning (for unlearning, for new learning) and adaptivity (for conceptual and behavioral plasticity) in a fast-changing world. Not remembering is not seen as wholly positive or negative. (Even if people had perfect memories, only a limited number of objects may be held in working memory.) What is lesser known is just how forgetting may occur based on human choices and preferences, human actions, and human interactions with others, both as individuals (egos) and as members of groups (entities, social networks, and societies):

- How something is learned (encoded into long-term memory)
  - The emotions around the learning
  - The practice behind the learning
- Belief preferences ("confirmation bias" or preferring information that aligns with one's preferences and ignoring information that is disconfirming to that bias)
- The agency to forget purposefully
- How one is directed to forget (by agency and will)
- The conversations one has with others around a topic and what is focused on in conversation (to induce forgetting)
- The selection of what is seen as important vs. unimportant (based on underlying value systems)
- Lying to self (self-deception) and lying to others (deception)

Learning / Encoding

How something is learned may also affect how it encodes into long-term memory. For example, researchers have long identified context dependency in various types of learning. The ability to transfer learning from one context to another requires additional and effortful learning and even practice, often in simulations of the real-world environment where the learning may be applied.

The atypicality (novelty) of the encountered learning object may also enhance its induced forget-ability and the potential effects of retrieval-induced forgetting (RIF) (how people's focus on a particular depiction of information leads to forgetting of other related but unmentioned information): "We found that object memorability (as determined by typicality) influenced RIF with significant forgetting occurring for the memorable (non-typical), but not non-memorable (typical), objects." (Reppa, Williams, Worth, Greville, & Saunders, 2017, p. 51). Selective remembering induces forgetting (Cue, Koppel, & Hirst, 2007), so there are built-in risks of omissions. "Mnemonic silence—the absence of expressing a memory—is public in nature and is embedded within communicative acts, such as conversations" (Stone, Coman, Brown, Koppel, & Hirst, 2012, p. 39). Retrieval-induced forgetting has been shown to affect even personal, autobiographical memories (Stone, Barnier, Sutton, & Hirst, 2012). In public, such omissions may have far-reaching implications, including social propagation. The lengths of time of retrieval-induced forgetting from research can be less than a day to even a month (Hirst & Coman, 2018, p. 89).

Social learning also has implications on human learning (and forgetting). In general, it is thought that there is more effective encoding into memory for individuals working in isolation rather than collaboratively potentially because "collaborative encoding produces less effective cues for later retrieval" (Barber, Rajaram, & Aron, 2010, p. 255). Based on the assumption of the "pooling of abilities," though, groups of people should recall more than they do, in a phenomenon known as "collaborative inhibition" (Weldon & Bellinger, 1997, as cited in Barber, Rajaram, & Fox, 2012, pp. 1–2). Collective groups do tend to recall more than individuals, and group recall tends to be more stable over time than individual recall (Weldon & Bellinger, 1997). For groups co-creating shared memories, they engage in "communicative acts of remembering" on which they may "build a collective memory" (Hirst & Coman, 2018, p. 88). Such shared memories may have powerful effects: "The community may be as small as a couple or as large as a nation, but the reality its members share will be grounded in part by memories held across the community" (Hirst & Coman, 2018, p. 88).

Emotional arousal around particular learning may affect how well new learning is encoded into long-term memory. Some types of memories are thought to be so surprising and consequential that they are maintained as "flashbulb memories" in permanent memory (Brown & Kulik, 1977). If the emotional arousal is too high, the learning is interrupted and ineffective. If it is too low, then the new learning is not seen as relevant and may not be attended to. Directed forgetting is less powerful over negative information (Yang, Lei, & Anderson, 2016), which seems to have a more powerful retention impact on people's memories. In an experimental study, negative words were harder for participants to forget. Researchers found evidence of "impeded inhibitory control (that) suggests that forgetting negative words is harder" than neutral ones (Yang, Lei, & Anderson, 2016, p. 44), reaffirming earlier research that there are "emotion constraints (to) mental control by capturing mental processes including memory retrieval" (Payne & Corrigan, 2007, p. 780) and also that emotional items have "a higher degree of salience and tend to attract more attention than neutral items" (Nørby, Lange, & Larsen, 2010, p. 73). In terms of emotion-related research, other researchers have explored to see whether purposeful forgetting may aid in forgiveness (Sell, 2016, p. 10).

Some people seem to have higher capabilities in directed and purposive forgetting. One description of this mix of personality traits is in terms of "mental toughness," "a generally positive constellation of personality traits" that in relation with conscientiousness is associated with the ability to enact forgetting (Delaney, Goldman, King, & Nelson-Gray, 2015, p. 183).

Reinforcement of the learning based on various types of practice, review, and even overlearning can affect how well the memories are retained.

Belief Preferences

Confirmation bias, the tendency to view new information as fitting existing beliefs and rejecting disconfirming information, may also apply to remembering and forgetting. Preferred information may be remembered in a more salient way, and undesirable information may be forgotten. People, as individuals and as social entities, tend to invest more deeply into their existing belief systems than in counter viewpoints. Prior stances affect how something is seen, and the relative willingness or unwillingness to see.

Agentic Forgetting

People have preferences for the memories that they prefer (pleasure over pain, for example). Based on their preferences, people may engage in "motivated forgetting" or the incentivized control of their own awareness. Researchers explain: "Not all memories are equally welcome in awareness. People limit the time they spend thinking about unpleasant experiences, a process that begins during encoding, but that continues when cues later remind someone of the memory" (Anderson & Hanslmayr, 2014, p. 249).

They can intentionally suppress memory (Geraerts & McNally, 2008), with varying degrees of effectiveness. The duration of voluntary suppression of neutral and emotional memories may differ, with more effective suppression of neutral memories. Suppressed memories may return after a time duration, such as a week, resulting in the findings that "intended memory suppression interferes with immediate retrieval but does not lead to long-term forgetting" (Nørby, Lange, & Larsen, 2010, p. 73). If some memories are too traumatizing, people may not engage in purposeful forgetting:

Most studies have shown that trauma survivors, especially those with post-traumatic stress disorder, are characterized by a breakdown in the ability to forget disturbing material. Studies on individuals reporting repressed or recovered memories of trauma have not confirmed predictions regarding heightened forgetting skills for trauma-related words. However, recent research on suppressing disturbing autobiographical memories suggests that people who report spontaneously recalling childhood abuse outside of psychotherapy may, indeed, possess skills for not thinking about disturbing material (Geraerts & McNally, 2008, p. 614).

Or, in some cases, for some people, difficult memories may be suppressed temporally but retrieved at a later date when desired (Geraerts & McNally, 2008, p. 622).

There are other methods of intentional agentic forgetting, too, such as through "divided attention." One research study showed this could be achieved with people engaging in a non-related task while working to forget something intentionally (Lee & Lee, 2011). The application of inhibitory control to suppress memories has different effects than that caused from associative interference (distraction or interruption) (Wang, Cao, Zhu, Cai, & Wu, 2015, p. 31). Directed forgetting can be applied to "otherwise continuous events" in an effortful process and can result in "impoverished representation of the unwanted information in memory" (Fawcett, Taylor, & Nadel, 2013, p. 332). Different sorts of forget cues have differing "retention intervals" (Abel & Bäuml, 2017). Multiple studies suggest that there is a cognitive cost to forgetting.

Directed and Induced Forgetting

People are capable of retrieving properly stored memories, and they are also able to purposefully forget information as an act of will. This capability of inhibiting memory may increase with maturity in childhood, with retrieval inhibition and "mnesic access of irrelevant or unwanted information increases with age during secondary school" (Todor, 2012, p. 1402).

Retrieval-induced forgetting (RIF) refers to the social sharing of particular information that induces forgetting of other related information in the hearers. The RIF may occur in individuals [within-individual retrieval-induced forgetting (WI-RIF)] and in groups [socially shared retrieval-induced forgetting (SS-RIF)] (Stone, Barnier, Sutton, & Hirst, 2009, p. 170). Retrieval-induced forgetting has implications and effects on follow-on social behavior (Fernandes & Saunders, 2013).

In terms of forgetting methods, they affect different types of retrieval cues:

Inhibition-induced forgetting generalizes to other retrieval cues, while interference-caused forgetting is restricted to directly interfered cue-target association (Wang, Cao, Zhu, Cai, & Wu, 2015, p. 34).

When people reason through inconsistent information, some information is given more relevance than others, and some ideas are retained and others forgotten. Forgetting is "variable," with particular pieces of information retained to maintain a consistent framework and based on "preferred recoveries" (Lang & Marquis, 2010, p. 799). (Certainly, people can also hold mutually contradictory ideas at the same time, without necessarily committing to one over the other.)

There is a risk in issuing the "instruction to forget" because of its association with the emotional devaluation of what the individual is to forget (Vivas, Marful, Panagiotidou, & Bajo, 2016, p. 85).

Certainly, memory cuing may be deployed with particular intentions in mind, but there may be unintended and even opposite effects. To-be-forgotten (TBF) items may end up with "a greater memory trace" than the non-cue condition in which people naturally forget information over time albeit in a non-directed way (Gao, Cao, Zhang, Qi, Li, & Li, 2016, p. 1).

Individuals and groups may engage in practicing memories, through various means. The study of remembering and forgetting involves different types of memories; in one experimental design, there were "practiced memories," "unpracticed memories related to the practiced memories," and "unpracticed memories related to any practiced memory" (Stone & Hirst, 2014, p. 318), which gives a sense of some of the nuanced complexities in the space.

Selectivity

Underlying belief and value systems may inform what people pay attention to and reinforce into memory. Humans engage in "motivated-recall," with group membership and points-of-view affecting what is remembered vs. forgotten (Coman, Stone, Castrano, & Hirst, 2014). Different social actors engage large-scale topics in different ways (Vinitzky-Seroussi & Teeger, Mar. 2010, p. 1105).

This phenomenon of selective and strategic recall has been observed in governments and government leaders, with portrayals of historical events framed in often nation state-serving ways. Public figures in their speeches shape public memory and public forgetting (Stone & Hirst, 2014). In part, they help set agendas by sharing particular information through mass media. Some types of forgetting by nation-states include the following types:

Nation-states and their work in forgetting, including "narrative forgetting: the formation and dissemination of an historical narrative; physical forgetting: the destruction of physical remains; and symbolic forgetting: the creation of a new symbolic geography of new places and street names. (Ram, Sept. 2009, p. 366)

The available meta-narratives of nation-state scale entities is also constrained by history and prior population narratives and culture and shared cultural values—all of which inform citizen identities. Collective memories are "treated as memories shared across a group that help to shape the identity of the group" (Wertsch & Roediger, 2008, as cited in Stone, Barnier, Sutton, & Hirst, 2009, p. 170), and this messaging may create senses of closeness or rifts and other relational impacts. Large-scale remembering and forgetting are socially constructed, with the risks of revisionist and reconstructed history, self-mythologizing and other mythmaking, false memories, backstopped lies, and more comfortable fictions, and the broadening of propagandas and retouched photos. Worse yet, misinformation can have continuing effects on "memory and reasoning" even if that information is retracted and "is well remembered" (Ecker, Lewandowsky, & Tang, 2010, p. 1087) in a phenomenon terms "continued influence effect" (Johnson & Seifert, 1994). While human memory is reconstructive and takes into account new information to revise an erroneous earlier version, initial impressions tend to retain, sometimes at a subconscious or unconscious level.

Each new generation has differing points of reference and so have to be read into collective memory and designed history. A dark extreme of the in-group membership is that selective memories may affect moral-disengagement of atrocities (Coman, Stone, Castrano, & Hirst, 2014). The remembrance of past events may be manipulated for political expediencies. At a macro level, the people who remember particular events and serve as "crucial carriers of collective memories of an event" tend to be those who experienced the event "during their critical ages of adolescence and early adulthood" (Shuman & Rodgers, June 2004, n.p.). Collective memories of "old events can be saved from extinction, at least temporarily, by new occurrences that bring them to mind" (Shuman & Rodgers, June 2004, n.p.). More recent superseding events may overshadow historical ones (Shuman & Rodgers, June 2004).

A simplistic approach may be that "talk and representation" enable collective recollection (Vinitzky-Seroussi & Teeger, Mar. 2010, p. 1103), and silence achieves collective forgetting. There is the idea that remaining silent is tantamount to taking a stance towards ignoring and forgetting. A more passive approach to selective memory may be to simply let events and information lapse and letting memories fade for collective forgetting.

The notion of silencing the past and thus burying specific events is not new. But in a world that demands talk and memory even about pasts that contain embarrassing moments, human right (sic) violations, shameful events and little to be proud about, silence may conquer a new position and social space. Most immediately silence is connected in our mind with forgetting, while talk is tied to remembrance. (Vinitzky-Seroussi & Teeger, Mar. 2010, p. 1116)

And yet, silence can "facilitate recollection" and "talk" can "enhance amnesia" (Vinitzky-Seroussi & Teeger, Mar. 2010, p. 1104). The various acts of remembering and forgetting may look similar, so the intentionality matters as well as the outcomes. Talk that focuses on particular topics and not others may induce forgetting, and silences that are coaligned with other messaging may be antithetical to accurate commemoration. Researchers propose four types of public silences:

(1. Overt and literal silences aimed at enhancing memory; (2. Overt and pervasive silences aimed at forgetting; (3. Covert silences that inhere in the mnemonic talk of agents intending to construct and maintain memory; (4.

Covert silences used to enhance forgetting in situations where complete and overt silences are neither possible nor desirable (Vinitzky-Seroussi & Teeger, Mar. 2010, p. 1108)

Some overt silences are "heavily ritualized, bounded, short and escorted either by a siren or by much mnemonic talk that comes before or after the moment of silence…" and there are silences "in the domain of forgetting" and led by those who "object to the commemoration" and who use silence as a way to "withdraw from participating in the mnemonic activity and who have perhaps despaired at the possibility of being equally and fully integrated as part of a democratic community." (Vinitzky-Seroussi & Teeger, Mar. 2010, p. 1117) Understanding the respective roles of these communications acts will require deeper analyses of surrounding behaviors and histories and contexts.

The authors describe covert silences in more depth in the context of "difficult pasts":

In between these extremes of literal silence, we find covert silences: silences that are contained within and disguised by much mnemonic talk. First, there are covert silences in the domain of memory. These are used by agents of memory who choose to give up on part of their preferred interpretation of the past (often the context of the event) so as to enable various collectives to participate in mnemonic activities, to enlarge the potential mnemonic audience, and thus to enhance memory. The second kind of covert silence is embedded in an expectation that the past can be commemorated coupled with little desire to do so. This type of covert silence thus falls within the domain of forgetting and is achieved through cacophonous commemorations where a mnemonic time and space are shared with many other issues. Thus, what looks like remembrance, may in fact, be aimed at forgetting. (Vinitzky-Seroussi & Teeger, Mar. 2010, p. 1117)

To understand public silences, there has to be a sense of "intentionality underlying the silence" (Stone, Coman, Brown, Koppel, & Hirst, 2012, p. 40). The "science of silence" is in its nascent phases of study (Stone, Coman, Brown, Koppel, & Hirst, 2012, p. 49).

Finally, selective remembering and selective forgetting speak to both the past, the present, and the future, and these actions are freighted with implications. The forgetting risks are not only at nation-state level but may result in "perpetuating questionable behavior in a systematic fashion" for businesses and organizations (Mena, Rintamäki, Fleming, & Spicer, 2016, p.

734). What is brought up to public consciousness is a mix of "retrospective and prospective" given the role of news media mediating "prospective memory" (Tenenboim-Weinblatt, 2013, p. 91).

This phenomenon has been observed in terms of organizational remembering and forgetting [also known as "organizational unlearning" (de Holan, 2011, p. 317)]. Strategic unlearning is part of organizational management to enable organizations to change; prior learning may obstruct the acquisition of new knowledge and its activation. What needs updating is the "stable organizational memory" that retains even as employees arrive and depart (de Holan, 2011, p. 317). Some of the mechanisms for enacting voluntary organizational forgetting include four elements: "assets and technologies, routines and procedures, structure and understandings" (collective understandings informed by organizational values and beliefs) (de Holan, 2011, p. 317). There are other tools that corporations may use to affect corporate memory:

Forgetting work involves manipulating short-term conditions of the event, silencing vocal 'rememberers,' and undermining collective mnemonic traces that sustain a version of the past (Mena, Rintamäki, Fleming, & Spicer, 2016, p. 720).

Such forgetting has been applied to the non-remembrance of past misdeeds, in order to protect company reputation and brand (Mena, Rintamäki, Fleming, & Spicer, 2016, p. 720). "Forgetting work" includes efforts to manipulate, silence, and undermine (Mena, Rintamäki, Fleming, & Spicer, 2016, p. 725), and these are often based on power relationships. To mitigate the concentrations of power, some advocate "assemblies for deciding collective actions on collective matters-of-concern" (Galloway, April 2006, p. 1), given the need to learn from past mistakes. Regular practices of organizations and groups may also reconfigure collective memory and collective forgetting, based on what is seen as relevant. Rituals are often conducted to enhance remembering, and language is a common medium for memory and forgetting.

The analogy between formal workplace organizations and more freeform electronic hive minds apply to some degree. While workplaces are often more formal and tightly coupled, with formal and often centralized leadership, defined policies and values, and formal methods of propagating workplace culture, electronic hive minds tend to be informal, loosely coupled, supported by distributed leadership (with technological stand-ins), defined by evolved and emergent values, with technological methods for propagating social norms and cultures. And yet, what an EHM values affects what is learned and what is forgotten. This is a kind of "cognition through social network" (Coman & Hirst, Sept. 2011), with different types of mnemonic traces (digital vs. analog). Induced forgetting in online spaces may be a factor of focus, and a matter of interactional conversations between speakers and listeners that may propagate through social networks. What is retained and valued depends on "how people exposed to attitudinally biased selective practice propagate the practice and forgetting effects into subsequent conversations with attitudinally similar and dissimilar others and, through these conversations, affect subsequent acts of remembering" (Coman & Hirst, 2012, p. 321). The mnemonic influence of what people say and what they fail to say and where they are silent affects "retrieval-induced forgetting…(which) is transitive" and propagates through social networks (Coman & Hirst, 2012, p. 321) and the conversational remembering between dyadic pairs (Coman & Hirst, 2015, p. 1).

Also, distractive forgetting may also be deployed online by sending out a number of messages and making it difficult for people to attend. Interestingly, the process is not just linear: "Changes in memory lead to changes in attitude" (Coman & Hirst, 2012, p. 333), and attitude affects what is remembered, and so on. This would suggest that cycles may become virtuous or vicious, positive or negative, constructive or destructive.

Unintended Forgetting

Some forms of forgetting are apparently unintentional and occur under the level of consciousness. One study involved participants who exaggerated their own prior actions while trying to impress an experiment confederate and ended up harming their own memory's accuracy (Brady & Lord, 2013). In a sense, this prior result may come from the "saying-is-believing paradigm" and "the close connection between shared reality and shared memories" (Echterhoff, Higgins, & Levine, 2009, as cited in Hirst & Coman, 2018, p. 88). Public testimonials through "saying-is-believing" (Hausmann, 2005) apparently affirms personal belief in and commitments to what is spoken and shared.

In the same way that people may acquire true (actually experienced) memories, they can also acquire false ones and report out on planted memories that they may not be aware were not actually acquired from their own experiences. (People also do not always pay attention to where information comes from. In "breaking" events, oftentimes, the available information is incomplete and often incorrect; yet, people are susceptible to the rumors, even those of opaque origins, and they have a hard time corrected incorrect initial impressions even if they are given chances to revise their ideas. The initial impressions can leave residual trace memories even when the person knows that the information is inaccurate. This is a little like the Internet joke of not being able to "un-see" something.)

Online Sociality and Forgetting

When people interact socially, there is an exchange, a give-and-take, and in conversation, "speakers and listeners will often influence each other's memories, and in doing so, promote the formation of a shared, or collective, memory." (Coman & Hirst, 2015, p. 1) There are reinforcements of ideas through "conversational remembering" (Hirst & Coman, 2018, p. 89). Some groups may end up with "mnemonic convergence" or the clustering around particular shared memories (Hirst & Coman, 2018, p. 89). In socializing, people tend to engage in concurrent retrieval of memories and to synchronize them, enabling socially shared retrieval-induced forgetting (Coman & Hirst, 2015, pp. 5 - 6). The collective memories reside in individuals and in groups. The larger the sizes of groups, the more diverse the sub-groups and motifs may be, and maybe the broader the diversities of ideas. In virtual groups, there may be center-periphery dynamics, with those preferring the center as lower-case "conservative" and those preferring the periphery as lower-case "liberal". There are some early research questions in this space:

Why do some individual memories, and not others, become shared across a community? When might one expect a collective memory to form? What cognitive mechanisms are involved, and how do these mechanisms interact with the social relationships within a community? (Hirst & Coman, 2018, p. 88).

Based on long-term research, (social) forgetting is tied to "unpracticed memories" (Hirst & Coman, 2018, p. 89), a lack of focus on the "unmentioned."

Online communities, such as electronic hive minds, are about intercommunications, if nothing else. As such, they serve as "mnemonic community" (Zerubavel, 2004, as cited in Stone & Hirst, 2014, p. 314), with communicative acts of remembering that "can induce collective selective forgetting, clearly one component of any collective memory" (Hirst & Coman, 2018, p. 88). People can be highly sensitive and socially attuned, in ways that may make them susceptible to non-relevant messaging. Older research suggests that people may be unduly influenced by others' reportage of whether a messenger is likeable or not and that such second-hand impressions may lead to skewing perceptions of the related messaging (Higgins & Rholes, 1977). The study of collective memories generally includes both the psychological and social construction approaches (Stone & Hirst, 2014, p. 314), with implications for individuals and social entities. The space is rife for analysis, with different frameworks for interpretation, such as "whether a silence is accompanied by covert remembering, whether the silence is intentional or unintentional, and whether the silenced memory is related or unrelated to the memories emerging in a conversation" (Stone, Coman, Brown, Koppel, & Hirst, 2012, p. 39).

The induction of forgetting may be exacerbated on social media, which is often about people connecting around the purposeful sharing of their respective inner states to enable social bonding and the development of some level of relating:

According to a current definition (Echterhoff, Higgins et al., 209; also see Echterhoff, 2010), shared reality is the product of the motivated process of experiencing a commonality of inner states (e.g. attitudes, impressions, or judgments) about the world. Shared reality requires that people infer or know another person's inner state and are aware of the target of this inner state... (Echterhoff, 2014, p. 105)

This purposeful sharing may involve the exchange of intercommunications, which may enhance some aspects of remembrance and some aspects of forgetting. The social aspects mean that such conversations are shared further, sometimes leading to the propagation of forgetting. (Echterhoff, 2014, p. 106)

REMEMBERING AND FORGETTING IN THE ELECTRONIC HIVE MIND

Understanding what may have been forgotten by an EHM involves looking for invisibilities, absences, white spaces, what Sherlock Holmes observed as the dog that didn't bark (in "Silver Blaze"). A simple approach works in research, where an official account of a historical event may be compared against historically known and documented data. While there are known-knowns, there are "known unknowns" and "unknown unknowns," which can contribute confusion. Or there may be fast unfolding events for an EHM that lessens the capabilities of fact checking. Some data may not have the focus of historians, who can explore and apply high-level standards to the vetting work.

The information in social media is incomplete, even when public facing data is captured fully (N=all), the private channel data are unavailable (and form a "black box"). Also, what is seen in social communications shows a "survival bias"; these are the details that made it into articulations and interchanges. What is not mentioned is everything else. Part of this "everything else" may be relevant (in the past and today and into the future). What is mentioned is whatever survives inattention, apathy, lack of knowing, and other challenges. So what does this all mean for EHMs? How does remembering and forgetting relate to the main objectives of the particular EHMs? What needs to be remembered with accuracy—history, personages, events, processes and methods, values, and others? (Table 1)

The sharing of this knowledge is to bolster people's consciousness of their own remembering and forgetting, and to help them make decisions about how to proceed with proper remembering and forgetting in communities that are virtual and distributed, such as EHMs. What knowledge should be valued, and why? What social norms should be promoted to be more inclusive of knowledge? What should the "authorizing environment" look like, and why? How can new members be read into the conventions of the community? How can new voices be encouraged and broadcast? How should social tuning be supported to promote a growing and healthy EHM? How can what is relevant be explored with higher levels of emotional salience for increased remembrance? This information may help inform people's imaginations.

This knowledge can bring with it sinister implications, particularly if remembering and forgetting are in the hands of malevolent individuals or groups. The selective erasure of history from social forgetting and social tuning, or the substitution of falsified stories (myths) and "revisionist history" in place of actual history, or the harnessing of counter messaging to enforce forgetting, all have very risky and dangerous outcomes. These have dangerous implications for the decisions that people would make and the misunderstandings they would use to justify their actions. Planted hostilities can spark people to acts of mass violence, as in the "tall trees" messaging leading to the Rwandan genocide in 1994. With the variance in people's respective perspectives and life experiences, and the need to enable learning for each new generation to avoid forgetting from population attrition), and the polysemous (many-meaninged) nature of writing and multimodal communications, even an accurate history can be misread and responded to in unconstructive or anti-humanity sorts of ways.

Table 1. Four Parts to the Analysis of Remembering/Forgetting in Electronic Hive Minds

Part 1: Remembering / Forgetting Phenomena in the Electronic Hive Mind
• What does natural forgetting look like over time in an EHM? What are some natural rates of memory decay? What percentage retention and what percentage decay may be seen in EHMs?   o What does accelerated forgetting look like over time? Why?   • What does artificial forgetting look like over time in an EHM? What are some artificial rates of memory decay in this state? What percentage retention and what percentage decay may be seen in EHMs?   • What does mass forgetting look like in an electronic hive mind (EHM)? Is there a normal rate of forgetting for general EHMs or EHMs of particular types? If so, how and why? How it is possible to see absences or what is not there or what is no longer remembered?   • What does partial forgetting look like in an EHM? How is it possible to see absences or what is not there or what is no longer remembered? How is it possible to identify skew in memories?   o How are absences understood in terms of forgetting? How can absences be seen without being presumptive about what EHMs should cover?   • What does mass remembering look like in an EHM? What does partial remembering look like in an EHM?   o What are ways to identify what the focuses of remembering are in an EHM?   o What are ways to identify partial understandings or partial memories? Partially developed memories?   • What does it look like when an issue is top-of-mind on an EHM? What does short-term working memory look like in an EHM?   o What does short-term forgetting look like?

Part 2: "Folk" History-Keeping, Commemoration, and Fact-Checking Roles in EHMs
• Are there ways to set up tripwires for EHMs to become aware when the remembering and forgetting are misfocused? Are there ways to set up sensors (of people, of technologies, of cyborgs) to understand the state of an EHM in terms of remembering and forgetting?   • Who are those in an EHM that take on the roles of historian or commemorator? Of fact checker? How do they express into the space? What are their apparent motivations? What sorts of effects and outcomes can they have?   o How is data vetted for remembering (if it is)? For attention? What is the role of EHM values in the selection of data for remembering? How are critical ideas and information identified in a particular EHM? What types of information are valued vs. others in a particular EHM? (Are there larger patterns of valuing across a variety of similar types of EHMs?)   • How can the distributed leaders of EHMs support accurate remembering and accurate forgetting?   o What are group behaviors conducive to collective remembering? What are group behaviors conducive to collective forgetting?   ▪ How can pro-remembering activities be encouraged and those conducive to inappropriate forgetting be discouraged?   ▪ What are ways for EHMs to encourage adaptive remembering and adaptive forgetting?   • What are the roles of technology in remembering? In forgetting? What can memes provide in terms of focus? Are there more effective ways of keeping important values to the fore?   • How can the respective identities in an EHM be formed to be more open to differing messaging? To different types of remembering and forgetting?

Part 3: Content for Remembering; Content for Forgetting
• What memories are selected for remembering over time? What level of time duration? Which part of the population is targeted?   • Which memories are selected for targeted or purposeful forgetting, and why? What sorts of memories are inconvenient? Difficult? Non-aligned with social identity? Emotionally painful?   o How is remembering aligned with certain desirable behaviors? How is forgetting aligned with certain desirable behaviors?   • What are some of the constructive effects of mass forgetting in an electronic hive mind? What are some of the destructive effects of mass forgetting in an EHM?

Part 4: Directed and Induced Actions for Social Remembering and Forgetting
• How can new learning be written into EHMs in an effective way? What are effective ways to rehearse, reinforce, refresh, and retain?   • When does remembering get in the way of adaptivity? When does forgetting get in the way of adaptivity?   • What are "remember" cues in EHMs?   • What are "forget" cues in EHMs? Are there ways of targeted forgetting for particular purposes?   • Are there analogical methods of interrupting incorrect memories, so these are not coded into the EHM? Substitution? Distraction? Interruption? Multitasking? Selective recall? If there are non-obvious methods of malicious group memory manipulation in an EHM, is there a way to identify this?   o Are there ways to head off memory (and forgetting) manipulations?   • What are ways to instantiate long-term memory for an EHM? How can new members be read into particular ideas, to maintain long-term memory? Social norms? Cultural values? Authorizing environment? Leadership? What are routines and subroutines that may enhance proper remembering and proper forgetting? And other aspects?   o In a context of mass forgetting on EHM, what are some ways to bring back memories (with reminders and other efforts)?

While some types of forgetting are temporary, others may lapse into permanent irretrievability and oblivion for future populations, potentially leading to ahistoricity about some topics (or the filling in of gaps in the record with fictional stories and ripe imaginations). (With the speed and directionality of time, some information—like extinct animal species—disappear forever, without the potential of recoverability. Unrecorded memories are also lost forever when people pass on.)

The idea is that members of an EHM should be aware of what they are focusing on by commission but also by omission. The idea is to have EHMs advance in knowing and conscious ways, without subconscious cues to forgetting from preferences, identity, expression, social signaling, and other approaches.

Even if the entire EHM is not read into the issue, individuals (even as "isolates") in the space may work on themselves to move beyond their own confirmation bias and filter bubbles. They can widen the aperture to a wider range of information, and they can serve in the role of folk historians and commemorators and fact checkers. An initial first "check" may be to see if they fit the definition of being a "true believer" (in the Eric Hoffer vein, 1951) and have subsumed themselves unthinkingly into the EHM; if so, it would be healthier to have a full extrication first, so freethinking is enabled.

They can work on memes that make an important fact memorable and places it top-of-mind for others. They may bridge between different communities. They may enlarge the social space for unwanted and discomfiting memories. They may bring people together, those who are "conservative" (lower case) and prefer the *status quo* and those who are "liberal" (lower case) and who may be interested in a direction change for the virtual community. Perhaps there are ways to constructively call out others who are sharing erroneous information, so the community can benefit. Perhaps there can be counter-messaging to the silences and expressions that lead to selective forgetting or accelerated forgetting. Perhaps some types of messaging may be restorative.

Understanding Social Forgetting in a Fandom Context (an Early Case)

A superficial walk-through of this concept is based on the idea of "fandom" and "followership," by focusing on a one-to-many broadcast account of a singer who is in the top 10 Twitter accounts. A hypothesis here is that people are willing to believe certain things about a star whom they idolize, and that they will defend their star with various expressions of loyalty and care and framing of news reports. An assumption is that followers (fans) may also empathize deeply with whomever they follow and want to emulate them. (An example of this includes the fans of the Barbie doll who have gone through various cosmetic surgeries and tens of thousands of dollars in costs, in order to look more like their fictional idol.) At the time of the data capture, this accomplished performer had shared 10,204 Tweets. She had 1,101 following, and 88,116,621 followers. Her account, which was started in October 2009, had 998 likes. A surface read-through of her Tweetstream (with 2,654 original messages a fourth of the 10,204 in the account) showed one-to-many sharing of ads for her makeup line, a jewelry line, a fashion line, and her performances. These messages range from the day of capture in November 2018 back to May 2018, for seven months' worth of messaging. She shares information about her globetrotting. The photos are high-fashion high-glamor fantasy ones. She had many shared messages about national politics and voting. Interestingly, other data sources—mainline mass media, a Wikipedia page, and other sources—contribute to this performer's good name and fame. They report on generous personal contributions to charities like hospitals and disaster recovery efforts. While her entertainment persona is edgy, her personal comments to the public have been judicious and apparently supported by a professional public relations team. Responses do not seem on the whole anything but laudatory, with little derogatory. Her tone is inclusive of her fans, and she expresses appreciation for their affection. In terms of interactivity, the dynamics of this account do seem to be one-to-many, without long chains of interactions.

A map of the people engaged in the Tweetstream for this account is a global one, with broad interest and engagement (Figure 1).

The out-degree for the following accounts (those that the singer's account follows) may be seen in Figure 2.

An auto-extraction of the available themes shows focuses on birthday, photo shoots, various seasonal collections, and others. The themes themselves seem generally fairly light. (The "http" and "https" themes were removed in order to get past the URLs to see what the main topics are. For all the close-in messages about voting in recent weeks, the main focuses seem to be on-message for the commercial brand and the persona behind the social performances.) (Figure 3)

A machine analysis of the sentiment in the messaging finds that most trend "Very positive" (Figure 4). Broadly speaking, people respond well to positivity.

Figure 1. A global map of the followers of the target star

Figure 2. Sociogram of outlinks from the target account on Twitter

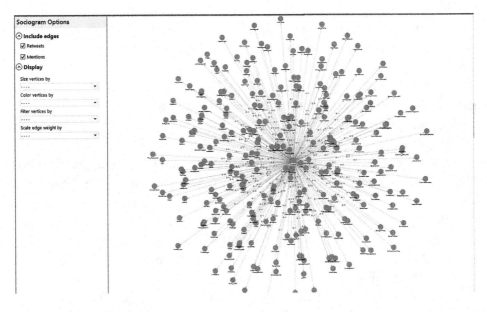

Figure 3. Autocoded themes from the tweetstream of the singer's account

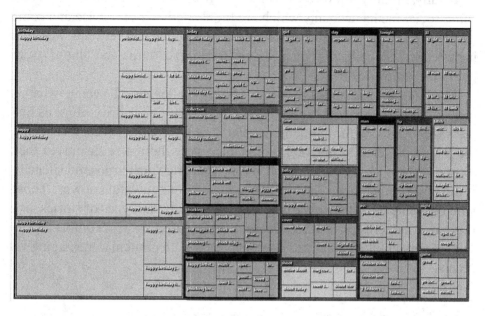

Figure 4. Autocoded sentiment analysis from the tweetstream of the singer's account

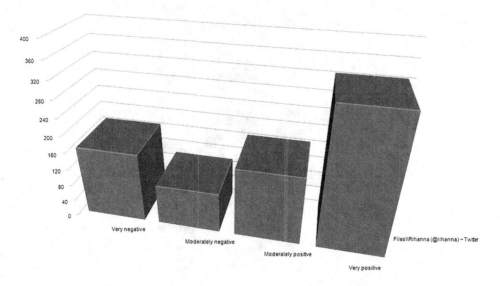

Finally, Figure 5 shows a word cloud of the Tweetstream, which suggests some social media accounts which are highly active in the space and some hashtag (#) terms that draw wide attention. Replies and retweets were not included in this collection of messages. Also, the "http" and "https" were put in the stopwords list.

This initial look suggests some of the challenges of seeing what is unspeakable and unseeable and taboo. The nature of celebrity suggests that messages outside of the momentum will not be speakable or seeable, not until the grip on power relaxes (over time). If there were alternative narratives, then it is possible to identify silences. It is clear that there are purposeful silences, some known unknowns…as well as numerous unknown unknowns. Those who consume the fantasies of celebrity want particular types of stories, and they are not interested in others. Executives of entertainment companies can sell the personality and related products better with particular messaging vs. others.

Figure 5. A word frequency word cloud from the tweetstream

DISCUSSION

In distributed electronic hive minds, some ephemeral, some semi-permanent, the work of remembering and forgetting are important aspects of EHM adaptivity and well-being, particularly of its members. Being aware of how knowledge may be written into group memory may be important for collective mind management (and to protect against remembering and forgetting manipulations). Collective focus is a limited resource, and directing people's focus has both remembering and forgetting implications. Understanding the tendencies of a particular EHM—its values, its collective identity, its messaging, its membership (including its folk historians and fact checkers, its leadership, and others), its aide- aide-mémoire—may provide insights on where invisibilities and blind spots are.

FUTURE RESEARCH DIRECTIONS

This chapter proposes an informal approach to understanding EHMs and their respective tendencies to remembering and forgetting. A more objective and formalized mapping of what EHMs tend to forget and have forgotten would be valuable. Also, how can forgetting be accurately and objectively measured?

Also, this work touches lightly on the roles of social media and ICT in social remembrance and social forgetting. Experimental and empirical based research would strengthen understandings of the varying roles of technologies. (Some sociotechnical sites, such as some popular imageboards and electronic bulletin boards, maintain an enforced forgetting by archiving threads and taking them offline and of supporting communities with fast-moving ideas that have seconds to attain attention before they are replaced by other ideas. The ephemera means that people cannot fix ideas with any consistency.) The uses of technologies for learning (normal acquisition) and consolidation of ideas is another angle that may be effectively studied.

The ethics of remembering and forgetting are also critical to this space, particularly given the wide ranges of EHMs in the world. Malicious employment of induced forgetting *en masse* may also be another line of study.

CONCLUSION

Memories are perishable; in digital spaces, even if 1's and 0's are thought to persist, these biodegrade and go defunct. Even as technologies extend human perceptual and experiential capabilities, human attention itself is not infinite, and even if digital data may be retrieved into forever, there has to first be the interest in the data and in the remembering; otherwise, the findability of the information may be moot. Large-scale attentional focus is expensive because of opportunity costs (the populations of individuals can be spending their time and energy on other more relevant endeavors). Collective memories are generally more resilient than single-held memories because of the remembering by multiple members and the potential for sharing, but groupness may also be collectively inhibitory of remembering in other ways, with possibly "less effective cues for later retrieval" (Barber, Rajaram, & Aron, 2010, p. 255). The work of remembering with accuracy requires sophistication and hard effort—to ensure that shared information in accurate, that histories are vetted and objective, that depictions of the world are accurate to it. This requires that people filter precious signal from noise. This requires that people struggle against their own worst instincts—their tendencies to place their own egos at the center of their "worlds" (loving flattery, loving others' agreement with them), their tendencies to select messaging that aligns with their own senses of the world and to downplay whatever does not align(confirmation bias), and their tendencies to take the easy way forward and not engage in the hard work of research and learning.

Different features of social media may exacerbate this challenge of accurate remembering. Filter bubbles are formed easily based on algorithms that deliver information to people based on preferences. Online, "relationships" are superficial, ephemeral, and fast moving; they are hard to validate to a person. In most cases, the cost of joining an EHM is negligible. Moderators of social networks may be there informally, and they have little power to vet for informational accuracy—based on social norms, based on social media policies, and based on legal liabilities if moderators take on too much of an editorial role. Digital memory is long (even if it is potentially not "forever"), and contents that are released online may be eminently findable and discoverable, including conspiracy theories and hoaxing.

In electronic hive minds, the various members would benefit from understanding the dynamics of remembering and forgetting, and how who they are and how they engage with others can affect their memory stores, both in terms of remembering and forgetting. They would benefit from knowing that understanding something with accuracy is important, so they do not have a store of falsehoods and half-truths, given how misinformation can affect people's decision making. This work has implications on record-keeping, so that what is stored has informational value and not just noise. It has implications for how to talk…to remember (encode)…and to forget ("learn over," "re-learn" more than "unlearn")…strategically. In the end, it is important to keep relevant and accurate information top-of-mind, in working memory as well as in long-term memory storage in electronic hive minds, so their members' well-being and interests may be protected, with a proper selected bouquet of "forget-me-nots."

REFERENCES

Abel, M., & Bäuml, K.-H. (2017). Testing the context-change account of list-method directed forgetting: The role of retention interval. *Journal of Memory and Language, 92*, 170–182. doi:10.1016/j.jml.2016.06.009

Anderson, M. C., & Hanslmayr, S. (2014). Neural mechanisms of motivated forgetting. *Trends in Cognitive Sciences, 18*(6), 279–292. doi:10.1016/j.tics.2014.03.002 PMID:24747000

Averell, L., & Heathcote, A. (2011). The form of the forgetting curve and the fate of memories. *Journal of Mathematical Psychology, 55*(1), 25–35. doi:10.1016/j.jmp.2010.08.009

Barber, S. J., Rajaram, S., & Aron, A. (2010). When two is too many: Collaborative encoding impairs memory. *Memory & Cognition, 38*(3), 255–264. doi:10.3758/MC.38.3.255 PMID:20234016

Barber, S. J., Rajaram, S., & Fox, E. B. (2012). Learning and remembering with others: The key role of retrieval in shaping group recall and collective memory. *Social Cognition, 30*(1), 121–132. doi:10.1521oco.2012.30.1.121 PMID:25431516

Brady, S. E., & Lord, C. G. (2013). When liars fool themselves: Motive to impress alters memory for one's own past evaluative actions. *Social Cognition*, *31*(5), 599–612. doi:10.1521oco.2013.31.5.599

Brown, R., & Kulik, J. (1977). Flashbulb memories. *Cognition*, *5*(1), 73–99. doi:10.1016/0010-0277(77)90018-X

Coman, A., & Hirst, W. (2012). Cognition through a social network: The propagation of induced forgetting and practice effects. *Journal of Experimental Psychology*, *141*(2), 321–336. doi:10.1037/a0025247 PMID:21910558

Coman, A., & Hirst, W. (2015). Social identity and socially shared retrieval-induced forgetting: The effects of group membership. *Journal of Experimental Psychology*, 1–6. PMID:25938179

Coman, A., Stone, C. B., Castrano, E., & Hirst, W. (2014). Justifying atrocities: The effect of moral-disengagement strategies on socially shared retrieval-induced forgetting. *Psychological Science*, *25*(6), 1281–1285. doi:10.1177/0956797614531024 PMID:24747169

Connerton, P. (2008). Seven types of forgetting. *Memory Studies*, *1*(1), 59–71. doi:10.1177/1750698007083889

Cue, A., Koppel, J., & Hirst, W. (2007). Silence is not golden: A case for socially shared retrieval-induced forgetting. *Psychological Science*, 727–733. PMID:17680945

de Holan, P. B. (2011). Agency in voluntary organizational forgetting. *Journal of Management Inquiry*, *20*(3), 317–322. doi:10.1177/1056492611408265

Delaney, P. F., Goldman, J. A., King, J. S., & Nelson-Gray, R. O. (2015). Mental toughness, reinforcement sensitivity theory, and the five-factor model: Personality and directed forgetting. *Personality and Individual Differences*, *83*, 180–184. doi:10.1016/j.paid.2015.04.020

Dodge, M., & Kitchin, R. (2007). 'Outlines of a world coming into existence': Pervasive computing and the ethics of forgetting. *Environment and Planning. B, Planning & Design*, *34*(3), 431–445. doi:10.1068/b32041t

Ebbinghaus, H. (1885). *Ueber das Gedächtnis* [Memory: A contribution to experimental psychology] (H. A. Ruger & C. E. Bussenius, Trans.). Retrieved Nov. 12, 2018, from http://psychclassics.yorku.ca/Ebbinghaus/index.htm

Echterhoff, G. (2014). Achieving commonality in interpersonal communication: Shared reality and memory processes. *Asian Journal of Social Psychology*, *17*(2), 104–107. doi:10.1111/ajsp.12048

Ecker, U. K. H., Lewandowsky, S., & Tang, D. T. W. (2010). Explicit warnings reduce but do not eliminate the continued influence of misinformation. *Memory & Cognition*, *38*(8), 1087–1100. doi:10.3758/MC.38.8.1087 PMID:21156872

Esposito, E. (2008). Social forgetting: A systems-theory approach. In Media and Cultural Memory. Berlin: Walter de Gruyter.

EU GDPR.org. (2018). *Trunomi*. Retrieved Nov. 13, 2018, from https://eugdpr.org/

Fawcett, J. M., Taylor, T. L., & Nadel, L. (2013). Event-method directed forgetting: Forgetting a video segment is more effortful than remembering it. *Acta Psychologica*, *144*(2), 332–343. doi:10.1016/j.actpsy.2013.07.005 PMID:23933003

Fernandes, M., & Saunders, J. (2013). Does retrieval-induced forgetting affect future social behavior? *Acta Psychologica*, *144*(1), 1–5. doi:10.1016/j.actpsy.2013.04.017 PMID:23739579

Galloway, A. (2006, April). Collective remembering and the importance of forgetting: a critical design challenge. In *Designing for Collective Remembering Workshop, CHI* (Vol. 23, pp. 1-5). ACM.

Gao, H., Cao, B., Zhang, Q., Qi, M., Li, F., & Li, H. (2016). Intending to forget is not easy: Behavioral and electrophysiological evidence. *International Journal of Psychophysiology*, *104*, 1–9. doi:10.1016/j.ijpsycho.2016.03.007 PMID:27021846

Garaerts, E., & McNally, R. J. (2008). Forgetting unwanted memories: Directed forgetting and thought suppression methods. *Acta Psychologica*, *127*(3), 614–622. doi:10.1016/j.actpsy.2007.11.003 PMID:18164273

Hai-Jew, S. (2019). The electronic hive mind and cybersecurity: Mass-scale human cognitive limits to explain the 'weakest link' in cybersecurity. In *Global Cyber Security Labor Shortage and International Business Risk* (pp. 206–262). Hershey, PA: IGI Global. doi:10.4018/978-1-5225-5927-6.ch011

Hausmann, L. R. M. (2005). *Developing group perceptions through communication: Extensions of the saying-is-believing effect* (Doctoral thesis). University of Pittsburgh.

Higgins, E. T., & Rholes, W. S. (1978). 'Saying is believing': Effects of message modification on memory and liking for the person described. *Journal of Experimental Social Psychology*, *14*(4), 363–378. doi:10.1016/0022-1031(78)90032-X

Hirst, W., & Coman, A. (2018). Building a collective memory: The case for collective forgetting. *Current Opinion in Psychology*, *23*, 88–92. doi:10.1016/j.copsyc.2018.02.002 PMID:29459336

Hirst, W., & Echterhoff, G. (2018). More to episodic memory than epistemic assertion: The role of social bonds and interpersonal connection. *Behavioral and Brain Sciences*, *41*, E17. doi:10.1017/S0140525X17001388 PMID:29353571

Hoffer, E. (1951). *The True Believer: Thoughts on the Nature of Mass Movements*. New York: Harper & Row, Publishers, Inc.

Johnson, H. M., & Seifert, C. M. (1994). Sources of the continued influence effect: When misinformation in memory affects later inferences. *Journal of Experimental Psychology. Learning, Memory, and Cognition*, *20*(6), 1420–1436. doi:10.1037/0278-7393.20.6.1420 PMID:7983472

Koops, B.-J. (2011). Forgetting footprints, shunning shadows. A critical analysis of the 'right to be forgotten' in bit data practice. *Scripted*, *8*(3), 229–256.

Koppel, J., Wohl, D., Meksin, R., & Hirst, W. (2014). The effect of listening to others remember on subsequent memory: The roles of expertise and trust in socially shared retrieval-induced forgetting and social contagion. *Social Cognition*, *32*(2), 148–180. doi:10.1521oco.2014.32.2.148

Kraemer, P. J., & Golding, J. M. (1997). Adaptive forgetting in animals. *Psychonomic Bulletin & Review*, *4*(4), 480–491. doi:10.3758/BF03214337

Lang, J., & Marquis, P. (2010). Reasoning under inconsistency: A forgetting-based approach. *Artificial Intelligence*, *174*(12-13), 799–823. doi:10.1016/j.artint.2010.04.023

Loftus, E. F., & Loftus, G. R. (1980, May). On the permanence of stored information in the human brain. *The American Psychologist*, *35*(5), 409–420. doi:10.1037/0003-066X.35.5.409 PMID:7386971

Mayer-Schönberger, V. (2007, Apr.). *Useful void: The art of forgetting in the age of ubiquitous computing*. RWP07-022. Faculty Research Working Papers Series. John F. Kennedy School of Government, Harvard University.

McGeoch, J. A. (1932). Forgetting and the law of disuse. *Psychological Review, 39*(4), 352–370. doi:10.1037/h0069819

Mena, S., Rintamäki, J., Fleming, P., & Spicer, A. (2016). On the forgetting of corporate irresponsibility. *Academy of Management Review, 41*(4), 720–738. doi:10.5465/amr.2014.0208

Michaelian, K. (2011). The epistemology of forgetting. *Erkenn, 74*(3), 399–424. doi:10.100710670-010-9232-4

Nørby, S., Lange, M., & Larsen, A. (2010). Forgetting to forget: On the duration of voluntary suppression of neutral and emotional memories. *Acta Psychologica, 133*(1), 73–80. doi:10.1016/j.actpsy.2009.10.002 PMID:19906363

Payne, B. K., & Corrigan, E. (2007). Emotional constraints on intentional forgetting. *Journal of Experimental Social Psychology, 43*(5), 780–786. doi:10.1016/j.jesp.2006.07.005

Ram, U. (2009, September). Ways of forgetting: Israel and the obliterated memory of the Palestinian Nakba. *Journal of Historical Sociology, 22*(3), 366–395. doi:10.1111/j.1467-6443.2009.01354.x

Reppa, I., Williams, K. E., Worth, E. R., Greville, W. J., & Saunders, J. (2017). Memorable objects are more susceptible to forgetting: Evidence for the inhibitory account of retrieval-induced forgetting. *Acta Psychologica, 181*, 51–61. doi:10.1016/j.actpsy.2017.09.012 PMID:29049936

Rosen, J. (2010, July 25). The end of forgetting. *The New York Times Magazine*, 32 – 45.

Schuman, H., & Rodgers, W. L. (2004, June). Cohorts, chronology, and collective memories. *Public Opinion Quarterly, 68*(2), 217–254. doi:10.1093/poq/nfh012

Sell, A. J. (2016). Applying the intentional forgetting process to forgiveness. *Journal of Applied Research in Memory and Cognition, 5*(1), 10–20. doi:10.1016/j.jarmac.2015.10.003

Stone, C. B., Barnier, A. J., Sutton, J., & Hirst, W. (2009). Building consensus about the past: Schema consistency and convergence in socially shared retrieval-induced forgetting. Psychology Press.

Stone, C. B., Barnier, A. J., Sutton, J., & Hirst, W. (2012). Forgetting our personal past: Socially shared retrieval-induced forgetting of autobiographical memories. *Journal of Experimental Psychology*, 1–16. PMID:23148464

Stone, C. B., Coman, A., Brown, A. D., Koppel, J., & Hirst, W. (2012). Toward a science of silence: The consequences of leaving a memory unsaid. *Perspectives on Psychological Science*, 7(1), 39–53. doi:10.1177/1745691611427303 PMID:26168421

Stone, C. B., & Hirst, W. (2014). (Induced) forgetting to form a collective memory. *Memory Studies*, 7(3), 314–327. doi:10.1177/1750698014530621

Tenenboim-Weinblatt, K. (2013). Bridging collective memories and public agendas: Toward a theory of mediated prospective memory. *Communication Theory*, 23(2), 91–111. doi:10.1111/comt.12006

Todor, I. (2012). Age-related differences in directed forgetting. In the proceedings of the International Conference on Education and Educational Psychology (ICEEPSY 2012). *Procedia: Social and Behavioral Sciences*, 69, 1402–1409. doi:10.1016/j.sbspro.2012.12.079

Vinitzk-Seroussi, V., & Teeger, C. (2010, March). Unpacking the unspoken: Silence in collective memory and forgetting. *Social Forces*, 88(3), 1103–1122. doi:10.1353of.0.0290

Vivas, A. B., Marful, A., Panagiotidou, D., & Bajo, T. (2016). Instruction to forget lead to emotional devaluation. *Cognition*, 150, 85–91. doi:10.1016/j.cognition.2016.02.005 PMID:26872249

Wang, Y., Cao, Z., Zhu, Z., Cai, H., & Wu, Y. (2015). Cue-independent forgetting by intentional suppression – Evidence for inhibition as the mechanism of intentional forgetting. *Cognition*, 143, 31–35. doi:10.1016/j.cognition.2015.05.025 PMID:26113446

Weldon, M. S., & Bellinger, K. D. (1997). Collective memory: Collaborative and individual processes in remembering. *Journal of Experimental Psychology*, 23(5), 1160–1175. PMID:9293627

Yang, T., Lei, X., & Anderson, M. (2016). Decreased inhibitory control of negative information in directed forgetting. *International Journal of Psychophysiology*, 100, 44–51. doi:10.1016/j.ijpsycho.2015.09.007 PMID:26386395

ADDITIONAL READING

Hoffer, E. (1951). *The True Believer: Thoughts on the Nature of Mass Movements*. New York: Harper & Row, Publishers, Inc.

KEY TERMS AND DEFINITIONS

Adaptive Forgetting: The use of forgetting to help individuals and/or groups to better adjust to the larger ecosystem.

Agenda Setting: The identification of topics that populations should focus on as important or relevant (such as via the role of mass media).

Aide-Mémoire: An aid to memory, a mnemonic device.

Cognition Through Social Network: Learning through social means.

Commemorator Role: The position of reminding the larger community of particular historical facts in an electronic hive mind (and in other contexts).

Electronic Hive Mind: A synchronous temporal and informal patchwork of emergent shared social consciousness (held by geographically distributed people, cyborgs, and robots) enabled by online social connectivity (across a range of social media platforms on the web and internet), based around various dimensions of shared attractive interests.

Flashbulb Memories: A detailed memory of a particular moment or situation.

Induced Forgetting: Prompted disremembering.

Lethotechnics: The techniques for forgetting.

Mass Forgetting: To not think about or to not remember on a large-population scale.

Mnemonic: A device that aids or supports memory, an aide-mémoire.

Mnemonic Silence: Using silence to aid in public memory.

Motivated Forgetting: Purposive forgetting or avoidance of non-remembering.

Motivated Recall: Purposive remembering.

Organizational Forgetting: The practice of unlearning within an organization.

Retrieval-Induced Forgetting (RIF): The calling up of selected memories resulting in the forgetting of non-retrieved related and unrelated memories (includes within-individual RIF and socially-shared RIF), with initial research of this phenomenon in 1994.

Saying-Is-Believing: A testimonial-based remembering of a phenomenon, the reinforcement of an underlying idea through public sharing.

Silencing: Muting, the preventing of sharing of information with others.

Social Tuning: The phenomenon of people adjusting their own ideas in order to align socially with the ideas of those around them.

Socially-Shared Retrieval-Induced Forgetting (SS-RIF): The forgetting of particular information when an individual is induced to remember some aspects of learning through social interactions and inter-communications (social sharing) but not others.

Sousveillance: Bottom-up or within-group surveillance by a participant in the activity (in a term coined by Steve Mann.

Within-Individual Retrieval-Induced Forgetting (WI-RIF): The forgetting of particular information when an individual is induced to remember some aspects of learning but not others.

Chapter 8

Micro– to Meso– to Macro–Scale Coordinated Individual and Group Action(s) on Electronic Hive Minds

ABSTRACT

So many human endeavors are dependent on others' actions and interests. On an electronic hive mind (EHM), coordination online may spark and sustain actions by the body (the members of the EHM). Such coordination occurs over a range of human endeavors and continuously at different scales: micro (individual, dyadic, and motif levels), meso (small to large groups), and macro (system-wide, societal, web-scale levels). This chapter explores EHMs as planned-action entities and offers some early insights about some common practices based on multiple exemplars and the application of abductive logic.

INTRODUCTION

What do you have? What do you want? What will you give up? - Jack Ma, Alibaba (2018)

The time to take counsel of your fears is before you make an important battle decision. That's the time to listen to every fear you can imagine! When you have collected all the facts and fears and made your decision, turn off all your fears and go ahead! - General George S. Patton

DOI: 10.4018/978-1-5225-9369-0.ch008

Progress in America does not usually begin at the top and among the few, but from the bottom and among the many. It comes when the whispered hopes of those outside the mainstream rise in volume to reach the ears and hearts and minds of the powerful. - Jon Meacham, The Soul of America: The Battle for Our Better Angels (2018)

In some senses, "electronic hive minds" (EHMs) are transitory and abstract. Online interests are ephemeral, and fads by definition exist for brief and passing moments. EHMs exist in virtual space on the Social Web generally and on social media platforms and apps more specifically. And yet, they do not just exist as individual and collective consciousnesses (enabled by digital technologies) but also as bodies, with a mind-body connection; after all, underlying EHMs are the thinkers, the people and cyborgs (people augmented with automated agentry) (Hai-Jew, 2019). EHMs and bodies may be conceptualized as having body-awareness based on proprioception (with people serving as "human sensors" and the body's nerve endings that inform proprioception for the collective physical body). In this cyber-physical confluence, what sparks in the mind may affect the body, which can achieve actions online and in the physical real life (RL).

Individual members can spark others' through their knowledge, enthusiasms, and behaviors. They can "model" ways of being and expression that inspire others and galvanize some to action. Sometimes, even a small piece of information may be sufficient to cause a wide ranging number of different effects. Outcomes can be unpredictable (think "chaos theory" and "butterfly effects"). These effects may occur even if the relations between individuals are ephemeral weak ties. Individuals, in groups, can give each other courage for group actions. Their individual and cooperative actions may create reverberations that magnify some effects and nullify others. Spontaneous actions may spark unpredictably, and so, too, can planned or coordinated ones. Planned activities in EHMs can magnify out virally into online and physical spaces. Such coordination may occur at three main scales: micro (individual, dyadic, triadic, motif levels), meso (small to large group levels), and macro (mass-scale levels, such as country or societal). Depending on the objectives of the endeavor, the EHM membership size, the available member skills and expertise, the socio-technical and other tools available for coordination, the larger ecosystem, and other factors, varying levels of coordination may be required.

In this work, several EHMs focused around a particular action-oriented objective with implications at the micro, meso, and macro levels was identified and studied to understand some of the types of coordination at the respective levels. The exemplar was selected as an EHM with different constituencies. The idea is that at the respective scales, there would be different enablements and potential (and real) outcomes, not just higher magnitudes of influence at the larger levels. This topic was selected also to ensure that there are actual dependencies in the issue and collaborative reliance of people on each other to achieve particular aims.

REVIEW OF THE LITERATURE

For all the affordances and enablements of the Social Web, one of the major ones involves the use of "social media as organizing mechanisms" (Segerberg & Bennett, 2011, p. 197), used for logistical coordination (p. 198). Those who run the respective social media platforms and "set its rules" hold outsized power over how people engage with each other and the world (Singer & Brooking, 2018, p. 21). Other researchers have suggested that social media are not neutral and have real-world implications. One research team observed: "Far from being neutral platforms, social media are affecting the conditions and rules of social interaction" (van Dijck & Poell, 2013, p. 3). One of the main ways is to engage in "online conflict" with "terrible consequences" (Singer & Brooking, 2018, p. 16). Some see the online space as a highly contested and conflictual one:

From the world's most powerful nations to the pettiest flame war combatants, all of today's fighters have turned social media into a weapon in their own national and personal wars, which often overlap. They all fight to bend the global information environment to their well. The Internet, once a light and airy place of personal connection, has since morphed into the nervous system of modern commerce. It has also become a battlefield where information itself is weaponized. (Singer & Brooking, 2018, p. 19)

Online, what is shared becomes part of the forever record and may make real "an ever-present watcher" or electronic panopticon (Singer & Brooking, 2018, pp. 57 - 58) and lifelong dossiers (p. 61). People share information without realizing what the implications may be for their own unimagined futures. Information that may seem innocuous on its own may be accrued with other information for different impacts. ["Nothing truly disappears online. Instead, the data builds and builds, just waiting to reemerge at any moment"

(Singer & Brooking, 2018, p. 60).] This designed space rewards those who can gain others' attention, whether or not the information is "truthful":

Social media has rendered secrets of any consequence essentially impossible to keep. Yet because virality can overwhelm truth, what is known can be reshaped. 'Power' on this battlefield is thus measured not by physical strength or high-tech hardware, but by the command of attention. The result is a contest of psychological and algorithmic manipulation, fought through an endless churn of competing viral events. (Singer & Brooking, 2018, p. 22)

The implications of the socio-technological design are that unvetted information may spread through social networks in viral ways and spark unthinking actions that have high impacts, including negative and / or destructive ones. Social media and scripted agentry capabilities have released externalities into the social environment, with potentially far-reaching effects.

Such effects may be especially problematic for those in filter bubbles and echo chambers, which may reinforce their senses of the world and provide authorizing environments for their actions. The harnessing of scripted agents and social "cyborg" accounts (managed by both people and scripted robots) may create the false impression of volume and intensities of commitments. In cases of malicious "hidden hands," online manipulations can result in dire consequences, such as manipulated elections and power takeovers. The advent of scripted agents (social robots or "socialbots") and artificial intelligence-enablements means that simulated computerized agents that emulate people have gone well beyond chatbots but involve speaking intonations and physical appearances online. Synthetic versions of people as "deep fakes" may fool many (Singer & Brooking, 2018, pp. 253-254) and require digital literacy based on national security needs (Singer & Brooking, 2018). Online, people may parachute into others' realities and discover some gruesome worldviews. A perusal of high profile court cases have found susceptible individuals lured into violence through falsehoods, through "sock puppet" (false online identity) accounts, charismatic personalities, and other messaging "triggers" to action.

(IT-enabled) communications play a central role in collective actions both from access to "high levels of organizational resources and the formation of collective identities" and "the less familiar logic of connective action based on personalized content sharing across media networks" (Bennett & Segerberg, 2011, p. 739). There are more deeply planned and less spontaneous actions collective coordinated actions, such as the harnessing of social media for mass-scale and sustained protests, including across geographies. More spontaneous collective actions may include "flash mobs," where groups of strangers are inspired to gather in a defined physical location, engage in a defined social performance or act, and then disperse. The point of such acts is to make a statement and to gain larger attention to the interests of the particular group. One term for such actions is "digitally networked action (DNA)" (Bennett & Segerberg, 2011, p. 743). Such digitally enabled "collective action" through social media comments "that represent, reinforce, or spur social mobilization" presents a sense of threat to authoritarian governments (King, Pan, & Roberts, May 2013, p. 326).

People are also socialized by the communities they grew up and live in, so they are influenced by others. People often act in concert with their social identities and social affiliations. People may be triggered as small groups, such as those acting in trust and friend networks. And then, mass numbers of people may also be influenced simultaneously, for mass effects. Social media platforms play important roles "in the process of creating the collective" (Kavada, 2015, p. 884). As such, it is possible to view a social movement as "a phenomenon emerging in communication" and collective identity (Kavada, 2015, p. 884). Shared culture also plays a "central role...in shaping social action" (Melucci, 1996, p. 18). Social media removes barriers to participation by strengthening in-group identities and interrelationships:

A second way movements may undergo subtle change due to the Internet is that the very same strategic factors that liberate people to express their identity toward the out-group also liberate them from in-group strictures and remove barriers to participation. (Brunsting & Postmes, Oct. 2002, p. 532)

A later work suggests that social media are used "in the organization, unfolding, and diffusion of contemporary protests..." and their use to "develop a joint narrative and a collective identity" (Milan, July-Dec. 2015, p. 1). "Cloud protesting" (Milan, July-Dec. 2015, p. 1) may stay virtual, or it may spill over into real space and real lives.

The triggers-to-action from social media may inspire people as individuals, as small groups, and as mass ones. At every scale level, individuals have to decide to act or not. The rise of "personal action frames" given "structural fragmentation and individualization" has led to more individualized societies as compared to collective ones (Bennett & Segerberg, 2011, p. 744).

Collective action itself is a dynamic process: "To study collective action means redefining the relationship between the observer and the observed, because we are not dealing with a thing, but with a process continuously activated by social actors" (Melucci, 1996, p. 395).

"Collective action" has been traditionally defined as any action that aims to improve the status, power, or influence of an entire group" through mass scale social change (van Zomeren & Iyer, 2009, p. 646). For example, the changes of social norms and laws have advanced the human rights of various groups in the West over time. Prior to the advent of social media, social movements and mainstream media were "interacting systems" (Gamson & Wolfsfeld, July 1993, p. 114), with activists striving to reach a wider audience to gain more followers and to attract the attention of those in power. Media strengthens the public sphere and enables influence on political processes (Shirky, Jan./Feb. 2011). Activists had to understand "the importance of organization, professionalism, and strategic planning" for effective attention-getting and engage other strategic thinking for advancing an agenda to the public (Gamson & Wolsfeld, July 1993, p. 114). It is important to look at collective action strategically, such as through a game theory lens (Jasper, Jan. 2004).

Online collective action elicitations have to be mentally processed, to some degree, at the individual level.

This means that online collective action is relatively more reliant on group members' mental representation of the group(s) involved and their considerations about the nature and effectiveness of the collective actions—a cognitive calculus of costs, benefits, and the strategic consequences of participation. This is likely to be reinforced by the way in which social movement Web sites are structured primarily to persuade people with rational arguments to take part in their actions. These Web sites also signal that a number of individuals are undertaking the action, and they rarely include Web site visitors as members of or sympathizers with the organization and, therefore, as part of the group of concerned people that is about to undertake a collective effort. (Brunsting & Postmes, Oct. 2002, pp. 531 - 532)

Researchers divide those engaged in social change in three main roles: activists, sympathizers, and nonactivists (Brunsting & Postmes, Oct. 2002, p. 525). Those who take on different roles may be thought of as acting based on different motivations:

Using structural equation modeling, it was examined whether online activism was predicted by different factors than offline activism. A wide range of predictors was derived from central theories about mobilization and collective action, including identification, relative deprivation, attitudes, subjective norm, perceived efficacy of action, and self-efficacy. Results show that when compared with offline actions, participation in online actions was slightly more motivated by cognitive calculations (efficacy) and less by affective factors (identification). Moreover, results reflect the popularity and potential of the Internet for activities that surpass the individual (Brunsting & Postmes, Oct. 2002, p. 525).

A major challenge in collective action is to distribute the work and address the so-called "free-rider problem," or the fact that many will benefit from social changes, even those who do not contribute to the effort.

Most analyses of collective action agree that overcoming the free-rider problem requires organizing potential contributors, thus making their decisions interdependent. The potential for organizing depends on the social ties in the group, particularly on the overall density or frequency of ties, on the extent to which they are centralized in a few individuals, and on the costs of communicating and coordinating actions through these ties. Mathematical analysis and computer simulations extend a formal microsocial theory of interdependent collective action to treat social networks and organization costs. As expected, the overall density of social ties in a group improves its prospects for collective action. More significant, because less expected, are the findings that show that the centralization of network ties always has a positive effect on collective action and that the negative effect of costs on collective action declines as the group's resource or interest heterogeneity increases. These non-obvious results are due to the powerful effects of selectivity, the organizer's ability to concentrate organizing efforts on those individuals whose potential contributions are the largest (Marwell, Oliver, & Prahl, 1988, p. 502).

Albert Bandura's work on social cognitive theory and "enabling media" informs the work of achieving social change, through the social diffusion of thinking and practices. This psychologist suggests the importance of an empowered individual and populace to make change through knowledge, analysis, and expectancy of outcomes. He wrote:

Social cognitive theory provides an agentic conceptual framework within which to analyze the determinants and psychosocial mechanisms through which symbolic communication promotes personal and social changes

(Bandura, 1986, 2001a). To be an agent is to influence intentionally one's own functioning, and life circumstances. In this transactional view of self and society, people are producers as well as products of their social environment. By selecting and altering their social environment, they have a hand in shaping the course that their lives take (Bandura, 2004, p. 76)

In a sense, people speak into their social space even as they are influenced by the social. On contested issues, there would be messaging and counter-messaging, moves and counter-moves. In societal level changes, communications are thought to operate in "two pathways":

In the direct pathway, communication media promote changes by informing, enabling, motivating, and guiding audience individuals. In the socially-mediated pathway, media influences are used to link participants to social networks and community settings. (Bandura, 2004, p. 76)

The first is about directed action, and the latter is about sociality and social connectivity. People work within social spaces to achieve change: "The major share of behavioral and valuational changes are promoted within these social milieus. People are socially situated in interpersonal networks." (Bandura, 2004, p. 77) People recruited into social movements tend to be "recruited through preexisting social ties and that mobilization is more likely when the members of the beneficiary population are linked by social ties than when they are not (e.g., Tilly 1978; Oberschall 1973, as cited in Marwell, Oliver, & Prahl, 1988, p. 502). Social networks "matter when decisions are interdependent" (Marwell, Oliver, & Prahl, 1988, p. 505).

Social media are harnessed in different ways to support popular movements. Such movements are not a direct follow-on of the existence of the social technologies and are not particularly "spontaneous" or "leaderless" (Gerbaudo, 2012, p. 13) but are planned. There is a need to "choreograph" protest through "bodily assembling" in space (Gerbaudo, 2012, p. 39) through "liquid organising and choreographic leadership," described as "Follow me, but don't ask me to lead you" (Gerbaudo, 2012, p. 134). Distributed leadership may be seen in "activist clusters" and in near-continuous acts of communications to sustain activist momentum (Gerbaudo, 2012, p. 136).

Kurt Lewin's field theory of change suggests that people exist in a temporal equilibriums based on "a complex field of forces" that act on those realities. To make change, he suggested, people have to "unfreeze" the status quo, move that reality, and enable refreezing to a new social equilibrium, based on new learning, in this unfreeze-change-refreeze three-step model of change (Lewin, 1947a, as cited in Burnes, Dec. 2004, p. 313).

COORDINATED INDIVIDUAL TO GROUP TO MASS-SCALE ACTIONS VIA PLANNED-ACTION EHM's

Some beginning assumptions of planned-action electronic hive minds (EHMs) is that its members are generally inertial. Those who are in motion will have a tendency to stay in motion, and those who are not in motion have a tendency to not activate to activities or contribution. The basic assumptions are that, practically speaking, to enable coordinated action using online means, one has to be able to do the following:

- Collect data
- Identify others with similar interests
- Identify others with relevant skills
- Identify others with relevant contexts
- Identify others with relevant social networks
- Identify resources (of various types)
- Share information in a motivational action-framed way
- Elicit information from others
- Elicit planning from others
- Define values
- Define principles
- Set goals
- Plan actions
- Coordinate actions
- Evaluate actions
- Maintain the community
- Plan future actions, and so on

While the information is shared socially, on public and private channels, people may choose to remain in the background or volunteer their ideas, resources, skills, and actions, among others. The EHM may be formal and declared, or it may be informal and non-declared. Strategically, Tables 01 and 02 show the considerations first for those in the EHM considering collective actions and offerings to potential participants, and the second table considers

Table 1. An escalating level of commitment by the planned-action EHM to contributors based on perceived level of contribution

1. motivating values / principles						
2. motivating values / principles	information					
3. motivating values / principles	information	guidance				
4. motivating values / principles	information	guidance	support			
5. motivating values / principles	information	guidance	support	resources / payment		
6. motivating values / principles	information	guidance	support	resources / payment	credit	
7. motivating values / principles	information	guidance	support	resources / payment	credit	power / influence / formal role / leadership / responsibility …

potential participants' considerations about what they might contribute. The provisioning in various efforts may be decentralized and piecemeal, so even though the escalating support is shown on the diagonal, and there is numbering along the left-most column, it may be that participants may be provided resources from different parts of the EHM and may end up with a piecemeal set of resources. Table 1 suggests that some participants may be sparked to action by motivating values / principles alone, and they may offer the range of resources to the planned-action themselves. Others may require information, guidance, support, and so on.

Table 2 suggests that some participants in planned-action EHMs may provide an escalating level of resources to the effort. A light offering may be a word of encouragement, a shout out, a microblogging message, at minimum. Maybe a next step is some invested thought and some proposed ideas. On the diagonal is an intensification of commitment. In the same way as Table 1 is actually piecemeal in real life, it may be that the offerings by participants vary over time and depend on various factors.

One way to conceptualize the melding of Tables 1 and 2 is in a spider chart showing what an EHM provides an individual and what that individual gives back. This can be mapped for a particular endeavor or movement and an individual.

Table 2. An escalating level of commitment by the EHM members to the planned-action EHM

1. encouragement						
2. encouragement	idea sharing					
3. encouragement	idea sharing	resource sharing				
4. encouragement	idea sharing	resource sharing	line work online			
5. encouragement	idea sharing	resource sharing	line work online	line work in real life (RL)		
6. encouragement	idea sharing	resource sharing	line work online	line work in RL	recruitment (friend and acquaintance sharing)	
7. encouragement	Idea sharing	Resource sharing	line work online	line work in RL	recruitment (friend and acquaintance sharing)	longer (and escalating) term commitments…

An exchange may be depicted between an EHM and a participant in Figure 1. In a way, this might be a typical case for mass-scale behavior, without too much personal interaction between the EHM and the individual and maybe limited outputs on both sides.

Figure 2 shows a conceptual mapping of a multi-institutional planned-action (meso-scale) EHM.

And Figure 3 shows a micro-scale project-level sort of conceptual mapping.

Figures 1 to 3 show that EHMs at all three scaler levels require synergy and mesh with the potential participants, and it is possible that the sizes of the respective endeavors may affect the exchanges between the EHM and the participants. Certainly, the EHMs are comprised in part of the participants, but recall, too, that EHMs may have a large number of passive and lurking individuals.

On both sides are the tensions between "cheap talk" and "costly signaling." There are interests in protecting resources on both sides, so the propositions have to result in measurable outcomes. The table sequences may not exactly work in the implied order because what each side values may not be in that order. An EHM may have messaging platforms but not much in the way of monetary resources and so will emphasize more of the first than the latter, to motivate participation. A person who has a lot of money may find it easier to write a check than to participate in person, or a person who values direct

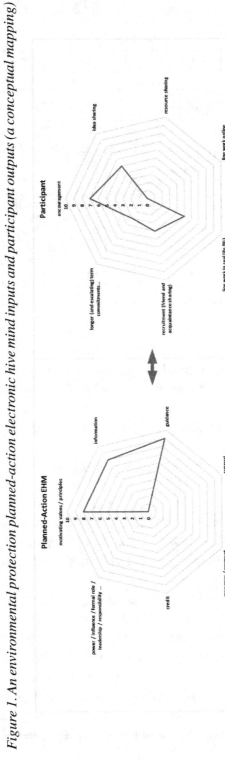

Figure 1. An environmental protection planned-action electronic hive mind inputs and participant outputs (a conceptual mapping)

An Environmental Protection Planned-Action Electronic Hive Mind Inputs and Participant Outputs (a conceptualized mapping)

Figure 2. A meso-scale multi-institution collaborative planned-action electronic hive mind inputs and participant outputs (a conceptual mapping)

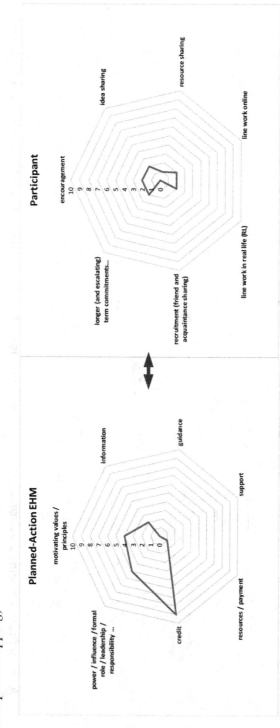

A Meso-Scale Multi-Institution Collaborative Planned-Action Electronic Hive Mind Inputs and Participant Outputs (a conceptual mapping)

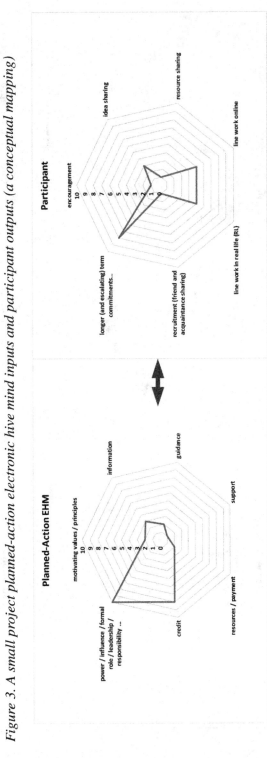

Figure 3. A small project planned-action electronic hive mind inputs and participant outputs (a conceptual mapping)

284

engagement may show up at demonstrations instead of doing something more distant like contributing knowledge alone.

Finally, as noted earlier, the participation may be at the micro (individual, dyadic, triadic, or motif levels), meso (small to large groups), and macro levels (mass-scale levels, such as societal or country-wide or others). In terms of coordination, smaller groups may be easier to work with to achieve the objectives, which are likely much more humble than what can be achieved in bigger groups. Smaller scale coordination can be kept private more easily than coordination with larger groups. Most large-scale endeavors have micro and meso pieces. For example, in an educational context, individuals and groups may work to support adoption of a virtual immersive world for learning—for simulations, for social networking, for particular lessons in courses, and so on. They may work as part of macro level individuals by creating virtual resources online and freely available. They may contribute to wikis about the technologies, and they may also contribute to the professional formal literature to support the usage of the software. They may create machinima videos to share on social video sharing sites. They may contribute to commercial efforts to monetize scripted objects. And so on. All three levels—micro, meso, and macro—are present here. This can apply to the support for learning management systems (LMS), with individual and small group supports for online teaching and learning…but also macro-level supports by upvoting and downvoting updates to the technologies, sharing research articles about the uses of the technologies, free contributions to the "commons" spaces using the LMS technologies, and so on, to collaborate at the macro level. At the micro level are advances to the uses of the tool and local successful projects; at the macro level is the advancement of the technology and the shared learning resources.

DISCUSSION

Coordination towards various objectives requires a fair amount of trust and effort even with the affordances of social technologies. Yet, for all the advances that may be achieved by singletons and by small groups, there are some endeavors that totally require large-scale collective endeavors.

FUTURE RESEARCH DIRECTIONS

Electronic hive minds that are action-oriented stand to contribute broadly to many spaces, through effective planned actions, at differing scalar levels. As yet, this area is quite under-theorized. For example, how can leaders in an EHM better understand the collective physical body in the real world... through proprioception? Do the different scaled parts of the planned-action EHM have different senses of somatosensation—or differing understandings of the extensions of the EHM's physical soma or body (and its sizing of a few members to large swaths of humanity)? (A "soma" is the physical body, separate from the psyche or mind.) Is there an expansion of psychological possibilities along with the conceptualized or perceived size of the network? How far in the membership does the collective size of the body reach? If there are social networks within the EHM, how are they structurally comprised? Are they in sparse or thick social networks? Where are the respective networks in terms of geographical space?

If the underlying technologies are a critical part of the "brain" on which the EHM exists, are there ways to redesign and rewire those technologies for more effective coordination and reach? What are physical in-world elements that also enable more effective coordination and reach?

Given the effects in the real world, how can various prosocial actions be encouraged and supported? How can planned-action EHMs be studied to predict their future directions and potential effects? (How do EHMs evolve into planned-action ones?) And beyond abductive logic and the study of exemplars, what are some effective research methods to better understand planned-action EHMs? What different categories of EHMs are there? How do the different types of EHMs differ from each other?

CONCLUSION

Ready? Set? Go! This work introduces the idea of planned-action EHMs and offers two examples of them from the educational context. This offers an understanding of how motivations may be created by EHMs for its membership to participate, and it offers an understanding of how people on-ground might decide whether or not to engage. This work also proposes the idea of scalar understandings of the size of participation, from individual to mass-scale levels and suggests that the coordination and outputs are different at the respective levels. This is a nascent work but a potentially fruitful one given the uses of EHMs to achieve ends online and in the world.

REFERENCES

Bandura, A. (2004). Social cognitive theory for personal and social change by enabling media. In A. Singhal, M. J. Cody, E. M. Rogers, & M. Sabido (Eds.), *Entertainment-education and social change: History, research, and practice*. Mahwah, NJ: Lawrence Erlbaum.

Bennett, W. L., & Segerberg, A. (2011). Digital media and the personalization of collective action. *Information Communication and Society, 14*(6), 770–799. doi:10.1080/1369118X.2011.579141

Brunsting, S., & Postmes, T. (2002, October). Social movement participation in the Digital Age: Predicting offline and online collective action. *Small Group Research, 33*(5), 525–554. doi:10.1177/104649602237169

Burnes, B. (2004, December). Kurt Lewin and complexity theories: Back to the future? *Journal of Change Management, 4*(4), 309–325. doi:10.1080/1469701042000303811

Gamson, W. A., & Wolfsfeld, G. (1993, July). Movements and media as interacting systems. *The Annals of the American Academy, 528*(1), 114–125. doi:10.1177/0002716293528001009

Gerbaudo, P. (2012). *Tweets and the Streets: Social Media and Contemporary Activism*. London: Pluto Press.

Hai-Jew, S. (2019). The electronic hive mind and cybersecurity: Mass-scale human cognitive limits to explain the 'weakest link' in cybersecurity. In *Global Cyber Security Labor Shortage and International Business Risk* (pp. 206–262). Hershey, PA: IGI Global. doi:10.4018/978-1-5225-5927-6.ch011

Jasper, J. (2004, January). A strategic approach to collective action: Looking for agency in social-movement choices. *Mobilization: An International Journal, 9*(1), 1–16.

Kavada, A. (2015). Creating the collective: Social media, the Occupy Movement and its constitution as a collective actor. *Information Communication and Society, 18*(8), 872–886. doi:10.1080/1369118X.2015.1043318

King, G., Pan, J., & Roberts, M. E. (2013, May). How censorship in China allows government criticism but silences collective expression. *The American Political Science Review, 107*(2), 326–343. doi:10.1017/S0003055413000014

Marwell, G., Oliver, P. E., & Prahl, R. (1988). Social networks and collective action: A theory of the critical mass. III. [AJS]. *American Journal of Sociology, 94*(3), 502–534. doi:10.1086/229028

Melucci, A. (1996). *Challenging codes: Collective action in the information age.* Cambridge, UK: Cambridge University Press. doi:10.1017/CBO9780511520891

Milan. S. (2015, July-Dec.). When algorithms shape collective action: Social media and the dynamics of cloud protesting. *Social Media + Society,* 1 – 10.

Segerberg, A., & Bennett, W. L. (2011). Social media and the organization of collective action: Using Twitter to explore the ecologies of two climate change protests. *Communication Review, 14*(3), 197–215. doi:10.1080/10714421.2011.597250

Shirky, C. (2011). The political power of social media: Technology, the public sphere, and political change. *Foreign Affairs, 90*(1), 28–41. Retrieved from http://www.jstor.org/stable/25800379

Singer, P. W., & Brooking, E. T. (2018). *LikeWar: The Weaponization of Social Media.* Boston: Houghton Mifflin Harcourt.

Van Dijck, J., & Poell, T. (2013). Understanding social media logic. *Media and Communication, 1*(1), 2–14. doi:10.17645/mac.v1i1.70

Van Zomeren, M., & Iyer, A. (2009). Introduction to the social and psychological dynamics of collective action. *The Journal of Social Issues, 65*(4), 645–660. doi:10.1111/j.1540-4560.2009.01618.x

ADDITIONAL READING

Linden, D. J. (2018). *Think Tank: Forty Neuroscientists Explore the Biological Roots of Human Experience.* New Haven, CT: Yale University Press.

KEY TERMS AND DEFINITIONS

Collective Action: Mass coordinated social actions in order to achieve shared objectives for large-scale social change.

Coordination: Organizing different persons and activities in order to achieve goals.

Electronic Hive Mind: A synchronous temporal and informal patchwork of emergent shared social consciousness (held by geographically distributed people, cyborgs, and robots) enabled by online social connectivity (across a range of social media platforms on the web and internet), based around various dimensions of shared attractive interests.

Flash Mob: A sudden gathering of people at a defined location where people perform a particular act and then disperse, usually based on messaging from social media or information and communications technology (ICT).

Group Action: Acts taken by a number of individuals.

Mass Action: Coordinated actions involving large numbers of people.

Planned Action Entity: An organizational unit created to achieve collective aims and objectives.

Proprioception: Awareness of a body's spatial orientation and movement (based on sensory information from the body's nerves).

Sock Puppet: False online identity.

Somatosensory System: A term including touch sensations and proprioception to understand the position and state of the body.

Chapter 9
Expanding the Imagination, Thinking, Knowledge, and Relevant Skills:
True Innovation With Electronic Hive Minds?

ABSTRACT

"Creatives" online, those who innovate as a regular part of their work and lifestyles, are likely one of the most diverse electronic hive minds, with often highly dissimilar and heterogeneous members. As a general group, they are specialists in their respective areas but often engage online with professionals in their respective communities of expertise as well as with others in disparate fields in order to benefit from the cross-fertilization of ideas. They are by nature and practice exploratory and often sharing. This chapter explores what the pursuit of inspiration looks like for the EHMs based around creative work.

INTRODUCTION

Dominick Cobb: What is the most resilient parasite? Bacteria? A virus? An intestinal worm? An idea. Resilient... highly contagious. Once an idea has taken hold of the brain, it's almost impossible to eradicate. An idea that is fully formed - fully understood - that sticks, right in there somewhere." - Christopher Nolen (screenplay author and film director), Inception (2010)

DOI: 10.4018/978-1-5225-9369-0.ch009

A revised version of Bloom's Taxonomy for levels of learning suggests that people have to acquire particular capabilities in order to wield more complex skills. At the base of the Bloom's Taxonomy triangle is remembering, then understanding, then apply, analyzing, evaluating, and creating. It is no accident that the ability to create is at the pinnacle (1956, mid-1990s, as cited in Anderson, Krathwohl, Airiasian, Cruikshank, Mayer, & Pintrich, 2001). The imagination seen as a "higher mental function" as "a consciously directed thought process that is learned through collective social interactions" (Vygotsky, 1931, pp. 14 – 16, as cited in Smolucha & Smolucha, Aug. 1986, p. 3). Another researcher points to creativity as "the epitome of cognitive flexibility" Dietrich, 2004, p. 1018).

It is one thing to understand the world accurately and to function effectively in it, but to be able to see possibilities (with imagination) and actualize them in the world (with innovation) requires expertise in the target domain combined with imagination—for an informed imagination. There needs to be "the collaboration of imagination and thinking in concepts" as a necessity for "both artistic and scientific creativity" (Vygotsky, 1931, pp. 14 – 16, as cited in Smolucha & Smolucha, Aug. 1986, p. 3). Expertise without imagination, and imagination without expertise will leave people short of the goal. It one thing to retroactively look back at a set of facts and assume that a particular advancement was fated, but in the real, such discoveries are challenging. Actualizing new innovations in the world is a hard problem, with real world constraints. Expertise in one area can be difficult to apply to other contexts, and prior paradigms may exert undue influences on thinking, making new thinking difficult.

A number of fields may be considered ones for "creatives," those who create new contents (writers, designers, editors, marketers, and others). There are those who invest much effort into exploring new thinking (artists, performers, and others). Those who work in research have to be creative because they are advancing their respective fields with new discoveries. Engineers, chemists, and other scientists also work in spaces where constant new thinking and new doing are *de rigueur.* For many, invention is the job. How creativity is actualized may differ based on the respective domains, the available technologies, the collaborating teams, the work context, and the creativity processes of individuals. Indeed, there are collections of books about how to be creative and all sorts of tools and methods designed to encourage creativity.

An earlier work suggests that electronic hive minds inform knowledge and actions (Hai-Jew, 2019). What does an innovation-based electronic hive mind look like? For the "creatives" electronic hive mind, this is conceptualized as including all those who work in fields that require new thinking both as a part of "daily innovating" and as creating new thinking, novel methods, original products, inventive services, fresh combinations, and ingenious other parts of a domain…and who go online to find inspiration. An initial theorized concept is that this EHM is likely pervasive and ever-present because of the universality of human creativity. It is also likely diffuse with heterogeneous populations. And it will likely be elusive to define, with patchworks of interests across the human population. It is likely that this EHM also will pursue different methods of inspiration given the different ways that people find their respective Muses.

REVIEW OF THE LITERATURE

Creativity is considered a core part of human thinking. A child's imaginative play may enrich creativity in adulthood. For example, "childhood worldplay" (paracosm) may enrich creativity in adulthood (Root-Bernstein & Root-Bernstein, 2006, p. 405). "Daydreaming and fantasy" are important in enhancing people's "everyday problem-solving abilities" (Singer, 2009, p. 190). Creativity is not about chasing a muse per se, but is a learned thought process (Vygotsky, 1931, pp. 14 – 16, as cited in Smolucha & Smolucha, Aug. 1986, p. 6), which not only occurs on conscious levels but also sub-conscious and unconscious levels. "Free play" enhances "human health and creativity" (Elkind, 2008, p. 1). For one researcher, "play" is one of three critical elements in life (along with "work" and "love") (Elkind, 2008, pp. 2-3).

One definition of creativity is that it results in "divergent production" (Woodman, Sawyer, & Griffin, Apr. 1993, p. 298); it results in something novel—new thinking, new procedures, new products, and new approaches. Another conceptualization of creativity suggests that there are "four basic types of creative insights, each mediated by a distinctive neural circuit" (Dietrich, 2004, p. 1018). In the "Knowledge Domain" are the "emotional" and "cognitive" aspects, and in the "Processing Mode" are "deliberate" and "spontaneous" (Dietrich, 2004, p. 1018). Domain knowledge is critical for creative thinking (Dietrich, 2004, p. 1020). It is not enough to be creative in a freestanding non-contextualized way. What is produced has to be "novel…

and appropriate" (Sternberg & Lubart, 1999, p. 3, as cited in Dietrich, 2004, p. 1018).

In terms of practical production, corporations have an interest in "organizational creativity" as in "the creation of a valuable, useful new product, service, idea, procedure, or process by individuals working together in a complex social system" (Woodman, Sawyer, & Griffin, Apr. 1993, p. 293). In the workplace context, to broadly over-simplify, "individual characteristics, group characteristics, (and) organizational characteristics) provide inputs to the creative process, and the "creative behavior" and "creative situation" result in "organizational creativity" (Woodman, Sawyer, & Griffin, Apr. 1993, p. 309). Corporations that use social media for innovation require particular capabilities, including "social media managers who orchestrate social media activities across the innovation process; top management that cultivates support, team empowerment, and test-and-learn cycles; and agile processes that facilitate rapid decision making and knowledge flows across teams" (Muninger, Hammedi, & Mahr, 2019, p. 116). There should be a fit between the collaborative business need and the platform technology selected (Chi, Wang, Lu, & George, 2018). Formal innovation methods tend to be locked-down and protected.

By contrast, open innovations subscribe in some level of interchange of ideas with individuals and corporations outside a company. Some crowd-source hard questions, or they hold public competitions with large payouts to try to solve hard problems. Some go online to find innovation partners to get over particular design hurdles or to advance particular projects.

The cross-fertilization of ideas by people who specialize in different domains but who have occasion to meet and socialize can result in so-called "regional advantage" of AnnaLee Saxenian, albeit non-place-based and non-place bound (1994, 1996). In a sense, online spaces can provide a kind of cross-fertilization of ideas and advantageous cross-fertilization of ideas, provided people can engage in a sufficient level and depth of interchange to enable the diversity of thought. The idea is to avoid being trapped in cultural, personal, and domain blind spots. One downside of going broadly public with innovations is that "product innovation rumors" can be informative of innovation. This provisional knowledge can affect organizational "innovation decisions." Further, the "paradox of openness" may result in others' appropriation of promising ideas and practices (Hannigan, Seidel, & Yakis-Douglas, 2018, p. 953).

At the societal level, innovation requires inputs from four sectors: "Government, University, Industry, and Civil Society (referred to as the Quadruple Innovation Helix)" (Carayannis, Goletsis, & Grigoroudis, 2017).

The members need to differentiate between fruitful pursuits that can benefit people against unfruitful ones, at the risk of losing resources and human talent to wasteful efforts. Being in a "high trust country" enables higher production of co-owned joint patents (Brockman, Khurana, & Zhong, 2018, p. 2048). In the absence of legally enforceable trust, "opening up to external knowledge also entails substantial risks of appropriation and opportunism" (Brockman, Khurana, & Zhong, 2018, p. 2048). The authors explain: "This effect is more pronounced when perceived opportunism is higher (i.e., firms in high-tech industries, or in countries with less disclosure transparency), and when formal contracts are less enforceable (i.e., in countries with relatively weak legal systems)." (Brockman, Khurana, & Zhong, 2018, p. 2048) Another research team observed the importance of civic culture (including the positive effects of "trust, control, work ethic and honesty" on innovation and the negative effects of "obedience") at the societal level based on data from 34 OECD countries from 1980 to 2010 (Kostis, Kafka, & Petrakis, 2018, p. 306). They observe categorically: "Countries have varying levels of technological development and investment capacity because their cultural backgrounds differ" (Kostis, Kafka, & Petrakis, 2018, p. 311). An important element of culture involves social norms, which emerge from social relations, to define collective behaviors. Crises may serve as forcing functions: "It originates in out-of-the-ordinary 'extramundane' social situations in which people may come to feel their emergent collective behavior is feasible, timely, permissible, necessary, or duty-bound behavior. Their collective action is seen as appropriate" (Aguirre, Wenger, & Vigo, June 1998, p. 302). The challenge at the nation-state level is to create "sustainable innovation" (Kostis, Kafka, & Petrakis, 2018, p. 311).

The so-called STEM pipeline (science, technology, engineering, and math) is conceptualized as starting in toddler-hood and extending well into post-retirement years, the near full span of human life, with the importance of creating the intellectual and innovation skills to compete globally. One sub-movement in this endeavor are so-called "makerspaces" to help people conceptualize themselves as creators and tinkerers, and to directly think spatially and to conceptualize physical objects and representations. Such makerspaces have relatively high innovation rates ("53%" in one study) and diffusion rates (18%) (Halbinger, 2018, p. 2028).

Besides encouraging innovation in a broad sense, companies benefit by accurately identifying "innovation indicators" to know whether work in development may bear fruit. A review of the academic literature from 1980 – 2015 resulted in the identification of 82 unique indicators of innovation

(Dziallas & Blind, 2018). An "indicator" is "a measured value that provides information about a specific phenomenon or a status quo" (Dziallas & Blind, 2018, p. 1). Indicators may be based in the general categories of "product definition, product concept, validation phase, production phase, market launch, innovation process management" (Dziallas & Blind, 2018, p. 10). In the business context, "innovation" is defined as "invention plus exploitation" (Roberts, 1998, p. 13, as cited in Dziallas & Blind, 2018, p. 1). For another researcher, the concept of innovation is comprised of three (interrelated) things: "an outcome," "a process," (and) "a mindset" (Kahn, 2018, p. 453). The innovations do not have to be "completely new and radical in nature" but may include "minor incremental innovation" (Kahn, 2018, p. 453).

How important are innovations for businesses? Conventional wisdom and research offer some insights. Working towards innovations can be costly and incur risks for companies. Directions for research may be non-obvious in some cases. Researcher potential can be hard to assess. Exploratory firms "incur a higher failure-to-success ratio" (Jia, 2018, p. 155). (This may be seen also in corporations that are "first movers" on a scene. One observed pattern is that "second movers" may be the ones to gain the advantage once a market has been created by first movers.) The type of company may affect the criticality of innovation. Manufacturing firms that survive long-term "overwhelmingly gravitate away from non-innovative strategies toward incremental or more far-ranging innovation orientations" (Wojan, Crown, & Rupasingha, 2018, p. 1801). In a study of patent records in British firms in the 19th and 20th centuries, researchers found the following: "The number of patent applications seems to increase the survival probability of the manufacturing firms, but not of the service ones" (Ortiz-Villajos & Sotoca, 2018, p. 1418). Study of big data suggests that companies starting out in the "informal sector" (the ungoverned and untaxed "informal economy") may have negative effects on their technological innovations potentially due to such firms' negative "perceptions on the need to innovate" and their "severe informational disadvantages" (Mendi & Mudida, 2018, p. 326). Starting out informally has detrimental "lasting effects on firms' innovativeness" (Mendi & Mudida, 2018, p. 334).

It would stand to reason that some corporations require innovations to survive, such as in the healthcare industry, pharmaceuticals, high-technology, automotive industry, and others. And yet, sales (as a service) also requires innovation—such as electronic sales companies. If companies are not adapting to the competitive space, they are falling behind and losing ground to others.

Competitor companies in a space engage in patent races in attempts to gain competitive advantage.

This sense of competition to innovate may be seen in even more macro structures. In each university graduation cycle, there is a rush by corporations in many countries to hire new talent to advance their objectives. Nation-states have an interest in preventing brain drains to other nation-states, particularly rivalrous competitor ones. Research suggests that "innovative SMEs (note: subject matter experts) are more likely to export than non-innovative SMEs," with these practices differing "according to the type of innovation introduced and the degree of novelty of the innovation" (Saridakis, Idris, Hansen, & Dana, 2019, p. 250). In other words, subject matter experts that innovate tend towards internationalizing or exporting their skills and discoveries (based on what the researchers term "export propensity") (Saridakis, Idris, Hansen, & Dana, 2019, p. 252).

Online spaces have much lower thresholds for "innovation." One example is the idea that Internet memes are creative production and expressions of "symbolic values" and "symbolic innovation" (Benaim, 2018, p. 901).

DRAWING INSPIRATION FOR CREATIVITY AND INNOVATIONS FROM ELECTRONIC HIVE MINDS

"Desperately seeking inspiration" can be a descriptor for any number of individuals and groups at any time in the "creatives" EHM. Perhaps they are starting with a known question or problem and are looking for answers or solutions. Perhaps they are taking a break from other work and just looking for something that might catch the eye or ear, jog the memory, or arouse the Muse and compel imagination. As described in the title, the "creatives" EHM involves the pursuit of inspiration to engage and strengthen the human imagination, thinking, knowledge, and relevant skills.

In the Preface, an early definition of an electronic hive mind is as follows:

a synchronous temporal and informal patchwork of emergent shared social consciousness (held by geographically distributed people, cyborgs, and robots) enabled by online social connectivity (across a range of social media platforms on the Web and Internet), based around various dimensions of shared attractive interests. (Hai-Jew, 2019)

Based on that conceptualization, a "creatives" EHM is likely perennial and diffuse and diverse because of the diversity of creative work in the world (which cuts across virtually all fields).

On the Internet and Social Web, there are some other insights about what "creativity" may look like. A formal trawl of books published in English between the 1800s to 2000 shows "innovation" as a more commonly cited term than "creativity," which only apparently caught fire in the 1920s onwards. (Figure 1)

In terms of mass search, "creativity" as a search term on Google Search shares high correlational weekly time patterns with other terms (Tables 1 and 2). The first table shows search term correlations in descending order for the United States, and the second table for the United Kingdom (highlighting regional differences at mass scale). The correlated search terms are suggestive of focuses on methods and other practical considerations for both tables, but with differing emphases. These data tables were acquired using Google Correlate.

Figures 2 and 3 show the line graphs for the respective top correlational search terms by time pattern for the U.S. ("creativity" and "aspects of") and the United Kingdom ("creativity" and "approach to"). The data in Google Correlate cover January 2003 to present (late 2018). ("Google Correlate FAQ," 2011).

Figure 1. "Creativity" and "innovation" over time in the Google books ngram viewer

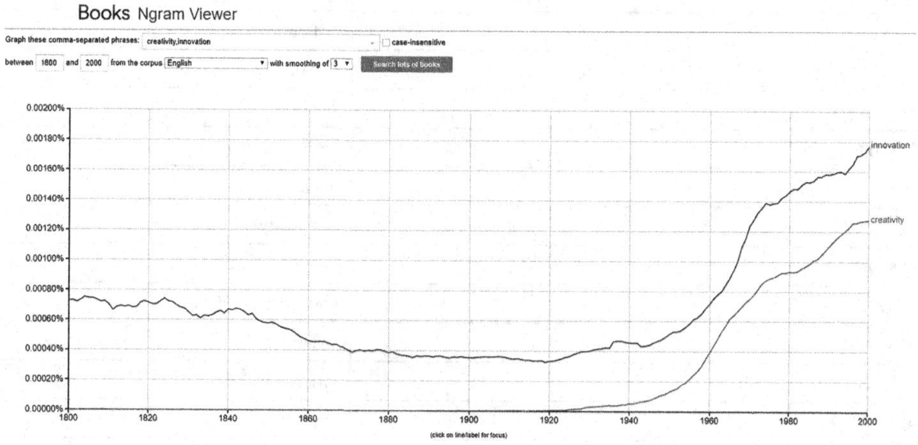

Table 1. "Creativity" in mass-search data on Google correlate (in the u.s.)

0.9151	aspects of
0.9125	aspects
0.9118	development of
0.9051	differences
0.9005	structure
0.8961	structure of
0.8948	morality
0.8903	mechanisms
0.89	concerning
0.8898	relating
0.8891	in society
0.888	the nature
0.887	disadvantages
0.8869	theories of
0.8868	use of
0.8866	problem of
0.8865	advantages
0.8855	description of
0.885	on technology
0.8837	importance
0.8824	composition of
0.8819	analyzing
0.8816	synthesis
0.8812	difficulties
0.8807	role of
0.8805	symbolic
0.8803	decision making
0.8799	interaction
0.8795	case study
0.8794	psychology
0.8792	government policies
0.8792	spherical
0.8788	differences in
0.8787	structures
0.8776	importance of
0.877	literary analysis

continued on following page

Table 1. Continued

0.8767	representation
0.8762	evolutionary
0.8761	quality of
0.8761	outline
0.8752	coefficients
0.8747	social issues
0.8745	the society
0.8736	discussion of
0.8728	advantages of
0.8719	the effects
0.8718	influencing
0.8716	relating to
0.8706	perspective on
0.8704	symbolism
0.8703	technology
0.8702	fallacies
0.8701	the culture
0.8699	ethical
0.8696	comparing
0.8693	participation in
0.8692	well known
0.8689	study on
0.8684	stress
0.8678	essay on
0.8677	sociology
0.8674	the modern
0.8672	in art
0.8668	methods of
0.8661	the effects of
0.8654	of substance
0.8652	buoyancy
0.8649	impact of
0.8645	technological
0.8642	a summary
0.8632	primary sources
0.8632	composition

continued on following page

Table 1. Continued

0.8626	of
0.8622	media in
0.8621	relation
0.8615	in communication
0.8615	perturbation
0.8612	problem solving
0.861	ethic
0.8609	mass media
0.8607	mechanism
0.8606	explanation of
0.8605	salinity
0.8603	disadvantages of
0.86	experiences
0.8599	economic growth
0.8597	economic factors
0.8595	absorption
0.8592	the uses
0.8584	phase diagram

Table 2. "Creativity" in mass-search data on Google correlate (in Great Britain)

0.9305	approach to
0.918	limitations
0.916	impact of
0.9158	approaches
0.9114	effectiveness of
0.909	ethical issues
0.9067	theoretical
0.9052	relationship between
0.9048	the use
0.9048	the use of
0.903	influence
0.9026	case study
0.8994	motivation
0.8987	considerations

continued on following page

Table 2. Continued

0.8982	the impact of
0.8979	model of
0.8974	essay
0.8973	discourse
0.8966	the role
0.8963	principle of
0.8951	relation
0.8929	deviation
0.8928	standard deviation
0.8927	strategies for
0.8926	importance
0.8923	the role of
0.8922	effect of
0.8914	method of
0.8906	mechanism
0.8898	effectiveness
0.8884	decision making
0.8868	receptors
0.8865	the impact
0.8864	role
0.8846	use of
0.8834	implications
0.8814	why use
0.8805	implications of
0.8804	inclusion
0.8801	issues in
0.88	mechanism of
0.879	hypothesis
0.8781	importance of
0.878	coefficient
0.8778	absorption
0.8777	concept of
0.8776	significance
0.8775	differential
0.8771	model for
0.8769	promoting

continued on following page

Table 2. Continued

0.8762	correlation
0.8758	the concept of
0.8753	interaction
0.8749	measures
0.8747	physiological
0.8743	a case study
0.8741	criticism
0.874	qualitative
0.8732	the concept
0.8731	the need for
0.8731	perspective on
0.8729	ideology
0.8719	impacts
0.8717	barriers
0.8715	ethnography
0.8714	imperialism
0.8713	changes in
0.8712	research methods
0.8712	autonomic
0.8709	physical activity
0.8702	the effect
0.8695	principles of
0.8692	study
0.869	inequalities
0.8689	affecting
0.8687	the development
0.8686	the effect of
0.8679	principle
0.8671	expenditure
0.8666	swot analysis
0.8664	criticism of
0.866	stratification
0.8654	organisational
0.8654	differences in
0.8651	nervous system
0.865	role of

continued on following page

Table 2. Continued

0.864	economic growth
0.864	characteristic
0.8639	process of
0.8636	problem of

Figure 2. "Creativity" and "aspects of" correlation in mass search in the us (Google correlate)

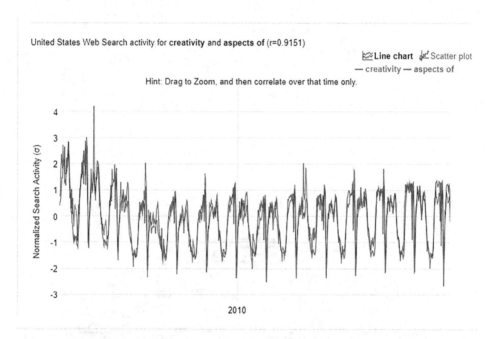

An article-article network on Wikipedia with "Creativity" as the seeding page shows outlinks to a number of articles to personages, methods, human psychological characteristics, and other topics. Figure 4 was laid out using the Harel-Koren Fast Multiscale Layout algorithm.

A retired subreddit focused on "creativity" was explored both manually and through computational text analysis means (mostly for text contents, with less focus on the included images and linked videos). The eight months of extracted messaging showed references to creativity in general but not much in terms of specific problem-solving challenges or specific personal pursuits

Figure 3. "Creativity" and "approach" correlation in mass search in the United Kingdom (Google correlate)

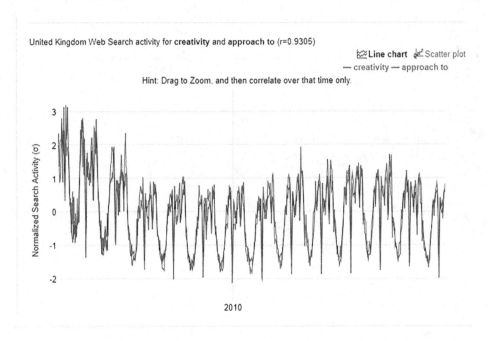

Figure 4. "Creativity" article-article network on Wikipedia (1 deg.)

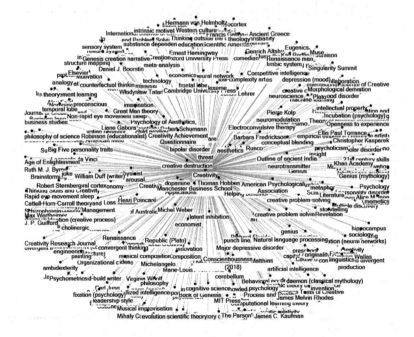

of inspirations. A word cloud of the collected messaging shows some of the participants and some of the areas of focus (Figure 5). Some words were added to the stopwords list, including "share, save, posted, ago, comment, months, (and) year" in order to see some of the more specific topics; however, the word cloud does not really show much in the way of coalesced topics around creativity. Many of the messages were about driving traffic to short videos. There were some comments on movies. One posting engaged questions about the time of day or night when people are more creative.

A word tree shows not that many direct references to "creativity." (Figure 6)

Top-level topics extracted through autocoded themes showed three: "creativity," "comments share," and "box." (Figure 7)

In general, autocoded sentiment showed a high tendency for most of the messages to be "Moderately positive" and "Very positive" (Figure 8). From a close human read, the messages were fairly superficial and fairly impersonal.

Socially shared imagery may offer a visual sense of "creativity." A related tags network based on "creativity" was extracted from the SmugMug Flickr image-sharing site. A one-degree network shows that the images uploaded with the folk tagging of "creativity" also tend to include the other tags in Figure 9. In this grid layout, "creativity" is at the top left of the graph. Many

Figure 5. A word cloud from eight months of messaging from an archived "creativity" subreddit

Figure 6. A "creativity" word tree from an archived "creativity" subreddit

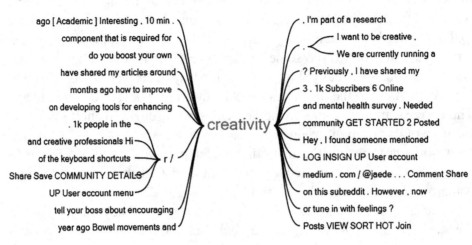

Figure 7. Autocoded top-level themes and sub-themes from the eight months of messaging on an archived creativity subreddit

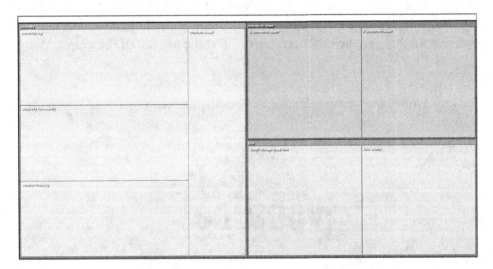

of the co-tags have visual aspects, like "texture, artwork, colorful, pink, white, black, drawing, artistic," and so on. This suggests that the modality of the communications and the underlying social networks affect the sense of the term.

A 1.5 degree related tags network was also captured on SmugMug Flickr around "creativity" as the tag. This larger network graph was analyzed for clustering, using the Clauset-Newman-Moore clustering algorithm for

Figure 8. Autocoded sentiment from eight months of messages on an archived creativity subreddit

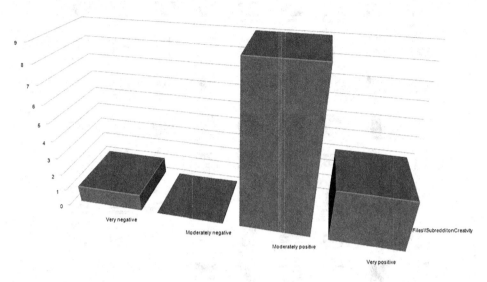

grouping. Three clusters were identified: Group 1 (far left) about people and aspects of the physical world, Group 2 (top right more about imagery, and Group 3 (bottom right corner about artworks) (Figure 10).

For more in-depth views of the contributions of social imagery to a topic, two sets were studied: 597 images from Google Images and 862 from Flickr. (Figures 11, 12, and 13)

The tags for the Google Images image set were the following, inclusively: "art, kids, design, innovation, brain, drawing, imagination, quote, mind, technology, nature, home, word, education, love, cartoon, music, business, paper, poster, advertising, background, school, craft, pencil, thinking, clip art, abstract, logo, (and) tumblr." The first set showed

This social image set includes flowcharts describing different conceptualizations of the creative process, autobiographical cartoons describing the cartoonist's creative life, a national creativity day event, animated gifs of motion visuals, close-in macro imagery (for new ways of seeing), informational graphics, drawings on white boards, book covers of creativity-inspiring books for children, quotes about creativity, word clouds, mixed media illustrations, musical scores, and others. There are recurring visual depictions of the human brain. There are many depictions of lightbulbs, a symbol of creativity indicating Eureka moments. Several visuals show rows of scrunched up papers (representing discarded ideas) and then one that

Figure 9. "Creativity" related tags network on Flickr (1 deg.)

Figure 10. "Creativity" related tags network on Flickr (1.5 deg.)

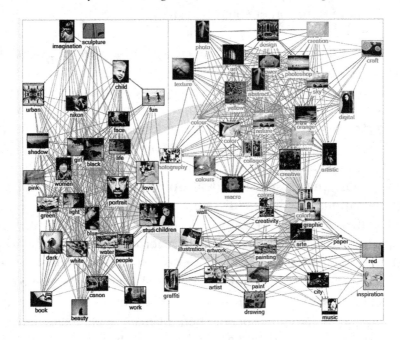

results in a Eureka lightbulb moment. There are lessons about creativity (such as how it is non-linear, how it can be learned/practiced/improved). Children figure into many of the images…as painters and photographers. (Figure 11)

In the Flickr social image set, these tend to include more artistic works including Dali-esque photos, creative post-processed images, artworks, custom jewelry, paintings, statues, physical art installations, photo mosaics, digital artworks, jewelry, analog and digital portraits, and others. There is creative physical journaling depicted. There is a close-up photo of jelly beans. One image shows religious iconography. Several photos depict cityscapes. Some of the images show optical illusions. Some photos show performances—plays, concerts, light shows, and others. One image shows an avatar on Second Life. Some images clearly make statements with visuals, such as a human forearm with batteries embedded. One image shows a carved apple with slices splayed out to display a butterfly, with the apple core as part of the butterfly's antennae. These images suggest a focus on visual expression and wit (Figures 12 and 13).

Figure 11. "Creativity" social imagery from Google images

Figure 12. "Creativity" social imagery from Flickr

Figure 13. "Creativity" social images in Flickr downloadr app

DISCUSSION

What can be said about a "creatives" electronic hive mind? Initial hypothesizing suggested that it would be a fairly dispersed and divergent group, with different methods for innovation…and different needs from the Internet and WWW. This collective was thought even initially to be elusive to map, without obvious boundaries, since creativity is a part of people and therefore relevant in every work domain and in being. It was hypothesized that this EHM would be too big to be represented on any one platform or even a number of them. Even though a number of methods were used to sort of map this, the mapping itself is provisional and incomplete. The explorations in this work suggest some glimmers, including that many members of this EHM may trawl the general space as lurkers to find inspirations. Lurking precludes the need to bring others up to speed on the particular challenges, often with most in the public sphere unaware of the challenge and not trained to provide a suitable solution. The risk of data leakage is another challenge. Many spaces focused on "creativity" directly seem to show creative works but in limited ways. Others express into the space as creatives, so they can share their artistic vision.

The main finding may be that this space has its limits for targeted creative sparking. In many ways, for creatives, having defined spaces where problem-solving can be done may be more directly inspirational. This might also suggest that respective creatives may collaborate as individuals and as groups in order to solve particular specific challenges on-ground. After all, creativity is applied to specific challenges, and while a main task for a creative individual is to find and make their own inspirations and innovation, harnessing what is in digital spaces should offer some ideas and ways forward.

FUTURE RESEARCH DIRECTIONS

The work of learning domains in depth, innovating in the space, and continuously broadening the "imagination, thinking, knowledge, and relevant skills" seems like a lifelong challenge. The long reach enabled by the collective Internet and WWW enables "creatives" to reach far beyond their local circumstances and gain rich understandings from co-practitioners as well as those far outside their domains of expertise. Understanding the "creatives" EHMs in particular areas and local contexts may be powerful and informative and may help advance work in the particular spaces. This work took a macro view, but more micro ones may provide different insights. Studying observable creative EHMs may inform on future phenomena and be used predictively. Perhaps there are socio-technical tools that may be built to support the work of creative EHMs in advancing respective thinking and production goals.

Perhaps those who are creative individuals and groups and collectives may provide *sousveillance* insights from within the EHMs to describe their experiences and observations. How to advance the creative work by using socially shared contents and engaging socially with others may provide valuable insights. How are people sparked to creativity—by word combinations, a concept, imagery, music, stories, simulations, film characters, a data point? What are ways to assess others online, to understand the depth of expertise, motivations, and creative potential? What are ways to engage socially without giving away advantage? Are there EHM moods that are more conductive to exploration and innovation? What are ways to encourage the right type of sharing for mutual creativity? How can the wisdom of crowds be harnessed constructively? From within the "creatives" EHM, how aware are the respective members of the nature of the whole, the various fragmented initiatives, and the individual and group motives?

How people process their creative work differs depending on the individual and the domain and the objectives, among other things. Sometimes, coming at a topic directly is non-productive, but coming at it through elision (joining abstract ideas) and through indirectness, allowing the subconscious to process the ideas, may work better.

Innovating in the world requires seeing the world for what it is, "rejecting the default and exploring whether a better option exists" or "vuja de" or seeing the familiar in new ways (Grant, 2016, p. 7). It requires translating original ideas into entrepreneurial (or other) action and risk-taking in the world while hedging against that risk by controlling for the other aspects of their lives.

CONCLUSION

EHMs of "creatives" looking for disparate inspiration is a topic amenable to dispersed exploration, touching different social media platforms and different data acquisition methods. The amorphousness and size of this EHM make it impossible to use just a few limited sources. This entity does not have clear defined edges in terms of membership and may truly stretch the bounds of EHM "membership." As it is, this hybrid research approach provides slivers of insights and snippets. It relies on some degree of researcher subjective framing.

REFERENCES

Aguirre, B. E., Wenger, D., & Vigo, G. (1998). A test of the emergent norm theory of collective behavior. *Sociological Forum*, *13*(2), 301–320. doi:10.1023/A:1022145900928

Anderson, L. W., Krathwohl, D. R., Airiasian, W., Cruikshank, K. A., Mayer, R. E., & Pintrich, P. R. (2001). *A Taxonomy for Learning, Teaching and Assessing: A Revision of Bloom's Taxonomy of Educational Outcomes: Complete Edition*. Longman.

Benaim, M. (2018). From symbolic values to symbolic innovation: Internet-memes and innovation. *Research Policy*, *47*(5), 901–910. doi:10.1016/j. respol.2018.02.014

Brockman, P., Khurana, I. K., & Zhong, R. (2018). Societal trust and open innovation. *Research Policy*, *47*(10), 2048–2065. doi:10.1016/j. respol.2018.07.010

Carayannis, E. G., Goletsis, Y., & Grigoroudis, E. (2017). Composite innovation metrics: MCDA and the Quadruple Innovation Helix framework. *Technological Forecasting and Social Change*, *131*, 4–17. doi:10.1016/j. techfore.2017.03.008

Chi, M., Wang, W., Lu, X., & George, J. F. (2018). Antecedents and outcomes of collaborative innovation capabilities on the platform collaboration environment. *International Journal of Information Management*, *43*, 273–283. doi:10.1016/j.ijinfomgt.2018.08.007

Dietrich, A. (2004). The cognitive neuroscience of creativity. *Psychonomic Bulletin & Review*, *11*(6), 1011–1026. doi:10.3758/BF03196731 PMID:15875970

Dziallas, M. & Blind, K. (2018). Innovation indicators throughout the innovation process: An extensive literature analysis. *Technovation*, 1 – 27. (in press)

Elkind, D. (2008). The Power of Play: Learning What Comes Naturally. *American Journal of Play*, 1–6.

Google Correlate F. A. Q. (2011). Retrieved Dec. 14, 2018, from https://www.google.com/trends/correlate/faq

Grant, A. (2016). *Originals: How Non-conformists move the world*. New York: Viking.

Hai-Jew, S. (2019). The electronic hive mind and cybersecurity: Mass-scale human cognitive limits to explain the 'weakest link' in cybersecurity. In *Global Cyber Security Labor Shortage and International Business Risk* (pp. 206–262). Hershey, PA: IGI Global. doi:10.4018/978-1-5225-5927-6.ch011

Halbinger, M. A. (2018). The role of makerspaces in supporting consumer innovation and diffusion: An empirical analysis. *Research Policy*, *47*(10), 2028–2036. doi:10.1016/j.respol.2018.07.008

Hannigan, T. R., Seidel, V. P., & Yakis-Douglas, B. (2018). Product innovation rumors as forms of open innovation. *Research Policy*, *47*(5), 953–964. doi:10.1016/j.respol.2018.02.018

Jia, N. (2018). Corporate innovation strategy and stock price crash risk. *Journal of Corporate Finance*, *53*, 155–173. doi:10.1016/j.jcorpfin.2018.10.006

Kahn, K. B. (2018). Understanding innovation. *Business Horizons*, *61*(3), 453–460. doi:10.1016/j.bushor.2018.01.011

Kostis, P. C., Kafka, K. I., & Petrakis, P. E. (2018). Cultural change and innovation performance. *Journal of Business Research*, *88*, 306–313. doi:10.1016/j.jbusres.2017.12.010

Mendi, P., & Mudida, R. (2018). The effect on innovation of beginning informal: Empirical evidence from Kenya. *Technological Forecasting and Social Change*, *131*, 326–335. doi:10.1016/j.techfore.2017.06.002

Muninger, M.-I., Hammedi, W., & Mahr, D. (2019). The value of social media for innovation: A capability perspective. *Journal of Business Research*, *95*, 116–127. doi:10.1016/j.jbusres.2018.10.012

Ortiz-Villajos, J. M., & Sotoca, S. (2018). Innovation and business survival: A long-term approach. *Research Policy*, *47*(8), 1418–1436. doi:10.1016/j.respol.2018.04.019

Root-Bernstein, M., & Root-Bernstein, R. (2006). Imaginary worldplay in childhood and maturity and its impact on adult creativity. *Creativity Research Journal*, *18*(4), 405–425. doi:10.120715326934crj1804_1

Saridakis, G., Idris, B., Hansen, J. M., & Dana, L. P. (2019). SMEs' internationalization: When does innovation matter? *Journal of Business Research*, *96*, 250–263. doi:10.1016/j.jbusres.2018.11.001

Saxenian, A. (1994, 1996). Regional Advantage: Culture and Competition in Silicon Valley and Route 128. Cambridge, MA: Harvard University Press.

Singer, J. L. (2009). Researching imaginative play and adult consciousness: Implications for daily and literary creativity. *Psychology of Aesthetics, Creativity, and the Arts*, *3*(4), 190–199. doi:10.1037/a0016507

Smolucha, L., & Smolucha, F. C. (1986, Aug.) L.S. Vygotsky's theory of creative imagination. *Proceedings of the 94th Annual Convention of the American Psychological Association*, 1 – 15.

Wojan, T. R., Crown, D., & Rupasingha, A. (2018). Varieties of innovation and business survival: Does pursuit of incremental or far-ranging innovation make manufacturing establishments more resilient? *Research Policy*, *47*(9), 1801–1810. doi:10.1016/j.respol.2018.06.011

Woodman, R. W., Sawyer, J. E., & Griffin, R. W. (1993, April). Toward a theory of organizational creativity. *Academy of Management Review*, *18*(2), 293–321. doi:10.5465/amr.1993.3997517

ADDITIONAL READING

Catmull, E., & Wallace, A. (2014). *Creativity, Inc*. New York: Random House.

Csikszentmihalyi, M. (2013). *Creativity: Flow and the Psychology of Discovery and Invention*. New York: HarperCollins Publishers.

KEY TERMS AND DEFINITIONS

Electronic Hive Mind: A synchronous temporal and informal patchwork of emergent shared social consciousness (held by geographically distributed people, cyborgs, and robots) enabled by online social connectivity (across a range of social media platforms on the web and internet), based around various dimensions of shared attractive interests.

Imagination: The ability to conceptualize non-extant realities or possibilities.

Innovation: The origination of new methods, processes, concepts, understandings, or objects.

Conclusion

A proposed book is often an amorphous construct. The initial contract asserts something simple: there is a topic about which a researcher might be able to explore and come out with sufficient information to fill the pages. How it shapes out thereafter depends on too many factors outside of a researcher's control. At least that is the experience of this author. Other authors may ensure that they have a draft Table of Contents (TOC) or a few drafted chapters or some datasets or something else to go on first. (There is something to be said for trusting a publisher enough to be able to sign a contract for a work that only exists notionally and about which one has an irrational obsession.) Every book manuscript is resistant to creation, and every finished work has to have been willed into existence. Even as alluring as this topic was, this work was no different and involved a fair amount of hard work and exploration. Ultimately, there is a lack of self-satisfaction…because this could have included more data and additional analytical strategies. Additional electronic hive minds (EHMs) could have been explored. New insights are there for the discovery and construction. This is probably a good thing for a Research Insights text, which is at least partially about sharing ideas with others for ways to advance fields and broaden research methods.

Electronic Hive Minds on Social Media: Emerging Research and Opportunities was based on a simple "theory of mind" at macro scale—that from the *residua* from online interactions enabled by social media platforms and other forms of information and communications technology (ICT), EHMs may be studied for research insights and even predictivity (Figure 1). The online data are observable, but they are proxies into what is hidden, the electronic hive minds (which exist in part online and in part offline, in people's heads and minds and bodies). This work serves as an initial work focused around hypothesizing and light research exploration (based on partial and imperfect data, subjective analytical lenses, and only some reproducible research).

Figure 1. "Theory of mind" to understand electronic hive minds (EHMs)

"Theory of Mind" to Understand Electronic Hive Minds (EHMs)

So how well did the analogy of "electronic hive minds" map to the space? Some initial observations have been made in Table 1. The mapping seems light but sufficient.

Another way to conceptualize this EHM construct is as layers. The layers may be understood horizontally across the layers, and vertically (as cross-sections). (Table 02) All the layers are conceptualized as being in flux and fluidity, with messaging changing the fastest and membership changing the slowest (being the most static). However, these features can differ widely depending on the particular EHM. This approach suggests that the unit of

Table 1. Applicability of the "electronic hive mind" analogy to the social media space

Analogy of "Electronic Hive Mind"	Social Media Space
Electronic	Internet World Wide Web Social Web Social Media Platforms
Brain	Social Web Social Media Platforms
Synaptic Activity	Social Messaging Social Interactivity
Mind	Collective Thought Collective Interests Collective Conscious, Subconscious, and Unconscious
Mindset	Collective Personalities, Dispositions, Temperaments, Collective Moods
Personality	Collective Patterned Values Collective Patterned Behaviors
Hive	Mass Actions Collective Actions Inspired Actions
Physical Body	EHM Membership Physicality of Human Members

analysis does not have to be the whole EHM but pieces and parts, at more granular levels.

At micro and meso levels, there may be messaging among dyads, triads, and other motifs and small groups. There may be actions taken at ego and entity levels. There may be studies of members as individuals and as parts of small groups (including co-located ones). And the "whispers and shadows" level may also be studied at a smaller than EHM-scale-level.

Then, there are macro levels, including the intersections of multiple EHMs, perhaps, or a slice-in-time view of a multiple EHMs around particular topics, and so on. It is not infeasible to conceptualize of computational analyses of all extant EHMs on particular platforms…or around particular topics…or in particular physical regions…or other categorization approaches.

Where do electronic hive minds come from? In a simple sense, they are produced by human living organisms, so they are biogenic. They are influenced or partially determined by social forces, so they are sociogenic. They are influenced by human personalities, so they are somewhat social conformed and idiosyncratic. They are enabled by socio-technical spaces and technologies, so they are technogenic.

To recap, this work is comprised of nine chapters, with an opening Preface and a closing Conclusion.

Table 2. Layers of an electronic hive mind

Some Layers of an EHM (at a Macro Level)	Observability
1. Messaging (public consciousness)	Low, medium, and high observability (depending on the technological understructures of the social media platforms)
2. Actions (public consciousness)	Low, medium, and high observability (depending on social documentation and other documentation of the actions)
3. Membership (human, cyborg, robot/scripted agent)	Low, medium, and high observability (depending on social documentation and other documentation of membership; access to corporate information)
4. Whispers and shadows [people's intentionality, people's emotions, people's unexpressed and tacit thoughts; private electronic messaging, in-world messaging, unspoken; hidden actions (online and in-world); private membership, cutouts, hidden hands/ secret actors/secret influencers, and others]	Low observability Invisibility [These "whispers and shadows" may be partially projected (suspected, guessed at, inferred) and partially validated / invalidated. In general, latency is more of a natural state than expressivity or revelation. The latent is about potential, including mass thought / mass action outbreak potential.]

Preface

Conclusion

The number of chapters was delimited by the book type with the publisher. However, within that limit, the author strove to remain open to having each chapter evolve in new directions. Each title, abstract, focus, and other aspects of each chapter changed multiple times before a work was in a sufficient draft format for review. Even as the chapters started coalescing, the author worked to remain flexible and to accept divergence and range in the topics. Perhaps the sense of EHMs would be quite different if different topics were selected instead through which to understand EHMs. Perhaps theorizing about EHMs without their in-world instantiations would be more powerful, with imagined counterfactuals along with the factuals.

In part, the work of a conclusion is to offer a kind of retrospective. A simple angle is to recall the initial start point and the initial conceptualized objectives then.

PHASE 4: IN RETROSPECT (JAN. 2019)

This work began with a partial description of an "electronic hive mind" from an earlier work of the author's in a topic-based context of general user cybersecurity (Hai-Jew, 2019b). For this work, the initial definition of an electronic hive mind (EHM) is as follows:

a synchronous temporal and informal patchwork of emergent shared social consciousness (held by geographically distributed people, cyborgs, and robots) enabled by online social connectivity (across a range of social media platforms on the Web and Internet), based around various dimensions of shared attractive interests.

This suggests that through social engagement, distributed individuals may experience coalescences around particular ideas and values and practices. The initial intuition suggests that an electronic hive mind is comprised of some distributed coalescence of people around an issue and / or practice online forming some sort of entity (entitivaty), not necessarily in agreement or consensus or dissensus, but interest and focus. The members may have different individual and shared agendas. The coalescence may be sudden or gradual. But some shared engagement with the topic holds the hive mind somewhat loosely (or tightly) as a temporary body (with the presumption that they may act in some sort of cohesion or semi-cooperative mass). These seem to be the essentials. In many ways, this somewhat unwieldy definition still works and is still relevant at the completion of the text. While it is possible to add other potential dimensions to that definition, the basics still hold, nine chapters later, with a handful of real-world examples.

One way to enhance this definition is to identify phenomenon and entities that seem like electronic hive minds but are not. For example, a social network is not necessarily an EHM, which is more ephemeral and distributed and exists across multiple social media platforms. (To illustrate, a "sleuthing" EHM focused on a case may access a range of disparate social networks and online communities to acquire the requisite information for the potential problem solving. This is also true for anything EHM dealing with hard problems or complexity.) For another example, a grouping on a particular social media platform may be a distributed social group, but it may not function at the level of an EHM. A free-floating idea without human adherents would not be an EHM. Identifying other non-EHMs as (non)exemplars may be insightful.

Perhaps exploring the various seeding types of EHMs may be informative of non-EHM examples at a more granular level. To refresh from the Preface, EHMs may be seeded in various ways, such as those based on the following aspects (and others): who, what, when, where, why, and how. A non-EHM may be limited seeded ones with few to no adherents or limited reach, for example.

What about the general ten-step research trajectory proposed in Chapter 1 (Figure 02)? The steps used to capture the information in Chapter 1 works generally, but Steps 5 and 6 (empirical data capture and data analysis) is where the heart of the unique future approaches will lie; certainly, Step 8, the validation or invalidation of the research, is also an area of interest (although it is likely most will like a provisional or contingent approach to the framing). [Certainly, social media contents have been shown to be somewhat difficult to engage in a naïve way because of massive problems of manipulation—with widespread frauds of various types, scripted agents, swiped real-world identities, and poor oversight by both social media companies and respective governments. The attempts at manipulation will likely always be a part of any media because of media's reach and the potential rewards of controlling massminds. Whoever controls the mind has access to everything else that the person controls—knowledge, resources, actions. Oftentimes, people do not set up the sufficient controls on their own suggestibility. Biologically, there are ways to bypass the conscious mind and elicit unwanted behaviors. Some suggest that there are no such things as conscious thoughts and that what comes to mind come through hidden channels (Ayan, Dec. 20, 2018). Even if that is the *status quo*, it clearly is high-risk to have non-sentient unwilled and unaware minds.]

So is this work about "mind-reading" electronic hive minds (EHMs) and predicting from that information? Yes, and no. This seems more to be about listening closely to different types of communications to understand loosely connected human collectives. This work is about formalizing some of the nascent ideas around EHMs.

Some Takeaways about EHMs

So what are some of the main takeaways from this book (beyond the observations in the Preface and in each of the prior nine chapters)? Particularly, what parts of an EHM are most important? And what are some insights about researching them? Six main ideas emerged:

Conclusion

Figure 2. Exploring the Online Space for Electronic Hive Minds (EHMs)

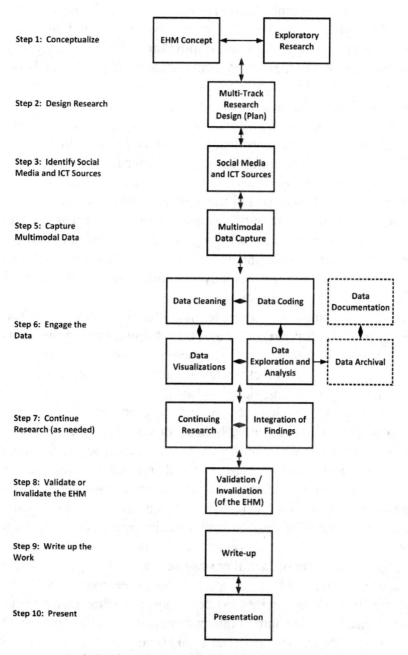

Exploring the Online Space for Electronic Hive Minds (EHMs)

First is that, of the three elements of an "electronic + hive + mind," the electronic (socio-technical tools) + hive (activated humanity, linked to individual and group action) + mind (awareness, analytical thinking, cogent decision making), maybe **the most important is the engagement of the human mind**, to best harness the "electronic" and "hive" aspects. Humanity has primacy, with all the implications of human striving and the human condition. In EHMs, the members exist as individuals, as motifs, as groups, and as larger wholes, and understanding the micro (ego), meso (entity), and macro (network) levels is important. Overlaid over the electronic + hive + mind is the social and the cultural and the intentional.

This work has shown the presence of malicious actors and their manipulations in EHMs, to activate desirable impressions and reactive behavioral actions, often without due consideration. Smart engagement means understanding the context and selecting influences with care. People have power in their respective online and physical environments, and they can engage constructively and pro-socially and positively in many ways. This is so, too, on electronic hive minds.

Second, in the same way that people's minds can be attractive, **EHMs have a range of methods for attracting and maintaining human membership**. Initial "come-ons" may be attractive members (with public reputations), alluring ideas or stories, direct invites to particular organizations or social groups, engaging platforms, delightful or productive activities, appealing group identities, free or low-cost resources, promises of spectacle (like conflict) or pleasure (eye-candy, humor) or entertainment (drama), eye-catching imagery, and attractor click-bait. There has to be satisfaction of the initial promise and follow-on substance and continuing novelty (and some consistency) for people to continue engaging. The EHMs in this work show a range of motivations for participation. Again, the assumption is that the EHM forms around an interest around a particular phenomenon or idea or mix of factors, but it does not assume that the members are in alignment or agreement. As a matter of fact, there can be a wide divergence of opinions and practices within an EHM. (People can cooperate even in the absence of group agreement.) While EHMs can be highly ephemeral, many are not and have some histories. With fairly high replacement rates and some committed core of membership, EHMs may last a long time. A core assumption is that EHMs, like most human collectives, have some interest in survival and may act accordingly. There is also an interest in the maintenance of its membership, by meeting their felt needs. Also, while this work only used data that was publicly available, if EHMs exist mostly in the minds of the membership, perhaps there should be outreaches to the membership to understand their thoughts…for more direct human subjects research.

Third, **researchers have a number of qualitative/quantitative/mixed methods and tools that they can use to learn about respective electronic hive minds**. In this work, there were a range of data sources, including social media platforms (microblogging sites, social networking sites, image-sharing sites, video-sharing sites, crowd-sourced encyclopedias, and others), information and communications technology (ICT), non-consumptive mass book data, non-consumptive mass search data, social imagesets, and others. Manual coding of data was applied. Computational text analyses, content network graphing, and other efforts were also applied.

Fourth, **understanding EHMs is provisional and somewhat tentative.** The researcher subjectivity, the applied framework(s), the theory(ies), the research method(s), the selected (or available non-private) data, and all will speak to the interpretive space and limit what is understood. Given the dynamism of some EHMs, refreshing the research will be important because research understandings will expire in time. And yet, for all the limitations, there are benefits to even initial impressions and initial learning. These may be informative of some level of predictivity, although this feature was not directly explored in this work. (In this work, the EHM profiles were sketched fairly quickly, and the assertions were made lightly. Suffice it to say that the first impressions of EHMs did not ever hold, and there were always surprises.)

This work also suggests the incompleteness of EHMs in terms of how issues are engaged and how touch-and-go particular focuses may be depending on the participants, the technologies, and serendipity.

Fifth, **EHMs do take on different characteristics on different social media platforms,** in part because of the affordances and constraints of the respective socio-technical spaces…in part because of the different members… in part because of the different communications modalities…in part because of the cultural practices and social norms and values in those communal spaces…and so on. It would seem important to always assume EHMs exist in a number of locations online and to explore as many of these as possible through data skims and fuller data collection in some cases.

They also instantiate differently in the face of different challenges or experiences or contexts. An EHM may function one way in a relaxed environment vs. a high-stress or pressured one. To this end, it is important to study beyond the limits of the online EHM and explore beyond, to better understand the larger environment or context.

Sixth, **EHMs are physically embodied**. They link people who are physical beings with access to physical resources and positionality in the world and power. These interconnections suggest varying levels of current implications and potential future implications in the world.

These are some foundational elements. In this space, there are numerous open questions (addressed later in Phase 5).

First Principles of Electronic+Hive+Minds

These are some of the larger broad-scale insights from this work. Are there supportable "first principles" or "foundational ideas" about electronic hive minds? A slow read of the working definition may be insightful. Here, an EHM is...

a synchronous temporal and informal patchwork of emergent shared social consciousness (held by geographically distributed people, cyborgs, and robots) enabled by online social connectivity (across a range of social media platforms on the Web and Internet), based around various dimensions of shared attractive interests.

Some initial fundamental principles may be asserted from this research. Ten early ones follow (segmented by general areas of focus):

Focus Area 1: About social practices and social humans (and cyborgs and socialbots)

1. **Human-bot membership.** The members of EHMs are humans, cyborgs, and socialbots, where cyborgs are social accounts animated by both human(s) and automated agent(s), and where socialbots are scripted agents that behave as if they were human (and are generally undiscernible from actual humans on the public facing sides of the social media platforms). These socialbots may be "deep fakes," backstopped with created impressions that hint at their faux humanness. This mixed membership would not be possible without the many technologies available in the world for human manipulation and expression.
2. **Patchwork social consciousness.** EHMs are comprised of a patchwork of shared social consciousness, with ways to partition by membership (macro, meso, and micro levels); by demographics; by cultures; by languages; by interests, and other forms of membership; by positional

stances; by actions; by behavioral roles, and other dimensional elements. (Where there are more connected patchworks, these form when people are in agreement around particular ideas and visions and endeavors.)

3. **Social practice.** Social practices (values, social norms, collaborations, and others) inform electronic hive minds. They inform how people interact. They inform what people do in the service of the electronic hive minds and what roles and activities they take on.

4. **Survival.** As (egos and) entities, EHMs behave somewhat collectively in terms of retaining human membership, being socially relevant, attracting social attention, striving for survival or continued existence (in some form), and creating a legacy (or legacies). EHMs are in constant flux, with some parts stable and some parts engaging in change. These are not self-contained per se, with spillages into other areas, and parts breaking off and redefining themselves more meaningfully for their membership.

Focus Area 2: About distributed social communications on virtual spaces

5. **Social expression.** In any social expression online…

    a. …the communicators are engaging intentionally and purposefully. (It is hard to engage in effortful messaging without any personal or group interests on the line. The self-interests of various egos and entities are always in play.)

    b. …only a portion of ideas are expressed (with the rest existing in silences or left unexpressed). It is never the whole communications even in multi-dimensional multimodal communications like imagery, video, and others. And in every expressed message, there will be leakage of subconscious and unconscious thoughts (and even intentions).

    c. …there is an assumed third-person audience, even in narrowcast one-to-few or one-to-one expressions. Communicants may have partial awareness of the actual publics, and they likely over- or under-estimate the size of the audience, and they will mis-describe who the individuals are. Part of the communications involves a nod to the assumed third-person audience.

6. **Technological understructure.** A given "hidden hand" and outsized influencer in any EHM involves the underlying technologies or the enabling analog-digital "brain" structures. In part, the system sets up the incentives for people to behave within them in particular ways. The

human members of an EHM who know how to work the systems will have an outsized voice and outsized power over the other members.

7. **Across social platforms and Social Web and real space.** EHMs are diffuse and distributed over a number of social platforms and physical spaces. Even so, it is possible to discern and map them. If some social presences and messaging are minimal, it may well be that real social needs are being met elsewhere—in online multi-channel spaces and in offline real spaces. The scant presences and messaging may be only part-worths of a whole amount of people's expressed interests.

Focus Area 3: About time (in all its forms) and space (in all its forms)

8. **Time.** EHMs are temporal and share some time overlap or synchronicity. As in most (all?) things, they are impermanent. They evolve and change dynamically over time. There are times of heightened intensities and times of fallowness and latency. Even as EHMs arise, they also sunset.

9. **Space.** Members of EHMs (and EHMs) are geographically distributed, so the members may come from concentrated or diverse ranges of physical areas. Power may be projected in distributed spatial ways.

Focus Area 4: In-world interests

10. **The real.** Humans can be triggered to action by various forms of belief, messaging, and alluring ideas. They can fix on attractive identity messaging and wear those identities with pride and long-term loyalty. They can be mesmerized by the charisma of other people (even faux people like digital avatars); they can "worship" these individuals through followership, emulation, and fanatical true believing. Humans can be highly suggestible based on what they see in the world and what appeals to them intellectually, sensually, emotionally, and otherwise. For some, the allurements remain a phenomenon in their minds, but for others, these commitments affect choices in the real world, resulting in action taken, resources spent, connections made, and other observable phenomena. All EHMs arise from in-world self-interests and have both diffuse and concentrated effects in the real world and in real space and on real peoples. The self-interest is at every level and scale: individual, dyadic, small-group, and up to the macro level. If self-interest wanes, in all likelihood, those members will pull back on their participation and contributions and ultimately leave the EHMs. They will "ghost"

their peers by being unreachable. (Understanding the complexities of human motivations, though, is required in understanding the various egos, entities, and other nodes within an EHM.)

Some of the listed first principles of electronic hive minds are compound, with multi-faceted dimensions. There are likely others dimensions as well. These concepts, abstracted from observations of social trace data, enable more in-depth reasoning from first principles and not analogy alone.

Pressure-Testing the Collected Data for Presence of Prospective EHM

It may help to pressure-test the social and other data to detect whether an electronic hive mind (EHM) exists. Some valid questions in a checklist may include the following:

Human, Cyborg, and Robot Membership

- Do some of the human members of the prospective EHM have awareness of the distributed EHM as an entity (via the sense of entiativity)?
- Are the sentient members somewhat geographically distributed (or spatially localized or co-located)?
- Are there some recognizable human personalities with indicators of unique personhood? Created cyborg and robot entities with indicators of unique simulated personhood?
- Does the probable EHM enable a mix of human interests and motivations?
- Is it possible to differentiate between the various types of membership in the EHM: human, cyborg (mix of human- and scripted-agent), and robot membership?

Existence in Time

- Has the potential EHM been in existence for some period of time? Is there a sense of origin and maybe even (brief) history, in terms of information? (historicity)
- Is there a sense of shared time in the EHM, some synchronicity, or some time overlap?

- Is there a reasonable understanding of how the EHM originated (bottom-up or top-down ways)? Was there a sense of purposiveness early on? Did the EHM emerge from collective grassroots interests, or was it started in other ways?

Exchanged Ideas

- Is there some level of coherence and coalescence of ideas in the prospective EHM? Is there diversity of messaging and disagreements? Is there convergence of messaging in some aspects?
- Is there some tradition of information sharing, including some original user-generated information? Is the information shared done so across various modes?

Common Practice(s)

- Is there a sense of common practice among some or all of the members in the potential EHM?
- Does the EHM have a proprioception or physical body-awareness?

Collective Mindfulness

- In the prospective EHM, is there a sense of remembering and forgetting and "working memory" (top-of-mind)?
- In the potential EHM, is there a sense of personality, disposition, temperament, and mood?

Multiple Underlying Socio-Technical Platforms (Brain or "Neural Architecture" Analogy)

- Are there multiple social media platforms and other sites used as research data sourcing? Has the data been cleaned against "impression management" and "manipulations"?

Adaptivity

- Does the potential EHM show adaptive and survival capabilities? Does it show resilience in the face of challenges? Is it able to change? Is it able to evolve? Is it able to attract members and keep them (and encourage their contributions)?

There may be other dimensions of the titular EHM that may be indicative of its reality, but these seven dimensions are a start: human membership, existence in time, ideas, common practice, collective mindfulness, multiple underlying platforms (brain analogy), and adaptivity. [A new wrench in this involves the sense that much of the Internet is "fake" and illusory with scripted personas to fake "views" in order to justify advertising costs, counterfeit personas to steal votes, and numerous other types of fakery online (Read, Dec. 26, 2018).]

PHASE 5: ABOUT FUTURE RESEARCH (JAN. 2019)

Electronic hive minds are more ephemeral than defined social networks, with memberships defined by formalized following relationships and online interactivity (replies, forwarding, retweeting, commenting, tagging, and others). They are more dispersed than local geographically co-located communities. They are somewhat amorphous and yet somewhat designed. They are built up and connected around various issues and phenomena (per the 5Ws and 1H in the Preface). There is still much that has not been defined about EHMs.

Some open questions: Finally, what of the "research agenda" related to EHMs? In some ways, the foundational questions are still left extant and still open questions.

- **Electronic hive minds:** What are electronic hive minds (EHMs)? How do they instantiate? What are the strengths and weaknesses of respective EHMs, and why? What are their formative stages? What are their trajectories over time? Their typical lifespans? What contributes to their starts, their achievements, and their conclusions? What do spinoff EHMs look like? Where are the boundaries and edges of EHMs, and why? How do these electronic social entities engage with other EHMs? What are characteristics of short-lived EHMs? Middle-lived ones? Long-lived ones?
- *Sousveillance*: What are EHMs like as experienced by members (individuals and groups) from inside? What insights may be captured from this "emic" perspective than an "etic" one? How are members motivated to engage, and what do they get out of these?

- **Technological understructures:** What are their technological understructures? (With the waxing and waning of various technologies, how do these affect the respective EHMs?)

- **Resourcing:** How are EHMs resourced? What resources move through them? Informational ones? Moneys? Others? What are common inputs and outputs (I/Os)?

- **Memberships:** What attracts individuals and groups to EHMs? What contributions do members make? What are the various memberships of EHMs, and how do they differentiate from each other? What types of people join particular EHMs? What sorts of robots are deployed on particular EHMs, and why? What sorts of cyborgs (humans and robots) are deployed on particular EHMs, and why? Are there ways to understand the contributions and roles of various social members in EHMs?

- **EHM dispositions and moods:** What are various factors that affect EHM personalities / dispositions / temperaments? Moods (more transient)? What are some ways to affect both?

- **Combined or overlapping EHMS:** What about studying mixes of electronic hive minds (EHMs) and not just single ones? What about studying melded ones? What about studying cross-cultural ones (albeit based around a core phenomenon of interest)?

- **EHMs in longitudinal time:** What about stretching time in the research and moving to longitudinal time, from starts to ends of EHMs (instead of the slice-in-time approaches here)? There is more need to understand the lifespans of EHMs and critical moments in their existence (such as when major changes occur). How do EHMs evolve? What are critical periods when their essential natures change?

- **Real-time EHMs:** What do EHMs look like in the midst of various experiences (in a dynamic mapping sense)?

- **EHMs in the world:** What do the EHMs look like globally? What is the thinking? What geographical ties are there for the respective minds (and why)? In the global mind space, what are the most salient issues, and why? What excites such EHMs, and what provides them satiety?

- **Planned-action EHMs:** In terms of EHMs that activate its member bodies, what are some of the main issues of interest? What sparks or excites actions? How aware are the members of the particular EHMs? What sorts of observable in-world effects do they have? What are constructive ways to engage in planned-action EHMs? To have voice?

- **Multimodal contents in EHMs:** What sorts of various modalities (text, audio, video, image, and mixed modality) of digital contents do people in EHMs share? Analog contents? How does modality of shared objects affect what is shared and what is communicated?
- **EHM theorizing:** What sorts of theories and frameworks inform on various aspects of EHMs?
- **Predictivity and EHMs:** How can EHMs be harnessed to understand population shifts (at present and the near-future)? Shifting people's interests? Resonant topics? Anticipated behaviors in the near-term, mid-term, and long-term?

If I were to write new chapters along these same lines, I might pursue other aspects of the human mind that may have some potential equivalencies to the EHM: mindfulness, concentration and focus; mental states / states of mind (celebratory, mournful, high-emotion, paranoia / suspicion / fear, obsessiveness, habituation, meditativeness, and other states), hypnotic, high-energy, precognition, curious/engaged, excitement-pursuing, lizard brain minds, social, insatiable (vs. sated), visual-based, playful, split minds, traditional vs. modern mindsets, pressured minds and related perceptions/ misperceptions, religious or spiritual minds, and various other aspects of minds and mental functions. If nothing else, the prior brainstorm gives a little of the sense of what the initial approach to this work—formless and messy, creative.

Also, I think there may be a real benefit in taking a wholly different approach to the idea of EHMs by beginning with explorations of various types of online data and *not* starting with human senses of mind as I did (as noted in the Preface). I went out looking for aspects of mass-scale human minds on the Social Web and on social media. Perhaps working in the other direction may shed new light. Or perhaps another approach can be from using brain maps and functions to see if analogues may be found in online EHMs.

This work employed a range of research methods for trying to understand the state of mostly macro-level electronic hive minds, including harnessing web search data, book data, formalized second-hand research, article-article network data, textual messaging (microblogging site tweetstreams, social networking site post streams, discussion threads, and others), social imagery, and others. The data analytic methods include manual coding as well as computational analytics (computational text analysis, sentiment analysis, social network analysis, linguistic analysis with psychometric analysis, and other approaches). Suffice it to say, there is plenty of other techniques and methods and applied technologies left. Technologically, scripted agents may be used to collect data. Various types of machine learning and data models may be applied to identify EHMs and to understand their dynamics. For example, decision trees may be used to understand what determines particular paths or membership that social accounts may take in EHMs. Population segmentation methods—through clustering and other approaches—may define the membership of an EHM and identify what people (and 'bots and cyborgs) cluster around. Artificial neural networks may enable insights about EHM members and what determines the categories of membership.

Not only are there many open questions about the nature of EHMs, but there are open aspects to research into them.

- **Data capture and data analytics methods:** The data acquisition methods and the data analytics methods here are by no means exhaustive. Also, this method requires some amount of close-in human reading and engagement and interpretation, with those attendant subjectivities. Using the concept of the EHM, researchers may use any number of other methods to acquire and analyze the available unstructured, semi-structured, and structured data around EHMs.
- **Ns of all:** What about capturing larger datasets for an N of all? What about using internal data to understand what is seeable from within the corporations that own the respective social networking and social media platforms?
- **Machine learning insights:** And what about using machine learning and other computational methods to extract "inherent" data patterns and other insights? When are automated insights relevant and more manual close-in human analytics important? When it is best to apply mixed methods?
- **Active research data elicitation:** Instead of just using available information in "natural" spaces, what about online survey elicitations? What about ethical research in which the researcher and his/her confederates also actively engage? What about using electronic Delphi methods to talk to experts or core informants (well situated insiders)? What about eliciting insights from participants in particular EHMs for "sousveillance" or monitoring from within or below?
- **Unique case studies:** What sorts of unique case studies are there about different types of EHMs?

- **Typologies:** What other types of EHMs exist in the world? What are variations on the different types (based on functionalities) identified in this work?
- **Situational awareness, predictivity, and decision making:** EHMs, theoretically and likely practically, can be used to predict and anticipate what may be to come (to some degree) and to enhance decision making. How this may be done would be helpful to know.
- **More:** Then, too, the respective research questions brought up in this book can benefit from follow-on or wholly independent research.

Certainly, there is no one-size-fits-all in this approach. A variety of techniques will be needed for the respective research questions, researcher needs, and the EHM contexts.

Ultimately, the "electronic hive mind" is a composite analogy and construct, drawing from ideas of online connectivity, hive-unthinkingness, and collective thinking/feeling/being/doing in a social brain (with a variety of sensors and indicators of the hidden or latent). Because of the dynamism on the elements here—the socio-technical spaces, the changing human and robot and cyborg memberships of the respective EHMs, the changing social norms and online cultures, and other elements, what may be true for a short online moment may well be highly untrue and / or irrelevant a short moment later.

An observation of the structure of the human brain seems to apply effectively to electronic hive minds. David J. Linden, professor of neuroscience at The Johns Hopkins University School of Medicine, wrote of the human brain:

The evolution of brains or any other biological structures is a tinkering process. Evolution proceeds in fits and starts with lots of dead ends and errors. Most important, there's never a chance to wipe the slate clean and do a totally new design. Our human brains were not designed all at once, by a genius inventor on a blank sheet of paper. Rather, the brain is a pastiche, a grab bag of make-do solutions that have accumulated and morphed since the first neurons emerged. It is a cobbled-together mess that nonetheless can perform some very impressive feats. (2018, p. 6)

The electronic hive mind, while not a "brain," often has a cobbled-together, make-do feel, and evolved feel (with "punctuated equilibrium" jumps to different directions) based on the varying and competing interests of the particular egos and entities at work within. These are spaces sensitive to loud voices and strong personalities, as well as the technological manipulations of those controlling "troll armies."

From a personal angle, I am a member of multiple EHMs, based on a combination of professional interests and self-indulgent personal whimsies and exploratory dabbling. On the professional front, there are research EHMs, education-related ones, educational technology, academic publishing, instructional design, and data analysis. On the personal side, there are those based on cooking, political science, history, biographies, inventions, and fiction-based mysteries. EHMs mostly have negligible costs of entry, and it is possible to be a member without paying much in the way of dues, except attentional ones. My sense is that most modern people have a wide range of interests, and there are many EHMs that may help meet their needs.

Finally, this book helps lay the concept of an electronic hive mind and some practical research approaches for studying coalescences of distributed people around shared issues of interest (even with divergent thinking and divergent opinions) and practices. It is hoped that others may engage in this space and find some small value in this approach to a complex human-created space. This is an initial first word and hopefully not the last.

PHASE 6: ABOUT RESEARCH ETHICS AND THE EXPLORATION OF ELECTRONIC HIVE MINDS (FEB.-MAR. 2019)

One of the reviewers of this text astutely observed that it would be helpful to explore the research ethics around the exploration of electronic hive minds.

Of course, there are the fundamental ethics of research surrounding human subjects. Briefly, this includes having the need to run research designs and instruments through an institutional review board (IRB) for their review and to enable their continuing oversight for especially sensitive research. There is the need for informed consent of research participants. There is the need to enforce the beneficence and constructiveness and prosocial aspects of the research. There have to be efforts to protect research participants and to avoid any potential harm, for all, and especially for protected classes. There are protocols for protecting research data against data leakage, identity leakage, misappropriation, misuse, and privacy compromises.

In terms of electronic hive minds, the principles of ethical research still apply, but there are some different features. Moral principles apply as well, in terms of general ideas of right and wrong, good or bad, and tradeoffs between different decisions and paths.

- **Recruiting informants online? Engaging the crowd in crowd-sourcing information? (Yes, but...)** If researchers are conducting research as active participants in an electronic hive mind, how much do they have to self-identify as a researcher? How much informed consent do they have to provide to those with whom they engage? Given the high bar for research that involves deception of other humans (and the potential for abuse), when should researchers active in EHMs engage in deceptive practices? And how can social media platforms and other spaces be informed of such research, if approved at the researcher's institution of higher education or corporation? What are the limits of ethical elicitation in EHM spaces? Where does the overlap happen between the personal individual (person as self) and the personal researcher (person as researcher)? If there are some who do not want to be "informants," how can their interests be addressed?
  - In terms of self-representations, how can researchers of EHMs avoid appropriations of others' deeply-held identities? How can they avoid even the appearance of any sort of usurpation?
  - How can they avoid getting in the way of other people engaging on the respective sites for their own interests and needs?
  - How can researchers put the needs of those around them ahead of the research? How can they avoid behaving in ways that may be manipulative? How can they be mindful of potential impacts of their work while also being realistic about how difficult it may be to anticipate potential effects in complex environments?
- **Public data, so anything goes? (Nope.)** While those who use social media platforms do have to agree to end user license agreements (EULAs) of the corporations hosting the platforms, and generally release these contents to the broad public, many of them may not be aware of how their data may be used to train artificial intelligence, to profile particular populations for commercial purposes, to influence elections, or other applications. Many have no idea how easy it is to scrape data en masse...or how to re-identify people from de-identified data. They may not realize how particular snippets of information may be revelatory (as a "tell") in ways that they did not intend. What responsibility does a researcher have to a broad public about the uses of broadly available public data? Should that data be published second-

hand, third-hand, or not (going with non-consumptive data analysis instead of making the underlying datasets available)? Or should the datasets be de-identified and published?

    ◦   In terms of using social idea, how can a research of EHMs avoid free-riding those who've created user-generated data or shared analytical tools or other elements?

- **Duty to warn? (Sometimes.)** If a researcher in the EHM space discovers what seems to be a threat, what is the scope of the "duty to warn"? In the absence of any "good Samaritan" legal protections, how can a researcher deal with the extant issues effectively and in a timely and accurate way? How can others' private data be protected in such a scenario? How should that move through a sequence? Whom should be notified? What about the social platform provider? Local law enforcement?

    ◦   Given how complex the world is, how can social messaging be understood in terms of follow-on actions, in first-order, second-order, third-order, and other effects?

    ◦   In identifying EHMs, the "signals" and "noise" can be mistaken one for the other. What threshold of evidence should be achieved before assertions are made about such ephemeral and transitory phenomena? If a researcher identifies what seems to be hidden hands or malicious agents, what level of proof should there be? And how can a researcher not assign himself / herself the role of "social police" or "social law enforcement" and potentially ruin others' online sociality experiences by calling out others publicly or reporting on them to the powers-that-be in social platforms? There are serious considerations about using collective intelligence to support law enforcement, which brings up such questions of roles and responsibilities and privacy (Furtado, et al., 2010). How can researchers strive for the social good without falling into traps of mistaking human-embodied social accounts with robot ones or cyborg (both human and scripted agent) ones? How can researchers definitively identify sock puppets, given how difficult verifiable information is to come by about social account identities without platform host "insider" data. (Hai-Jew, 2019a) Given the need for safety for all online, how can negative messaging be handled without negative externalities?

- **Scripted research agents and automated tools? (Yes, but…)** In the online space, there are various types of very low-cost scripted agents (robots) that are used for data collection, data elicitation (from humans), data elicitation from data systems, and a range of other applications. How should these be used in the detection of EHMs? Its members? Its messaging? Its data patterns? Its purposes?
  - Can the uses of collective swarms to control against "malicious users" in online collectives (Mazzara, et al., 2013) be a solution in EHMs without negative externalities (or with controlled negative externalities)? How much should computational capabilities be applied to this space, in what ways, and to what ends?

These offer some early thoughts in this space, but a more formal and orderly exploration may be in order. Certainly, some of the early work in terms of how to deal with social media research inform this.

Finally!

I would like to express gratitude to IGI Global and their Research Insights imprint for taking a chance on a book topic about which I could describe little and then didn't blink when I sent in a very drafty proposed Table of Contents (TOC). I've been around long enough to know that such opportunities are rare, and it may be that our years of collaboration have enabled a moment such as this. Thank you!

Shalin Hai-Jew
Kansas State University, USA
March 2019

REFERENCES

Ayan, S. (2018, Dec. 20). There is no such thing as conscious thought. *Scientific American.* Retrieved Dec. 27, 2018, from https://www.scientificamerican.com/article/there-is-no-such-thing-as-conscious-thought/

Furtado, V., Ayres, L., de Oliveira, M., Vasconcelos, E., Caminha, C., D'Orleans, J., & Belchior, M. (2010). Collective intelligence in law enforcement – The WikiCrimes system. *Information Sciences*, *180*(1), 4–17. doi:10.1016/j.ins.2009.08.004

Hai-Jew, S. (2019a). Multidimensional mappings of political accounts for malicious political socialbot identification: Exploring social networks, geographies, and strategic messaging. In *Global Cyber Security Labor Shortage and International Business Risk* (pp. 263–348). Hershey, PA: IGI Global. doi:10.4018/978-1-5225-5927-6.ch012

Hai-Jew, S. (2019b). The electronic hive mind and cybersecurity: Mass-scale human cognitive limits to explain the 'weakest link' in cybersecurity. In *Global Cyber Security Labor Shortage and International Business Risk* (pp. 206–262). Hershey, PA: IGI Global. doi:10.4018/978-1-5225-5927-6.ch011

Linden, D. J. (2018). *Think Tank: Forty Neuroscientists Explore the Biological Roots of Human Experience*. New Haven, CT: Yale University Press.

Mazzara, M., Biselli, L., Greco, P. P., Dragoni, N., Marraffa, A., Qamar, N., & de Nicola, S. (2013). Social networks and collective intelligence: A return to the Agora. In *Social Network Engineering for Secure Web Data and Services* (pp. 88–113). IGI Global. doi:10.4018/978-1-4666-3926-3.ch005

Read, M. (2018, Dec. 26). *How much of the Internet is fake? Turns out, a lot of it, actually. Life in Pixels. Intelligencer section.* Retrieved Dec. 29, 2018, from http://nymag.com/intelligencer/2018/12/how-much-of-the-internet-is-fake.html

Related Readings

To continue IGI Global's long-standing tradition of advancing innovation through emerging research, please find below a compiled list of recommended IGI Global book chapters and journal articles in the areas of social media, virtual communities, and swarm intelligence. These related readings will provide additional information and guidance to further enrich your knowledge and assist you with your own research.

Agrifoglio, R., & Metallo, C. (2018). Knowledge Management and Social Media in Tourism Industry. In F. Di Virgilio (Ed.), *Social Media for Knowledge Management Applications in Modern Organizations* (pp. 92–115). Hershey, PA: IGI Global. doi:10.4018/978-1-5225-2897-5.ch005

Ahmed, A. A. (2019). Online Social Capital Among Social Networking Sites' Users. In J. Thakur (Ed.), *Modern Perspectives on Virtual Communications and Social Networking* (pp. 90–119). Hershey, PA: IGI Global. doi:10.4018/978-1-5225-5715-9.ch004

Akpojivi, U. (2018). Euphoria and Delusion of Digital Activism: Case Study of #ZumaMustFall. In F. Endong (Ed.), *Exploring the Role of Social Media in Transnational Advocacy* (pp. 179–202). Hershey, PA: IGI Global. doi:10.4018/978-1-5225-2854-8.ch009

Alamaniotis, M., & Tsoukalas, L. H. (2018). Assessment of Gamma-Ray-Spectra Analysis Method Utilizing the Fireworks Algorithm for Various Error Measures. In Y. Shi (Ed.), *Critical Developments and Applications of Swarm Intelligence* (pp. 155–181). Hershey, PA: IGI Global. doi:10.4018/978-1-5225-5134-8.ch007

Amer, T. S., & Johnson, T. L. (2017). Information Technology Progress Indicators: Research Employing Psychological Frameworks. In A. Mesquita (Ed.), *Research Paradigms and Contemporary Perspectives on Human-Technology Interaction* (pp. 168–186). Hershey, PA: IGI Global. doi:10.4018/978-1-5225-1868-6.ch008

Angélico, M. J., Silva, A., Teixeira, S. F., Maia, T., & Silva, A. M. (2017). Web Accessibility and Transparency for Accountability: The Portuguese Official Municipal Websites. In A. Mesquita (Ed.), *Research Paradigms and Contemporary Perspectives on Human-Technology Interaction* (pp. 140–166). Hershey, PA: IGI Global. doi:10.4018/978-1-5225-1868-6.ch007

Angiani, G., Fornacciari, P., Iotti, E., Mordonini, M., & Tomaiuolo, M. (2018). Participation in Online Social Networks: Theories and Models. *International Journal of Interactive Communication Systems and Technologies*, 8(2), 36–55. doi:10.4018/IJICST.2018070103

Angiani, G., Fornacciari, P., Mordonini, M., Tomaiuolo, M., & Iotti, E. (2017). Models of Participation in Social Networks. In M. Brown Sr., (Ed.), *Social Media Performance Evaluation and Success Measurements* (pp. 196–224). Hershey, PA: IGI Global. doi:10.4018/978-1-5225-1963-8.ch010

Arif, T., & Ali, R. (2017). Social Media Metrics in an Academic Setup. In N. Rao (Ed.), *Social Media Listening and Monitoring for Business Applications* (pp. 116–130). Hershey, PA: IGI Global. doi:10.4018/978-1-5225-0846-5. ch006

Arrigo, E. (2016). Deriving Competitive Intelligence from Social Media: Microblog Challenges and Opportunities. *International Journal of Online Marketing*, 6(2), 49–61. doi:10.4018/IJOM.2016040104

Asunka, S. (2018). Use of Social Media for Knowledge Sharing by Instructors in a Higher Education Institution: An Exploratory Case Study. In F. Di Virgilio (Ed.), *Social Media for Knowledge Management Applications in Modern Organizations* (pp. 116–143). Hershey, PA: IGI Global. doi:10.4018/978-1-5225-2897-5.ch006

Ayscue, L. M. (2016). Perception of Communication in Virtual Learning Environments: What's in It for Them? In B. Baggio (Ed.), *Analyzing Digital Discourse and Human Behavior in Modern Virtual Environments* (pp. 25–39). Hershey, PA: IGI Global. doi:10.4018/978-1-4666-9899-4.ch002

Baggio, B. G. (2016). Why We Would Rather Text than Talk: Personality, Identity, and Anonymity in Modern Virtual Environments. In B. Baggio (Ed.), *Analyzing Digital Discourse and Human Behavior in Modern Virtual Environments* (pp. 110–125). Hershey, PA: IGI Global. doi:10.4018/978-1-4666-9899-4.ch006

Bailey, L. W. (2017). Social Media: A Discussion of Considerations for Modern Organizations and Professionals. In M. Brown Sr., (Ed.), *Social Media Performance Evaluation and Success Measurements* (pp. 64–77). Hershey, PA: IGI Global. doi:10.4018/978-1-5225-1963-8.ch004

Barbosa, V. A., Pinheiro dos Santos, W., Emmanuel de Souza, R., Ribeiro, R. R., Feitosa, A. R., Araújo da Silva, V. L., ... Dias, Í. J. (2018). Image Reconstruction of Electrical Impedance Tomography Using Fish School Search and Differential Evolution. In Y. Shi (Ed.), *Critical Developments and Applications of Swarm Intelligence* (pp. 301–338). Hershey, PA: IGI Global. doi:10.4018/978-1-5225-5134-8.ch012

Bouraga, S., Jureta, I., & Faulkner, S. (2019). Functional and Non-Functional Requirements Modeling for the Design of New Online Social Networks. In J. Thakur (Ed.), *Modern Perspectives on Virtual Communications and Social Networking* (pp. 28–57). Hershey, PA: IGI Global. doi:10.4018/978-1-5225-5715-9.ch002

Bouraga, S., Jureta, I., & Faulkner, S. (2019). Users Holding Accounts on Multiple Online Social Networks: An Extended Conceptual Model of the Portable User Profile. In J. Thakur (Ed.), *Modern Perspectives on Virtual Communications and Social Networking* (pp. 120–145). Hershey, PA: IGI Global. doi:10.4018/978-1-5225-5715-9.ch005

Briziarelli, M., & Karikari, E. (2016). Mediating Social Media's Ambivalences in the Context of Informational Capitalism. *International Journal of Civic Engagement and Social Change, 3*(1), 1–22. doi:10.4018/IJCESC.2016010101

Brown, M. A. Sr. (2017). SNIP: A Survey Instrument. In M. Brown Sr., (Ed.), *Social Media Performance Evaluation and Success Measurements* (pp. 15–45). Hershey, PA: IGI Global. doi:10.4018/978-1-5225-1963-8.ch002

Brown, M. A. Sr. (2017). Social Networking and Social Media Comparisons. In M. Brown Sr., (Ed.), *Social Media Performance Evaluation and Success Measurements* (pp. 1–14). Hershey, PA: IGI Global. doi:10.4018/978-1-5225-1963-8.ch001

Brown, M. A. Sr. (2017). Understanding Social Communication. In M. Brown Sr., (Ed.), *Social Media Performance Evaluation and Success Measurements* (pp. 47–63). Hershey, PA: IGI Global. doi:10.4018/978-1-5225-1963-8.ch003

Campbell, D. M., & Chollier, M. (2018). Trans-National Advocacy and the Hashtag Black Lives Matter: Globalisation and Reception in the UK and France. In F. Endong (Ed.), *Exploring the Role of Social Media in Transnational Advocacy* (pp. 101–135). Hershey, PA: IGI Global. doi:10.4018/978-1-5225-2854-8.ch006

Castellano, S., & Khelladi, I. (2017). Play It Like Beckham!: The Influence of Social Networks on E-Reputation – The Case of Sportspeople and Their Online Fan Base. In A. Mesquita (Ed.), *Research Paradigms and Contemporary Perspectives on Human-Technology Interaction* (pp. 43–61). Hershey, PA: IGI Global. doi:10.4018/978-1-5225-1868-6.ch003

Chamakiotis, P., & Panteli, N. (2016). The World is your Office: Being Creative in a Global Virtual Organization. In B. Baggio (Ed.), *Analyzing Digital Discourse and Human Behavior in Modern Virtual Environments* (pp. 87–108). Hershey, PA: IGI Global. doi:10.4018/978-1-4666-9899-4.ch005

Chedid, M., & Teixeira, L. (2018). The Role of Social Media Tools in the Knowledge Management in Organizational Context: Evidences Based on Literature Review. In F. Di Virgilio (Ed.), *Social Media for Knowledge Management Applications in Modern Organizations* (pp. 31–57). Hershey, PA: IGI Global. doi:10.4018/978-1-5225-2897-5.ch002

Cheng, S., Chen, J., Qin, Q., & Shi, Y. (2018). An Analysis on Fireworks Algorithm Solving Problems With Shifts in the Decision Space and Objective Space. In Y. Shi (Ed.), *Critical Developments and Applications of Swarm Intelligence* (pp. 119–153). Hershey, PA: IGI Global. doi:10.4018/978-1-5225-5134-8.ch006

Dadoo, S. (2018). From Jenin to Johannesburg: The Digital Intifada and Transnational Advocacy for Palestine. In F. Endong (Ed.), *Exploring the Role of Social Media in Transnational Advocacy* (pp. 73–100). Hershey, PA: IGI Global. doi:10.4018/978-1-5225-2854-8.ch005

Dhal, K. G., Sen, M., & Das, S. (2018). Multi-Thresholding of Histopathological Images Using Fuzzy Entropy and Parameterless Cuckoo Search. In Y. Shi (Ed.), *Critical Developments and Applications of Swarm Intelligence* (pp. 339–356). Hershey, PA: IGI Global. doi:10.4018/978-1-5225-5134-8.ch013

Di Virgilio, F. (2018). Exploring Determinants of Knowledge Sharing and the Role of Social Media in Business Organizations: Overview and New Direction. In F. Di Virgilio (Ed.), *Social Media for Knowledge Management Applications in Modern Organizations* (pp. 1–30). Hershey, PA: IGI Global. doi:10.4018/978-1-5225-2897-5.ch001

Di Virgilio, F., & Antonelli, G. (2018). Consumer Behavior, Trust, and Electronic Word-of-Mouth Communication: Developing an Online Purchase Intention Model. In F. Di Virgilio (Ed.), *Social Media for Knowledge Management Applications in Modern Organizations* (pp. 58–80). Hershey, PA: IGI Global. doi:10.4018/978-1-5225-2897-5.ch003

Elazab, A., Mahmood, M. A., & Hefny, H. A. (2018). Social Media and Social Networking: The Present and Future Directions. In F. Di Virgilio (Ed.), *Social Media for Knowledge Management Applications in Modern Organizations* (pp. 144–167). Hershey, PA: IGI Global. doi:10.4018/978-1-5225-2897-5.ch007

Endong, F. P. (2018). Hashtag Activism and the Transnationalization of Nigerian-Born Movements Against Terrorism: A Critical Appraisal of the #BringBackOurGirls Campaign. In F. Endong (Ed.), *Exploring the Role of Social Media in Transnational Advocacy* (pp. 36–54). Hershey, PA: IGI Global. doi:10.4018/978-1-5225-2854-8.ch003

Endong, F. P. (2018). Using Social Media to Advocate LGBT Rights in Black Africa: A Study of Nigerian and Cameroonian Gay Bloggers and "Facebookers". In F. Endong (Ed.), *Exploring the Role of Social Media in Transnational Advocacy* (pp. 203–227). Hershey, PA: IGI Global. doi:10.4018/978-1-5225-2854-8.ch010

Erragcha, N. (2017). Using Social Media Tools in Marketing: Opportunities and Challenges. In M. Brown Sr., (Ed.), *Social Media Performance Evaluation and Success Measurements* (pp. 106–129). Hershey, PA: IGI Global. doi:10.4018/978-1-5225-1963-8.ch006

Ezziane, Z. (2019). Social Networking: A Tool for Enhancing E-Services. In J. Thakur (Ed.), *Modern Perspectives on Virtual Communications and Social Networking* (pp. 1–27). Hershey, PA: IGI Global. doi:10.4018/978-1-5225-5715-9.ch001

Farmer, L. S. (2016). Using Virtual Environments to Transform Collective Intelligence. In B. Baggio (Ed.), *Analyzing Digital Discourse and Human Behavior in Modern Virtual Environments* (pp. 149–163). Hershey, PA: IGI Global. doi:10.4018/978-1-4666-9899-4.ch008

Gur, S., Blanchard, A. L., & Walker, L. S. (2016). Impacts on Society: Informational and Socio-Emotional Support in Virtual Communities and Online Groups. In B. Baggio (Ed.), *Analyzing Digital Discourse and Human Behavior in Modern Virtual Environments* (pp. 181–195). Hershey, PA: IGI Global. doi:10.4018/978-1-4666-9899-4.ch010

Hai-Jew, S. (2017). Capturing the Gist(s) of Image Sets Associated with Chinese Cities through Related Tags Networks on Flickr. In N. Rao (Ed.), *Social Media Listening and Monitoring for Business Applications* (pp. 245–315). Hershey, PA: IGI Global. doi:10.4018/978-1-5225-0846-5.ch011

Hai-Jew, S. (2017). Employing the Sentiment Analysis Tool in NVivo 11 Plus on Social Media Data: Eight Initial Case Types. In N. Rao (Ed.), *Social Media Listening and Monitoring for Business Applications* (pp. 175–244). Hershey, PA: IGI Global. doi:10.4018/978-1-5225-0846-5.ch010

Hai-Jew, S. (2017). Exploring Public Perceptions of Native-Born American Emigration Abroad and Renunciation of American Citizenship through Social Media. In N. Rao (Ed.), *Social Media Listening and Monitoring for Business Applications* (pp. 338–382). Hershey, PA: IGI Global. doi:10.4018/978-1-5225-0846-5.ch013

Hai-Jew, S. (2017). Finding Automated (Bot, Sensor) or Semi-Automated (Cyborg) Social Media Accounts Using Network Analysis and NodeXL Basic. In N. Rao (Ed.), *Social Media Listening and Monitoring for Business Applications* (pp. 383–424). Hershey, PA: IGI Global. doi:10.4018/978-1-5225-0846-5.ch014

Hai-Jew, S. (2017). Real-Time Sentiment Analysis of Microblog Messages with the Maltego "Tweet Analyzer" Machine. In N. Rao (Ed.), *Social Media Listening and Monitoring for Business Applications* (pp. 316–337). Hershey, PA: IGI Global. doi:10.4018/978-1-5225-0846-5.ch012

Hai-Jew, S. (2017). *Social Media Data Extraction and Content Analysis* (pp. 1–493). Hershey, PA: IGI Global. doi:10.4018/978-1-5225-0648-5

Hein, D., Hentschel, A., Runkler, T. A., & Udluft, S. (2018). Particle Swarm Optimization for Model Predictive Control in Reinforcement Learning Environments. In Y. Shi (Ed.), *Critical Developments and Applications of Swarm Intelligence* (pp. 401–427). Hershey, PA: IGI Global. doi:10.4018/978-1-5225-5134-8.ch016

Hersey, L. N. (2017). CHOICES: Measuring Return on Investment in a Nonprofit Organization. In M. Brown Sr., (Ed.), *Social Media Performance Evaluation and Success Measurements* (pp. 157–179). Hershey, PA: IGI Global. doi:10.4018/978-1-5225-1963-8.ch008

Ingle, S., & Kuprevich, C. L. (2016). Workforce Development in Behavioral Healthcare and the Increased Use of Technology: Is It Working or Not? Are We Asking the Right Questions? In B. Baggio (Ed.), *Analyzing Digital Discourse and Human Behavior in Modern Virtual Environments* (pp. 40–59). Hershey, PA: IGI Global. doi:10.4018/978-1-4666-9899-4.ch003

Islam, A. Y. (2017). Technology Satisfaction in an Academic Context: Moderating Effect of Gender. In A. Mesquita (Ed.), *Research Paradigms and Contemporary Perspectives on Human-Technology Interaction* (pp. 187–211). Hershey, PA: IGI Global. doi:10.4018/978-1-5225-1868-6.ch009

Kang, Y., & Yang, K. C. (2016). Analyzing Multi-Modal Digital Discourses during MMORPG Gameplay through an Experiential Rhetorical Approach. In B. Baggio (Ed.), *Analyzing Digital Discourse and Human Behavior in Modern Virtual Environments* (pp. 220–243). Hershey, PA: IGI Global. doi:10.4018/978-1-4666-9899-4.ch012

Karnaukhova, O., & Hinkelbein, O. (2018). Expert Knowledge in the University-Industry Cooperation: The Cases of Germany and Russia. In F. Di Virgilio (Ed.), *Social Media for Knowledge Management Applications in Modern Organizations* (pp. 218–236). Hershey, PA: IGI Global. doi:10.4018/978-1-5225-2897-5.ch010

Kasemsap, K. (2017). Mastering Social Media in the Modern Business World. In N. Rao (Ed.), *Social Media Listening and Monitoring for Business Applications* (pp. 18–44). Hershey, PA: IGI Global. doi:10.4018/978-1-5225-0846-5.ch002

Kasemsap, K. (2018). The Role of Knowledge Transfer in Modern Organizations. In F. Di Virgilio (Ed.), *Social Media for Knowledge Management Applications in Modern Organizations* (pp. 190–217). Hershey, PA: IGI Global. doi:10.4018/978-1-5225-2897-5.ch009

Ketshabetswe, L. K., Zungeru, A. M., Chuma, J. M., & Mangwala, M. (2018). Swarm-Intelligence-Based Communication Protocols for Wireless Sensor Networks. In Y. Shi (Ed.), *Critical Developments and Applications of Swarm Intelligence* (pp. 271–300). Hershey, PA: IGI Global. doi:10.4018/978-1-5225-5134-8.ch011

Khaleel, M., & Chelliah, S. (2018). Employee Wellbeing English Language Proficiency a Key to Knowledge Sharing and Social Interaction. In F. Di Virgilio (Ed.), *Social Media for Knowledge Management Applications in Modern Organizations* (pp. 237–262). Hershey, PA: IGI Global. doi:10.4018/978-1-5225-2897-5.ch011

Khedhaouria, A., & Beldi, A. (2017). Continuance Use Intention of Mobile Internet Services: Does Gender Matter? In A. Mesquita (Ed.), *Research Paradigms and Contemporary Perspectives on Human-Technology Interaction* (pp. 212–234). Hershey, PA: IGI Global. doi:10.4018/978-1-5225-1868-6.ch010

Klepac, G. (2018). Using Particle Swarm Optimization Algorithm as an Optimization Tool Within Developed Neural Networks. In Y. Shi (Ed.), *Critical Developments and Applications of Swarm Intelligence* (pp. 215–244). Hershey, PA: IGI Global. doi:10.4018/978-1-5225-5134-8.ch009

Kowalsky, M. (2016). Analysis of Initial Involvement of Librarians in the Online Virtual World of Second Life. In B. Baggio (Ed.), *Analyzing Digital Discourse and Human Behavior in Modern Virtual Environments* (pp. 126–148). Hershey, PA: IGI Global. doi:10.4018/978-1-4666-9899-4.ch007

Kumar, G. V., Rao, B. V., Chowdary, D. D., & Sobhan, P. V. (2018). A Computational Comparison of Swarm Optimization Techniques for Optimal Load Shedding Under the Presence of FACTS Devices to Avoid Voltage Instability. In Y. Shi (Ed.), *Critical Developments and Applications of Swarm Intelligence* (pp. 182–214). Hershey, PA: IGI Global. doi:10.4018/978-1-5225-5134-8.ch008

Liang, C., Chang, C., Rothwell, W., & Shu, K. (2016). Influences of Organizational Culture on Knowledge Sharing in an Online Virtual Community: Interactive Effects of Trust, Communication and Leadership. *Journal of Organizational and End User Computing*, 28(4), 15–32. doi:10.4018/JOEUC.2016100102

Lichy, J., & Kachour, M. (2017). Insights into the Culture of Young Internet Users: Emerging Trends – Move Over Gen Y, Here Comes Gen Z! In A. Mesquita (Ed.), *Research Paradigms and Contemporary Perspectives on Human-Technology Interaction* (pp. 84–115). Hershey, PA: IGI Global. doi:10.4018/978-1-5225-1868-6.ch005

Liu, L., & Mo, H. (2018). Magnetotactic Bacteria Optimization Algorithm (MBOA) for Function Optimization: MBOA Based on Four Best-Rand Pairwise Schemes. In Y. Shi (Ed.), *Critical Developments and Applications of Swarm Intelligence* (pp. 97–118). Hershey, PA: IGI Global. doi:10.4018/978-1-5225-5134-8.ch005

Lu, Q. S., & Seah, Z. Y. (2018). Social Media Influencers and Consumer Online Engagement Management. In F. Di Virgilio (Ed.), *Social Media for Knowledge Management Applications in Modern Organizations* (pp. 81–91). Hershey, PA: IGI Global. doi:10.4018/978-1-5225-2897-5.ch004

Lubua, E. W. (2018). Enhancing E-Transparency in Public Governance Through Social Media. In F. Endong (Ed.), *Exploring the Role of Social Media in Transnational Advocacy* (pp. 136–152). Hershey, PA: IGI Global. doi:10.4018/978-1-5225-2854-8.ch007

Macedo, M. G., Bastos-Filho, C. J., Vieira, S. M., & Sousa, J. M. (2018). Multi-Objective Binary Fish School Search. In Y. Shi (Ed.), *Critical Developments and Applications of Swarm Intelligence* (pp. 53–72). Hershey, PA: IGI Global. doi:10.4018/978-1-5225-5134-8.ch003

Makhwanya, A. (2018). Barriers to Social Media Advocacy: Lessons Learnt From the Project "Tell Them We Are From Here". In F. Endong (Ed.), *Exploring the Role of Social Media in Transnational Advocacy* (pp. 55–72). Hershey, PA: IGI Global. doi:10.4018/978-1-5225-2854-8.ch004

Manjunath Patel, G. C., Krishna, P., Parappagoudar, M. B., Vundavilli, P. R., & Bhushan, S. N. (2018). Squeeze Casting Parameter Optimization Using Swarm Intelligence and Evolutionary Algorithms. In Y. Shi (Ed.), *Critical Developments and Applications of Swarm Intelligence* (pp. 245–270). Hershey, PA: IGI Global. doi:10.4018/978-1-5225-5134-8.ch010

Maravilhas, S. (2016). Social Media Intelligence for Business. *International Journal of Organizational and Collective Intelligence*, *6*(4), 19–44. doi:10.4018/IJOCI.2016100102

Marichelvam, M. K., & Tosun, Ö. (2018). Using Cuckoo Search Algorithm for Hybrid Flow Shop Scheduling Problems Under Makespan Criterion. In Y. Shi (Ed.), *Critical Developments and Applications of Swarm Intelligence* (pp. 379–400). Hershey, PA: IGI Global. doi:10.4018/978-1-5225-5134-8.ch015

Marovitz, M. (2017). Social Networking Engagement and Crisis Communication Considerations. In M. Brown Sr., (Ed.), *Social Media Performance Evaluation and Success Measurements* (pp. 130–155). Hershey, PA: IGI Global. doi:10.4018/978-1-5225-1963-8.ch007

Matilda, S. (2017). Big Data in Social Media Environment: A Business Perspective. In N. Rao (Ed.), *Social Media Listening and Monitoring for Business Applications* (pp. 70–93). Hershey, PA: IGI Global. doi:10.4018/978-1-5225-0846-5.ch004

McKay, E., Barefah, A., Mohamad, M., & Bakkar, M. N. (2019). Advances in E-Pedagogy for Online Instruction: Proven Learning Analytics Rasch Item Response Theory. In J. Thakur (Ed.), *Modern Perspectives on Virtual Communications and Social Networking* (pp. 58–89). Hershey, PA: IGI Global. doi:10.4018/978-1-5225-5715-9.ch003

Melonashi, E. (2017). Social Media and Identity: Understanding Identity Communication and Creation through Social Media. In A. Mesquita (Ed.), *Research Paradigms and Contemporary Perspectives on Human-Technology Interaction* (pp. 62–83). Hershey, PA: IGI Global. doi:10.4018/978-1-5225-1868-6.ch004

Papadopoulou, P. (2017). Exploring M-Commerce and Social Media: A Comparative Analysis of Mobile Phones and Tablets. In A. Mesquita (Ed.), *Research Paradigms and Contemporary Perspectives on Human-Technology Interaction* (pp. 1–21). Hershey, PA: IGI Global. doi:10.4018/978-1-5225-1868-6.ch001

Peixoto, C., Branco, F., Martins, J., & Gonçalves, R. (2017). A Multi-Perspective Theoretical Analysis to Web Accessibility. In A. Mesquita (Ed.), *Research Paradigms and Contemporary Perspectives on Human-Technology Interaction* (pp. 117–139). Hershey, PA: IGI Global. doi:10.4018/978-1-5225-1868-6.ch006

Popescu, F., & Scarlat, C. (2017). Human Digital Immortality: Where Human Old Dreams and New Technologies Meet. In A. Mesquita (Ed.), *Research Paradigms and Contemporary Perspectives on Human-Technology Interaction* (pp. 266–282). Hershey, PA: IGI Global. doi:10.4018/978-1-5225-1868-6.ch012

Rao, N. R. (2017). Social Media: An Enabler for Governance. In N. Rao (Ed.), *Social Media Listening and Monitoring for Business Applications* (pp. 151–164). Hershey, PA: IGI Global. doi:10.4018/978-1-5225-0846-5.ch008

Rao, N. R. (2017). Social Media: An Enabler in Developing Business Models for Enterprises. In N. Rao (Ed.), *Social Media Listening and Monitoring for Business Applications* (pp. 165–173). Hershey, PA: IGI Global. doi:10.4018/978-1-5225-0846-5.ch009

Rathore, A. K., Tuli, N., & Ilavarasan, P. V. (2019). Tweeting About Business and Society: A Case Study of an Indian Woman CEO. In J. Thakur (Ed.), *Modern Perspectives on Virtual Communications and Social Networking* (pp. 196–212). Hershey, PA: IGI Global. doi:10.4018/978-1-5225-5715-9.ch008

Rive, P. B. (2016). Virtual Design Teams in Virtual Worlds: A Theoretical Framework using Second Life. In B. Baggio (Ed.), *Analyzing Digital Discourse and Human Behavior in Modern Virtual Environments* (pp. 60–86). Hershey, PA: IGI Global. doi:10.4018/978-1-4666-9899-4.ch004

Roth, S., Clark, C., & Berkel, J. (2017). The Fashionable Functions Reloaded: An Updated Google Ngram View of Trends in Functional Differentiation (1800-2000). In A. Mesquita (Ed.), *Research Paradigms and Contemporary Perspectives on Human-Technology Interaction* (pp. 236–265). Hershey, PA: IGI Global. doi:10.4018/978-1-5225-1868-6.ch011

Sabao, C., & Chikara, T. O. (2018). Social Media as Alternative Public Sphere for Citizen Participation and Protest in National Politics in Zimbabwe: The Case of #thisflag. In F. Endong (Ed.), *Exploring the Role of Social Media in Transnational Advocacy* (pp. 17–35). Hershey, PA: IGI Global. doi:10.4018/978-1-5225-2854-8.ch002

Sambhanthan, A., Thelijjagoda, S., Good, A., & Scupola, A. (2016). Virtual Community Based Destination Marketing with YouTube: Investigation of a Typology. *International Journal of Web Portals*, 8(1), 32–49. doi:10.4018/IJWP.2016010103

Scalabrino, S., Geremia, S., Pareschi, R., Bogetti, M., & Oliveto, R. (2018). Freelancing in the Economy 4.0: How Information Technology Can (Really) Help. In F. Di Virgilio (Ed.), *Social Media for Knowledge Management Applications in Modern Organizations* (pp. 290–314). Hershey, PA: IGI Global. doi:10.4018/978-1-5225-2897-5.ch013

See-To, E. W., Del Rio, P. A., & Ho, K. K. (2016). Social Media Effects in Virtual Brand Communities: The Case of Facebook and Twitter. *International Journal of Systems and Service-Oriented Engineering*, 6(2), 66–88. doi:10.4018/IJSSOE.2016040104

Sezgin, A. A., & İplik, E. (2018). From Personal Knowledge Management to Corporate Knowledge Management. In F. Di Virgilio (Ed.), *Social Media for Knowledge Management Applications in Modern Organizations* (pp. 169–189). Hershey, PA: IGI Global. doi:10.4018/978-1-5225-2897-5.ch008

Shahrokh, Z. D., & Behyar, P. (2017). Consumer's Participation Model in Virtual Communities. *International Journal of E-Business Research*, 13(4), 15–36. doi:10.4018/IJEBR.2017100102

Shi, Y. (2018). Unified Swarm Intelligence Algorithms. In Y. Shi (Ed.), *Critical Developments and Applications of Swarm Intelligence* (pp. 1–26). Hershey, PA: IGI Global. doi:10.4018/978-1-5225-5134-8.ch001

Sillah, A. (2017). Nonprofit Organizations and Social Media Use: An Analysis of Nonprofit Organizations' Effective Use of Social Media Tools. In M. Brown Sr., (Ed.), *Social Media Performance Evaluation and Success Measurements* (pp. 180–195). Hershey, PA: IGI Global. doi:10.4018/978-1-5225-1963-8.ch009

Singh, S., & Saluja, D. (2019). Effects of Social Media Marketing Strategies on Consumers Behavior. In J. Thakur (Ed.), *Modern Perspectives on Virtual Communications and Social Networking* (pp. 146–173). Hershey, PA: IGI Global. doi:10.4018/978-1-5225-5715-9.ch006

Smith, K. H., Méndez Mediavilla, F. A., & White, G. L. (2017). The Impact of Online Training on Facebook Privacy. In A. Mesquita (Ed.), *Research Paradigms and Contemporary Perspectives on Human-Technology Interaction* (pp. 22–42). Hershey, PA: IGI Global. doi:10.4018/978-1-5225-1868-6.ch002

Soler-Labajos, N., & Jiménez-Zarco, A. I. (2017). Productivity on the Social Web: The Use of Social Media and Expectation of Results. In N. Rao (Ed.), *Social Media Listening and Monitoring for Business Applications* (pp. 45–68). Hershey, PA: IGI Global. doi:10.4018/978-1-5225-0846-5.ch003

Sudarsanam, S. K. (2017). Social Media Metrics. In N. Rao (Ed.), *Social Media Listening and Monitoring for Business Applications* (pp. 131–149). Hershey, PA: IGI Global. doi:10.4018/978-1-5225-0846-5.ch007

Switzer, J. S., & Switzer, R. V. (2016). Virtual Teams: Profiles of Successful Leaders. In B. Baggio (Ed.), *Analyzing Digital Discourse and Human Behavior in Modern Virtual Environments* (pp. 1–24). Hershey, PA: IGI Global. doi:10.4018/978-1-4666-9899-4.ch001

Tai, Z., & Liu, X. (2016). Virtual Ties, Perceptible Reciprocity, and Real-Life Gratifications in Online Community Networks: A Study of QQ User Groups in China. In B. Baggio (Ed.), *Analyzing Digital Discourse and Human Behavior in Modern Virtual Environments* (pp. 164–180). Hershey, PA: IGI Global. doi:10.4018/978-1-4666-9899-4.ch009

Tellería, A. S. (2016). Liquid Communication in Mobile Devices: Affordances and Risks. In B. Baggio (Ed.), *Analyzing Digital Discourse and Human Behavior in Modern Virtual Environments* (pp. 196–219). Hershey, PA: IGI Global. doi:10.4018/978-1-4666-9899-4.ch011

Vaidyanathan, S., & Sudarsanam, S. K. (2017). Social Media in Knowledge Management. In N. Rao (Ed.), *Social Media Listening and Monitoring for Business Applications* (pp. 94–114). Hershey, PA: IGI Global. doi:10.4018/978-1-5225-0846-5.ch005

van Niekerk, B. (2018). Social Media Activism From an Information Warfare and Security Perspective. In F. Endong (Ed.), *Exploring the Role of Social Media in Transnational Advocacy* (pp. 1–16). Hershey, PA: IGI Global. doi:10.4018/978-1-5225-2854-8.ch001

Venkatesh, R., & Jayasingh, S. (2017). Transformation of Business through Social Media. In N. Rao (Ed.), *Social Media Listening and Monitoring for Business Applications* (pp. 1–17). Hershey, PA: IGI Global. doi:10.4018/978-1-5225-0846-5.ch001

Wang, Q., & Liu, H. (2018). Optimized Base Station Sleeping and Smart Grid Energy Procurement Scheme to Improve Energy Efficiency. In Y. Shi (Ed.), *Critical Developments and Applications of Swarm Intelligence* (pp. 357–378). Hershey, PA: IGI Global. doi:10.4018/978-1-5225-5134-8.ch014

Wang, Y. (2017). Framing and Mis-Framing in Micro-Blogging Sites in China: Online Propagation of an Animal Cruelty Campaign. In M. Brown Sr., (Ed.), *Social Media Performance Evaluation and Success Measurements* (pp. 78–105). Hershey, PA: IGI Global. doi:10.4018/978-1-5225-1963-8.ch005

Yang, Y. (2018). City Group Optimization: An Optimizer for Continuous Problems. In Y. Shi (Ed.), *Critical Developments and Applications of Swarm Intelligence* (pp. 73–96). Hershey, PA: IGI Global. doi:10.4018/978-1-5225-5134-8.ch004

Yarchi, M., Wolfsfeld, G., Samuel-Azran, T., & Segev, E. (2017). Invest, Engage, and Win: Online Campaigns and Their Outcomes in an Israeli Election. In M. Brown Sr., (Ed.), *Social Media Performance Evaluation and Success Measurements* (pp. 225–248). Hershey, PA: IGI Global. doi:10.4018/978-1-5225-1963-8.ch011

Yaslioglu, M., & Yaslioglu, D. T. (2018). Demystifying the Power of Digital to Become a Cleverer Enterprise: The Concept of "Digital Quotient". In F. Di Virgilio (Ed.), *Social Media for Knowledge Management Applications in Modern Organizations* (pp. 264–289). Hershey, PA: IGI Global. doi:10.4018/978-1-5225-2897-5.ch012

Yüksel, H. (2018). Social Media Strategies of Political Power: An Analysis of the Ruling Party in Turkey. In F. Endong (Ed.), *Exploring the Role of Social Media in Transnational Advocacy* (pp. 153–178). Hershey, PA: IGI Global. doi:10.4018/978-1-5225-2854-8.ch008

Zhou, J., Yang, J., Lin, L., Zhu, Z., & Ji, Z. (2018). Local Best Particle Swarm Optimization Using Crown Jewel Defense Strategy. In Y. Shi (Ed.), *Critical Developments and Applications of Swarm Intelligence* (pp. 27–52). Hershey, PA: IGI Global. doi:10.4018/978-1-5225-5134-8.ch002

About the Author

Shalin Hai-Jew works as an instructional designer at Kansas State University (K-State), where she has worked since January 2006. She has taught at the university and college levels for many years (including four years in the People's Republic of China) and was tenured at Shoreline Community College but left tenure to pursue instructional design work. She has Bachelor's degrees in English and psychology, a Master's degree in Creative Writing from the University of Washington (Hugh Paradise Scholar), and an Ed.D in Educational Leadership with a focus on public administration from Seattle University (Morford Scholar). She tested into the University of Washington at 14. She reviews for several publishers and publications. She has worked on a number of instructional design projects, including those based on public health, biosecurity, one health, mental health, PTSD, grain science, turfgrass management, social justice, and others. Dr. Hai-Jew has analyzed data for federally funded projects. Hai-Jew was born in Huntsville, Alabama, in the U.S. She is working on several publishing projects currently.

Index

Ensure Quality Research is Introduced to the Academic Community

Become an IGI Global Reviewer for Authored Book Projects

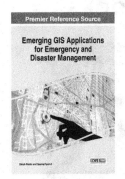 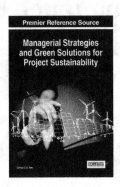  

The overall success of an authored book project is dependent on quality and timely reviews.

In this competitive age of scholarly publishing, constructive and timely feedback significantly expedites the turnaround time of manuscripts from submission to acceptance, allowing the publication and discovery of forward-thinking research at a much more expeditious rate. Several IGI Global authored book projects are currently seeking highly qualified experts in the field to fill vacancies on their respective editorial review boards:

Applicants must have a doctorate (or an equivalent degree) as well as publishing and reviewing experience. Reviewers are asked to write reviews in a timely, collegial, and constructive manner. All reviewers will begin their role on an ad-hoc basis for a period of one year, and upon successful completion of this term can be considered for full editorial review board status, with the potential for a subsequent promotion to Associate Editor.

If you have a colleague that may be interested in this opportunity, we encourage you to share this information with them.

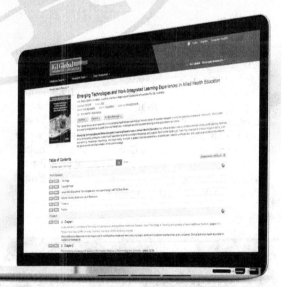

Printed in the United States
By Bookmasters